THE POLITICAL CLINIC

New Directions in Critical Theory

NEW DIRECTIONS IN CRITICAL THEORY
Amy Allen, General Editor

New Directions in Critical Theory presents outstanding classic and contemporary texts in the tradition of critical social theory, broadly construed. The series aims to renew and advance the program of critical social theory, with a particular focus on theorizing contemporary struggles around gender, race, sexuality, class, and globalization and their complex interconnections.

For a complete list of books in the series, please see the Columbia University Press website.

The Political Clinic

Psychoanalysis and Social Change
in the Twentieth Century

Carolyn Laubender

Columbia University Press   New York

Columbia University Press
Publishers Since 1893
New York   Chichester, West Sussex
cup.columbia.edu

Library of Congress Cataloging-in-Publication Data
Names: Laubender, Carolyn, author.
Title: The political clinic : psychoanalysis and social change in the
    twentieth century / Carolyn Laubender.
Description: New York : Columbia University Press, [2024] |
    Series: New directions in critical theory | Includes bibliographical
    references and index.
Identifiers: LCCN 2024002779 | ISBN 9780231214940 (hardback) |
    ISBN 9780231214957 (trade paperback) | ISBN 9780231560542 (ebook)
Subjects: LCSH: Psychoanalysis—History—20th century. |
    Psychoanalysis—Political aspects. | Social change. | Critical theory.
Classification: LCC BF173 .L2468 2024 | DDC 150.19/50904—dc23/eng/20240205
LC record available at https://lccn.loc.gov/2024002779

Cover design: Milenda Nan Ok Lee
Cover art: Ho Jae Kim, *Day 16: Therapy* (2021)

Contents

Acknowledgments

The acknowledgments section of a first book presents a unique challenge. Because first books seem like the culmination of both a finite research project and an entire life, it can feel especially impossible to take account of all the debts accrued along the way. This has been a particular struggle for me here. I am a great believer in the idea that any writing worth its salt contains numerous voices—both past and present, recognized and not—and so I can only begin to name those who have enabled my thinking and writing. My hope is that those who find themselves contained within these pages will take this inclusion as an acknowledgment, finally realized, in one form or another.

I am grateful to have presented portions of this work to many generous and engaged audiences who helped me clarify my arguments. Discussions at the British Psychoanalytical Society, the Freud Museum, Cornell University, Birkbeck University, University of Sussex, the South African Contemporary History and Humanities Seminar at the University of the Western Cape, Duke University, the American Comparative Literature Association, the Modernist Studies Association, the Modern Language Association, the Association of Psychosocial Studies, and many, many forums at the University of Essex improved the clarity and relevance of my interventions. Talks are one of the most immediate and tangible embodiments of an author's ever-present but always spectral "audience," and these venues provided valuable checkpoints for the project's evolution over time.

Numerous institutions have provided material support for this project along the way. Thanks to Duke University for six years of doctoral funding and countless research grants. Thanks to the University of Essex for a strategic research grant and for allowing my sabbatical. Thanks to the Melanie Klein Trust, the Winnicott Trust, the Wellcome Library, Ruth Runciman and the Ellen Hellmann Trust, and Ralph Bunche III for permission to use and reproduce their images throughout this book. Special thanks to Ho Jae Kim for permission to use his beautiful painting, "Day 16: Therapy," for the cover art.

I am grateful to several journals who published adapted versions of this work and who have generously granted me the rights to republish. Chapter 1 is revised from early work published as "On Good Authority: Anna Freud and the Politics of Child Analysis," *Psychoanalysis and History* 19, no. 3 (2017): 297–322. Portions of chapter 2 are taken from my article on Klein and reparative reading, "Beyond Repair: Interpretation, Reparation, and Melanie Klein's Play Technique," *Studies in Gender and Sexuality* 20, no. 1 (2019): 51–67. A short version of chapter 6 was first published with the Hidden Persuaders research blog and then was reprinted by *The Psychologist* (July 2019). Finally, I would also like to acknowledge Columbia University Press and specifically Wendy Lochner and Amy Allen, who helped shepherd this project from manuscript to book.

I am indebted to my colleagues at the University of Essex whose depth of engagement with and passion for psychoanalysis has qualified and improved this project immensely. Jess Battersby, Eben Cudjoe, Norman Gabriel, Emilia Halton-Hernandez, David Henderson, Sue Kegerreis, Kevin Lu, Zibby Loakthar, Roderick Main, Chris Nicholson, Leonardo Niro, Jordan Osserman, Renos Papadopoulos, Adrianna Pulsoni, Katharina Rowold, Mark Saban, Magda Schmukalla, Raluca Soreanu, Chris Tanner, Marita Vyrgioti, Julie Walsh, and Debbie Wright all helped with the everyday organization and operation of the department that formed the institutional setting for this book. Matt ffytche and Shaul Bar-Haim have been my stalwart historical anchors, saving me from many embarrassing factual and methodological mistakes. Those that remain are entirely my own. My gratitude goes to our graduate students, past and present—especially Öykü Türker, Max Maher, Rebecca Reynolds, Anusnigdha, Efi Koutantou, and Camilla Giambonini—who helped me stay afloat during term time at Essex through their indispensable work as TAs and RAs. Debbie Stewart, Ali Evans, Katrina Radford, Sarah Smith, Emily Gordon, Judith Ward, and Anne Snowling provided the daily logistical support without which nothing at all would get done.

This project first began at Duke University under the mentorship of some brilliant and inspiring teachers and advisers. Nancy Armstrong, Rey Chow, Anne Garréta, Elizabeth Grosz, Michael Hardt, Fredric Jameson, Wahneema Lubiano, Toril Moi, and Fred Moten all taught me early on, when I was still a grad student, and I am grateful to them for big thinking and bigger patience as I learned to both take risks and temper them. Ranjana Khanna was an early interlocutor for this work as it evolved, and I continue to find solace in her injunctive that I create space for myself in my writing, even if the climate of contemporary academic labor can feel increasingly alienating. No element of this book would have been possible without the decade-plus advisership and friendship embodied by both Robyn Wiegman and Antonio Viego. Together, they cochaired an unwieldy dissertation and, since then, have been a humbling and life-sustaining example of ongoing academic mentorship. Robyn remains my oracle of professional wisdom and her understanding of field formation and disciplinarity have transformed my thinking and writing more than anything else. With or without her consent, she is the voice in my head when I write and much of my professional savvy and success is due solely to her. Antonio was, in many ways, my first real teacher of psychoanalysis and he continues to be one of my most trusted advisers and closest friends. If one utopian reading of psychoanalysis is that it enables new forms of intimacy to emerge, then it has been through the hilarious, macabre, and affectionate conversational world that he and I have built over the past thirteen years that I have lived this possibility most fully.

My personal and intellectual community has evolved considerably as I have moved across cities, coasts, and continents, and I am grateful to many friends and family along the way. In Los Angeles, Kelsey Laity-D'Agostino and Michele Austin indelibly shaped who I would become; it was because of them that I first encountered Freud's work. In Durham, Carolin Benack, Carly B. Boxer, Brenna Casey, Bennett Carpenter, Kate Costello, Annu Dayha, Kita Douglas, Israel Durham, Zoë Eckman, Jaime Acosta Gonzalez, Rachel Greenspan, Nick Huber, Calvin Hui, Jess Issacharoff, Melody Jue, Cory Lown, Mitch Murtagh, Sonya Nayak, David Rambo, Renée Ragin Randall, Cole Rizki, Yair Rubinstein, Jessica Q. Stark, Abby Seeskin, Jake Silver, Jordan Sjol, Jake Soule, John Stadler, Phil Stillman, and Stefan Waldschmidt have all provided tremendous comradery, wit, intelligence, and fun. Through them, my capacity for thinking and partying have both improved considerably. In Wivenhoe, Neli Demireva, Robin West, Hersh Mann, and Anna di Ronco have curated a WhatsApp group for the ages and have provided me a much-needed social oasis in an otherwise sleepy fishing village. To them I say: here's to many more ex-pat Thanksgivings!

And then there are those who transcend time and place. To Rosemary, the best undergraduate adviser I could have asked for and an enabling example of friendship across institutional and generational divides. To Becky, still my favorite roommate and an easy friend across any distance. To David and Emily, for encouraging my passion for critique early on and for letting me know when I had reached my Prime. To Becky Blikslager and everyone at Windcroft Farm, for putting me back in the saddle and keeping me sane. To Shannan, for inspiring intellectual curiosity and the exceptional ability to make people feel welcome. To Julien, for Psyclops chatter and sex-person Lacanianism. To Chase, for indomitable good spirits in the face of my melancholy and for a grammatical passion that rivals my own. To Marina, for a decade of late-night processing and "fried-chicken Christmases." To Jessica, for calmly talking me through just about every crisis—real and imagined—and for babysitting Bandit over all those years. To Phoebe, for femme-radicalism, the Mermaid Express, and a back porch that feels like home. And, finally, to Audrey and Becky, for supporting me and my work even (and perhaps most especially) when they understood neither it nor me. This book is dedicated to everyone here but especially to them.

THE POLITICAL CLINIC

Introduction

On Neutrality and Other Clinical Fictions

In September 2019, in the auditorium of a north London high school, a conflict broke out among the participants of a two-day conference on psychoanalysis. The event, located around the corner from Maresfield Gardens, was sponsored by the Freud Museum and was the first in the newly resurrected "Psychoanalysis and the Public Sphere" series, which had led the British psychoanalytic scene for over a decade beginning in the late 1980s. Tensions had been mounting over the course of the event as those who viewed clinical psychoanalysis as an objective and politically neutral practice chafed against those who considered it a necessarily social and political endeavor. At one point, an audience member wondered aloud, in earnest, about how she could continue to maintain clinical neutrality in the face of her increasingly alt-right, white male clientele. By the event's end, Joanna Ryan had personally and publicly called out the British Psychoanalytical Society (BPS) for its ongoing institutional homophobia, citing her own firsthand experience of discrimination as a lesbian analyst. Directly addressing former BPS president, David Bell (who sat in the front row of the audience), Ryan charged, "And no one has still ever apologized to me for it!"

Silence followed.

At stake in these skirmishes was an unarticulated but fundamental difference in our collective understanding of the political function of psychoanalysis. Although clinicians and academics alike readily embrace the application of psychoanalytic theory to society, politics, art, and culture, the proposition that politics has any place in (or even near) the clinical consulting room is still heavily contested. To this day, appraisals of the clinic as a site of neutrality, objectivity, and apoliticality are a hallmark of many Global North clinical practitioners and training programs, with the Kleinian-dominated institutes in the United Kingdom and ego-psychological training programs in the United States being especially noteworthy in this regard. But, even among academic engagements with psychoanalysis, the clinic is habitually viewed as politically irrelevant (at best) or irrecuperable (at worst). According to Tim Dean and Christopher Lane's introduction to *Homosexuality and Psychoanalysis*, "One of the greatest paradoxes in the history of psychoanalysis is that psychoanalytic institutions have developed in directions antithetical to psychoanalytic concepts," a claim that performs a familiar splitting of theory and practice as a strategy for recuperating psychoanalysis's radical potential.[1] Twenty years earlier, in February 1981, at an ad hoc meeting of French and Latin American psychoanalysts in Paris, Jacques Derrida made a similar indictment, calling out the International Psychoanalytic Association (IPA) for its refusal to name and condemn the right-wing militaristic violence sweeping Latin America. But, as Derrida stressed in the very title of his talk—"Geopsychoanalysis: ... 'and the Rest of the World'"—the refusal to employ a proper name is, still, a practice of naming. Thus, when Ryan decried the failure of the BPS to address, engage with, or (to use Derrida's invitation) name psychoanalysis's institutional and clinical homophobia—homophobia that more often than not operates under the claim of political neutrality—she was highlighting both the continuing hegemony of the field's ideological investment in the promise of neutrality and, ironically, its practical impossibility.

The Political Clinic: Psychoanalysis and Social Change in the Twentieth Century therefore begins from a simple axiom that is still fervently disputed: the clinic *is* political. Throughout this book, I offer a reappraisal of the political work performed by—and in—the psychoanalytic clinic, ultimately arguing for the utility of clinical practice for critical thought. While much psychoanalytic scholarship has focused on its intellectual, social, and political impact outside of the clinic, this book makes the case for a theory of the psychoanalytic clinic as a vital site for novel political theorizing. To show this, I turn to an archive of specifically post-Freudian clinical encounters, exploring how prominent twentieth-century analysts developed unique and politically engaged clinical practices. Combining case studies and archival material from Britain and its former colonies, I examine across six chapters and five countries how some of the best-known European analysts of the twentieth century, such as Anna Freud, Melanie Klein, Wulf Sachs, D. W. Winnicott, Thomas Main, and John Bowlby, forged original clinical techniques for working with their patients while experimentally reimagining the political work that the clinic performs. I show how these analysts operationalized concepts like authority, reparation, anticolonialism, mothering, communalism, and security in the clinic as part of their daily practice to generate creative and inventive responses to the political exigencies of their day. I therefore consider how psychoanalysts became formidable political actors precisely through their clinical work, where they implicitly transformed the privatized space of the clinic into a protopolitical laboratory for reimagining the formations of race, gender, sexuality, childhood, nation, and democracy. By deliberately examining clinicians and techniques that represent some of the most conservative and orthodox traditions of psychoanalytic practice, part of this book's claim is that even the most "classical" psychoanalytic clinics perform implicit (and often explicit) political work. Refusing the institutional consensus that the clinic should be—or ever has been—politically neutral, *The Political Clinic* therefore maintains, at its most basic level, that psychoanalytic practice constitutes an important site of political thinking, theorization, and action.

• • •

Within academic circles, psychoanalysis—and especially clinical psychoanalysis—has often been an uncontroversial "bad object," the target of a set of practiced critiques about its limitations as a privatized and fundamentally middle-class affordance. Psychoanalysis, so the story goes, is a bourgeois luxury only accessible to those elite few who have ample discretionary time and income. By theorizing only in terms of personal psychology, it mistakes structural problems of political economy for individual maladies. It seeks individual assimilation over collective action; adaptation comes at the expense of revolution. The nuclear family adopts the status of ahistorical holy trinity, and there is a collective genuflection to that universalized idol: the phallus. The charge is that, stuck at the level of the personal, psychoanalysis (in both its academic and clinical uses) fails to be sufficiently political.

Yet, as I explore throughout this book, this reproach is only one side of a much more complex story. Beginning with Sigmund Freud and the first generation of psychoanalysts working in "Red Vienna," psychoanalysis was regularly conceptualized and instrumentalized as a means for social reform. Throughout his career, Freud, for instance, wrote essays on war, religion, group psychology, and the nature of civilization. As a matter of principle, he took on impoverished and low-wage patients (we could recall the Wolfman's impecunity here). Following the end of World War I, he oversaw the creation of a free clinic in Vienna known as the Ambulatorium that dealt extensively with soldiers suffering from shell shock. And, not insignificantly, both his personal and professional lives were scarred by some of the most violent political upheavals of the twentieth century, including an unprecedented racist genocide that claimed his sisters' lives and almost took his own. Even though Freud himself was rather politically quiescent—he was affiliated with the Social Democrats in Vienna but had little experience with direct political organizing—he lived and worked among a whole generation of social reformers during the interwar period who straddled the line between activist and analyst.

Indeed, Freud's own daughter, Anna Freud, would become a leading figure in children's social work through her creation of experimental residential institutions such as the Matchbox School, the Hampstead War Nurseries, and the Bulldogs Bank Home. She was inspired by the work of Siegfried Bernfeld and August Aichhorn, two men who adopted what would now, in the United Kingdom, be described as a psychosocial approach to the treatment of youth, education, and criminal justice reform in Vienna. But, beyond this early inner circle, there was also (to name just a few): Wilhelm Reich's communist activism and lecture tour in the Soviet Union; Otto Fenichel's global, Marxist-Freudian *Rundbriefe*, circulated covertly from his home in Los Angeles; D. W. Winnicott's fifty-plus postwar BBC lectures on mothering broadcast weekly to the British public; Harlem's short-lived but influential Lafargue Clinic, which catered primarily to poor Black patients and was cited in the reversal of U.S. segregation through *Brown v. Board of Education*; R. D. Laing and David Cooper's radical "antipsychiatric" refuge for psychotic and schizophrenic patients, Kingsley Hall, which refused standard medicalized interventions; Félix Guattari's anticapitalist, anti-colonialist "schizoanalysis" at La Borde Clinic and his involvement in the student protests of May 1968; West Germany's Socialist Patients' Collective, which issued the imperative "turn illness into a weapon!" as a way of pronouncing the link between capitalism and mental illness; and Austrian-born émigré Marie "Mimi" Langer's vocal opposition to the military dictatorship in Argentina, which resulted in her forced exile to Mexico in 1974 on threat of death. For these psychiatrists and analysts, psychoanalysis (often combined with Marxism) was a primary and indispensable vehicle for social reform.

Accounts such as these are just a snapshot of the growing record of psychoanalysis's variable forms of political engagement throughout the twentieth century. Elizabeth Danto explores this legacy at length in her landmark *Freud's Free Clinics*, where she disrupts any origin story of the clinic as originally apolitical by bringing to light an archive of forgotten leftist engagement by early European analysts for whom psychoanalysis was an unequivocally socialist exercise in combined economic-psychic liberation and freedom. As Danto shows, "From 1920 to 1938, in ten cities and seven countries, the activist generation of analysts built free treatment centers" that became material embodiments of their explicitly communist, socialist, or liberal political sensibilities.[2] From Max Eitingon and Ernst Simmel's founding work with the Weimar-era Berlin Poliklinik in 1920 and Wilhelm Reich's radical, Vienna-based network of free mental and sexual health clinics known as "Sex-Pol" to Ernest Jones's oversight of London's first public clinic in 1926 and Sándor Ferenczi's establishment, in 1929, of the first free clinic in Budapest, this generation of socially engaged psychoanalysts constructed a clear picture of the psychoanalytic clinic as part of a broader commitment to accessible public health and hygiene. For Danto, these analysts' work revealed that, far from the privatized bastion of bourgeois privilege, the clinic began as one of the clearest manifestations of the psychoanalytic commitment to social justice.

Since that inaugural heyday, psychoanalysts who have explicitly mixed their clinical work with political activism have been more the exception than the rule. Likely the most prominent and esteemed of these figures is the anticolonial psychiatrist and activist Frantz Fanon, who articulated a psychopolitical "sociogeny" of the nature of human oppression and liberation under racialized colonialism. As is now well known, Fanon's psychiatric work in both France and North Africa was informed by his political experience—first, as a young solider in the Free French Army and, later, as a member of the National Liberation Front, where he had become increasingly critical of (French) colonialism.[3] Fanon had originally done his psychiatric residency in France under the supervision of the famed Catalan psychiatrist François Tosquelles at Saint-Alban-sur-Limagnole, a hospital whose radical and unorthodox approaches drew some of France's most lauded clinical-intellectuals, including Michel Foucault and Félix Guattari.[4] Already by that point Fanon had had enough experience of French colonial racism, in psychiatric work and beyond, to develop his theory of the psychic self-alienation experienced by the Black person under colonialism.[5] But the move to colonial Algeria after his residency in 1953 further galvanized his anticolonial activism as he began daily work with Arab patients at Blida-Joinville Psychiatric Hospital.

Early in his tenure there, Fanon recognized that the suffering experienced by his Muslim patients especially was the systemic consequence of a violent and inexorable colonial structure.[6] For Fanon, "madness" under colonialism was not an individual or isolatable phenomenon; rather, it was a social pathology produced by the strategic and relentless dehumanization definitional to the colonial matrix. Put another way, the violence of colonialism was not just economic or political; it was psychic as well. Madness was, Fanon was apt to say, a "pathology of freedom."[7] By working clinically toward disalienation—that is, toward the reunification of the person with their social environment—Fanon advanced his clinical work as a form of anticolonial action.[8] Throughout his three-year directorship at Blida-Joinville, he developed creative, unorthodox, and often radical reconfigurations of daily clinical operations for both the Muslim men and European women in his charge. These included film screenings, ergotherapy stations, parties, day trips to the beach, football clubs, a café, a weekly newsletter, and (more contentiously) even insulin and electroconvulsive therapy. As Robcis has recently shown, these modifications were extensions of institutional psychotherapy, a unique form of psychosocial therapy developed by Tosquelles at Saint-Alban that used microcosmic recreations of social environments within the asylum to try to reunify the psychiatric patient with their social world.[9] At Blida-Joinville, Fanon recognized that the adjustments made for the European women in the ward had little effect on the Muslim men and so tried to deterritorialize this method in the service of colonial disalienation. "We had naively taken our division as a whole," reflects Fanon. "By virtue of what impairment of judgement had we believed it possible to undertake a Western-inspired social therapy in a war of mentally ill Muslim men? Was a structural analysis possible if the geographical, historical, cultural and social frames were bracketed?"[10] By differently tailoring the hospital environments to the Muslim men through the choice of films, celebration of holidays, types of activities provided, and the creation of a Moorish café, Fanon and his colleagues improved the participation of the Muslim residents considerably. For Fanon, the clinic was an unequivocal site of decolonial political praxis.[11]

Yet after the outbreak of the Algerian Revolution in 1954, Fanon's view on the political promise of the clinic darkened. He increasingly encountered patients who, as a result of their involvement with the Algerian resistance, had been tortured by the French Army using techniques the French had adopted directly from the Nazis. To complicate matters further, as the director of a state facility, Fanon was also charged with treating French soldiers and officers, many of whom had perpetrated grizzly acts of violence against Algerian citizens. By 1956, Fanon himself had become a target of the French police for his militant activism and, just before fleeing to Tunis, he penned a weary and withering letter of resignation to the French Resident Minister.

If psychiatry is the medical technique that aims to enable man to no longer be a stranger to his environment, I owe it to myself to affirm that the Arab, permanently an alien [aliéné permanent] in his own country, lives in a state of absolutely depersonalization.

What is the status of Algeria? A systematized de-humanization.

It was an absurd gamble to undertake, at whatever cost, to bring into existence a certain number of values, when the lawlessness, the inequality, the multi-daily murder of man were raised to the status of legislative principles.

The social structure existing in Algeria was hostile to any attempt to put the individual back where he belonged.[12]

Throughout his career, Fanon would never disavow his clinical psychiatric work and he continued to practice as a psychiatrist at the Neuropsychiatric Day Hospital of Tunis after his exile. Linear accounts that cast him as moving from psychiatry to politics are therefore inaccurate in this regard. But by 1956, Fanon was led to insist on the futility of this work when divorced from a larger anticolonial social reconfiguration.

In many ways, Fanon's overt politicization of his clinical psychiatric work bucked the trend of midcentury analysis. According to the common view of this period, as fascism flourished, antisemitism turned to full-blown genocide, and decolonial liberation movements gained ground, European and North American psychoanalysis especially retreated from its progressive political roots. To see one example of this, we could consider how the Vienna Psychoanalytic Society, once home to radicals like Wilhelm Reich, Sándor Ferenczi, and Otto Fenichel, publicly rescinded its political mission and declared formal "neutrality" in the face of amplifying antisemitic violence, directly prohibiting analysts from participating in activist organizations.[13] It was in direct response to this dramatic change of position that Langer left Vienna to join the Republican army in the Spanish Civil War, swapping her psychoanalytic training for anti-fascist medical service. One could also think here of the exodus of European (principally Jewish) analysts to the United States where, in a bid for assimilation to more conservative medical frameworks, they embraced normative psychological virtues like adaptation, reality testing, emotional regulation, and linear developmentalism—not to mention heterosexuality—as the cornerstones of their much-lambasted ego psychology. As Nathan Hale documents in his comprehensive two-part study of American psychoanalysis, *Freud and the Americans*, many of these refugees abandoned their previous political commitments to meet the institutional and disciplinary norms of North American practice.[14] On the whole, psychoanalytic practice in midcentury Europe and North America contracted its political aspirations, embracing ideologies of neutrality, apoliticality, and objectivity that had not characterized the progressivist trends of its early decades.

However, this turn toward a fantasy of a disengaged psychoanalytic practice was true perhaps only of North American and European clinicians. As many scholars have shown, psychoanalysis was, from its earliest days, a thoroughly global movement, with institutes and practitioners in India, South Africa, Germany, Brazil, Australia, Algeria, Argentina, Hungary, the United States, Russia, France, and Austria, among others.[15] Yet there were important distinctions between the way clinicians in these diverse locations interpreted their craft, with Global South practitioners showing a particular and intentional willingness to transform and improvise practice to meet differing local and cultural needs. If Freud's work was, famously, a local response to the specific forms of suffering experienced by the Viennese bourgeois, then, as many Global South practitioners realized, the rules, precepts, and techniques of the clinical practice he developed would inevitably need to change to address other cultural and political climates. Psychoanalysis, they argued, would need to be "provincialized." Analysts from these contexts were thus especially astute recreators of psychoanalytic practice, developing politically invested versions of the clinic that sought to address the realities of, for instance, poverty, racism, colonial oppression, and state violence. In this regard, Fanon was not an exception but rather a representative example of the way clinicians from the Global South— particularly those committed to decolonial, antiracist activism—used their clinical work as a form of liberatory activism.

In Argentina, for instance, Langer, who had begun her psychoanalytic career with a rather conservative book on the supposed psychological and pathogenic roots of female infertility, became a fierce and fearless critic of both the state-sponsored violence during the Dirty War and of the psychoanalytic institute's untenable and reactionary pledge to political neutrality.[16] In 1971, Langer delivered a factious tour de force paper at the International Psychoanalytic Association Congress in Vienna titled "Psychoanalysis and/or Social Revolution" in which she censured her colleagues' political complacency and urged them to embrace the link between individual and social change. The global student and worker protests of the late 1960s and early 1970s were an important backdrop for Langer's work since a generation of radicalized psychoanalysts had already been criticizing the IPA's stultification. During these years, activists had organized two counter-congresses in 1969 and 1971 to shadow the IPA's official biannual meeting, directly calling out its misuses of power. By 1974, Langer had quit the very Argentinian Psychoanalytic Association she had founded in protest to the institute's refusal to denounce the junta's escalating violence.[17]

In Brazil around the same time, the psychoanalyst Helena Besserman Vianna risked more than just her institutional affiliation when she covertly passed documents across the border to Langer in Argentina that detailed how Rio-based psychoanalytic trainee Amilcar Lobo Moreira was working as a torturer for the secret police. The "Lobo affair" is now well known within psychoanalytic circles, but what is far less frequently acknowledged is that, after Langer passed the evidence of Lobo's torture over to the IPA (then presided over by Serge Lebovici), the IPA not only refused to issue a public denouncement of Lobo but in fact returned the documentation to Lobo's training analyst—a man named Leo Cabernite, who had close ties to the military and was himself trained by former Nazi Party member Werner Kemper—thereby allowing Cabernite and Lobo to personally identify Besserman Vianna as the whistleblower.[18] Taken together, Besserman Vianna and Lobo are a testament to the political extremes adopted by a minority of analysts around the world throughout the twentieth century. But, as Besserman Vianna and Langer rightly lay bare in their respective denunciations, the IPA's institutional silence—its commitment, in other words, to a pseudoclinical ideal of neutrality—was no less political an action than any outright defense of Lobo would have been.

Accounts such as these have been made possible by an efflorescence of psychoanalytic historiography that has been especially interested in the diverse but previously underrecognized political involvement of psychoanalytic clinicians. As early as the so-called Freud Wars, which were catalyzed by Jeffrey Masson's mid-1980s allegation that Sigmund Freud had duplicitously "suppressed" evidence of the sexual abuse his female patients experienced in order to further psychoanalysis's wider social acceptance, critics were already beginning to document the sociocultural context and use of some of his most significant theories. Spanning the past forty years—and aided in large part by the relatively recent declassification of many psychoanalytic archives (including the Freud Archives housed in the Library of Congress)—this academic work moved beyond the insider mythmaking and biographically driven character studies that had largely defined psychoanalytic history of the midcentury. For instance, leaving aside Masson's publicly grabby but academically slapdash claims, intellectual historians such as Sander Gilman proposed bold and persuasive new readings of Freud's thought that placed psychoanalysis at the interstices of social, political, and medical history in fin de siècle Vienna. In *Freud, Race, and Gender,* Gilman showed how Freud's infamous claims about femininity—that racialized "dark continent"—could be read as a response to the racist feminization of male Jews prevalent in wider German discourse. For Gilman, the yield of this was not just a contextualization of Freud's thinking but a broader politicization of scientific theories of mind as local and contingent.[19] While much of this work—to name just a few, Janet Malcolm's *Psychoanalysis: The Impossible Profession,* Russell Jacoby's *The Repression of Psychoanalysis,* Stephen Frosh's *The Politics of Psychoanalysis: An Introduction to Freudian and Post-Freudian Theory,* Peter Gay's *Freud: A Life for Our Time,* Lisa Appignanesi and John Forrester's *Freud's Women,* John Forrester's *Dispatches from the Freud Wars: Psychoanalysis and Its Passions,* Sarah Winter's *Freud and the Institution of Psychoanalytic Knowledge,* and Mark Edmundson's *The Death of Sigmund Freud: Fascism, Psychoanalysis and the Rise of Fundamentalism*—took Freud and his inner circle of European disciples its gravitational center, it importantly deexceptionalized psychoanalytic theory, showing how it was part of a nuanced dialogue with its wider ideological and material environment.

More recently, this body of work has centrifugally spun scholarship on psychoanalysis out beyond its previous temporal and geographical centers. No longer just a story about a founding father developing one of the three great "hermeneutics of suspicion" in a major European capital, much of the psychoanalytic historiography of the past decade, which John C. Burnham christened the "New Freud Studies,"[20] has tracked its post-Freudian global reach.[21] While George Makari's *Revolution in Mind* dispenses with a biographical fixation on Freud as the navel of psychoanalysis in order to plot the global germination and expansion of a sweeping intellectual movement, Burnham's edited collection *After Freud Left* foregoes Europe itself to trace the development of psychoanalysis in midcentury America, a land Freud mordantly referred to as "Dollaria" where one was free only "to sell one's life as dearly as possible."[22] Meanwhile, Joy Damousi and Mariano Ben Plotkin, in *Psychoanalysis and Politics: Histories of Psychoanalysis Under Conditions of Restricted Political Freedom,* and Matt ffytche and Daniel Pick, in *Psychoanalysis and the Age of Totalitarianism,* together use their edited collections to map psychoanalysis's political malleability and ambivalence, showing how—from Europe, to the Americas, to Africa—it came to flourish in conditions of political unfreedom.[23] Indeed, as Erik Linstrum, Dagmar Herzog, and Warwick Anderson, Deborah Jenson, and Richard C. Keller all show in their respective works, psychoanalysis was far from a necessarily progressive or politically democratic ideology, especially when it came to its implementation in the colonies.[24] As psychoanalysis circulated globally throughout the twentieth century, at the height of empire, it was used to collaborate both with the forces of anti-imperial resistance *and* with those of metropolitical governance. Although psychoanalysis has been thoroughly (and often rightly) chastened for the Eurocentrism endemic to its universalizing claims, these types of more granular histories have effectively parochialized its practice, adding texture to our understanding of how and why local practitioners adopted, challenged, and transformed this tradition.

As even this brief review demonstrates, the question of psychoanalysis's politicality—whether as theory or as practice—is still one of the most pressing concerns for psychoanalytic historiography.[25] *The Political Clinic* contributes to this scholarship by situating each clinical case study within a larger political and historical context, from 1918–1989, that is anchored geographically by the ties each of these analysts had to the British metropole. As the rise of Naziism and World War II shifted both psychoanalytic persons and institutions westward, Britain became an undisputed fulcrum of midcentury psychoanalytic work in the Global North. Each figure I follow thus had some relationship to the practices of and standards set by the BPS: whether working at home or abroad, as British native or recent immigrant, each clinician discussed throughout this book was a member of the BPS at the height of its influence and renown. In this way, this book can be read as a partial microhistory of British analysts affiliated with the BPS, from those like Winnicott, who would twice serve as its president, to those like John Bowlby, who would eventually reject many of the orthodoxies of psychoanalytic practice.

Yet by following these analysts' transnational migrations, I am often taken far afield from London as I pursue, for instance: Anna Freud's emphasis on clinical authority amid debates in Red Vienna about the role of political authority in national democracy; Melanie Klein's valorization of psychic reparations during the rise and fall of European reparation claims as seen from her wartime refuge in Scotland; Wulf Sachs's experimental expansion of clinical boundaries as a way of contending with the racial injustices of British colonialism in South Africa; D. W. Winnicott's promotion of the analyst-as-mother as a means of grappling with the political upheavals of decolonization; Thomas Main's adaptation of a communal form of psychoanalytic practice amid multinational Cold War experiments with Leftist commune-clinics; and finally John Bowlby's promise of clinically born emotional security as an individualized answer to the transatlantic Cold War paranoia about global communism and the increasing prioritization of national security. While there is excellent scholarship on the clinical-political work of figures such as Langer and Fanon, far less has been said in this regard about some of Britain's leading post-Freudian analysts who were instrumental in establishing and institutionalizing many of the clinical norms still treated as canonical today. By focusing specifically on these clinicians—many of whom, like Klein, would insistently disavow any relation to politics, clinical or otherwise—this book emphasizes the politicality of the clinic as an ordinary state of affairs, not an exceptional provision necessitated by extreme political turmoil. Here, the very European analysts defining and policing so-called clinical orthodoxy, including ideals of neutrality, were also the ones, I argue, engaging in politicized forms of clinical practice.

Beyond psychoanalytic historiography, there are two other (not always distinct) bodies of work to which this book contributes. The first includes theoretical scholarship from the humanities, especially from the fields of feminist theory, queer theory, critical race theory, and postcolonial theory, where psychoanalysis has been a particularly welcome conceptual resource.[26] If one way to tell the story of psychoanalysis in the twentieth century is to note how, in the United States especially, psychoanalysis's decline as a prominent scientific epistemology and clinical practice coincided with its assimilation within universities as a noteworthy component of humanities curricula, then at least part of this narrative involves a recognition of just how much scholarship makes use of psychoanalysis in these fields. Within feminist theory, for instance, psychoanalysis was an early—and often antagonistic—discourse as radical critics like Kate Millet and Monique Wittig took aim at its phallocentrism, its paternalism, its heterosexism, and its pathologization of the feminine. By way of response, psychoanalytic feminists such as Luce Irigaray, Hélène Cixous, Juliet Mitchell, Julia Kristeva, Nancy Chodorow, Jessica Benjamin, and Carol Gilligan offered important defenses and qualifications, often building distinctly feminist alternatives to masculinist classics like penis envy and the Oedipus complex. While some of this work was squarely Freudian (such as Mitchell's famous defense of Freud as providing the analysis of, not the recommendation for, a patriarchal society),[27] much of it was inspired either by the more relational, two-body approach of Melanie Klein, who made the mother-daughter relationship the cornerstone of her theorizing, or by the more semiotic and symbolic interpretation of psychoanalysis furnished by Lacan, who debiologized some of Freud's more anatomical propositions. Since then, feminist theory's uses of psychoanalysis have become all the more varied and inventive, including the work of—to name a very few— Judith Butler, Hortense Spillers, Jacqueline Rose, Lauren Berlant, Toril Moi, Jane Gallop, Elizabeth Grosz, Joan Copjec, Laura Mulvey, Mari Jo Buhle, Jean Walton, Teresa de Lauretis, Teresa Brennan, Mary Ann Doane, Diana Fuss, Janice Doane, and Devon Hodges. Whether in the name of Freud, Klein, or Lacan, feminist theory was one of the earliest fields to diagnose the inherent politicality of psychoanalytic concepts and methods and to demonstrate how they could be flexibly repurposed for variable ends.

Many other fields have shared feminist theory's appreciation of psychoanalysis's nuanced theorization of the (often unconscious) vicissitudes of subjectivity. For the first generation of queer theorists— including Leo Bersani, Judith Butler, Tim Dean, Lee Edelman, and Eve Kosofsky Sedgwick—the central place that psychoanalysis accorded to sexuality in psychic life meant that it was an utterly indispensable resource for early elaborations of a nonnormative, anti-identitarian version of sexuality. Concepts like fantasy, polymorphous perversity, jouissance, the death drive, masochism, identification, unconscious bisexuality, and even shame became the de rigueur vocabulary for queer theorists' interest in the truculent and nonheteronormative aspects of queer sexuality and desire. While acknowledging psychoanalysis's troubled history of clinical homophobia—something Noreen O'Connor and Joanna Ryan document thoroughly in their published writing[28]— this thinking showed how some of psychoanalysis's most interesting and insurrectionary insights are ill-recognized by clinicians. As Adam Phillips quips in his dialogic response to Judith Butler in *The Psychic Life of Power*, "It is fortunate that writers are interested in psychoanalysis because, unlike analysts, they are free to think up thoughts unconstrained by the hypnotic effect of clinical practice. Good performers, like musicians or sportspeople or analysts, are often not that good at talking about what they do, partly because they are the ones who do it."[29] By pitting clinician against academic, Phillips performs the same splitting as Dean and Lane in order, implicitly, to bracket the ongoing homophobic violence perpetrated in psychoanalysis's name and, explicitly, to rehabilitate a version of psychoanalysis that intentionally refuses its moralizing and normative Oedipal frame. Indeed, psychoanalytic queer theorists have been among some of the best diagnosticians of Sigmund Freud's ambivalence on the topic of sexual normativity. While, on the one hand, Freud typologized male and female homosexuality as variously narcissistic, arrested, pre-Oedipal, and regressive, on the other hand, he also insisted—in a claim that would still find fervent objection today—that "all human beings are capable of making a homosexual object choice and have in fact made one in their unconscious" and that "from the point of view of psychoanalysis the exclusive sexual interest felt by men for women is also a problem that needs elucidating."[30] By taking up this latter, decidedly "queerer" version of Freud—felicitously christened "Pink Freud" in Diana Fuss's landmark special issue of *GLQ*[31]—queer theorists have drawn on psychoanalysis's capacity for amplifying, rather than contracting, the range of templates available for theorizing and valuing sexual multiplicity and nonnormativity.

Likewise, postcolonial theorists beginning with Fanon have produced similar readings of (especially Freudian) psychoanalysis that both challenge and reimagine its Eurocentrism, developmentalism, and primitivism. In her influential *Dark Continents: Psychoanalysis and Colonialism*, Ranjana Khanna describes how psychoanalysis (together with anthropology and archaeology) embodied an extension of the racist and sexist colonial episteme—while also, more daringly, arguing that it nevertheless constitutes a discourse through which a feminist, postcolonial resistance to the hegemony of the neoimperial European nation-state formation emerges.[32] Influenced by a generation of postcolonial theorists for whom psychoanalysis was indispensable (Fanon, Albert Memmi, Edward Said,

Homi Bhabha, and Gayatri Spivak), Khanna uses psychoanalysis to emphasize the subjective and ontological splits produced by the institution of postcolonial nation-statehood, splits that for Khanna engender an unassimilable loss—a ghostly melancholia—within the postcolonial subject that functions as both poison and cure. The same year Khanna published *Dark Continents*, Celia Brickman published her own analysis of psychoanalysis's colonial legacies, *Aboriginal Populations in the Mind: Race and Primitivity in Psychoanalysis*, where she unspooled the tension between Freudian psychoanalysis's liberatory aspirations and its moorings in colonialist paradigms such as "primitivity," which are still routinely used in clinical literature today.[33] Khanna and Brickman represent a discernible second generation of post- and decolonial psychoanalytic thinking that, to borrow Dipesh Chakrabarty's helpful slogan, "provincialized" psychoanalysis, diversifying our understanding of its philosophical lineages and geographical locations. More recently, post- and decolonial psychoanalytic work has entered yet another new phase, with scholarship since the mid-2010s (such as that by Gohar Homayounpour, Robert K. Beshara, Daniel Gaztambide, Lara Sheehi, Ankhi Mukherjee, Stefania Pandolfo, Karima Lazali, and Patricia Gherovici)[34] increasingly interested not just in tracking psychoanalysis's colonialist collaborations or Eurocentric biases but in theorizing its clinical capacity for decolonial action, particularly in the Global South.

While critical race theory has not found as much use for psychoanalytic theorizing as postcolonial theory—due largely, I suspect, to Freud's strategic deprioritization of race as a central axis of psychic difference—there have been noteworthy surges of scholarship that prove an exception to this trend. For instance, Khanna's embrace of melancholia as a critical concept for postcolonial feminism echoes a broader early-2000s trend within critical race theory, where texts like Anne Anlin Cheng's *The Melancholy of Race: Psychoanalysis, Assimilation, and Hidden Grief* hailed racial identification as itself a melancholic act.[35] Implicitly extending Butler's theory of gender melancholia,[36] Cheng (and, subsequently, David Eng, David Kazanjian, and Antonio Viego)[37] established how psychoanalytic accounts of loss can be metaphorized to diagnose the impasses of modern racial formation. During this same period, Kalpana Seshadri-Crooks published *Desiring Whiteness: A Lacanian Analysis of Race*, which used the Lacanian framework of sexual difference to make a case for racial difference as a structuring term in the unconscious.[38] More recently—but in a very different idiom—this thinking has been taken up in the debate within Black Studies around Afropessimism by both advocates and detractors such as David Marriott, Derek Hook, Jared Sexton, and Sheldon George, who alternately use Lacan to extend, complicate, and contest Orlando Patterson's original notion of "social death."[39] Although Frank B. Wilderson III, the founder of the Afropessimist school, is by no means a psychoanalytic theorist, many of the most inventive scholars following him in Black studies today draw on a specifically Lacanian interpretation of the trauma, negativity, exclusion, and affectively coded "pessimism" that his work hails for contemporary Black life. None of these fields is discrete—Khanna is as much a feminist as a postcolonial theorist; Eng can be considered in equal measure a queer and critical race theorist—and when taken together they evidence psychoanalysis's conceptual vitality across the humanities as a theoretical resource for critical theorizing.

The intentional and strategic disloyalty that critical theorists have adopted toward psychoanalytic doxa has arguably been the most formative influence for how I read the clinical archives of psychoanalytic practice throughout this book. Like these thinkers, in each chapter I aim to move beyond a purely historical frame—a "who did what when and where"—to interrogate the contemporary critical utility of the clinical concepts and techniques that these analysts developed. Taking the clinic as a political space, I am interested in elaborating how the specific forms of praxis engaged by clinicians constitute innovative political theories that implicitly speak to a larger understanding of identity, power, and justice. By viewing the clinic in this way—as a microcosm of society where experimental sociopolitical theories germinate and take root—my hope is to recuperate the critical relevance and utility of concepts that have previously been clinically circumscribed. Thus, I ask, for instance, what can Melanie Klein's clinical deployment of her psychological understanding of reparation tell us about critical and political demands for reparative justice today? Or to what extent does John Bowlby's security-minded attachment theory help articulate the collaboration between contemporary neoliberal imperial feminism (what Inderpal Grewal calls "security feminism")[40] and the security state? Or again, how does Wulf Sachs's boundary-crossing, cross-racial psychoanalytic practice in colonial South Africa productively reimagine the decolonial possibilities of clinical psychoanalytic intimacy?

As I explore throughout the book, such ideas often correspond to ambivalent political aspirations and can function in contradictory ways. This is part of what Eli Zaretsky has aptly described as the Janus-faced nature of psychoanalysis.[41] Even as psychoanalysis, broadly conceived, challenged the autonomous, rational, and unified subject of Enlightenment liberalism through its prioritization of the unconscious, affect, phantasy, drive, and relationality, so too it also, for instance, used the figure of the "good enough mother" to shore up the British welfare state during decolonization and emphasized individual emotional security as a supplement to the neoliberal Cold War security state. My interest here is not in defending one version of psychoanalysis as more authentic or accurate than another. Rather, I follow the field's variable evolution with curiosity in an effort to understand its larger social and political extensions and capacities. As inchoate political imaginaries that were in clear conversation with organized state formations like empire, liberal democracy, authoritarianism, fascism, colonialism, and decolonization, psychoanalysis's mutability indexes the idiosyncratic nature of clinico-political thought, which, by virtue of being removed from direct political engagement, was freed to make unique and unconventional contributions. In this way, *The Political Clinic* hails the clinic as a new horizon for social and political theorizing, reconstituting both critical and clinical understandings of the political thought and action performed within its walls.

This latter intervention—into contemporary *clinical* debates that have typically fallen beyond the purview of mainstream academic scholarship—constitutes this book's final (and most experimental) contribution. As with academic scholarship, there is a wide range when it comes to clinical thinking and writing. Differences of national location, clinical orientation, and even institutional affiliation have produced some distinct and recognizable intellectual signatures in the analytic world. Recently, for instance, there has been a small cadre of clinicians in both the United States and the United Kingdom whose work interrogates the dominant investment in the ideals of analytic neutrality, objectivity, and apoliticality. Among the first critics of these norms was Jungian analyst Andrew Samuels and Relational analysts Lewis Aron, Muriel Dimen,

Neil Altman, and Lynne Layton, who each, independently, began to attend to the role of identity politics in the clinic beginning in the early 2000s. While many, many analysts understand subjectivity as necessarily social and cultural, the work of Altman, Aron, Dimen, Layton, and Samuels is distinct for how it directly considers the analyst's subjective role in constructing clinical truth.[42] In everything from the location and organization of the analytic space, to the analyst's clothing and hairstyle, to her chosen interpretations and silences, these analysts reflect on the perhaps unconscious—but not, for this reason, less material—political significance of their personal analytic encounters. For instance, in the introduction to their edited collection, *Psychoanalysis, Class and Politics: Encounters in the Clinical Setting*, Layton, Hollander, and Gutwill pose a litany of rhetorical questions that challenge the analyst-qua-reader (that seductively interpolating "we") to face the clinician's inevitable political function.

> When patients express their anxieties about concerns related to politics and class, how do we take them up? How do we address fears about global warming? How do we explore concerns about the Iraq War? What do we say about potential terrorist attacks with weapons of mass destruction? How do we take up the real problems of unemployment, underemployment or lack of medical care? How do we understand patients' distrust or naïve acceptance of the media's presentation of political and social reality? On the other hand, what do we make of it when the external world is absent—when patients do not mention the Iraq War, or major weather events that signify effects of global warming, or controversial political struggles? What is our role when patients do not think about participating in civic life, either because of disinterest or the inability to imagine lively political engagement that might change current conditions? What happens when the patient and therapist have similar political positions or are as different poles of a polarized society? How do we challenge an official professional ethic of neutrality that requires us to evade and deny the personal impact of the sociosymbolic order? Is this neutrality collusion with our patients' denial? How do we respect psychological boundaries while venturing into the political aspect of personal experience without being polemical?[43]

Underwriting all of these questions is the understanding that every act of analytic interpretation that parses the psychic from the social, delimiting the supposed proper object of psychoanalytic work, entails a political calculus. Whether an analyst interprets a patient's concern about war, for instance, as a "real" threat or projective anxiety speaks as much to their own subjective investment in reifying distinctions between psychic and social, private and public, individual and collective as to any psychic interiority. The analyst's influence, in other words, is an unavoidable aspect of any clinical scenario. While working with the countertransference has been a major post-Freudian and post-Kleinian Anglophone technique that prioritizes the significance of the analyst's own conscious and unconscious feelings and associations, this framework still presumes that the analyst's response is, at least in part, reactionary—that is, that the countertransference response is a "communication" to the analyst originating from the patient. Even here, the patient is typically assumed to be the agent of the dyad's affective world. Yet there is a strategic interpretive separation being made since any attempt to parse transference/countertransference responses—deciding what belongs to the patient or which aspects of the analyst's response are diagnostically useful—inevitably relies on an exercise of the analyst's own power of interpretation, which always risks self-justification. In light of this, recourse to the idealized (but impossible) position of neutrality as the institutionally sanctioned analytic posture only ever disavows the analyst's constitutive power to (at least partly) define and shape clinical reality. By denying influence, neutrality itself harbors a significant reactionary force.[44]

The importance of the post-2001 political moment for the development of this critique among clinicians is difficult to overestimate. Amid the surge of jingoistic racist militarism parroted by much of the U.S. population in the sanctified name of antiterrorism, political concerns entered U.S. clinics with new magnitude and force. As Layton, Hollander, and Gutwill observe, "September 11 marks the moment at which the American people could no longer feel invulnerable to the devastating forces of violence and destruction throughout the world"— much of which the United States itself had deliberately orchestrated to shore up its own imperial and financial ascendency.[45] This material entered the clinic directly through patient narrative and discourse.

But it was also felt less overtly through the way changing political and economic conditions transformed what Layton describes as our "normative unconscious process" or those traces left by the distinctly inhuman contortions required by late-stage capitalism in a neoliberal, imperialist, and sexist nation-state. To this point, see: the steady accumulation of multiethnic daily racism; the erosion of the middle class and the increasing magnetization of wealth in the hands of an ever-smaller capitalist oligarchy; the continuing assault on gay, lesbian, and trans people's very right to exist and build diverse kinship relations; the dystopian encroachments on women's bodily and reproductive autonomy; the apocalyptic swell of numerous global climate emergencies; and the terrifying rise of a new transnational alt-right authoritarianism that has put even the flimsy affordances of liberal democracy in jeopardy. Over the past two decades, the 2008 financial crisis, Brexit, the triumvirate ascendancies of Donald Trump, Jair Bolsonaro, and Boris Johnson, and the COVID-19 pandemic have only accelerated this process. In a twenty-year span that has witnessed the swing from sensationalized extremism abroad to systemized extremism at home, the tenability of the boundary between the social and the psychic has been vitally called into question.

Yet for however much Layton, Hollander, and Gutwill may rightly mark a shift in the (un)consciousness of mainstream white America, it is worth noting that the precarity and violence of American exceptionalism has, for a long time, not been lost on those excluded from its protections. The poor, people of color (including Black Americans, the Latinx community, and Indigenous Americans), and many gay, lesbian, and trans people have been among those most willfully disposed of by the neoliberal U.S. state and have, consequently, been far more astute diagnosticians of its systematic brutality. Something similar can been seen within psychoanalytic establishments themselves. Beyond Ryan's censure of the BPS's ongoing, institutionally codified homophobia, analysts of color have long been some of the best interpreters of the mixed promise afforded by those spaces that claim ostensible neutrality and apoliticality. In Basia Winograd's excellent 2014 documentary *Black Psychoanalysts Speak*, many of the analysts interviewed reflect on their long-standing frustration with the reigning consensus that psychoanalytic theories and practice are objective. As they chart, racism is central not just to Anglophone society and history but to psychoanalytic institutes and consulting rooms as well. American psychoanalyst Annie Lee Jones recalls how, at yet another Freud Museum event, she was physically prevented from taking the stage by a white psychiatrist who grabbed her arm as she began to mount the steps—a physical repression that plainly expressed the Institute's larger stance on minoritized knowledges. In turn, the New York–based analyst Kirkland C. Vaughans recounts a story about how his former analyst had described his work with his only other Black patient. "The treatment didn't go well," the analyst tells Vaughans, "because all the guy wanted to do was talk about race. I couldn't get him off race!" Vaughans chuckles.[46]

Although we might be inclined to balk at an account like this and read it as an exceptional example chronicling the powerful intellectual blinders furnished by white supremacy, I think it would be a mistake to ignore its ordinary clinical relevance. Accounts like this provide a useful diagnostic of the extent to which political value systems subtend *all* clinical encounters. For Vaughans's former analyst, there is a clear sense that a good or successful analysis was one in which the discussion moved beyond the topic of race. The fact of the analyst's agenda is articulated best by his clearly frustrated ambition—"I couldn't get him off race!"—as though the analyst had already deemed race something secondary or merely symptomatic in psychic life, not the embodied and psychic facticity through which both men were communicating.[47] As Phillips has recently remarked, simply by virtue of believing in psychoanalysis—of deciding to implement one clinical orientation instead of another—all analysts necessarily have an ethico-political agenda. "The analyst has a sense of what the good is. . . . For example, your analyst may believe that it is a moral and emotional good to be able to free associate, to be able to see the way in which you actively narrow your mind. . . . So psychoanalysis can never be a neutral space, but it can generate a different kind of conversation."[48] For Vaughans's analyst, the exclusivity of the patient's focus on race constituted a hinderance, perhaps even an unconscious defense or sticking point. But it is easy to imagine how, for an analyst differently disposed, such unflagging attention to America's most simultaneously sensationalized and elided site of inequality would be an opening for vital psychical work. My point here is not to contend that one clinical approach is superior; I have neither the credentials for nor the interest in such an arbitration. Rather, I mean to demonstrate the impossibility of operating, in the clinic and outside of it, from a position of political neutrality.

As I sit writing this introduction in a political moment in the United States where the relatively minimal protections to women's autonomy and personhood afforded by *Roe v. Wade* have just been abruptly rescinded by the Supreme Court, the stakes of this project are not abstract. Without doubt, patients across the country will be bringing discussions of this political upheaval into the consulting room en masse—a similar phenomenon to what many analysts across the world witnessed following the #MeToo social movement and George Floyd's murder in the summer of 2020, on almost exactly this date. My advocacy throughout this book is not for a wave of overt analytic persuasion as though—in the highly unlikely event that such an approach was ever implemented—it would be the least bit effective in shifting what are often deeply moored unconscious and material ideologies. Rather, when it comes to clinical work, each chapter just begs a little more interrogation for clinical concepts and methods that are often held as naturalized fact. So, for instance, I wonder about what kinds of ethico-political judgments we are implicitly making when we detach our assessment of the moral value of ostensibly universal psychical processes—such as "splitting," "projection," or "reparation"—from their objects? Thought politically, it seems to me that the absolute and unequivocal disidentification with racist neo-Nazism has a different value than the idealization of a lover or friend, even as both of these phenomena could equally be described as the "immature" psychic process of splitting. Or, equally, I ask to what extent recent activist work publicizing the "White Silence Is Violence" slogan transforms the effects and use of analytic silence in the clinic? Does silence in the face of a patient's racist hate speech confer complicity? Or again, I ask if economic dispossession can be a condition of possibility for the dismantling of one of psychoanalysis's most cherished and most pilloried mainstays: the boundaried, privatized clinic? Such questions hover in the background of much of my thinking throughout this book, coming in and out of focus as I consider the larger implications of each figure's unique practice. As an academic who is not herself a clinician but who works in a largely clinical department and has experience with clinical training in both the United States and the

United Kingdom, my contributions to this field are without doubt the most speculative—but, for this reason, they are perhaps also the most provocative.

• • •

The first part of *The Political Clinic*, "Democracy's Children," considers the two most influential post-Freudian analysts, Anna Freud and Melanie Klein, whose divergent theories of human subjectivity vis-à-vis the child forever split the BPS in the 1940s. Following the transnational migrations of psychoanalysis from Austria to England to Scotland, I explore the politics of child analysis and discuss how the pliable figure of "the child" served as a tableau through which both women articulated their clinico-political imaginaries. In chapter 1, I chart how Anna Freud reimagined the shape of postimperial democracy in her clinic through her curation of a unique brand of clinical authority. Before fleeing to the United Kingdom and engaging in her well-documented wartime work in children's institutions,[49] Anna Freud worked in 1920s Red Vienna where, in conversation with radical educational reformists, she developed the first iterations of child psychoanalysis. Working across her case studies and miscellany from the 1920s, I excavate her clinical emphasis on the necessity of analytic authority, ultimately arguing that this nascent clinical technique constituted an experimental engagement with political theory. Drawing on scholarship from childhood studies, I establish how the figure of "the child" (as a representation of national futurity) was pivotal for her elaboration of this political-qua-clinical technique. As I show, through the child, Anna Freud's early clinical technique promoted authority in the clinic as a way to reenvision the organization of liberal democracy in the wake of the decline of empire.

The second chapter follows this discussion of the politics of child psychoanalysis with a focus on Melanie Klein's wartime clinical practice. Like Anna Freud, Klein was one of the founders of child analysis and she similarly used "the child" as an elastic category that licensed clinical innovation. In this chapter, I analyze Klein's clinical work throughout the 1930s and 1940s, focusing on her mammoth wartime case study, *Narrative of a Child Analysis*, in which she developed her thinking about psychological "reparative tendencies."[50] By putting

Klein's clinical technique in conversation with ethical, political, and economic reparations claims in interwar and postwar Europe, I show how her clinic experimentally spoke back to the political climates it inhabited. Through the language of reparation, Klein reimagined the clinic as both a part of and a potential solution to the sociopolitical aggressions manifested on the international stage. I claim that, although avowedly apolitical herself, Klein nevertheless mobilized the clinic as a site through which to envision and strive for an individualized form of sociopolitical justice. Yet, as I show, Klein's theorization ultimately complicates reparation's standing as a contemporary ethico-political ideal for critical theorists today.

In part II, "Empires of Mind: On Colonialism and Decolonization," I pursue a (de)colonial thread of psychoanalysis to consider how BPS-affiliated analysts used their clinics to address the racial and economic injustices produced by British colonialism and its aftermath. In chapter 3, I follow psychoanalysis beyond Europe to Johannesburg, South Africa, where the Lithuanian-born and London-trained psychoanalyst Wulf Sachs spent the 1930s working with an originally Southern Rhodesian medicine man named John Chavafambira. Expanding recent scholarship on the uses of psychology and psychoanalysis outside of the metropole,[51] I unpack Sachs's unique "traveling analysis" with Chavafambira, considering how the conditions of colonialism galvanized a reconfiguration of the typically boundaried, ostensibly neutral clinical relation. Readily foregoing clinical norms such as the consulting room itself, Sachs developed an unconventional intimacy with Chavafambira that involved his everyday participation in many parts of Chavafambira's life, including his growing anticolonial protest. Even as many scholars have rightly called attention to the racial, colonial, and gendered limitations of Sachs's endeavour,[52] I nevertheless argue that his practice contains the seeds of a progressive clinical practice insofar as it starkly calls out the nonneutrality of the clinical encounter and, in so doing, helps reimagine the boundaries of clinical intimacy as a decolonial act.

In chapter 4, I return to London to provide a critical analysis of how race and decolonization oriented D. W. Winnicott's clinical emphasis on "good enough mothering." To show this, I read Winnicott's 1964 case study of "The Piggle," which documents the psychoanalytic sessions of a two-year-old girl plagued by persecutory nightmares of a figure she calls "Black Mummy."[53] Winnicott never dealt openly with the racial and colonial tensions driving The Piggle's unconscious conflict; instead, as a white male analyst, he tried to cultivate a clinical experience of "good enough mothering" in his consulting room. This clinical technique would become one of his signature contributions. By putting Winnicott's clinical prioritization of the mother in conversation with the larger mid-century racist and colonialist pathologization of mothering practices, I argue that Winnicott's turn to the "good enough mother" constituted a fraught grappling with the larger social and political transformations in Britain caused by decolonization. As I show, Winnicott's analytic role as a "good enough mother" in the clinic is, for better *and* for worse, an explicitly political attempt to mitigate the racial conflict splitting the entire postcolonial British motherland. I thus reorient past scholarship on Winnicott that has primarily focused on the gendered dimension of his theory of the "good enough mother"[54] by calling attention to the intersectional racial work that this clinical technique also performs.

Part III, "From the Couch to the Iron Curtain: Psychoanalysis During the Cold War," shifts the historical perspective from decolonization to the Cold War and considers how the transatlantic paranoia about the spread of postwar Marxism and communism impacted psychoanalytic theory and clinical practice. I begin, in chapter 5, by taking up an important innovation in postwar psychoanalytic practice: the therapeutic community. As a communal form of clinical work, therapeutic communities flourished in Britain during the Cold War, becoming vital spaces for sociopolitical experimentations with direct democracy, egalitarianism, and horizontality that echoed the similar Marxist and anticolonial clinical innovations of global figures such as Fanon and Guattari. Here, I examine the work of the BPS psychoanalyst Thomas Main in one of Britain's most famous therapeutic communities—the Cassel Hospital—to unpack his particular approach to a "communal clinic." As I show, these clinical experimentations with communal sociality were part of a larger Cold War interest in exploring the political promise of the commune as a new social and institutional horizon. But, unlike other postwar iterations that used a combination of psychoanalysis and Leninist anti-imperialism to challenge the naturalized ascendency of capitalistic liberalism, I argue that Cassel's unique vision of therapeutic collectivity was wedded to a distinctly British ideology of the middle-class, hetero-sexual nuclear family as the seat of social democracy. Hence, I contend that Cassel did not so much reject the communalism socially definitional to Cold War communism; rather, the hospital used coupled, heteronormative sexuality to retool it for the economic ends of the capitalistic British welfare state.

In chapter 6, I explore how the language of individual maternal security that London-based psychologist and psychoanalyst John Bowlby promoted buttressed a growing Cold War emphasis on national security in an increasingly globalized setting of international hostility. Situating Bowlby's work within the economic and political climate of the Cold War United Kingdom, I consider how his idealization of infantile emotional "security" naturalized—and nationalized—the provision of "domestic" security by making the mother's reproductive labor with the child in the domestic home coextensive with the production of national security writ large. On a broad level, then, this chapter explores the link between Bowlby's security-minded "attachment theory" and contemporary so-called security feminism,[55] claiming that desecuritization of the state is tightly bound up with the urgent work of rethinking interpersonal relationality outside the vocabulary of safety and in/security.

Although the chronology of this book deliberately takes the closure of the Cold War in 1989 as its stopping point, the epilogue briefly considers how the legacy of these practitioners is being taken up today. For many decades, there has been a governing split between the clinical and the critical, with academic uses of psychoanalysis typically limited to the major theories of a few canonical figures and clinicians generally unaware of the breadth of academic social and political theorizing. Increasingly, however, there has been a growing interest in the convergence between these two spheres as academics embrace what I have come to think of as "a clinical turn" in their work while contemporary clinicians engage in intensified debate about the relationship between the clinic and social justice. Throughout the epilogue, I therefore bring my analysis of the clinic into the present moment by discussing some of these recent experiments with progressive practice, thinking specifically about what a justice-minded clinic can—and cannot—promise.

Taken together, these chapters consider the necessary historical-political contributions of clinical praxis while also making a larger case for the speculative political imaginaries furnished by originally clinical methods and practices. The invitation this thinking extends is thus intentionally bivalent. To historians and critical theorists, it offers more texture and nuance to our understanding of the political work performed by the clinic, detailing how six different clinical practices can be read speculatively as innovative political theory and engagement. To clinicians, it offers a provocative meditation on the mixed promise of the clinic and some of its most cherished mainstays. My hope is that these chapters will provide resources for new ways to theorize and practice psychoanalysis today.

PART ONE

Democracy's Children

CHAPTER ONE

On Good Authority

Anna Freud, Child Analysis, and the Politics of Authority

> If the unconscious becomes more intelligible—a source of coherent
> narratives—it also begins to be usurped by a new figure called the child.
> For some psychoanalysts . . . describing the child replaced describing
> the unconscious, or the dream work. Or rather, in their view, describing
> the child was to describe the unconscious. The child was as it were the
> unconscious live: you could see it in action. . . . With the advent of child
> analysis there was a growing sense that we could get closer to the source.
>
> —ADAM PHILLIPS[1]

In the foreword to a 1925 text on juvenile delinquency by August Aichhorn titled *Wayward Youth*, Sigmund Freud introduces the importance
of Aichhorn's work by hailing "the child" as the future of psychoanalysis.
He writes, "Of all the fields in which psychoanalysis has been applied
none has aroused so much interest, inspired so much hope, and accordingly attracted so many capable workers as the theory and practice of
child training. . . . The child has become the main object of psychoanalysis research and in this respect has replaced the neurotic with whom
the work began."[2]

Noting the interest in and wide appeal of the "application" of psychoanalysis to pedagogy, Freud concludes (almost a century before
Phillips) that the child has in fact become the "main object of psychoanalysis" itself, effectively displacing—or replacing—the neurotic. In this
foreword, Freud famously refers to psychoanalysis as a "re-education";

or, translated more accurately an "after-education," suggesting that an adult analysis is the necessary supplement to the child's primary schooling.[3] While these prefatory remarks are intended as a commentary on Aichhorn's work with so-called wayward youth, Freud's observation about the growing importance of the child for psychoanalysis writ large registers his more general recognition of the emerging body of work throughout Europe in the 1910s and 1920s produced by socially minded psychoanalytic reformers, such as Anna Freud, Siegfried Bernfeld, Willi Hoffer, and Hermine Hug-Hellmuth, all of whom put the child at the center of their psychosocial agendas. If the child had become the main object of psychoanalytic inquiry, then it seems hardly incidental that one of the most famous child psychoanalysts was in fact Sigmund Freud's own child, Anna Freud, who was born the same year as psychoanalysis and, from the first, counted herself as psychoanalysis's sibling, its "twin."[4]

This chapter analyzes the political stakes of child psychoanalysis by detailing the unique clinical technique that Anna Freud developed for her child patients. Before fleeing to the United Kingdom and engaging in her well-documented wartime social work in children's institutions,[5] Anna Freud was a clinical analyst in interwar Red Vienna where, in conversation with radical educational reformers, she developed the first iterations of child psychoanalysis. As I discuss, her early work was inspired by the climate of progressive social reform in interwar Vienna and she participated in many left-leaning experiments in radical pedagogy alongside progressive intellectuals throughout the city. But her clinical work tells a slightly different story. By working across her case studies and miscellany from the 1920s, I excavate her early emphasis on the necessity of authority in the child psychoanalytic clinic, ultimately arguing that this clinical priority complicates her political commitments. As I discuss, the status of naturalized political authority was a contested issue among intellectuals throughout interwar central Europe and it had particular significance for those grappling with the multinational rise of mass democracy. I thus suggest that Anna Freud's prioritization of authority in the clinic constitutes an experimental theorization of the shape of democracy in the wake of the Austro-Hungarian Empire, where she used the clinical relation between the analyst and the child patient to reimagine the relation between the governing and the governed. Drawing on scholarship in childhood studies, I establish how the figure of "the child" as a representation of national futurity was vital for the elaboration of this clinical-qua-political technique. If the child was to be psychoanalysis's future—the future of an international institution, profession, and, most importantly for this book, *practice*—then this chapter considers how, for Anna Freud, that future was invariably bound up with an open-ended and quickly changing political horizon that she used the space of the clinic to explore. I thus maintain that her clinical innovations—her impious departures from her father's approach—not only provide a vivid demonstration of how socioculturally embedded clinical practices necessarily are but also speak to their capacity to be sites of novel political theorizing.

PSYCHOPOLITICS: ANNA FREUD, EDUCATION, AND SOCIAL REFORM IN RED VIENNA

Born in Vienna on December 3, 1895, Anna Freud was the youngest of six children and the only one to pursue her father's profession.[6] Although she first trained as a public school teacher, her professional trajectory eventually returned her to her psychoanalytic twin and she carried the Freudian legacy forward to London, New Haven, Boston, and New York. From her early work in 1920s and 1930s Vienna, to her postwar institution-building in London, through to her training lectures in the United States, she pioneered the fields of child psychoanalysis and ego psychology.[7] Although her work has often been either ignored or, in the wake of the humanities' assimilation of Melanie Klein and Jacques Lacan in the 1980s and 1990s, dismissed by academics as a conservative relic of a misguided egoism whose function was purely adaptationalist in nature, Anna Freud remains one of the earliest and most influential innovators of an entirely new form of post-Freudian clinical practice: child psychoanalysis.[8]

Anna Freud began this work in the early 1920s after qualifying as an analyst when she delivered her first psychoanalytic paper, "Beating Fantasies and Daydreams," to the Vienna Psychoanalytic Society in May 1922.[9] From this point on—until the Gestapo's intensifying threats forced her entire family into exile in London—she worked in left-leaning Red Vienna where she honed her clinical technique for psychoanalysis with children. Her publications during this period reflect her focus on the nascent field of child analysis and include a range of books and essays in which she developed her unique clinical technique, such as *Introduction to the Technique of Child Analysis* in 1927 (1928 in English); "The Theory of Child Analysis" in 1928 (1929 in English); *Introduction to Psycho-Analysis for Teachers: Four Lectures* in 1930 (1931 in English); "Psychoanalysis and the Training of the Young Child" in 1934 (1935 in English); and *The Ego and the Mechanisms of Defence*—her most famous text—in 1936. Working between pedagogy and psychoanalysis, her early concern was with the elaboration of an adapted clinical technique that would be applicable to the child patient. Indeed, discussions of clinical practice were her priority because child analysis was a distinctly new direction for psychoanalysis and there was, up until that point, no standardized methodology for clinical work with a child patient.

True enough, in inventing psychoanalysis Sigmund Freud focused on the figure of the child, positing axiomatically that childhood experiences stood at the center of all adult psychic life. In 1909, he even published what many consider to be the first psychoanalytic case study of a child *avant la lettre*: "Analysis of a Phobia in a Five-Year-Old Boy"—or, more colloquially, "Little Hans."[10] Throughout this case, Freud narrates the phobias and anxieties of the case's five-year-old titular protagonist, "Hans," tracing his zoological fears back to their roots in his burgeoning Oedipus complex. However, Freud is the first to admit that he did not conduct this (child) analysis himself and actually only met Hans once throughout the period it was conducted. The bulk of the analysis was actually carried out by Hans's father, Max Graf, who was guided in his endeavors by an epistolary exchange with Freud in 1907 and 1908. Part narrative, part postal transcript, the case is thus a kind of bricolage of observations: as Graf observes his son, Freud observes Graf. The child remains at a location of one remove. For Freud, the significance of this case was therefore *not* that it furnished anything like a new program for clinical work with children; rather, its yield was purely theoretical: it provided "more direct, more immediate proof of [the] fundamental principles" of psychic life, especially those that Freud had elaborated a few years earlier in *Three Essays on the Theory of Sexuality*.[11]

It therefore fell to post-Freudian psychoanalysts, many of whom were women, to reconceive clinical psychoanalytic practice for the child patient. In 1920s Vienna, Budapest, and Berlin, Anna Freud, Melanie Klein, and Hermine Hug-Hellmuth, respectively, were the key figures embarking on this work, which necessitated the radical reimagining of the clinical relation. Even as these analysts lived and worked in relatively close geographical and historical proximity, they developed clinical vocabularies, techniques, and aspirations that were often worlds apart. Their conceptions of the child, and their attendant clinical practices designed to address its specificity, were exceptionally diverse. In other words, by the time Sigmund Freud wrote his foreword to Aichhorn's book, hailing the child as the future of the psychoanalytic enterprise, child analysis was already a varied subspecialty pioneered, importantly, by a coterie of rising female analysts, key among whom was Freud's own daughter. Child analysis would only gain in popularity and importance in the decades to come (especially in Britain), a fact clearly evidenced when, in the years immediately following Sigmund Freud's death, the entire institutional future of psychoanalysis writ large hinged upon the heated debates between two child analysts—Freud and Klein—whose "Controversial Discussions" split the BPS.[12]

However, before Freud ever made it to London and became affiliated with the BPS, she worked in interwar Red Vienna where her clinical practice was heavily informed by the radical pedagogy movements then in vogue. While not directly involved in politics herself, she actively collaborated with many political liberals, leftists, and social(ist) reformers.[13] In this regard, she was one among many since Red Vienna was, famously, a beacon of socialized municipal reform where expansive improvement programs in public housing, sanitation, education, and taxation were implemented to aid interwar recovery.[14] Austromarxists held powerful sway among the governing Social Democratic Worker's Party and the city was known, at the time, as a hub of leftist social engagement.

Children's health and education were some of the most important objects for these reformers, who sought to both expand and liberalize the provision of public education. Together with Hoffer, Aichhorn, and Bernfeld, Freud formed a weekly study group in the 1920s to discuss the relationship between psychoanalysis and pedagogy. While some, like Bernfeld and Hoffer, looked specifically to children's education as an exemplary site where the liberalization of oppressive strictures could facilitate large-scale political transformations, others, like Aichhorn, saw educational and criminal justice reform as pathways for dispossessed youth to gain greater social enfranchisement. Freud and Bernfeld—the former leader of Vienna's leftist Youth Movement—even created a short-lived antiauthoritarian school according to psychoanalytic principles known as the Hietzing School.[15] Alongside her small "Matchbox School" (co-run with Dorothy Burlingham), which combined psychoanalytic sessions with Montessori-style education, Freud collaborated with many educational reformers throughout her career to create experimental children's institutions as a mode of political engagement.[16] For these activists, education was central to the political promise of the city.

Psychoanalysis—especially in its liberationist, Frankfurt School iteration—was an indispensable resource for many of these left-leaning reform programs. According to Nick Midgley in *Reading Anna Freud*, "The radical reforms of education—understood as one aspect of a wider child welfare program—meant that many of the most idealistic and enthusiastic young people in Vienna chose to train as teachers. A significant proportion of these same young idealists were naturally attracted to psychoanalysis and wished to bring together their interest in educational reform with their enthusiasm for this new 'science of the mind,' which promised to revolutionize the way people thought about the psychology of the child."[17] Amid the unchecked hyperinflation, raging Spanish Flu, and dire food shortages that characterized interwar Red Vienna, a diverse cast of central European reformers such as Aichhorn, Wilhelm Reich, Erich Fromm, Erik Erikson, and Bruno Bettelheim drew heavily on psychoanalytic concepts for their revisions to crucial social institutions, including primary schools, but also churches, prisons, universities, government regulations, sexual mores, and gender conventions. Many relied on a particularly liberationist interpretation of psychoanalysis for their social and political pursuits, understanding it as a discourse and practice unequivocally allied with social progressivism. Indeed, this was the time and place where, as Elizabeth Danto has chronicled in her excellent *Freud's Free Clinics*, clinical psychoanalysis itself was explicitly aligned with a political commitment to social justice.[18] From the routinization of low-fee treatment, to the creation of free clinics like the Vienna Ambulatorium, to the incorporation of psychoanalytic consultations into various social services (including child guidance clinics), clinicians in Red Vienna actively widened the scope of their practices in an effort to use psychoanalysis for public outreach.

Reflecting retrospectively on the importance of this interwar political situation for the advent of child analysis, Anna Freud comments in an interview that "there is no doubt that child analysis began as a subspecialty of psychoanalysis, in the period after the First World War when several such subspecialties were initiated. What was later known under the slogan of the 'widening scope of psychoanalysis' were the attempts made from the 1920s onward to apply the therapeutic technique devised for adult neurotics to other ages or to other types of mental disorder."[19] In response to the pervasive experience of shell shock after the war, which powerfully and publicly demonstrated the susceptibility of ordinary, otherwise healthy individuals to psychic strain, interbellum psychoanalysis entertained what Sigmund Freud famously described as "a wider social stage" of engagement. Faced with the needs of not just individuals but entire populations, psychoanalysts openly modified and adapted their clinical techniques and theoretical insights to address various nodes of social welfare, mobilizing diverse versions of clinical practice for multiple fields. "Our dream was the dream of psychoanalysis—all it had to offer," reflected Anna Freud, "not only individuals, but schools and universities and hospitals and the courts and 'reform schools' that worked with 'delinquents,' and social service agencies."[20] According to her, these newly developed subspecialties were applications of earlier psychoanalytic theories and techniques to larger groups of people and to different and broader social and political issues. She counted child analysis among these interwar developments, contextualizing it as an attempt to expand psychoanalysis's purview beyond the limited scope of neurosis.

Yet, despite Freud's framing, many of these interwar offshoots of psychoanalysis—including child analysis—were far more than just simple "applications" of psychoanalysis. Indeed, they often radically transformed the nature of the previous psychoanalytic knowledge on which they were based, extending and modifying psychoanalytic orthodoxy in accordance with specific social and political ideals. Take, for instance, the controversial clinical innovations of Wilhelm Reich, who sought to undo the pernicious effects of capitalism's state-sponsored repression of sexuality through mobile clinics, free contraceptives, and different forms of touch therapy.[21] Or Karen Horney and Helene Deutsch, who in "applying" psychoanalysis to women not only developed unique theories that challenged the universalism of some of Freud's most (in)famous maxims (substituting "womb envy" for "penis envy," for example) but also prompted Freud's own well-known 1930s elaborations of psychoanalytic theories of sexual difference and femininity. Unsurprisingly, this was the context that likewise produced the first iterations of the Frankfurt School, whose members (such as Theodor Adorno, Erich Fromm, and Herbert Marcuse) mobilized psychoanalytic insights to generate powerful critiques of capitalism, authoritarianism, and (hetero)normative bourgeois family life. In making psychoanalysis relevant to new and different subsets of the population, these interwar "applications" thus fundamentally changed the nature of foundational psychoanalytic theories and methods. As Eli Zaretsky puts it in his social and cultural history of psychoanalysis, *Secrets of the Soul*, "In contrast to those that had propounded the classical liberal separation of public and private life, the thinkers of the 1930s recognized the unavoidably psychological and cultural character of modern politics, and thus the impossibility of separating the problems of democracy from those of personal autonomy, gender and sexuality, group identity, and the commodification of everyday life."[22] This style of psychoanalytically informed political theorizing gained further traction in the decades following World War II, especially, but its origins lie in the same historical mise-en-scène as those of child analysis.

No less than her male colleagues, then, Freud pursued a definitively political project when she began her psychoanalytic work with children. By combining clinical psychoanalytic practice with education, she merged two of the most energized spheres of leftist political engagement available in Red Vienna, thereby creating a new form of clinical practice. In what follows, I take up the nuances of her clinical work, showing how her approach both engages and resists the political promise of this social context. As I discuss, Freud began her career by advocating for the necessity of authority in the clinic, ultimately resolving that the child legitimately requires authoritative governance since the dismantling of authority would only ever result in the loosing of aggressive and sexual instincts that she found antithetical to the reproduction of a stable and nonviolent civil society. Contra socialist liberationist theorists like Reich or Marcuse who narrated the genesis of social malaise as a consequence of unnecessary repressions of the superego, which is classically represented by the patriarchal Oedipal father, Freud instead focused her clinical energies on the cultivation of precisely this psychic "institution," imagining the child to be developmentally immature and dependent and therefore in need of external (analytic) authority—which she herself sought to impose.[23] If, as Danto, Suzanne Stewart-Steinberg, and Michal Shapira have argued,[24] Freud's institutional work with children in schools and group homes testifies to her experimental production of horizontal, democratic power relations, then I discuss here how her interwar clinical work reveals an unexpected attachment to the political promise of hierarchical authority. Through her distinctive organization of the clinical space around the successful implementation of authority, Freud's interwar clinical practice can be seen participating in a broader political ambivalence about the viability and desirability of postimperial liberal democracy.

"ALLOWING HER DEVIL TO SPEAK": CHILD ANALYSIS AND AUTHORITY IN THE CLINIC

For Anna Freud, the child (as a psychological entity) was of a very different order than the primarily adult patients who had graced her father's couch since 1900. As the second generation of psychoanalysts worked to define what kind of being the child was, often developing a wide range of idiosyncratic theories, Freud advanced her own response, which relied on an overtly developmental rubric and emphasized the child's immaturity, incompleteness, and dependence.[25] Taking Sigmund Freud's structural model of the mind, with its now-famous nomenclature of the id, ego, and superego as the backbone of her theory of (childhood) subjectivity, Anna Freud turned her focus away from the excavation of the unconscious, emphasizing instead the relative instability of the young child's ego and superego and surmising from this that children are fundamentally bound to and dependent on external authorities. "Insofar as the childish superego has not yet become the impersonal representative of the demands taken over from the outer world, and is still organically connected with it," she writes in 1926, "to that extent the relevant external objects play an important role in the analysis itself."[26] If the child, according to Anna Freud, was essentially an "incomplete" version of the adult subject, then it only followed that any clinical work undertaken with children would need to operate with substantial modifications.[27]

To this, she proposed that there were two key alterations to Sigmund Freud's "classical" psychoanalytic technique that any clinician working with children needed to make. First, because of the unique circumstances of child analysis, she argued that the analyst needed to cultivate a specifically positive transference in the child patient. Whereas a defining aspect of psychoanalytic technique with adult patients is the transference wherein patients transpose past desires and anxieties—loves *and* hates—onto the person of the analyst, Anna Freud claimed that, because the child is still very much attached to and dependent on the presence of the actual parents themselves, the possibilities for any full-bodied transference are strictly limited. Explaining this in "The Role of Transference in the Analysis of Children" in *Four Lectures on Child Analysis*, she observes:

> Unlike the adult, the child is not ready to produce a new edition of his love relationships, because, as one might say, the old edition is not yet exhausted. His original objects, the parents, are still real and present as love objects . . . there is no necessity for the child to put the analyst fully in the parents' place, since compared to them he has not the same advantages which the adult finds when he can exchange his fantasy objects for a real person.[28]

Children, in other words, are creatures caught in the thrall of their everyday environments. Because of this, the child analyst must actively court the child's affection in order to secure her place in their psychic life. "I take great pains," Freud writes, "to establish in the child a strong attachment to myself, and to bring him into a relationship of dependence on me. . . . This affectionate attachment, i.e., the positive transference to the analyst, becomes the prerequisite for all later analytic work."[29] For her, these "great pains" are necessary because young children lack stable superegos and are therefore dependent on external, rather than internal, authority. Unable to regulate themselves, they must instead rely on external governance. Freud proposes that the analyst's clinical project is to aid the child in the introjection of a superego by, in fact, becoming the child's ego ideal—their ideal authority. This is, as she once wrote, an indispensable "period of preparation—a period of 'breaking the child in' for analysis."[30] Accordingly, it is the clinical role of the child analyst to buttress the parents' authoritative position, specifically using love and affection to encourage the child to develop socially acceptable sublimations and repressions. In contrast to her father, who theorized the superego—that psychic representative of paternal social authority—as the precipitate of anxiety and guilt, Freud here implicitly imagines the possibility of a less conflicted superego, one founded on unambivalent love and presence rather than anxiety and loss. "The really fruitful work," she summarizes, "always takes place in positive attachment."[31]

To elaborate this postulate about positive transference, Freud narrates her clinical work with a ten-year-old boy in which she actively curates the boy's positive transference and dependence by using her own authority to secure his attachment to her. This boy, who presented clinically with "an obscure mixture of many anxieties, nervous states, insincerities, and infantile perverse habits," distrusted her from the outset and refused to disclose what she speculated were his "sexual secrets."[32] In order to gain his trust, she embarked on a subtle process of one-upmanship, matching each of the boy's actions and behaviors with superior versions of her own: "If he came with a string in his pocket, and began to show me remarkable knots and tricks, I would let him see that I could make more complicated knots and do more remarkable tricks. If he made faces, I pulled better ones; if he challenged me to trials of strength, I showed myself incomparably stronger."[33] Her aim in performing this repertoire of Herculean feats is to make herself "useful" to the boy precisely by establishing herself as an authority on the subjects in which he is interested. She endeavors to show herself "incomparably stronger" so as to win his trust, bringing him to rely on her as an authority capable of shielding him from punishment and mitigating his destructive onslaughts. As she explains, "Besides an interesting and useful companion I had become a very powerful person, without whose help he could no longer get along. . . . I had made myself indispensable to him and he had become dependent on me. But I had only waited for this moment to demand of him in return the most extensive cooperation, though not in words and not all at one stroke: I asked for the surrender, so necessary for analysis, of all his previously guarded secrets."[34] By encouraging the boy's positive attachment and dependence in the clinic, Freud in effect became an authority without whom he could no longer make do. Love and authority work together here to produce the conditions that she believed to be the necessary groundwork for any further clinical work. "The child analyst, who in any case is bigger and older than his little patient . . . becomes a person of unquestioned power when the child feels that his authority is accepted by the parents even above their own."[35] According to Freud, this positive transference to an analytic authority yields yet another layer of the hierarchal relation: if all goes as planned, the child is then willing to "surrender" to the analysis, giving over "all his previously guarded secrets" as the final coup de grâce to the analyst's superior authority.

Not insignificantly, this narrative of a clinical practice based around a stronger, protectionist figure using their authority to secure the compliance of a younger, weaker initiate mirrors the daydreams that Freud herself used to compulsively record as a child. These daydreams, which she described as her "nice stories," followed the plot of a premodern political feud wherein "a medieval knight" takes a "fifteen-year-old noble youth" captive and holds him hostage as leverage, often threatening him with torture "to force him to betray his secrets."[36] In a structural dynamic that offers a fascinating parallel with the clinical technique she would come to invent only a few years later, Freud emphasizes that the significance of these daydreams is the hierarchical power relation they establish between the two male leads: the "antagonism between a strong and a weak person" is the formative aspect of the narrative drama that suffused her adolescent psychosexual life.[37] "The whole setting was one of apparently irreconcilable antagonism between one who is strong and mighty and another who is weak and in the power of the former."[38] Given how central conflict and (mis)recognition are to the dynamic, we might even say that these "nice stories" effectively function as a Hegelian parable of lord and bondsman in which political subjection is the condition of possibility for self-consciousness. In structure and affect, this fantasy tableau echoes the clinical technique that Freud developed for working with children, thus elucidating the latent political significance of her reconceptualization of the clinic as a space between the governing and the governed. In both scenarios, an interestingly sexualized and penetrative authority figure asks for the young child's surrender of secrets—of knowledge—as the basis of their improvised social contract. And, in both, there is the ultimate vindication of a good authority.

Beyond the positive transference, the second key modification that Freud implements for child analysis, already suggested by the above case study, is that the analyst be a pedagogical authority for the child patient. One of the main consequences of Freud's distinctive combination of psychoanalysis and education is her willingness to imagine the child analyst's function as quite different from the passive "mirror" that Sigmund Freud had proposed for analysts working with adults. "The child analyst must be anything but a shadow," she cautions, implicitly rejecting the statute of clinical neutrality that was the watchword of so many of her colleagues.[39] According to her advice, analysts should not simply act as passive reflectors of unconscious material since the young child suffers not from reminiscences but from current events. Given the fact that the child is actively negotiating the often-conflicted process of turning an external authority into an internal structure, she avers that the analyst ought to provide "support" throughout this process, helping the child to construct stable psychic structures through the authority of her presence, rather than prompting them to deconstruct solidified ones through transference and interpretation. Like a teacher or parent, the child analyst must mete out freedom with due discipline. For Freud, the analyst's authoritative presence is thus a prerequisite.

To give another brief example of the specifically pedagogical authority she promotes in clinical practice, Freud recounts her clinical work with a six-year-old girl who was brought to analysis because of an obsessional neurosis, which resulted in an overly inhibited demeanor. According to Freud, this inhibition was indicative of a repression of the girl's hostile and sadistic feelings against her mother, which she had split off into another part of her personality, calling this her "devil." By initially allowing the child to express these feelings without censure in the clinic, she "brought [her] young obsessional patient to the point of allowing her 'devil' to speak," a change that transformed not only the way the child behaved in the analytic hour but also her personality at home.[40]

But the tentative license that Freud gave her young patient did not go as she had planned. Having lifted the girl's external prohibitions and restrictions, she summarizes the results:

> In the absence of external condemnation, the child lost all moderation, carried over into her home all the ideas previously expressed only during analysis, and completely reveled, as she had with me, in her anal preoccupations, comparisons, and expressions. . . . My little patient had behaved like a pervert or a mentally ill adult, and thereby put herself beyond the pale of society. Since she was not removed from the company of others, they removed themselves from her. During this period she abandoned all restraints in other respects as well. In a few days she had become transformed into a cheerful, insolent, and disobedient child, by no means dissatisfied with herself.[41]

Freud interprets the little girl's abandonment of all social decorum as proof that children do not possess stable, self-regulating superegos and thus require the exercise of external authority if they are going to become other than a Hobbesian subject in the state of nature. This was a revelatory moment in the development of her analytic technique, and it solidified her conviction that clinical work with children, in order to be socially beneficial, should be decidedly authoritative.

> I had to acknowledge that I had made a mistake, in crediting the child's superego with an independent inhibitory strength which it did not possess. As soon as the important people in the external world had relaxed their demands, the child's superego, previously strict and strong enough to bring forth a whole series of obsessional symptoms, suddenly turned compliant. . . . I had changed an inhibited, obsessional child into one whose "perverse" tendencies were liberated. But, in doing so, I had also ruined the situation for my work. This liberated child now had her "rest hour" all day long [and] lost her enthusiasm for our joint work to a considerable degree.[42]

As a corrective to what she considered to be this early misstep in the analysis, Freud subsequently assumed a much more authoritative relation to the child and reinstated many of the original expressive prohibitions, especially those that related to the child's behavior outside of the clinic. She notes, "I fulfilled her apparent desire to have authoritative demands imposed on her."[43] She justified this unconventional intervention by (re)turning to an explicitly pedagogical idiom, emphasizing the importance of analytic "guid[ance]" and children's "learn[ing]." She opines further, in the same lecture:

> The analyst must claim for himself the liberty to guide the child
> at this important point, in order to secure, to some extent, the
> achievements of analysis. Under his influence the child must learn
> how to deal with his instinctual life; the analyst's views must in the
> end determine what part of the infantile sexual impulses must be
> suppressed or rejected as unsuitable in civilized society.[44]

Here, it is the analyst's job to "civilize" the (presumably "savage") child, taking what liberties she must in order to "guide" and "influence" the child toward the proper sublimations. Using a loosely colonial explanation that places the analyst's authority on the side of civilization, she suggests that the child analyst's ability to reproduce civil society is conditional on their authoritative suppression of unruly instinctual demands. Freud thus uses this case, which itself raises the question of the analyst's potentially pedagogical and disciplinary function, as a pedagogical object lesson for the reader, showcasing the moral failures of an undisciplined heroine—both the child given too free a rein and herself as an initially too-lenient analyst.

This case occupies an important place within Freud's early lectures since, through it, she justifies the implementation of the pedagogical preparatory period in child analysis, which she (as much as her many critics) acknowledges to be thoroughly unanalytic. She returns to the case frequently throughout her writings and uses it to argue that such pedagogical measures are not simply necessary in this one particular case but are a vital component in *all* child analyses. As Freud continually contends, because of the undeveloped nature of the child's mind it is incumbent on the analyst to be simultaneously psychoanalytic and pedagogical; the analyst must negotiate an unwieldy balance between the exercise of authority and its critique. She makes this statement a few pages later in the same lecture:

> I would not have enlarged upon this example if it did not serve to illustrate all the characteristics of the analysis of children put forward in this last section: the fact that a child's superego is weak; that his superego demands and consequently his neurosis are dependent upon the external world; that the child himself is incapable of controlling the instincts that have been freed; and that *for this reason the analyst must take charge and guide them.* The analyst accordingly combines in his own person two difficult and diametrically opposed functions: he has to analyze and educate, that is to say, in the same breath he must allow and forbid, loosen and bind again. If the analyst does not succeed in this, analysis may become the child's charter for all the ill conduct prohibited in society.[45]

Avowing the oppositional nature of these two pursuits—education and psychoanalysis—Freud nevertheless frames the technical uniqueness of child psychoanalysis as its almost impossible combination of them. The child's willingness and ability to conform to social expectations (primarily those having to do with sexuality and aggression) is a key part of how she narrates the "normal development" of the child, whose instinctual self-satisfactions must be tempered by cultural restrictions that are imposed as much by the authority of the analyst as by that of the forbidding teacher. In the pedagogical exercise of authority, the analyst, like the teacher, is a "real" person for the child, an external authority on which the child's superego can lean as a crutch: "The educational implications which, as you will hear, are involved in the analysis, result in the child knowing very well just what seems desirable or undesirable to the analyst, and what he sanctions or disapproves of."[46] In this way, Freud puts this case to work to prove the exceptional and unorthodox authority that the analyst must assume with children in order to avoid the collapse of society altogether.

Without doubt, this approach to authority has much in common with Sigmund Freud's *Group Psychology and the Analysis of the Ego* and his later *Civilization and Its Discontents.* But it is important to recall that Anna Freud advanced this ethic of authority, governance, and superegoic repression specifically in relation to the child in the clinic. While Sigmund Freud, in *Group Psychology*, described the social organization of groups and leaders through his theory of identification—astutely anticipating the multiple authoritarian "mass psychologies" that would soon be on the rise throughout 1930s Europe—Anna Freud adopted this social diagnosis as her clinical premise, prescribing it to children as the basis of clinical success. In a letter to family friend Max Eitingon in 1926, the same year that she delivered her lectures on child analysis, she confessed her personal attachment to her father's *Group Psychology*, telling Eitingon, "Everything was in there, my old daydreams and all I wanted."[47] *Group Psychology* functioned for Anna Freud as the authoritative text about authority. Her project, as she articulates it, is not one of speculative social theorization but of clinical construction and creation. She therefore took her father's political theory, with its emphasis on the psychosocial function of a regulatory social authority, and suggested that the subjects most in need of this particular kind of governance were children in analysis. In her own terms, Anna Freud argues that the child analyst's function ought to be the (necessarily prescriptive) production of subjectivity through the careful orchestration of good authority.

> We may say in short: the analyst must succeed in putting himself in the place of the child's ego ideal for that duration of the analysis; he ought not to begin his analytic work of liberation until he has made sure that the child is eager to follow his lead. For this purpose, it is essential that the analyst have *the position of authority* about which we spoke at the beginning. Before the child can give the highest place in his emotional life, that of the ego ideal, to this new love object which ranks with the parents, *he needs to feel that analyst's authority is even greater than theirs.*[48]

Implying that she knows how the psychic life of an adult ought to be structured in order to minimize suffering, she propounds a technique that seeks to lead children toward specific ends. From this, she maintains that clinical psychoanalytic practice ought to encourage children, as much as possible, to bring their instinctual needs under the guiding authority of the ego and superego; the analyst's work involves using her authority to transform socially unacceptable instinctual urges into what she understands to be socially useful and gratifiable ones, thereby reproducing stable, "civilized" society.

Freud said as much even in the latter decades of her career, after the human and material destructions of World War II, in the lecture series she gave in Boston for Harvard and Radcliffe students in 1952. In a talk titled "The Unconscious," she advised that "to change the environment of the child so that it fits the nature of the child . . . is all wrong. It does not work out well for the child, and for the adult community it means a loss in cultural values. It is the child who should go forward into the community."[49] This is perhaps the clearest demonstration of the ideological tension between Freud's institutional and clinical work. While the left-leaning educational experiments that she founded and directed with her socialist and communist colleagues—such as the Matchbox School, the Hietzing School, the Hampstead War Nurseries, and the Bulldogs Bank Home—developed new environments intentionally divested of excessive forms of authority in an effort to better meet children's instinctual needs, in the clinic she insisted on the importance of retaining these very hierarchical relations. In one respect, the Janus-faced nature of her politics is not new. While historians like Danto, Stewart-Steinberg, and Shapira have thoroughly documented Freud's socialist political leanings and her contribution to various democratic projects through her institutional work,[50] clinicians and academics inspired by Jacques Lacan have pilloried her as an emblem of the very forms of coercive adaptationalism that Lacan indicted as ego psychology's greatest political failing. Her adoption of analytic authority as a hallmark of her clinical method thus speaks to a noteworthy political ambivalence in her work, one that (as I will discuss) was as much a part of broader political as clinical discussion. For Anna Freud, the clinic was a compensatory, rather than revolutionary, space where the lived insufficiencies of liberal democracy could be supplemented and amended.

IN THE WAKE OF EMPIRE: AUTHORITY, DEMOCRACY, AND THE CHILD

In the psychoanalytic consulting room, child analysts like Anna Freud were actively (re)creating and implementing new clinical techniques to manage the child subject. These techniques, and indeed the very narratives they used to define "the child" as a particular kind of subjectivity, often pulled from the explicitly political vocabularies available to them. Terms like "authority," "liberation," "leadership," "attack," "defense," "tyranny," and "reparation" (to mention but a few) were a regular part of the rhetoric analysts used to theorize the child subject's metapsychology and craft clinical techniques. Take, for instance, Freud's brief description of the ego from her landmark 1936 *The Ego and the Mechanisms of Defence* in which she mobilizes politicized rhetoric to elaborate psychic structures: "Our proper field for observation is always the ego. It is, so to speak, the medium through which we try to get a picture of the other two institutions. When the relations between the two neighboring powers—ego and id—are peaceful, the former fulfills to administration its role of observing the latter."[51] Using language that registers the institutional, administrative, and even bureaucratic social structures that were the condition of possibility for Sigmund Freud's conception of the ego, Anna Freud shapes her understanding of the ego and the id—those "neighboring powers"—through the political idioms of peace and war. Poised on the brink of World War II, she argues in 1936 that the goal of analysis is negotiating "peace" between these conflicted institutions, whose personification as nation-states begs the question of their respective political signification. The geopolitical underpinnings of this metapsychology are far from novel, though, given that Sigmund Freud had been marshaling war imagery in his psychoanalytic papers from the very start. Indeed, the fact that Anna Freud's most enduring clinical legacy has been an unrelenting focus on the analysis of ego "defenses" already speaks to a lifetime spent caught between two world wars, a career embroiled in a major interinstitutional struggle for political power, and a subjectivity entrenched in racialized and gendered limitations. Psychoanalysts, as much as many other human scientists, were developing their conception of the child subject in the midst of a larger political discourse that was newly thinking about government, power, and (inter)national conflict on a global scale.

As historians of childhood have been quick to point out, it is difficult to overstate the importance of the frenzied political attention given to the child subject in this historical moment. Throughout industrialized Europe in the nineteenth and twentieth centuries, the figure of the child emerged as one of the most charged sites of professional and political interest, becoming the target of national as much as familial attention.[52] Such elevation was in large part to do with the expansion of industrialization since children played a vital role in the waged labor force during this time. In Britain, for instance, as urban industrialism ballooned in the early decades of the nineteenth century, the number of children in the public workforce likewise expanded. To slake the growing demand for a cheap, dexterous, and docile labor force, children's work moved out of the domestic sphere (where they had formerly served as apprentices and the like) and into the public sphere, where children become a key demographic of the industrial workforce.[53] The consequence of this was populous urban landscapes that brought the daily lived reality of children's harsh exploitation under the public eye, producing the child as an object of national concern.

Although industrialization developed more slowly in the Austro-Hungarian Empire and was generally better regulated by protective labor laws, the same link between industrialization and the public's sensationalized interest in children's welfare pertains. In the twentieth century, the welfare of the child throughout Europe was discursively, materially, and eventually legally united with the well-being of the nation, its value transformed from what sociologist Viviana Zelizer has described as an immediate economic "usefulness" to a prospective and future-oriented potentiality—in other words, an investment.[54] The interest in reforms to public education and child psychology were just two expressions of the expanding national investment in childhood as representative of both an economic and ideological future resource. The child thus came to represent what Lee Edelman, in his queer theoretical analysis of nineteenth- and twentieth-century culture, has termed "reproductive futurity," a locution that stresses how tied up the imaginary of national futurity that the child embodied is with specifically heteronormative modes of (social) reproduction.[55] Such scholarship highlights how, from the mid-nineteenth century on, the child became an unequivocally politicized entity, an abstract figure made to stand in the place of a fantasized collective future of national flourishing that is suspended permanently and purposefully on an open horizon, in everything from commercial marketing to scientific research and political campaigns to art, film, and literature. There is thus a paradoxical, if not unexpected, movement traceable wherein the very sentimentalized discourses born in the nineteenth century intended to advance progressive (labor) reform on children's behalf became the basis of a desubjectified rhetorical figuration deployed for a range of diverse political ends. (To see this, we need only think of how the figure of the child has been historically called on to contest everything from the end of Jim Crow, to LGBTQ adoption rights, to trans rights.) If Swedish feminist and educator Ellen Key was apt in hailing the twentieth century as the "century of the child," then childhood studies has gone some way toward theorizing on whose behalf this rhetorical "child" is often made to speak.[56]

Although only some child psychoanalysts were engaged in direct political work, their collective adoption of the child as the de facto subject of twentieth-century psychoanalytic practice registers the wide acceptance of this figure as a worthwhile object of social, political, and professional attention. Indeed, when reframed slightly, this newly magnetized focus on the child is exactly what Adam Phillips observes in the epigraph to this chapter since, from the 1920s to the 1970s, it was the child, far more than the adult, that became the privileged subject of psychoanalytic theory and practice, arguably "usurping" the unconscious. Whereas Sigmund Freud had unseated then-dominant theories of conscious, autonomous individualism by placing the unconscious at the helm of mental life, child analysts (Phillips suggests) to some extent walked this revolutionary postulate back, replacing it with more "coherent narratives" focused on the ego, normative development, psychological stability, and emotional maturity. In this telling, the definitional unintelligibility of the unconscious was replaced by the clean, coherent teleology of childhood development; the surrealism of the dreamwork was expropriated by realist narratives of growth and maturation. Where once the unconscious was, there the child had come to be. Phillips insinuates that psychoanalysis's refusal to leave any child behind meant, ironically, that it forgot the unconscious.

As I have been discussing, what makes analysts like Anna Freud particularly interesting is the extent to which their engagement with this spectral representation of national futurity goes beyond mere discourse and informs the organization and practice of an interpersonal, lived relation in the clinic. Working as a child analyst where many forms of experimental clinical engagement could be sanctioned, Freud invested ideologically in the salutary effects of the just operation of authority, imagining her clinic to be consonant with the reproduction of civil society. For the child, unlike for the adult, the liberatory potential of psychoanalysis is to be found—however paradoxically—in the judicious embodiment and exercise of authority. This treatment of authority represented a significant break with the thought of her various socialist colleagues who, largely, wanted to *de*emphasize the censures of the paternal superego since this rigid and repressive internal structure was understood to be the root of much unnecessary psychical conflict, an atavistic representation of patriarchal norms that many socialist and feminist psychoanalysts were struggling to undo. As the sweeping political appeal of authoritarianism was made more and more evident throughout the 1930s and 1940s, thinkers like Marcuse, Fromm, and Adorno grew increasingly wary of the psychic effects of authority and, as a tactical response to this zealotry, theorized authoritarianism as the political correlate of the psychic introjection of authority. Citing Fromm specifically, Frank Furedi observes in his comprehensive history of social theories of authority that there was an increasing tendency, throughout the interwar period but especially during the rise of global fascism, "to lose sight of the distinction between authority and power, and between terms like 'authority' and 'authoritarian.'"[57] In many interwar social and political discourses, authority and authoritarianism became synonymous; an emphasis on the former translated into a natural affinity for the latter. As the threat of multiple authoritarian regimes mounted in the 1930s, psychoanalytic rubrics that detailed the individual internalization of authority became powerful narratives for diagnosing the appeal of authoritarianism as a form of governance and for strategizing different kinds of social eugenics to stymie its recurrence.[58]

It was thus in contrast with these thinkers, who equated authority with authoritarianism and sought to retrench the hold of the superego as the internal representative of oppressive patriarchal political authority, that Anna Freud propounded a clinical technique in which children's "liberation" (to use her phrasing) was contingent on the successful internalization of precisely the internal authority that others meant to dispel: the superego. She emphasized the importance of the formation of the ego and superego through the instantiation of proper clinical authority, looking to the extant social order for the perimeters of the child's future instinctual gratification. By combining pedagogical with psychoanalytic methods in the clinic, she argued emphatically for the necessity of restrictive authority in the upbringing—and analysis—of the child. When it came to the child in the clinic, freedom, according to Freud, paradoxically came from obedience, authority, and analytic leadership. As Midgley confirms, "In contrast to the dominant view of psychoanalysis at the time, which many people understood to be promoting unfettered freedom of expression, Anna Freud emphasized that "'lack of restraint' can be as harmful to children as 'the injurious effect of too great repression.'"[59] Put simply, her primary concern in these early papers, during the socialist golden age of Red Vienna, was not with mitigating the injurious effects of too strong an authority but with curtailing those begat by too great a freedom.

Yet Freud was not alone in her conceptual turn to authority as a strategic solution for the problems incurred by excessive ungoverned liberty. While socialist antiauthoritarians on the cusp of World War II were highly critical of authority, rejecting it as the antithesis of (democratic) freedom, there was a large sect of transnational interwar pundits and intellectuals who were wary of democratic tenets and embraced instead a concept of authority as a potential solution to the problems inherent in mass democracies. After World War I ended and the Austro-Hungarian Empire was dismantled and partitioned into smaller, ethnic nation-states, the newly minted Austrian democracy struggled to articulate the legitimacy of its constitutional foundations.[60] In the abrupt transition from empire to democratic republic, many were ambivalent about not only the republic's legitimacy but also about its desirability. All three of the largest political parties at the time—the Social Democrats, the Christian Social Party, and the Greater German Nationals—had doubts about a liberal Austrian democracy: the conservative, antisemitic Christian Social Party would have preferred a return to monarchy; the Social Democrats were amenable to democracy but lobbied for a more fully socialist economy; and the German Nationals avidly vied for official unification with Germany.[61] Before World War II, many in Austria and Germany alike were thus skeptical of democratic republicanism, and there was much public ambivalence about the Allies' ideological project of enforced democratization. For many interwar Austrians and Germans, the imperative to democracy had the strong smell of cultural imperialism and its premises of majority rule often appeared as a threat rather than a promise. As Furedi speculates, it has perhaps only been retrospectively, after the disastrous realities of the twin authoritarian regimes of Stalinism and National Socialism, that democracy has come to be so idealized and enshrined as a broadly uncontested ethico-political virtue.[62] However, prior to the psychic and material violence of genocidal fascist and socialist regimes, democracy was treated with much more dubiety, in large part because its relationship to authority was ambiguous.[63] As Furedi writes, "In the inter-war era democracy was regularly depicted as the source of society's problem, rather than as its solution; and throughout most of the first half of the twentieth century democracy was regarded in highly ambiguous terms, even by its supporters."[64]

Harkening back to the crowd psychologists of decades before, this negative suspicion about the lack of legitimate, regulatory authority in democratic governments frequently took shape in a widespread anxiety about the irrational nature of "public opinion" and the deficiencies of the ungoverned "masses." Political commentators distrusted the sound decision-making of the public majority, likening them to "children" and "primitives" in a developmental framework reminiscent of Sigmund Freud's 1914 colonialist anthropological epic, *Totem and Taboo*. In his 1922 critique of democracy *Public Opinion*, the conservative American commentator Walter Lippmann wrote, "The mass of absolutely illiterate, of feeble-minded, grossly neurotic, undernourished and frustrated individuals, is very considerable, much more considerable there is reason to think than we generally suppose. Thus, a wide popular appeal is circulated among persons who are mentally children or barbarians, people whose lives are a morass of entanglements, people whose vitality is exhausted, shut-in people, and people whose experience has comprehended no factor in the problem under discussion."[65] Comparing the psychological sophistication of the masses, who he imagines are politically untrustworthy because of their susceptibility to uninformed public opinion, to children and "barbarians," he employs a familiar justification for disenfranchisement and political elitism on the basis of the risks posed by mass democracy. For Lippmann, authority was far from a threat to democracy; rather, it was democracy's solution, the necessary supplement to an internally flawed system.

In like kind, although with a less conservative bent, Max Weber, in his 1919 "Politics as a Vocation," turned to "charismatic authority" as an antidote to the deadening effects of the modern state's routinized bureaucracy. Writing against the hegemonic ascent of modernity, with its affinity for rationalism, secularism, capitalism, and professionalism—a historical movement Weber felicitously called "disenchantment"—Weber propounded his well-known tripart model of authority (traditional, charismatic, and legal) as a way of schematizing the different characteristics and functions of states. For Weber, all state formations (democracy included) are best defined as entities with a monopoly on the use of physical force—a claim that seems, at very least, questionable in today's political climate—and authority constituted the legitimating grounds for the exercise of this force. As he observes with a bleak realism in 1919: "The state is a relation of men dominating men, a relation supported by means of legitimate (i.e., considered to be legitimate) violence. If the state is to exist, the dominated must obey the authority claimed by the powers that be."[66] Although Weber's interest in the state remained abstract—he meant his triptych of authority to apply as much to the direct democracies of ancient Greece as to the monarchical empires of Europe—he was one of many thinkers during this time to make a notion of authority, however ahistorical, the lynchpin of political formation. As Andreas Anter puts it in his analysis of Weber's theory of the state, "The fact that the concept of authority was not defined by Weber and was only vaguely related back to 'command and compliance' reflects the thinking of the time, in which the old question 'what is authority?' remained unanswered in all contemporary writing."[67] As Furedi explains, "In the interwar era, widespread political insecurity encouraged antidemocratic ideals in which many people invested their hope in salvation through a decisive leader. It was in this context that ideas about charismatic leadership gained traction."[68] Authority was thus a keynote concern for many political theorists who struggled both with and against it during the interwar years as Europe grappled with whiplash multinational transitions from empire to democratic republic to authoritarian fascist state.

Anna Freud never consciously or explicitly entered into any of these political debates. In Vienna, she identified (as did her father) as a Social Democrat and her primary political engagements were at the level of her vast contributions to children's institutions and postwar social outreach work. Yet insofar as she took one of the most politicized figures of the turn of the century—the child—and used her work in the clinic to argue for the indispensability of a strong, paternal analytic authority for governing the child's unruly instincts, her clinical scenario echoed political debates about democracy and authority in the interwar period. By suggesting that the child, that paradigmatic figuration of national futurity, was the entity most in need of authoritative guidance, she created a clinical space that was actively reimagining political power—and, more specifically, the relationship between the governing and the governed in the transition from empire to liberal democracy. Her organization of the clinical relation through the value of properly instantiated authority thus constituted the practice of an ambivalence in relation to mass democracy.

Yet even though this turn toward authority carries with it a critique of liberal democracy's futures, it—like many other political theories of authority at the time—ought to be read as a supplement to rather than a rejection of the political promise of democracy. While her later, post–World War II social work would more strongly emphasize the value of horizontal and egalitarian relationality—the best example here would be her "An Experiment in Group Upbringing," coauthored in 1951 with Sophia Dann, which finds unexpectedly positive outcomes in a group of six bonded Jewish orphans in the Bulldogs Bank Home[69]—in her early clinical work we see enacted a different and more ambivalent relationship to lateral, nonauthoritative relations of power and governance. Taken as a combination of political theorizing and political action, then, Freud's clinic pursues a democratic agenda, to be sure—but one more interested in the maintenance of social hierarchy than in revolutionary transformation, understood personally or nationally. In this way, she used her clinic to experiment dually with the children of a nation and with the shape of the nation-state in its infancy. If Freud's interwar clinical techniques meditated on "good" authority, then it is my contention this was as a supplement to rather than a wholesale dismissal of the uncertain political futures of the new democratic nation-states born in the twentieth century.

Anna Freud was far from the only psychoanalyst to use the child analytic clinic in this way. As World War II took shape, in some measure as a response to the very problematics of authority that concerned Freud, psychoanalysts from across Europe fled to the United Kingdom. Consequently, the geography of psychoanalysis contracted and analysts of all stripes set up their clinical practices in London, where they grappled with the upheavals of twentieth-century global politics. Anna Freud was among the analysts of this diaspora and it was in London that her authoritative clinical technique would find its severest critic.

Beyond Repair

War, Reparation, and Justice in Melanie Klein's Clinic

It was May 1941, and Melanie Klein (like many other London-based psychoanalysts) had fled the daily London blitzkrieg by moving north to the small village of Pitlochry, Scotland. While there, Klein began the analysis of a "very unusual boy of ten" who she would come to call "Richard."[1] Klein saw Richard six times a week, for a total of ninety-three sessions, from April 28 to August 23, 1941.[2] During this time, Richard and Klein discussed the myriad anxieties and phobias that brought him to analysis, many of which were directly related to the ongoing violence of World War II. Every day, Richard read four newspapers, listened to the radio for updates about the war, and fervently tracked Hitler's advance across the continent. When Klein asked him, during their first session, to discuss some of the "difficulties" that caused him to be brought in for analysis, Richard answered with an expansive description of national conflict:

> He [Richard] also thought much about the war. Of course he knew that the Allies were going to win and was not particularly worried, but was it not awful what Hitler did to people, particularly the terrible things he did to the Poles? Did he mean to do the same over here? But he, Richard, felt confident that Hitler would be

beaten. (When speaking about Hitler he went to have a look at the large map hanging on the wall.)[3]

In a move that would become emblematic of the whole analysis, Richard responds to Klein's request that he map his psychological difficulties by providing a cartography of war. Throughout his analysis, Richard would continue to bring the political events occurring throughout wartime Europe into his daily psychoanalytic sessions, acting out everything from the Battle of Crete and the naval expeditions of the warships *Bismarck* and *Nelson* to Switzerland's precarious neutrality and Germany's gluttonous expansion. He brought his own set of toy battleships with him to most sessions and used the art supplies that Klein provided to create dozens of drawings that depicted air, sea, and railway attack, as well as the constantly shifting borders of a multi-state conglomerate he ominously called "The Empire."[4] These political concerns pervaded Richard's unconscious phantasies as well, and from his very first psychoanalytic session to his very last he discussed with Klein an astonishing cast of characters—some persecutory, others not—including his avowed enemy, the "bad Hitler-Daddy," and his paradigmatic good object, "Octopus Mummy."[5] As Richard detailed these politically informed phantasy configurations in his speech, in his play, and in his drawings, Klein honed her then-emergent theory of the depressive position and its attendant reparative processes. Through Richard's case, the geopolitics of world war would become the routine vernacular of Klein's consulting room, impacting not only Richard's own clinical encounter but also the future shape of Klein's entire theory and practice.

Combining scholarship from the history of the human sciences (by Eli Zaretsky, Adam Phillips, Michal Shapira, and Michael Roper)[6] with psychoanalytically informed political theory (from C. Fred Alford, Gal Gerson, David McIvor, and Amy Allen),[7] this chapter deepens part I's exploration of the politics of child analysis by turning to Klein's wartime clinical work. Like Anna Freud, Klein was one of the founders of child psychoanalysis and similarly used "the child" as a pliable figure to justify her unique reconfiguration of clinical practice. Focusing specifically on Klein's clinical work with her child patient, Richard, which she records in *Narrative of a Child Analysis*, I consider how, in the midst of World War II, Klein's consulting room became a hothouse for the elaboration of political phantasies and fears. It was in this context, while Richard fretted about the possibility of Nazi attacks, invasions, and bombings, that Klein elaborated her understanding of the importance of reparation. Putting her psychological theory of reparation, which she understood to be a relational ideal, in conversation with the fiercely contested economic reparations claims made throughout interwar and postwar Europe, I explore how Klein's work participates in a fraught grappling with the shape of justice in the twentieth century. I argue that, by envisioning the cultivation of reparation as a psychological priority in the clinic, Klein reimagined her clinical work as both a part of—and a potential solution to—the sociopolitical aggressions manifested in international wars. Although expressly apolitical herself, Klein's clinical practice nevertheless embraced a distinctly social and political agenda through its commitment to cultivating the capacity for reparation. As I contend throughout, Klein's child analytic clinic therefore constitutes a site through which she struggled to realize an individualized form of sociopolitical justice—albeit one that was being shown to be increasingly problematic on a global political scale. In this way, Klein's practice experimentally speaks back to the political climate it inhabited, offering novel—if not untroubled—theories of global justice.

CHILD'S PLAY AND WAR GAMES

Klein (née Reizes) was born in Vienna in 1882 to Jewish parents, the youngest of four children. Her early life was strained by her family's intermittent insolvency and by her elder brother's chronic illness, from which he died in 1902. She would not become a recognized figure in the psychoanalytic community until over twenty years later when, with the support of her analyst Karl Abraham and the help of Ernest Jones, she emigrated to London and became not only one of the founders of child psychoanalysis and the first European member of the BPS but also one of the most respected authorities on psychoanalytic theory and practice following Sigmund Freud's death in 1939.[8] Her work with children throughout the 1930s, 1940s, and 1950s established the field of Object Relations and inaugurated one of the most significant post-Freudian psychoanalytic orientations to date.[9]

Influential though Klein's theories undoubtedly were, her rise to prominence was dogged by constant criticism about the questionable orthodoxy of her interpretations of Sigmund Freud's work. These contestations were perhaps best exemplified by the "Controversial Discussions," a series of debates held by the BPS from 1941 to 1946 to settle the differences between the so-called Viennese camp—primarily composed of the newly arrived Anna Freud and her followers—and the more established "British" analysts, who were (ironically enough) led by Klein, a Viennese citizen by birth.[10] The disagreements and simmering animosities between Freud and Klein were long-standing and mutually held, going back as far as the mid-1920s when Jones had embraced Klein as a pioneer within the BPS while sidelining Freud. Adding insult to injury, Jones even leveled some waspish *ad hominem* attacks at Freud's character, calling her "a tough and indigestible morsel" in a letter to Klein and questioning, in a correspondence with Sigmund Freud, her "imperfectly analyzed resistances"—a dig not lost on Freud since it was, in fact, he who had analyzed his teenage daughter.[11]

Klein, for her part, was hardly neutral in the conflict. She disagreed vehemently with the pedagogical imperative of Anna Freud's method, insisting that the clinical treatment of children should adhere strictly to the original method that Sigmund Freud laid out. As J. B. Pontalis summarizes the dispute, "The technical debate opposing Melanie Klein to Anna Freud reflects the confrontation of two ethics: For Anna Freud, in the end, it was a question of making the child find the adult's alleged autonomy; for Melanie Klein, it was a matter of coming to meet the child's psychic reality and measuring adult knowledge against it."[12] In Klein's opinion, the child analyst's job, regardless of the patient's age, was to create conditions in the clinic that best facilitated the child's transference, which the analyst would then verbally interpret in order to lessen the child's resistance and alleviate their anxiety. Since this technique gave priority to interpretation and to the transference (both hallmarks of Sigmund Freud's original method) Klein stridently defended her approach on the grounds of its technical orthodoxy—a claim that, given Sigmund Freud's own penchant for heterodoxy, spoke more to Klein's own desire for intellectual and institutional legitimacy than to any universally accepted Freudian doctrine.

Much like her rival, then, Klein too departed from any standard "application" of classical psychoanalysis when dealing with the child patient. Along with other radical transformations of the clinical space (like Relational psychoanalysis's democratization of the analyst-patient dyad or Lacanian psychoanalysis's scanded hour), Klein arguably advanced one of the most significant and inventive reshapings of clinical practice in the whole of twentieth-century psychoanalysis. Her method's hallmark— and what would make it such a creative reimagining of the clinical dynamic—was her signature play-technique, which embraced the logic of clinical free association but applied it to children's physical actions rather than their verbal associations. Given that Klein often worked with children either too young to speak or whose speech was strongly inhibited, most of her clinical interpretations relied on what children did with their hands rather than with their mouths. Instead of listening to the (adult) patient's speech, Klein observed the (child) patient's play, rendering her verbal interpretations from their physical manipulation of objects. "Children," argues Klein, "substitute actions (which were the original precursors of thoughts) for words: with children, *acting* plays a prominent part."[13] According to Klein, acting not only plays a prominent part but playing acts as a due substitution for speech. Her conviction about the unimpeachable orthodoxy of her method thus rests on her belief in the fundamental substitutability of words for actions, of word play for child's play. Both word play and child's play, she argues, are forms of free association.

Klein was adamant that these modifications, however novel, were nevertheless entirely consistent with the fundamentals of Sigmund Freud's method. In this defense, Klein pursues a strategic (and rather spurious) separation of method and content, additionally suggesting that word, image, and action have an exchangeable status within the unconscious. "Just as children's means of expression differ from those of adults so the analytic situation in the analysis of children appears to be entirely different. It is, however, in both cases essentially the same."[14] Engaging what can only be described as a self-justifying tautology, Klein argues that the clinical substitution of objects for words is, if not unimportant, then a matter of only—and literally—*technical* difference: "It is a question only of a different technique, not of the principles of treatment."[15] Put another way, she insists that any differences manifested by her play technique are mere technicalities: issues of negligible importance that do not disrupt the more fundamental "principles of treatment."

Readers of Klein's work have ample opportunity to see demonstrations of this interpretive play technique in action since, perhaps more than any other analyst, she employed clinical case material to exemplify her theories. Take, for instance, this short clinical vignette from Klein's first monograph, *The Psycho-Analysis of Children*, the text in which she first proposes her play-technique. This passage records her interpretations of her patient, Peter, "an extremely timid, plaintive and unboyish child" aged three years and nine months who came to Klein for a prophylactic analysis.[16] Peter played with the toys that Klein provided,[17] and in describing one of his games, Klein offers the following interpretation:

> Once, when he had put the motor-cars, which symbolized his father's penis, in a row side by side and had made them run along, he lost his temper and threw them all about the room, saying: "We always smash our Christmas presents straight away; we don't want any." Smashing his toys thus stood in his unconscious for smashing his father's genitals. This pleasure in destruction and inhibition in play, which he brought into his analysis, were gradually overcome and disappeared together with his other difficulties during the course of it.[18]

Here, Klein reads Peter's fit of rage as a destructive attack aimed not at the toys themselves but at his father's penis, and she offers an apparently salutary interpretation. If the equation of motorcars with Peter's father's penis seems pellucid to Klein, it likely raises more than a few questions for readers who are not given any explanation for this abrupt comparison.[19] How, for instance, did Klein establish the symbolic capacity of the toy car? How much does Peter know about his father's genitals? What are the perimeters of the analyst's interpretations and according to what criteria would their accuracy be validated?

These questions were all the more pressing given Klein's capacity to push interpretation to its limits, testing the threshold of the plausible when it came to even the most quotidian actions. In a not-inaccurate pantomime, Anna Freud broaches this critique herself. "If the child overturns a lamppost or a toy figure," Freud speculates, "she [Klein] interprets this action, e.g., as an aggressive impulse against the father; a deliberate collision between two cars as evidence of an observation of sexual union between the parents. Her procedure consists in accompanying the child's activities with translations and interpretations, which themselves—like the interpretations of the adult's free associations— exert a further influence on the patient."[20] While Klein accuses Anna Freud of embodying an undue pedagogical authority that bullied the patient into compliance, Freud shoots back that Klein's "classical" interpretations are no less coercive. In the end, Freud's point is not simply that Klein gets her interpretations wrong—although there is a tacit accusation of "wild analysis" at work in her remarks—but rather that Klein's interpretive method is not nearly as neutral and benign as she might suggest. Through baroque interpretation, Klein "exert[s] a further influence on the patient," crossing the line from interpretation to out-and-out suggestion.[21]

Wild though they may indeed seem, Klein believed that such elaborate and sexually forthright interpretations were an honest rendering of the child's unconscious, which she argued operated far in advance of consciousness. Working against developmental models of mind (such as Anna Freud's), Klein considered even the smallest infant to be a temporally complex organism, riven by conflicted, phylogenetically inherent biological instincts that comprise the child's unconscious phantasies.[22] When prompted, for instance, to account for how a child of two or three could be made ill by unconscious phantasies about specific sexual acts or body parts with which they had little experience (such as the father's penis, the mother's vagina, the copulating "combined parent" figure, and their own internal children), she replies that these phantasies are the product of an instinctual species inheritance, which (in)forms the child's unconscious. "Even the quite small child, which seemingly knows nothing about birth, has a very distinct *unconscious* knowledge of the fact that children grow in the mother's womb," explains Klein.[23] Although it is often overlooked in scholarship on Klein that pits "Object Relations" squarely against the "instinct" or "drive" theory affiliated with Sigmund and Anna Freud, Klein's theory of unconscious phantasy is deeply invested in the interaction between the life and death *instincts*.[24]

Even as Klein's approach to instincts is not discharge-oriented (as is the Freuds' model), she nevertheless relies heavily on the language of *instinkt*/instinct rather than *trieb*/drive throughout her writing in German and in English (although almost all of her post-1920s writing was in English).[25] As Juliet Mitchell writes in her "Introduction" to *The Selected Melanie Klein*, "for Klein, what is unconscious is the biological and affectual condition of the human being. In essence, by the time of her later writings, the unconscious is equivalent to the instincts: to the life drive and death drive and their affects. . . . The Kleinian unconscious is a container full of contents; it is not another system of thought."[26] The consequence of this—and a noteworthy one at that—is a transformed understanding of what Klein means when she writes about "object relations" since objects, as the child perceives them, are never properly separable from instinctually informed unconscious phantasies. Objects, in her work, are best understood as the *internal representations* of objects, not as external or interpersonal realities. Relationality, for Klein, is therefore never entirely external and social since she thought that our subjective encounter with the broader social sphere—what is first the mother but gradually expands to encompass the whole domain of the sociopolitical—is governed, in large part, by instinctual, unconscious phantasies that kaleidoscopically turn our perception of the external object-world. Unconscious phantasies color, shape, and indeed determine a large swath of our object relations, and these relations are never properly separable from the body's instincts and their vicissitudes.

Although this bio-anatomism has now been largely supplanted in academic readings of Klein by a set of persuasive cultural and semiotic interpretations of her work, it was the target of severe criticism by many of her contemporaries and later interpreters. Radical psychoanalytic feminists such as Nancy Chodorow, for instance, rightly indicted Kleinian theory's tendency to implicitly bond women to the task of mothering, thereby reproducing the very psychological—and, for Chodorow, ultimately sociological—splits between masculinity and femininity that Klein's political intervention sought to undo.[27] Such a bio-anatomistic focus on the mother/child relation was the reason that critics like Chodorow initially embraced D. W. Winnicott, who seemed to offer a more gender-expansive theory of mothering—even as Winnicott's cultural and political impact, in Britain, was later shown to bolster the postwar entrenchment of gendered divisions of (reproductive) labor.[28] Arguably, it has only been retrospectively, through the vantage point offered by more poststructuralist feminist theorists such as Jacqueline Rose, Lyndsey Stonebridge, Julia Kristeva, and Ramón Soto-Crespo, that Klein's theory has been debiologized for those who continue to think with her in the humanities and social sciences.[29] To different ends, critics from the 1990s advanced a generally semiotic and often Lacanian account of Klein's work as part of feminist theory's abiding political wager that culture, not biology, is the true agent of radical, progressive change.[30] In so doing, they made Klein's work a viable and relevant critical interlocutor, not just for feminist theory but for many fields seeking to address questions of sociality, sexuality, fantasy/phantasy, femininity, childhood, aesthetics, and the persisting force of aggression and destruction in daily life.

While these critics (and many following them) typically swap Klein's biologistic language of "instincts" for the more cultural vernacular of "drives"—a collapse that is evident even in the passage from Mitchell I cited above—they nevertheless did justice to Klein's adamant insistence that the death instinct be understood as *the* crucial psychic force in the psychic life.[31] In contrast to Anna Freud, who rejected her father's 1920 theory of the death instinct, Klein embraced this idea and made it (and attendant experiences of aggression, anxiety, destruction, and reparation) the centerpiece of her theories about earliest infantile subjectivity. Indeed, the death instinct was integral to the processes of splitting and projection that Klein, in 1946, would come to organize under the umbrella of the "paranoid-schizoid position," meaning that, in some sense, death is the child's earliest and first antagonist. In order to safeguard its own survival against the threat of ego dissolution, the child's fledgling ego must ward off and expel the death instinct, projecting it into the external world where it can be more securely managed. Having done so, the child is then persecuted by paranoid phantasies of impending external assault, threatened now by anxieties related to the exterior world rather than the interior. In a radical reappraisal of metapsychology, Klein even linked the origins of the superego with the introjection of the death instinct, thereby imagining the superego not as the stable guardian of civilization and cultural reproduction (as Anna Freud had) but as yet another aggressive, persecutory force bent on subjective disintegration.[32]

Klein's theory of the child therefore departed quite radically from modernity's two dominant ideological constructions of childhood, which were derived from the political philosophy of the social contract theorists John Locke and Jean-Jacques Rousseau: the Kleinian child was neither *tableau rasa* nor uncorrupted innocence in the state of nature.[33] Rather, in a novel configuration, Klein theorized the child as a being besieged, a psychosocial subjectivity always already at war. Its mind is prepopulated by often-violent unconscious phantasies that stem from somatic origins and instinctual inheritances, whose strength and sophistication the child is psychically ill-equipped to handle. Because the unconscious is universal—it does not "develop," nor does it need to—Klein ultimately suggested that children and adults are not fundamentally different from one another, hence justifying her ostensibly unmodified clinical technique. If Sigmund Freud's work upended linear developmental temporality by emphasizing the determinative importance of childhood experiences in the psychic life of the adult, then Klein's child analysis flipped this equation, highlighting the incredible psychical sophistication of an infant no more than six months old.

Although it may be a habitualized vernacular for anyone—clinician or critical theorist alike—working seriously in the domain of Object Relations theory, the grammar of war, attack, and aggression so characteristic of Klein's theorizing merits pause. Suspending, for a moment, questions about this theory's psychological or sociological accuracy, what becomes clear when Klein's speculative psychoanalytic vocabulary is put in a historical context is how persuasively it ventriloquizes much of the midcentury political discourse common to wartime Europe. Not insignificantly, the most generative decades of Klein's career were sandwiched between two world wars, which saw unprecedented death tolls and new incursions of war into civilian life. During these years, Klein was geographically located in three of the wars' main urban epicenters: Budapest, Berlin, and London. Thus, when she posited a seemingly universal theory of subjectivity, describing as *the* prototypical subject a specifically besieged, embattled child whose first experiences were of paranoid anxiety and overt aggression, she (re)produced a psychoaffective stance that mirrored that of Britain's own citizenry, for whom constant discussion (not to mention direct experience) of conflict, aggression, attack, invasion, anxiety, and repair was the bread and butter of daily life. As Adam Phillips discerningly observes in his historical essay on child analysis, "Bombs Away," "if we cannot imagine psychoanalysis without the notion of war—psychoanalysis was partly made out of the materials of war, its casualties and its language—then the immediate experience of the Second World War seemed to put the finishing touches to a new description of the child that analysts had been struggling to articulate since before the First World War."[34] Put another way, war was the crucible in which child analysis, as both a theory and a practice, was formed. Hence, when Klein speaks of the "tyranny" of the superego, the child's "bombings" of the mother's body, "paranoia" as the child's earliest affective disposition, "death" as inextricably bound up with life, and the fact of "attack"—everywhere—she remobilizes much of the historically specific war vocabulary that saturated 1930s and 1940s discourse in Britain, ascribing it here to the child. For her, children's play is nothing more or less than international war games.

This ascription of the sociopolitical to the individual-psychological is seen perhaps most clearly in Klein's clinical work during World War II with her child patient, Richard. When Richard first came for treatment, he had been struggling with severe anxieties and phobias for two years, since the outbreak of the war in 1939. He was hypochondriacal, terrified of other children, unable to attend school, inhibited in learning, and frequently subject to depression.[35] Prior to his move to Scotland, Richard's house in London had been bombed and his older brother had enlisted in the British Army. Although Klein observed that he had precocious artistic sensibilities and a great love of nature and music, these interests were often stifled by his anxious concern for his mother's well-being, his paranoid fear of other children, and his obsessive interest in the daily developments of the war. World War II, particularly as it was epitomized by the conflict between Hitler's Germany as a singular "bad" and the British as a collective "good," was the subject of almost all of Richard's concerns throughout his treatment.

Although it might seem hardly surprising that a child in 1941 whose older brother was a soldier and whose house in London had already been bombed would be preoccupied by world events, for Klein this persistent interest in conflict, destruction, attack, and Hitler himself bespoke the internal—rather than external—dynamics of attack and repair. Relying on the play-technique she had developed over a decade earlier, Klein interpreted Richard's keen interest in international political conflict as a symptomatic projection of a deeper and more fundamental psychic conflict. When Richard talked about battleships, Hitler, and national alliance, Klein rejoined with the threats posed by Daddy's "bad Hitler-penis," Mummy's positioned body, and the copulating "combined parent" figure. Although Richard often strongly disagreed with these interpretations, Klein persisted. Her interpretive panache is dramatized in Richard's third session when he returns to the map on the wall (which he had noticed in the first session) and speculates about national conflict and alliance.

> He soon turned to the map and expressed his fears about the British battleships being blockaded in the Mediterranean if Gibraltar were taken by the Germans. They could not get through Suez. He also spoke of injured soldiers and showed some anxiety about their fate. He wondered how the British troops could be rescued from Greece. What would Hitler do to the Greeks; would he enslave them? Looking at the map, he said with concern that Portugal was a very small country compared with big Germany, and would be overcome by Hitler. He mentioned Norway, about whose attitude he was doubtful, though it might not prove to be a bad ally after all.
>
> *Mrs K* interpreted that he also worried unconsciously about what might happen to Daddy when he put his genital into Mummy. Daddy might not be able to get out of Mummy's inside and would be caught there, like the ships in the Mediterranean. This also applied to the troops which had to be retrieved from Greece.[36]

Richard's anxieties, as he expresses them, have to do with the political topography of Europe: ships stranded in the Mediterranean might not be able to get their wounded soldiers to Allied soil in time to save their lives; Greek citizens recently conquered in the Battle of Greece might be enslaved—or worse—by advancing Nazi soldiers under Hitler's command; Portugal, relatively small and neighboring fascist Spain, could easily be "overcome." But for Klein the realist purchase of these concerns had little appeal, and she interprets Richard's worries as manifestations of his unconscious phantasies, which are projected onto external events.

For instance, Richard's fear of Hitler as an aggressive and subjugating force represents his anxiety about his "Daddy's" alternately helpful and harmful penis; "Mummy," here figured as the vast expanse of earth and ocean on which this military drama was being literally mapped out, could engulf and capture the "good" father-penis, represented by the British warships. The idioms of "Father of a Nation" and "Mother Earth" are taken quite literally in Klein's interpretation, which proposes that familial and (hetero)sexual symbols are the deepest and most determinative objects for the child psyche.[37] According to Klein, the external political developments throughout World War II merely provided the stage dressing for Richard's deeper unconscious phantasies. To Klein's mind, Richard's interest in war indexes his *internal* conflict, what Shapira calls *the war inside*.[38]

But there are, of course, two sides to the coin here. As I have been discussing, even as it might appear that Klein is, time and again, ahistorically returning Richard's political anxieties to an ever-present "Mommy-Daddy-Me" triangulation that universalizes the European heterosexual middle-class nuclear family as the seat of all psychic life, in this very gesture she actually operationalizes some of the most politically salient concerns specific to that historical moment. As Richard rehearsed the dynamics of World War II in his play and in his drawings, Klein theorized that children as young as two are plagued by unconscious phantasies about "killing," "blowing up," "ambushing," "bombing," "invading," and "attacking" the "hostile" persecutors who appear allied against them. Klein does not date each of the sessions in the text of *Narrative*, but her pocketbook records that Richard's analysis lasted from April 28 to August 23 of 1941, a time span that witnessed the continued bombing of Northern Ireland, the fall of Greece, the sinking of the *Bismarck*, the invasion of the Soviet Union, and perhaps most notably the bizarre arrival of Rudolf Hess, Hitler's second-in-command, who fled Germany in the middle of the night and bailed out over Glasgow, less than a hundred miles from Klein, seeking asylum.[39] From a historical perspective, then, Klein constructs her instinctual, phylogenetic unconscious on and through modern political conflict narratives, emblemized in the swing between aggressive "attack" and conciliatory "reparation." During a time of attacks, bombings, and invasions—followed swiftly by monetary reparations—Klein's interest is not in the purchase of these phenomena in the external world but rather in the way they organize the internal, psychic life of children. As Phillips, Shapira, and Roper have all persuasively shown, Klein takes the political discourse of World War II and maps it onto—and into—the mind of the child.[40]

This historical contextualization offers a useful reorientation of the typical casting of Klein's life and work as apolitical. Klein herself was one of the most socially and politically disinterested of the midcentury psychoanalytic coterie. While Anna Freud was working in institutions for displaced children and D. W. Winnicott was broadcasting weekly BBC segments to British mothers, while Susan Isaacs was heading the Malting House School in Cambridge and John Bowlby was writing reports for the World Health Organization, Klein remained staunchly committed to her privatized clinical practice. Indeed, she rarely ever wrote about social or political issues, preferring to keep her speculations focused on metapsychology and clinical technique. Arguably, her only real political interest was to do with the institutional politics of the BPS and the "war" raging between herself and Anna Freud during the more-or-less exact years of World War II. Shapira puts this well when she observes that "war was something she [Klein] both recognized and denied; she incorporated violence into her work while mostly disavowing the reality of aerial bombardment. It was the war inside that was of interest to her. Her ideas stressed depth instead of surface; truth about violence could be found inside her patients, not in the newspaper reports on the war which they tried to read to her."[41] Although it might seem that this turn inward effectively removed Klein from the political sphere, Shapira (along with other scholars in the history of the human sciences) have importantly documented the substantive, if perhaps unintended, political collaborations produced by this ascription of sociopolitical exteriority to subjective interiority. According to Shapira, Klein's assimilation of martial discourse to and for the figure of the child helped justify the expansion of the state's management of psychological "welfare" in the coming postwar British welfare state. If (childhood) subjectivity was afflicted by the same threats and issues as the nation, then, Shapira argues, psychology could be newly reimagined as the proper province for similar forms of national intervention. By describing human subjectivity as a realm of cataclysmic war and violence, Klein lent Britain's burgeoning welfare-minded social democracy legitimacy and purpose.

Such a claim helps expand Zaretsky's influential argument that Klein's Object Relations theory advanced an ethics of interpersonal relationality that rearticulated modernity's establishment of a distinct sphere of "personal life," thereby contributing to a vison of radical collectivity for Britain's postwar social democracy. If "psychoanalysis . . . emerged as a theory and practice of 'personal life,' [whose] goal was *defamilialization*," then Zaretsky shows how Klein reshaped this injunctive by describing the child's ego through concrete economies of relational accountability and care.[42] The effect of this was the radical repositioning of modernity's ideals of freedom and autonomy as newly achievable through democratic collectivity, a psychosocial conviction that bolstered the emergent British welfare state. Even as Roper has usefully made the case that the origin of psychoanalysis's public involvement lies much earlier than the Second World War—he locates them in the *mise-en-scène* of the interwar years, a claim I similarly maintain in my first chapter on Anna Freud—these critical interventions, taken together, establish the covert political work that psychoanalysis performed on behalf of midcentury British social democracy.[43]

Building on this work—and combining its historical contextualization with a measure of my own political theorizing—I am interested, in the next section, in thinking through the political function performed by that sphere of Klein's psychoanalytic operation most privatized and thus most seemingly averse to sociopolitical engagement: her clinical practice. Notwithstanding her own apoliticality, I argue that Klein's clinic nevertheless participated in a form of political theorizing in fraught and inventive ways. By refusing to tarry in the realm of political practice, traditionally conceived, she reconceptualizes what counts as political in the first place, proposing that the clinical encounter is both a part of—and a potential solution to—the sociopolitical aggressions manifested in global politics. In what follows, I attend specifically to Klein's conception of reparation, arguing that in her clinical work reparation functions as a protopolitical theory of justice. Klein adopted reparation to name her understanding of the child's—and by extension the human being's—capacity for ethical relationality, and she used her clinical sessions with Richard as a testing ground for her attempt to cultivate this psychosocial orientation in her patients. But, as I show, in doing so she engaged with a particularly conflicted twentieth-century framework for assessing and redressing political injury, taking up this state-focused formation of justice and newly using it to theorize the operation of the individual subject's interpersonal relationality. While reparation debates in Europe foundered, reparation in Klein's clinic flourished. Such a confluence raises important questions about the shape of justice in the clinic—and, as I discuss, about the limits of individualized psychological intervention to meet the needs of global geopolitical redress.

MRS. K, RICHARD, AND "THE BAD HITLER-PENIS"

For Klein, Richard's case was an especially compelling demonstration of how clinical psychoanalysis assists in the consolidation of the patient's depressive position and the amplification of their reparative processes. Klein initially began her theorization of reparation in 1929 when she published an early paper on art and creativity. At that point, she was just as likely to refer to this process as "restoration" or "restitution" rather than "reparation." It was not until her writing in the 1930s and 1940s that she solidified her understanding of the two object-orientations as distinct psychic "positions," coining the unique "depressive position" and naming reparation as its primary process. Since Richard's case was situated in the midst of this, Klein took a special interest in it and focused on the manifestations of his reparative impulses in the clinic, seeing their steady increase as a mark of her technique's validity. Even though Richard's analysis was unusually short—its premature termination was the result of Klein's desire to return to London during the Controversial Discussions—she nevertheless considered it successful, reflecting in the appended "Final Remarks" section of the case study that, through the analysis, "[Richard's] envy, jealousy, and greed, which in my view are expressions of the death instinct, diminished because he became gradually able to face and integrate his destructive impulses. This was bound up with his capacity for love coming more fully into play, which made it possible for hate to be mitigated by love. . . . His sense of guilt, which had existed side by side with his persecutory anxieties, had diminished and this implied a greater capacity to make reparation."[44] A more than favorable account, Klein records that her clinical interventions led to the diminishment of Richard's destructive impulses, the integration of his life and death instincts, and the expansion of his capacity for love and reparation.[45] According to Klein, these were key metrics of analytic success since it was only by integrating love with hate that she thought that depressive anxieties could be mitigated and genuine reparation achieved. Ultimately, she concluded that it was "Richard's strong capacity for love" and his "wish to make reparation" that "made it possible for even this very short analysis to become fruitful."[46] As Klein wrote to her fellow BPS colleague and collaborator Clifford Scott six days after Richard's analysis ended, "It is surprising and gratifying to see how much the knowledge of the depressive position has advanced technique and theoretical and practical understanding."[47]

But the road to such a splendid outcome was hardly smooth. When Richard first entered analysis, Klein found him dominated by paranoid anxiety and aggression. In his play and in his speech, he was more concerned with attack than with repair, worrying constantly about the security threats posed by children passing on the street and about Klein's own potential for covert sedition given that she was originally an Austro-Hungarian citizen possibly allied with Hitler and the Third Reich. Such aggression was likewise on clear display in Richard's first drawings, which he completed in his twelfth session, roughly two weeks into the analysis (see figure 2.1). At the start of this session, Richard noticed that Klein had brought with her a number of art supplies. Eagerly taking up a pencil, Richard began two drawings, both featuring an assortment

FIGURE 2.1 Richard's drawings, sessions 12–15.
Compiled drawings from sessions 12–15. Klein Archives, Wellcome Library.

of German U-boats along with the real British battleships the *Salmon*, the *Truant*, and the *Sunfish*, all set against a blue-penciled backdrop of sea and sky. In them, the fleet of black British and German warships engaged in combat around (and sometimes with) various bright yellow sea creatures, including fish, starfish, and a rather striking character dubbed "Octopus Mummy" (Drawing 6/Session 14).

When Richard finished these two images, he explained that "there was an attack going on, but he did not know who would attack first, the *Salmon* or the [German] U-boat."[48] Interpreting these images became the focus of this analytic session as Klein encouraged Richard to associate the geopolitical conflict depicted in the drawings with a principally familial conflict that, she suggested, they unconsciously expressed. "*Mrs K* interpreted that the British represented his own family [who] he not only loved and wanted to protect but also wished to attack."[49] For Richard, such an interpretation was deeply offensive not just because it dealt a blow to family affections but also because it was an affront to his patriotism. As with his play, Richard and Klein debated the representational capacity of the images he created, with Richard alternately resisting and adopting the symbolic meanings that Klein assigned to them.

In spite of this early penchant for attack, Klein records that, as the analysis progressed, Richard's reparative impulses increased and the oscillation between his paranoid-schizoid and depressive positions became more frequent. Klein cited proof of this in Richard's play, which she carefully observed and liberally interpreted. A long passage from Richard's twenty-fourth session illustrates how she traced this oscillation between the paranoid-schizoid and depressive positions through even seemingly banal behaviors—a concerned question; a pointed silence—which she took as signifying a vital change in Richard's object-orientation.

Richard had in the meantime been all round the room, exploring, looking into books, and finding things on the shelves. He repeatedly touched *Mrs K*'s bag, obviously wishing to open and examine it. He squeezed a little ball between his feet and then began to do the goose-step, saying what a silly way of marching it was.

Mrs K interpreted that the little ball represented the world; Mummy and *Mrs K*, squeezed by German boots—the goose-step.

In doing this Richard expressed his feeling that he not only contained the good Mummy but also the Hitler-father, and was destroying Mummy as the bad father did.

Richard strongly objected, saying that he was not like Hitler, but he seemed to understand that the goose-stepping and the squeezing feet represented this. It was nearly time to go and Richard became very friendly and affectionate. . . . He asked her [Mrs K] to be silent, held his breath, and said, 'Poor old room, so silent.' Then he asked Mrs K what she was going to do over the weekend.

Mrs K interpreted his fear that she might die at the weekend—the poor old silent room. That was why he had to make sure about her bringing the drawings; this also expressed his wish to help in the analysis, and thus to put Mrs K right and preserve her. This was why he wished for Mrs K—the poor old radiator—to have a rest, not to be exhausted by her patients, particularly by him.[50]

In the first half of this passage, Richard plays at the military goose step while Klein interprets—much to Richard's dismay—that his parodic fascist parade represents an aggressive identification with the bad "Hitler-father" bent on destroying the good "Mummy-world." This aggressive attack is then followed by Richard's reparative concern, in the second half of the passage, for the consulting room and the "poor old radiator," which Klein construes as a representation of herself and an index of his concern that she might "die at the weekend" because of his goose-stepping assaults.

As Klein suggests in her interpretations, the depressive position characteristically follows on the coattails of the paranoid-schizoid position and involves the child's experience of responsibility, guilt, love, loss, mourning, and, eventually, the creative impulse to repair. Whereas in the paranoid-schizoid position the child attacks unadulterated "good" and "bad" part objects (the archetype of which is the breast), in the depressive position the infant becomes aware that the attacked breast is the same as the "good" feeding breast that provides warmth and comfort and therefore that its destructive onslaught is aimed also at a cherished object essential to the infant's survival. Prior to the recognition of these enigmatic "whole objects," the infant perceives the world according only to fractured parts: the infant, because of its limited cognitive and sensory palate, understands the mother as a series of disparate part objects (breast, skin, smell, gaze) that either satisfy or frustrate its instincts. As with all survival strategies that bluntly reduce complexity in order to ensure survival, the part object world definitional to the paranoid-schizoid position allows the infant to split into monolithic units what would otherwise be conflicted and ambivalent feelings. As Kleinian analyst Robert Hinshelwood puts it, "part object-relationships entail the freeing of the ego from ambivalence."[51] Only as the infant develops will it be able to bring these good and bad part objects together to form a whole object—the mother, for instance—who arouses a complexity of emotions. According to Klein, "Not until the object is loved *as a whole* can its loss be felt as a whole."[52] It is through this process that the depressive position is achieved and reparation attempted. Summarizes Klein:

> If the baby has, in his aggressive phantasies, injured his mother by biting and tearing her up, he may soon build up phantasies that he is putting the bits together again and repairing her. This, however, does not quite do away with his fears of having destroyed the object which, as we know, is the one whom he loves and needs most, and on whom he is dependent. In my view, these basic conflicts profoundly influence the course and the force of the emotional lives of grown-up individuals.[53]

The infant, phantasizing its paranoid attacks to be the cause of damage to the now-loved whole object, identifies with the object and attempts repair. The depressive position is thus marked by the infant's experience of ambivalent whole objects, which it understands itself as having injured and even destroyed, prompting new attempts at solicitous reparation and even mournful "pining." "This making reparation is, in my view, a fundamental element in love and in all human relationships."[54] Reparation, in other words, constitutes the child's relation to an object-world defined by injury but capable of redress.

Hence, when Klein proposes that Richard's concern for the "poor old room" be interpreted as a turn toward depressive reparation, she implies that his newfound compunction is galvanized by his unconscious recognition of the destruction he had previously unleashed. After trying to squash Klein under his heel, Richard feels guilty about his attempted murder and grows concerned for the survival of the room, the analysis, and "poor old" Mrs. K herself. Klein found that such reparative gestures increased throughout Richard's analysis, with his destructive assaults followed more and more closely and directly by reparative efforts. In his seventy-first session, for example, Richard brought his own set of toy trains to the session and, in a signature move, enacts a "disaster" with those that he had set on a course to London—the very city to which Klein herself was preparing to travel later that week. But, following the train's derailment, Richard engages in a heedful and attentive rescue mission, collecting the destroyed trains and sending "the wounded" to hospital. Given the explicit and quite literal pursuit of repair here, Klein saw in this game a clear indication that Richard's depressive anxieties and reparative impulses were ascendant.

> The cautious and anxious way in which he took the toys out of the bag and in which he decided that the damaged figures would have to go to hospital—asking me at the same time to mend the boy figure who represented himself—shows how both hope and the urge for reparation were operative side by side with his anxieties. . . . When destructive impulses and their consequences come closer together with a revived capacity for love and are mitigated by it, they become less overwhelming and reparation becomes possible.[55]

Richard's care with the toys, his assessment of their damage, and his investment in having them "mend[ed]" by Klein and the hospital indexes, for her, his "urge for reparation." As with this and previous descriptions, Klein's positive portrayal of reparation makes evident that her psychological matrix ascribes a moral weight to reparative dynamics, narrating their operation as less violent and destructive than their "paranoid" sibling. Experiences of love, creativity, gratitude, guilt, authenticity, empathy, interdependence, altruism, responsibility, and mourning are all stacked on the side of reparation, making it tantamount, in Klein's binary calculus, to an ethical relation to the world as such. Indeed, it is reparation that, in some of her later thinking especially, is said to resolve the anxieties characteristic of the depressive position. Although Klein does indicate that there are insincere, inauthentic, or false forms of reparation—which she groups under the umbrella of "manic reparation"—when it comes to reparation's "true" form, she unequivocally positions it as standing on the side of the life instincts and ego integration—in other words, of constructive sociality itself.

Richard's reparative gestures are given similarly generous plaudits and are variously associated with feelings of "reassurance,"[56] happiness and unity,[57] the diminishment of "depression,"[58] a "strong capacity for love,"[59] "more trust and hope,"[60] "greater sympathy,"[61] "the diminution of aggressiveness, envy, and jealousy,"[62] "less hate and despair and more hope,"[63] "harmony,"[64] and a "core of goodness"[65]—to name but a few. As Klein's thinking developed, reparation would increasingly provide, if not an outright solution to the negativity characteristic of her view of human subjectivity, then at very least an aspirational horizon on which one could glimpse the possibility of a mutually sustaining relationality, unburdened by either persecutory or depressive anxiety. Because reparation (like the depressive position itself) is never fully or finally achieved—as an aspect of Klein's nondevelopmental positional theory, it constantly turns back into a paranoid-schizoid orientation as part of every subject's ordinary object relationality—it can never promise any conclusive or encompassing resolution to the subject's (ongoing) historicity of aggression. But it does nevertheless function as a sustained—and sustaining—opening in Klein's thinking through which she imagines that the subject can experience personal and relational integrity.

As one might expect, this concept has been valuable to clinicians and critical theorists alike who, in working with Klein's characteristically negative, aggressive view of the human subject, nevertheless endeavor to move beyond a sphere of relationality fated to internecine destruction. Thinking clinically, the second-generation Object Relations analysts Hanna Segal and Marion Milner both made reparation a cornerstone of their emancipatory accounts of the role of creativity and aesthetics in psychic life, and it continues to be an important concept for leading Kleinian clinicians such as Karl Figlio.[66] From a critical theoretical perspective, C. Fred Alford, acknowledging Klein's proclivity for fracturing destructivity, nevertheless considered reparation to be a secure grounding for his Frankfurt School theory of sociality, art, and collectivity.[67] His work began a recognizable minor trend in political theory that specifically sources Object Relations psychoanalysis for theories about group dynamics, power, and the democratic polis to help make sense of the (de)formations of contemporary political life.[68] Even queer theorist Eve Kosofsky Sedgwick adopted reparation as the banner under which she launched her influential call for a new form of interpretive reading in the humanities and qualitative social sciences, inaugurating what has now become a fashionable trend in "post-critique" methodologies that intend to forego the supposed violence of more "paranoid," symptomatic approaches.[69] In many ways these thinkers, although aware of what Leo Bersani, Rose, Stonebridge, and Esther Sánchez-Pardo have described as the persisting "negativity" in Klein's thought,[70] nevertheless mine the optimism implicit in her account of reparation to enable a vision of social and political life beyond that produced by a focus on the so-called negative affects.

Seductive as this desire for a form of collaborative sociality is given how it opens a psychosocial horizon characterized by fantasies of mutuality and recognition, the critical embrace of reparation nevertheless rests on the tacit acceptance of Klein's strategic, and not altogether straightforward, idealization of reparation's ethico-political promise. Throughout her work, Klein's view of human subjectivity is unequivocally binary: whole object versus part object; life instinct versus death instinct; depressive versus paranoid-schizoid; gratitude versus envy. Although these spheres interact, they carry a clear moral weight within her thinking where love, creativity, and mutually sustaining sociality are the pledged horizon of depressive reparation. As her work progressed throughout the 1950s, Klein would commit more and more thoroughly to the possibility of a "true object love" in which identification with and recognition of the (flawed) whole object exists as a distinct relational accomplishment separate from the ambivalent and libidinal gratification models typical of most psychoanalytic theorizing. However, Klein's conviction about our ability to fully apprehend "whole objects"—and thus to love and repair them in ways that are genuinely conducive to their own flourishing—hinges crucially on a theory of interpersonal recognition that her own convictions about constitutional instincts and unconscious phantasies make impossible. As I discuss at greater length in the final section of this chapter, our ability to perceive others is always and necessarily mediated by processes of projection, introjection, and identification, meaning that there can be no guarantee that any attempt at recognition will ever perceive the object in its wholeness, fullness, or complete alterity. Indeed, one of the theoretical precepts of the unconscious is that the subject's most authentic core is precisely that which escapes recognition, signification, and capture. In this regard, Klein (and many of the critical theorists following her) idealize the ethical essence of reparation by imagining that it provides an inherently nonappropriative relational matrix, one in which there is no gap between intention and effect in interpersonal reconciliation.

From this, we can understand that Klein's theory of reparation is significantly more complex and fraught than her preliminary idealizations would have us think. As a self-preserving process operating mainly at the level of phantasy, reparation may aspire to redress the object-world, but its potential for external realization is always secondary and precarious. On this point, it is useful to recall that the most famous of Klein's critical contributions—those euphonious "paranoid-schizoid" and "depressive" positions—were only fully codified between 1935 and 1946, and it was through this conceptual development that reparation came to the fore in her thought. Not insignificantly, this was the same period during which reparation was popularized in Britain and in Europe as a distinctly political concept, albeit one that was highly mutable, undergoing significant transformations in both scope and reception throughout the twentieth century. For instance, after World War I, monetary reparations against Germany were first publicly lauded and then publicly decried as critics made the link between national impoverishment and the rise of National Socialism.[71] The growing sense, throughout the 1930s, that the Allies had mistreated Germany by levying such punishing fiscal reparations was due largely to the 1919 publication of John Maynard Keynes's *The Economic Consequences of the Peace*, which became an immediate, trans-Atlantic bestseller.[72] In it, Keynes—a prominent member of the Bloomsbury Group who was deeply influenced by psychoanalysis—forcefully admonished the architects of the Treaty of Versailles and reproved the treaty's mandates about reparations on economic and political grounds, calling the treaty a "Carthaginian Peace." What Keynes suggested was that the reparations claims were a form of fiscal punishment meant to chasten Germany for its bellicosity. Keynes's text, perhaps more than any other single document, brought about the widespread public opinion that reparations were anything but an expression of political justice.

Yet, curiously, after World War II, reparations resurfaced through-out Europe and the world as one of the foremost terms through which victims of national or international violence sought justice. To see examples of this, we might think here of the postwar reparations agreement between the newly created state of Israel and West Ger-many for the resettlement of Jews displaced by the Holocaust; the still incomplete claims for reparation in Argentina for human rights vio-lations throughout its Dirty War; or the ongoing reparations debates in the United States about the horrors of chattel slavery, which have been repopularized by public intellectuals like Ta-Nehisi Coates.[73] In the postwar decades, reparations expanded from being a principally monetary negotiation to being a transnational victim- and citizen-fo-cused framework that sought justice by and through the emergent language of human rights. This framework is most often employed to parse injuries that either cross national boundaries (thereby inval-idating the state's internal juridical system) or that past formations of the state have enacted against its own citizenry. In contrast to initiatives that adjudicate justice through the legal system, through perpetrator-focused procedures of discipline and punishment, rep-aration attempts to identify injury and redress harm specifically by recognizing victims as victims through their status as rights-bearing national (or world) citizens. In other words, what defines reparation as a unique program for (international) justice is the victim-focused nature of its pursuit. As legal scholar and political theorist Ruth Rubio-Marìn explains in her book on reparation, "the main aim of reparations [is] to be [able] to give victims due recognition as citizens, something which, I argue, requires all of the following: the recogni-tion of the wrongful violation of victims' rights; the acknowledge-ment of state responsibility for such violations; the recognition of harms ensuing from the violations; and the attempt to help victims cope with the effect of the harms in their lives, and to subvert, how-ever minimally, the structures of subordination that might have led to the violations of their rights in the first place."[74] Insofar as reparation operates conceptually (at either national or international levels) by recognizing the subject of injury through the grammar of national cit-izenship or human rights, it is a particularly twentieth-century frame-work for conceptualizing the relationship between injury and repair.

Although the narrow, legal sense of the term as juridical compensation can be seen as emerging from as far back as the Talmudic law of Talion, only throughout the twentieth-century global consolidation of nation-states and the postwar transnational affirmation of human rights (through global bodies like the United Nations) did it take on an extrajudicial relevance to justice.

What all of this means is that when Klein adopted the term "reparation" to describe the ethical efforts of the infant in its depressive attempts to ameliorate harm, she was entering into an explicitly political conversation about shifting and highly contested approaches to global justice. Importantly, reparation is not just—or even originally—a psychological concept; reparation could only ever become the grammar of the infant's Object Relations because it had first been the unique vernacular of the state's (inter)national relationships. Despite the fact that it is a habituated idiom within psychoanalytic theory, reparation is historically a principally political language for negotiating claims for individual or collective justice in the face of unresolved histories of state violence. Regardless of whether or not Klein had any of these political uses of the term in mind when she theorized the way that paranoid attack and aggrieved reparation structure the mind of the child, her ability to even think the subject along these lines testifies to the broader conception of interwar and, eventually, postwar justice enabling her theory.

Read in this context, the grammar of individual psychological repair emerges in connection with what appear to be clear and identifiable state aggressions, which reparative justice projects would increasingly strive to recognize as fundamentally irresolvable. Klein's attempt to foster reparation in her private clinic therefore comes to light as a fraught grappling with a crisis in geopolitical thinking about the possibility for and shape of justice. Indeed, it is worth noting the curiosity of Klein's initial deployment of this term in the interwar period, when (politically speaking) reparation would have carried its strongest international distaste. As World War II progressed and public faith in the achievability of either political justice or human ethics reached a crisis point in antisemitic genocide, Klein interestingly looked to the clinic as a space where the jeopardized promise of reparative justice could be realized.

BEYOND REPAIR: ON REPARATION AND JUSTICE

Understanding reparation's theoretical and historical complexity has some important consequences for how we envision Klein's clinical project. First, as I have been suggesting, the recognition that reparation is a political concept tied to different imaginaries for justice reorients what had been her previously purely psychological appreciation. Although Klein may have consciously and intentionally depoliticized her clinical work, her analysis with Richard—a child who staunchly refuses to divest from the political as a primary axis of psychic life—is helpful for how it highlights her practice's necessary embeddedness in the sociopolitical sphere.

Second, this broader framing helps elaborate the complex ethical and political stakes of reparation, which are otherwise elided in Klein's more restricted psychological focus. To see this, we need only look back to Klein's "Final Remarks" on Richard's analysis, where she emphasizes the development of Richard's reparative capacity by giving a politically provocative example from his play: "I have referred to the fact that Richard, who so strongly hated the enemies threatening Britain's existence at that time, became capable of feeling sympathy for the destroyed enemy. This was shown, for instance, when he regretted the damage done to Berlin and Munich and, at another occasion, when he became identified with the sunk *Prinz Eugen*."[75] Although Klein means this précis to be a tribute to Richard, when considered politically, her claim that Richard's clinical progress should be marked according to his ability to identify and sympathize with the "destroyed enemy" raises important questions about the idealization of reparation as an abstract, psychological ethic somehow detached from its political and historical context. Although most clinicians working through a "reparative" idiom do not mention this, Klein is insistent that the depressive position and reparation derive from the child's ability to put itself in the object's place, scripting the object's injury according to the perimeters of its own guilt. Klein alternately describes this as "true reparation," "genuine sympathy," or "authentic sympathy," all terms that speak to the self–other identification at the heart of reparative relations. Indeed, in a public lecture Klein gave in 1936, she explicitly listed reparativity under the subheading "Identification and Making Reparation," explaining (again through the language of authenticity) that "to be genuinely considerate implies that we can put ourselves in the place of other people: we can 'identify' ourselves with them . . . [this is] a condition for real and strong feelings of love."[76] Even as Klein writes constantly about how reparative tendencies aim to love the object, ameliorate harm, repair injury, and generally "make good," she means this language to describe the child-subject's own affective climate in relation to the object world. Insofar as identification, in a psychoanalytic understanding, involves a mapping of the self—of the ego—onto the other, it necessarily entails a redaction and refusal of the other's alterity in favor of reproducing more of the subject's own self-same. As even Hinshelwood reports in his *Dictionary of Kleinian Thought*, in reparation "it is primarily a repair of the internal world that is intended, through repairing the external."[77] In other words, reparativity is important in Klein's psychoanalytic theory not because it constitutes an ethical relation to the world per se—there is, after all, no guarantee that its intention to "do good" translates in any way to material consequences, or that the objects of one's reparative intentions are politically desirable—but because it gives the child the feeling of ethical action and thereby allows it to expiate its own guilt and reinvest in the world of object relations.

As I have already discussed, Klein's work thus ascribes this object-orientation a moral weight, narrating its operation as less violent and destructive than its "paranoid" sibling. But it is precisely the ethical status of reparation, especially as enacted by identification, on which I want to pause. In this passage, where Klein is reflecting on the case and considering the beneficial effects of the analysis, she marks Richard's progress by his ability to sympathize, to identify with, the "destroyed enemy." Klein downplays the political implications of this assessment by naming cities as the objects of Richard's sympathetic solicitude, highlighting—from her secure editorial position in the postwar 1950s—that it was "the [fascist] enemy" who was "destroyed" and thereby lending Richard's sympathy the air of magnanimity. However, taken from a different angle, what she suggests here is nothing less than that Richard's achievement of the depressive position and his impulse toward reparation are best exemplified by his identification with Nazi Germany at the height of a genocidal extermination. For Klein, the ethical aspect of reparation—a term not unburdened by the history of state wars and genocidal logics—is the child's self-sustaining identifications, which exculpate its own guilt by adjudicating injury and repair. In this process, the child constructs the object's injury according to its own expectations and desires, its own ability to position itself as the agent of repair. This is a process undertaken with little attention to the ethical pitfalls of identification (which derive from the recognition and repro-duction of similitude) or of the political consequences of the particular objects both taken up and cast aside. Indeed, the very fact of Germany as the object of Richard's potential reparative attention is historically evocative given how the contestation about the justness of interwar mon-etary reparations centered, famously, on the tension between Britain and Germany as the then-leaders of the Allied and Axis powers. Reparations, as a historical and material form of interstate political justice, are thus implicitly referenced in the very play scenarios that Klein interpreted as a manifestation of their psychological alter egos.

This recognition profoundly transforms any judgment and assess-ment of ethical action—political and clinical—in Klein's framework. In her clinical work with Richard, for instance, Klein is only able to valorize his reparative tendencies by strategically depoliticizing the status of the objects toward which his actions are geared. In this way, reparation is separated from its affiliation with justice and valued only as an ostensibly abstract psychological orientation, a move that extends psychoanalysis's troubling and politically conservative tendency to sever psychological norms and ideals from their social and historical contexts in the name of scientific neutrality and objectivity. Although concepts like "splitting," "projection," and "reparation" are typically treated as universal psychic processes, when thought politically the different objects to which they are applied necessarily transform their ethico-political value. Are there not substantial differences, for instance, between a white American's feeling of identificatory solicitude for the imagined victimization of Donald Trump and an Israeli's empathetic drive toward restitution for the decades of violence perpetrated against Palestinians—even as both of these object orientations, when thought clinically, could feasibly be described as "true reparation"? Can an individual's internal feeling of reparative care ever itself be enough?

Returning this question to Klein, what I am concerned with here are the dangers of a method that downgrades the potential violence of defining injury and ascribing repair, be it with children, texts, movements, populations, art objects, or concepts. This violence is far from abstract and is materialized quite plainly in the lecture Klein delivered at Caxon Hall in London five years before her analysis with Richard began. In this lecture, which she gave with Joan Riviere, Klein offers a rare social example intended to illustrate, for her audience, the clinical concept of true reparation. Comparing the child's early relationship with the mother to settler-colonialism, she explains how:

> The child's early aggression stimulated by the drive to restore and to make good, to put back into his mother the good things he had robbed from her in phantasy, and these wishes to make good merge into the later drive to explore, for by finding new land the explorer gives something to the world at large and to a number of people in particular. In his pursuit the explorer actually gives expression to both aggression and the drive to reparation. We know that in discovering a new country aggression is made use of in the struggle with the elements, and in over-coming difficulties of all kinds. But sometimes aggression is shown more openly; especially was this so in former times when ruthless cruelty against native populations was displayed by people who not only explored, but conquered and colonized. Some of the early phantasied attacks against the imaginary babies in the mother's body, and actual hatred against new-born brothers and sisters, were here expressed in reality by the attitude towards the natives. The wished for restoration, however, found full expression in repopulating the country with people of their own nationality.[78]

Taking the scene of colonial conquest as her object—and making sure her 1936 British audience knows that all of this happened in "former times" rather than their own political present—Klein literally maps the paranoid-schizoid and depressive positions onto the ongoing history of ostensibly Western colonial invasion, subjugation, and extermination. While the invasion of foreign lands and the slaughter of "native populations" is a clear display of the infant's hostile attacks on its mother's body (again figured as the world), Klein somewhat unbelievably argues that the "repopulate[ion]" of the ravaged country by the colonist's own people constitutes reparation, her psycho-ethical ideal. Read from this vantage point, colonial repopulation is a demonstration of the "creativity" of a conqueror's response to his or her own decimation of indigenous peoples.

David Eng comments on this passage as well, noting how this vision of reparation enters into an established liberal narrative of retroactive justice for past histories of colonial violence and exploitation that naturalizes love as the "property of the European liberal human subject, foreclosing in the process any possibility for racial reparation and redress."[79] Read in this context, the vocabulary of reparative justice emerges in connection with (and seems inextricable from) the history of state injustice that proposes the tidy closure of past aggressions by the state's liberal promise of fiscal compensation for physical violence. This more sinister geopolitical reading of reparation suggests, according to Eng, that even deciding which objects count as objects deserving of repair is already a political calculus inseparable from national histories of oppression and subjection.

However, my own point is that if the "native populations" massacred by the "ruthless cruelty" of imperial conquest do not even register as a loss, it is only because the identificatory optics of reparation script injury according to their own (colonial) desires. The injury of colonial aggression is registered only as depopulation, an assessment that is stubbornly insensible to the racial and national politics enabling such an event. Given this logic, repopulation seems a natural (indeed, "ethical") solution. Yet as most readers can clearly recognize, this calculation is a strategic one that refuses to account for the violence produced by the identificatory relation mobilizing it or the political consequences of its enactment. Neither Richard's reparative sympathy for Nazi Germany nor the explorer's colonial repopulation takes into account the particular political status of the object being offered reparation, nor does either weigh the ethical hazards of such identificatory relations in the first place.

To give but one final instance of the disquieting underside of such reparative responses, in another piece of cultural analysis Klein analyzes a woman's sudden desire to paint—her need to fill the empty hole on her wall—as an instance of maternal reparation, willfully blind to what she includes as merely the incidental fact that the image painted in this "blank space" was the body of a "naked negress."[80] Klein turns to the story of this painter, who she names "Ruth Kjar" (but who is likely Ruth Weber),[81] as an example of what she calls "true reparation," a form of authentic ethical action from which creativity is born. Yet it is easy to see from a political perspective that, much like her colonial expedition, such a frivolous appropriation of racialized femininity offers a selective reading of *what* counts as ethical action based on *who* counts as a qualifying subject of redress. For certainly the "naked negress's" occupation of the blank space is far from the first time that Black women's bodies have been appropriated to slake the emotional needs of white women under the auspices of care. Here, the "injury" is the "empty wall" and the painter's own internal sense of emptiness, not the frivolous decorative appropriation of racialized femininity. As Jean Walton rightly argues in her analysis of the racial elision in this case study, "Klein's theory is predicated upon an example containing this unexamined representation [which] suggests that it is, in itself, a theory of a specifically white female subjectivity."[82] Klein considers reparation to name only the subject's ability to sustain itself through "creative" action, where "creativity" can just as easily present as Nazi sympathy, colonial "repopulation," or the continued aesthetic fetishization of Black women's bodies.

When it comes to Klein specifically, this is a particularly complex elision since, as a Jewish Austrian living in midcentury England, Klein herself was a racialized subject not afforded the privileges of metropole whiteness, either Germanic or British. Read biographically in connection with her own racial identity, it would hardly be a stretch to consider that Klein's affinity for a universalizing psychology was a strategic, if not necessarily intentional, antiracist bid to reject the kind of desubjectivizing racist discourses with which she herself was threatened. Therefore, even as her clinical practice and theoretical work refuse to consider the political significance of racialized colonialism, the overall political import of her work is complex and (as postcolonial critics like Homi Bhabha, Edward Said, and Gayatri Spivak have importantly shown in relation to Freud's work) potentially contradictory.

From this, my concluding question is a simple one: What picture of reparation do we get if we shift the focus from Klein's narration of the child's own feeling of ethical action to an assessment of the variable political ends—clinical as well as critical—toward which this fraught concept has been made to work? What theory and practice of reparation emerges if we wager that through reparation the clinic is bound up with the vital work of reparative justice, making its endeavor an inescapably ethico-political one?

My answer here is that Klein's theory of reparation, although insufficient in some respects, provides an opportunity to reimagine clinical practice as a vitally political operation whose methods and content are not distorted but rather strengthened and finessed by an understanding of their political implications. In both Klein's psychological work and in the work of international politics, reparations claims are claims about history: they are claims that involve the recognition of a history of injury juxtaposed against a present moment geared toward creation and repair, terms that for Klein are invariably thought of together. This emphasis on Klein's theory as itself historical is an admittedly unconventional interpretation. While psychoanalysis has provided much leverage for rethinking history to the extent that, at an individual level, the operation of repression and the constellation of the unconscious inaugurates the fact of historicity itself—of pastness—the novelty of Klein's work is typically ascribed to the positional (and thus spatialized) oscillation between the paranoid-schizoid and the depressive positions, which implicitly reject a developmental narrative of historical progress. For Klein, temporality is thus more cyclical than linear, with paranoid attack and depressive reparation constituting a hermetically sealed circular orbit.

But reparation can only ever emerge as a virtue, psychological or political, in a historical framework that has, in its past, privileged destructive assault. The fact of a past that is understood as being destructive and inadequate—as necessarily insufficient and, more than this, the locus of harm—is what makes reparation seem necessary, moral, and sufficient. Without injury, there can be no repair. There is thus an implicit temporality at work in the oscillation between destruction and reparation and it is through this positional tension that the historical and political stakes of reparation enter the scene. History, in Klein, is imagined not as the progression of a linear narrative but as the space necessarily held open between an irreparable harm and the imperative to justice. I therefore think that the complexity of Klein's theory of reparation—as positional and as relational—lies in how it reveals that political claims to reparation paradoxically announce the impossibility of their own project: they depend on a unique historical gap that binds destruction to reparation, making full restitution impossible because of the very fact of injury's temporal pastness. The promise of reparation—its appeal but also its limitation—is that it could somehow be sufficient to an injury in and of the past.

Thus, to the extent that reparation articulates historical trauma, it subtly suggests the impossibility of ever fully closing the gap between past injury and present redress; the need for reparation itself signals an irreparable harm, one that can only ever be recognized, never resolved. This is the space from which history emerges. Undoubtedly, attempts at recognition are important and, I would venture, indispensable to the pursuit of justice. But the historical narrative that reparation is defined by and through introduces a necessary limitation to the full or sufficient closure of injury. Indeed, I have been brought to question the utility of thinking in terms of an injury/repair framework in the first place since my sense is that such a narrative always enforces, however subtly, a normative ideal of health, wholeness, and well-being. From this, I suggest that the justice reparation strives for (both clinical and political) is an impossible one but that the fact of striving for an impossible justice—a justice that the world historical narrative necessarily cannot give—is justice's most politically desirable form. Reparation constitutes the psychological, political, and historical relation, but it still indexes that relation's entrenchment in past narratives of destruction and aggression to which any present-tense reparation can never be fully sufficient. Given this, might there not be some ethical value in a methodological orientation that considers, from the beginning, that a past of violent destruction cannot and should not be redeemed, is importantly beyond repair?

This reading highlights how Klein's clinical psychoanalytic work constituted a fraught grappling with the problematic of political justice. For Klein, reparation was the grammar through which she contended with the unstable function of global claims to justice in a modern world. Her clinical work might therefore best be understood as suggesting that reparation is politically desirable not because it can ever secure the promise of justice's closure but rather because it embodies the value of the struggle for it in the first place.

Theorizing the relationship between psychoanalysis and justice would become even more pressing for analysts working outside the metropole in Britain's vast colonial empire. While Klein may have used colonialism allegorically, as a rhetorical device to demonstrate reparation's sociopolitical scope, for many clinicians settler colonialism's myriad violences were the daily reality structuring their clinical practices. Wulf Sachs, the originally Lithuanian BPS analyst who worked in South Africa and Southern Rhodesia (now Zimbabwe), was among the earliest of these transnational analysts who grappled with a potential clinical-political form of justice head-on. In the next chapter, I follow his struggle to renegotiate racial and decolonial justice in the consulting room through his unconventional "traveling analysis" with the Black healer-diviner John Chavafambira.

PART TWO

Empires of Mind

On Colonialism and Decolonization

CHAPTER THREE

Traveling Analysis

Wulf Sachs, Racial Justice, and the (De)colonial Clinic in South Africa

Early every morning in 1933, a Southern Rhodesian healer-diviner (*nganga*) named John Chavafambira set out from his home in New Doornfontein, Johannesburg, to his analyst's clinical consulting room a few blocks away. The walk took Chavafambira from his one-room, tin-walled apartment in an overcrowded Black "slum" named Rooiyard to a fashionable white neighborhood where his analyst, Wulf Sachs, conducted his medical (and nascent psychoanalytic) practice. Chavafambira arrived each day at the preappointed time in the same clean but worn coat and tie. Upon entering the room, he would shake Sachs's hand, take off his jacket, and lay down on Sachs's couch, spending the next hour engaged in a disjointed narrative process familiar to all those who have ever been in analysis. Through his free associations, Chavafambira slowly narrativized his life experiences for Sachs, meditating on love, loss, family, sex, dreams, migration, dislocation, racism, illness, conflict, depression, and joy. United by their mutual commitment to the healing professions, the two men also shared the secrets of their respective trades, using the psychoanalytic relation between patient and analyst to help bridge the divide between Black Manyikan and white European forms of medical practice. At the end of each hour, Chavafambira would stand, gather his coat, and depart, either returning to Rooiyard or else visiting other neighborhoods in segregated Black Johannesburg to attend his own patients.

This, at least, describes what we know of Sachs and Chavafambira's psychoanalytic encounter as it unfolded within the four walls of Sachs's clinic. But unlike much contemporary psychoanalytic practice where the analytic relationship is confined to the space of the consulting room (at least in theory, if not always in practice), Chavafambira and Sachs's psychoanalytic intimacy extended far beyond the physical walls of Sachs's clinic. While the clinical portion of their relationship lasted two and a half years, the Jewish-Lithuanian Sachs and the Black Manyikan Chavafambira maintained an unconventional, extraclinical relationship for well over a decade. From their first meeting in 1933—organized by their mutual acquaintance, the social anthropologist Ellen Hellmann— through at least 1945, Sachs was directly involved in many aspects of Chavafambira's life: he traveled with Chavafambira, gave him money, treated his wife, visited his family, collaborated with him in his medical practice, and even bailed him out of prison, where he had been incarcerated (on four different occasions) for minor infractions of various race laws. What began, for Sachs, as a loosely ethnopsychological interest in Chavafambira as a case study in "African psychology" ended with a cooperative mutual regard that found Sachs, as much as Chavafambira, politically radicalized by the realities of racism in Johannesburg. In the context of British colonial South Africa, analytic neutrality became a practical and political impossibility.

In this chapter, I follow a (de)colonial thread of British psychoanalysis outside of the metropole to Johannesburg, South Africa, where Sachs spent the 1930s and 1940s working with the originally Southern Rhodesian medicine man he referred to as John Chavafambira.[1] Expanding recent scholarship on the uses of psychology and psychoanalysis in the colonies,[2] I unpack Sachs's unique "traveling analysis" with Chavafambira, considering how Sachs's interracial psychoanalytic work under the political conditions produced by British colonialism galvanized a reconfiguration of the privatized, boundaried, and ostensibly neutral clinical relation. While many scholars have written on the 1937 text that Sachs published about his experiences with Chavafambira—first titled *Black Hamlet* but later updated and republished in 1947 in the United States with the more militant title, *Black Anger*—none have yet considered how it chronicles a radical transformation of the boundaries and conventions of clinical practice.[3] Even for scholars such as Jacqueline Rose, Saul Dubow,

Chesca Long-Innes, Ranjana Khanna, and Andreas Bertoldi, who carefully unspool the racial and colonial complexity of Sachs's undertaking, there is a near-universal agreement that, although *Black Hamlet* is many things, it is principally *not* the record of a clinical analysis.[4]

In light of this, I explore what might be gained by nevertheless retaining psychoanalytic practice as the frame through which to understand the unconventional intimacy that Sachs and Chavafambira develop. By putting their analysis into conversation with recent postcolonial scholarship that explores the great range of local receptions, adaptations, and permutations of psychoanalysis beyond its Viennese birthplace, I consider how Sachs's experimental extraclinical psychoanalytic relationship with Chavafambira constituted an attempt at decolonial psychoanalytic practice. As I show, Sachs departed from orthodox psychological and psychoanalytic protocols as a way of trying to adapt the clinic to function in conditions of political unfreedom. Working in colonial Johannesburg made evident to Sachs that the clinic was not—and could never be—a politically neutral, hermetically sealed separate sphere since he found that racial and economic injustice on the streets of Johannesburg was the origin of much of his patients' mental strife. I thus argue that Sachs expanded the boundaries of the clinic as a form of antiracist, decolonial psychoanalytic praxis. Although this attempt was undoubtedly flawed—and potentially even failed—I maintain that this failure ought to be read not as a (re)confirmation of psychoanalysis's necessary orthodoxy but as a productive diagnosis of the limitations of dominant narratives that imagine the clinic as apolitical. By experimenting with the boundaries between analyst and patient—and by reconceptualizing how an analyst might best serve a (Black) patient in colonial Johannesburg—Sachs both literally and figuratively puts the political function of the clinic in motion.

KING GEORGE GOES TO SOUTH AFRICA

The night before Chavafambira met Sachs in mid-1933, he had what he considered to be a prophetic dream. In the dream, King George V, then king of England, traveled to Johannesburg in order to help remedy the racial and economic strife in the city caused by rapid colonial urbanization, industrialization, mass migration, and segregation. According to Chavafambira, who later reported the dream to Sachs in the clinic, when "King George came to Johannesburg" both Black and white South Africans greeted his arrival with buoyant enthusiasm, embracing him as a great benefactor for their country. "Plenty of whites and natives meet him . . . the big man, the big king. All very friendly, natives and whites. I was very surprised. They all shouted, 'The King has come to help the people.' All sang, blacks and whites. After this, the King left us and went back to England."[5] According to Chavafambira, both the king's arrival in the dream and the dream's occurrence in his life were auspicious omens. As he told Sachs months later in the analysis, they were clear signs that "even better luck was coming" since they heralded an improved fortune for both himself and for the rest of the oppressed Black majority in South Africa who Chavafambira described as his "fellow sufferers."[6] Given the racial politics of the dream, Chavafambira was convinced that this "better luck" was to come in the form of a white man—a prediction that was then quickly realized when Sachs arrived in Rooiyard the next day to treat Chavafambira's wife, Maggie, who had been suffering from a painful swelling in her legs. "So sure was I that a white man would come to my help," Chavafambira later told Sachs in the analysis, "that I was not at all surprised when one day the white woman [Hellmann] came to the yard and brought you."[7] Even though Sachs acknowledges that this sanguine association could have been a figment of Chavafambira's retrospective fantasy, Sachs nevertheless lived in Chavafambira's mind clad in the garb of a beneficent sovereign.

Sachs would not make much, analytically, of the link Chavafambira proposed between this dream and Sachs's timely arrival. But this inaugural association, which proleptically equates the figure of the white analyst with that of the British king, established a prescient triangulation between race, colonialism, and the role of psychoanalysis in South Africa that would come to define much of Sachs and Chavafambira's future relationship. On one level, the dream indicates how a placeholder was created for Sachs in Chavafambira's mind that granted Sachs exceptional authority and proclaimed him to be an emissary of progressive transformation. But this same equation, where an analyst comes to occupy the place recently vacated by the king, also performs a double movement, tacitly indicting Sachs—and by extension psychoanalysis itself—in the operation of colonial governance and rule. For if Sachs, as a white analyst, could so smoothly step into the place of a colonial monarch, then subtly the dream suggests that the distance separating the analyst's authority from colonial sovereignty might not be as great as it would first appear. The dream implies that psychoanalysis inevitably runs the risk of being, as Gilles Deleuze and Félix Guattari have famously written, "colonization pursued by other means."[8] Although the dream may manifestly hail Sachs as the fulfillment of a wish, read psychoanalytically it also latently diagnoses the colonial and racial power inequities that would characterize Sachs and Chavafambira's psychoanalytic intimacy for the decade to come. As both men realized, when the psychoanalytic clinic traveled to colonial South Africa, all pretense of objectivity, orthodoxy, and apoliticality evaporated.

· · ·

When Sachs first met Chavafambira in 1933, he had already been working in South Africa for eleven years. Born in Lithuania in 1893, Sachs spent his youth moving throughout Europe—from St. Petersburg to Cologne and then London—while completing his medical training. He eventually took his degree from London University in 1922 and then immediately emigrated to South Africa, where he served as a physician at the Pretoria Mental Hospital. His experience working with the schizophrenic patients, both Black and white, in Pretoria throughout the late 1920s galvanized his interest in psychology and in 1929 he travelled to Berlin for six months to undertake an analysis with Theodor Reik.[9] On returning to South Africa, he gave a series of lectures organized by the University of the Witwatersrand Philosophy Department on psychoanalysis and literature, which were eventually published in 1934 as *Psychoanalysis: Its Meaning and Practical Applications*. With this book, Sachs was inducted into the BPS and he began his own South African Psychoanalytic Study Group: the first organized instance of psychoanalysis in South Africa and the widely acknowledged basis of the current South African Psychoanalytical Association, now headed by Mark Solms.[10] In addition to his work as a doctor and psychoanalyst, Sachs was also a passionate Zionist and socialist and, from 1943 to 1947, he edited the socialist magazine *The Democrat*. In 1946, Sachs became the first (and only) training analyst in South Africa and, until his untimely death in

1949, he served as a lecturer at the Boston Psychoanalytic Institute, the New York Psychoanalytic Institute, and the Department of Social Science at the University of the Witwatersrand.[11]

Yet the work that he is perhaps best known for is *Black Hamlet*, his book-length account of the life and analysis of John Chavafambira, his former patient and longtime friend and associate. This record of their decade-long relationship is difficult to classify. Part psychoanalytic case study, part novel, part ethnography, and part biography, *Black Hamlet* combines case notes from Sachs's clinical work with Chavafambira with his direct personal experience of Chavafambira's life and that of the local Black community. Through this amalgamation, Sachs creates a sort of psychobiographical chronicle of Chavafambira, an East African man grappling with the internal and external changes produced by British colonialism. Sachs serves as the narrator throughout the text, and he presents the work as a roughly linear biography that follows Chavafambira's reconstituted life story, which began years before the two met. As Sachs puts it, he wanted "to give the story of [Chavafambira's] life in chronological order instead of in the disconnected manner in which I encouraged him to talk to me."[12] The result, as Rose and Dubow aptly note in their 1996 introduction to the reissued text, is a genre-defying work that asks, as its central question, "What dialogue is possible across boundaries of race, nation, and culture?"[13] And, beyond this, what role does psychoanalytic practice—that famous talking cure—play in sustaining, or stymieing, this exchange?

The challenge that this dialogue presented should not be underestimated. Given their differences of language, nationality, race, class, and religion, any attempt at a discussion required both literal and figurative forms of (self-)translation that often intensified the power differentials undergirding their relationship. Sachs reports that Chavafambira spent the whole first two weeks of the analysis recounting his early life and explaining, "in broken though fluent speech," the circumstances that brought him from Southern Rhodesia to Johannesburg.[14] According to Sachs, Chavafambira was born in a small village (*kraal*) in what is now southeastern Zimbabwe around 1904 (figure 3.1). His father was a distinguished *nganga*, much respected in the community, who died when Chavafambira was a child. In keeping with the local custom, Chavafambira's uncle, Charlie, then married Chavafambira's widowed mother,

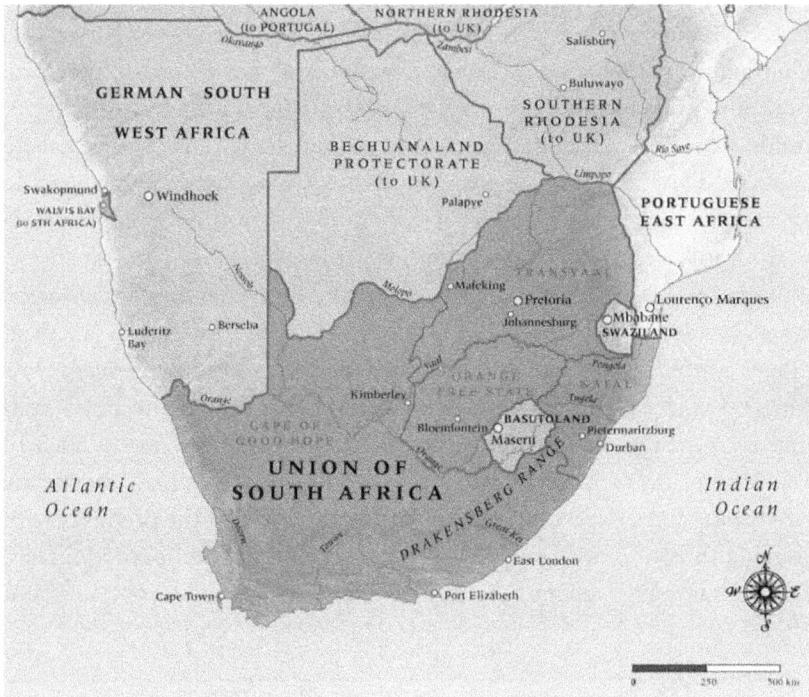

FIGURE 3.1 Map of South Africa, 1914.
"Map of South Africa in 1914," https://nzhistory.govt.nz/media/photo/map-south-africa-1914,
Ministry for Culture and Heritage.

Nesta—a union that would be the source of much conflict throughout his life, prompting Sachs to title the first version of his book *Black Hamlet* in recognition of the familiar Oedipal geometry. While the intention was always for Chavafambira to follow in his father's ancestral footsteps and train as a *nganga* himself, he had been advised that he must first reach a more mature age so that he would be less subject to illicit sexual temptations. Chavafambira thus sought employment outside his *kraal* for most of his youth, working as a children's nurse, a kitchen aid, and a domestic servant before eventually setting out for Johannesburg in 1921.

However, Chavafambira would not actually reach Johannesburg until 1927. After being waylaid on the road by a mystical encounter with a witch in a village not far from his own, he arrived in Pietersburg (now Polokwane) South Africa, where he found work in a commercial hotel as a domestic servant and waiter. During his years working there, Chavafambira met his wife, Maggie, who worked as a maid in the same hotel and whose painful limp evoked his pity. Theirs was far from a happy union and Chavafambira became increasingly frustrated with what he described as Maggie's performed laziness and dependency. At the same time, he grew ever more irritated by the entitled white clientele at the hotel, who treated the Black staff with unvarnished condescension and contempt. In a dramatic denouement, Chavafambira and Maggie were forced to flee the hotel when a white patron falsely accused Chavafambira of sexual assault, an experience Dubow describes as "an archetypical South African situation."[15] Although the hotel staff and even managers were well aware of this woman's recurrent fantasy of Black rape and trusted Chavafambira's innocence (a rather noteworthy predisposition in its own right) he was still hurried off the premises with Maggie in tow. It was only after this incident that he boarded a train to Johannesburg, secured employment in a boarding house there, and

FIGURE 3.2 John Chavafambira photographed at Rooiyard, 1935.
Photograph by Ellen Hellmann, Rooiyard, 1935. Historical Papers Research Archive, University of the Witwatersrand. Series: ZA HPRA A1419-8-8.2-16.

shuttled between various living quarters until he eventually arrived in Rooiyard around 1931 (figure 3.2).

While Chavafambira's story is unique in many ways—he came from a long line of distinguished *ngangas*, maintained intimate interracial friendships, and eventually became a respected political organizer and community leader—in many other ways his life was typical of the numerous Black migrants in South Africa at the time. In the interwar period, prior to the official implementation of apartheid, the Union of South Africa was deeply segregated by both convention and law. While the effects of colonialism were unevenly felt since colonial authority held far less sway outside of the major urban centers, a series of so-called Native bills, including the controversial antecedent Natives Land Act of 1913, severely restricted the rights of the Black majority to acquire, own, and occupy land outside of preordained "reserves."[16] As cities like Johannesburg rapidly industrialized and expanded throughout the early twentieth century under their new colonial governments, many Africans were driven from their rural *kraals* into the overcrowded urban centers in search of work, housing, and reliable income.

However, the restrictions of the Native bills (and other segregation legislation) forced these migrants onto tiny plots of land within the cities, producing much congestion, crowding, and unrest. Urban segregation was further reinforced by the 1937 Native Laws Amendment Act, which curtailed Black mobility in the city and effectively legalized the eviction of any Africans who could not prove their necessity as laborers "ministering to the needs of whites."[17] As many South African historians have established, much of the racist ideology and legislation throughout this period of rapid industrialization was tied to colonial insecurities about the reliance on Black labor power, since this was both essential for capitalist development and expropriation and simultaneously the biggest insurrectionary threat to the ruling white minority.[18] According to Dubow, who treats *Black Hamlet* as an intimate ethnography of race relations in pre-apartheid South Africa, the basic story of Chavafambira's life evidenced the "pattern of proletarianisation which drove Africans from the entire southern African region to the industrial areas of the Witwatersrand."[19] As one of these migrants, Chavafambira "fitted into a network of labour migrancy in which many young Manyika workers travelled to South Africa, often finding employment as waiters or domestic servants."[20] As labor migration increased throughout the late 1920s and 1930s, conditions in the city only worsened.

Rooiyard, where Chavafambira was living when he began his analysis with Sachs, was a prime, centrally located example of the poor conditions produced by this race legislation. With 107 rooms, Rooiyard sat on not more than 1,183 square yards of land and its roughly 400 residents (235 adults and 141 children) were serviced by one water tap, two garbage bins, and just six latrines.[21] The single-room dwellings, with ten to twelve square feet of living space, were shoddily tin-sided with broken windows or gaping seams that did little to protect the residents from the extremes of the climate. According to Hellmann, who was studying Rooiyard and other residences like it, the residents of Rooiyard were vocal about the derelict conditions; they complained "bitterly of the high rents which they rightly maintain are out of all proportion to the value received. They revolt against the filth and congestion of their surrou[n]dings. They inveigh against the appalling state of the sanitary arrangements."[22] Yet Hellmann also observed that the conditions of Rooiyard were "typical of the many yards which exist in those suburbs of Johannesburg where Natives are still allowed to reside," an indication of the scope and scale of racial segregation in the city-center.[23] Given the pressurized dual forces of land restriction and urban migration, squalor among Black African migrant communities in the city was a nearly guaranteed outcome of racist urban planning.

For its part, the municipality agreed that the conditions were inhospitable and, by 1933, had already placed Rooiyard and other "slum yards" like it on a list of "unsanitary" buildings slated for demolition. This was hardly the first time the municipality would enforce such evictions of Black communities in the name of "public health and security."[24] But the government's program for eradicating these dwellings—without provisioning any affordable and accessible housing in their stead—only compounded the problem since the urban demand for the cheap labor provided by migrant Africans continued to grow. As Dubow documents, "employment for Africans in secondary industry almost doubled between 1936 and 1945, while the urban African population increased by some 50 percent to reach 1,689,000."[25] With more and more migrants coming to the city and less and less housing accessible to them, vast informal shantytowns cropped up around the city's periphery and many workers were forced to make a daily, multihour commute from the surrounding suburbs to their jobs. These conditions, combined with the rampant criminalization of Blackness—notably, Chavafambira's first meaningful encounter when he arrived in Johannesburg was with a chain gang of recently arrested Black prisoners who were forced to make the daily exodos from the courtroom to the jail—meant that there was much racial unrest as the Black (lumpen)proletariat increasingly began to organize and resist. As a speaker at one of Chavafambira's political clubs aptly put it, "Where are we to live? In 1913 they passed the Land Act, by which they drove us from the land, our natural dwelling-place. Now they have passed the Urban Area Act, and tell us to get out of the towns and go back to the land we do not possess. We stand between the devil and the deep blue sea. What are we to do? Where are we to go?"[26] By the 1940s, Johannesburg was home to frequent protests, strikes, and boycotts as the struggle for self-determination intensified.

Because Sachs was one of the privileged colonial minority living and working in Johannesburg, he had had little direct experience with the pervasiveness and extent of colonial oppression in the city center until he began working with Chavafambira. Although the racialized nature of colonial oppression would become one of Sachs's, as much as Chavafambira's, dedicated political causes by the late 1930s and 1940s, when Sachs first began his analytic work his main research interest was concerned with academic debates in colonial ethnopsychology, a distinct field of colonial research investigating the intersection between race and psychology. Ethnopsychology was hardly a unified field (even within British Africa), but in general, in the interwar and immediate postwar periods, African ethnopsychologists held that the indigenous African mind, both in sanity and in insanity, was typologically different from that of the white European. In East Africa, the most well-known figure in this field during the postwar period was the East African (Kenyan) colonial administrator and minor ethnopsychological celebrity J. C. Carothers, whose work at the Mathari Mental Hospital in Nairobi on the so-called frontal lobe defect of the indigenous Africans dominated colonial ethnopsychology—on both sides of the African continent—for some two decades.[27] Carothers argued that, because of this supposed defect, the African brain was tantamount to that of the leucotomized European brain, leading to developmental deficiencies in the areas of independence, self-governance, and personal responsibility.[28]

Given how well his research dovetailed with the colonial "civilizing mission," Carothers would eventually become an official mouthpiece for the ideology of British colonialism writ large. In the postwar period, he was separately contracted by the British government and the World Health Organization to carry out studies on "the African mind" designed to quell anti-imperialist rebellion.[29] But prior to this national exaltation, Carothers's preliminary work largely just extended and popularized much earlier claim-making in the East African context. In particular, it provided scientific justification for the widely held "detribalization" thesis, which maintained that the numerous recorded cases of madness among urban Blacks were not "madness" in the European sense of the term since, as the African medical historian Megan Vaughan has argued, this would be to acknowledge that Black African mental life was fundamentally similar to that of the European.[30] Rather, madness in the indigenous Black population was thought to be the result of the corrosive impact of European culture and education on minds developmentally incapable of assimilating it. Thus, various structural, functional, and anatomic tests on Africans' brains by interwar physicians such as H. L. Gordon, the former president of the Kenyan branch of the British Medical Association, and F. W. Vint, a government-appointed pathologist, helped bolster the widespread colonial investment in scientific and psychological accounts of racial difference and inferiority.[31]

Sachs's early work was characterized by both interest in, and disagreement with, the tenets of this influential field. Prior to beginning the analysis with Chavafambira, Sachs had already come to reject the claim that white and Black psychology (and pathology) were different in type. As Dubow records, Sachs delivered a paper to the South African Association for the Advancement of Science (SAAAS) in 1933 in which "he concluded that 'the delusions, and hallucinations of the insane native were in structure, in origin and, partly in content, similar to those of the European.'"[32] This was the conviction that compelled Sachs to seek out an analysis with a Black African since he believed, in contrast to the colonial fad for different kinds of psychological testing, that it was only by "probing into the depths of the human mind, into the wide range of desires, conflicts, [and] strivings" that genuine psychological insight could be gained.[33] In the first pages of *Black Hamlet*, Sachs echoes the conclusions he drew in his SAAAS presentation, arguing that by following the procedure of a typical psychoanalysis (including talk therapy, free association, and dream interpretation) his clinical work with Chavafambira had revealed "that insanity in its form, content and causation is identical in Blacks and whites."[34] His insistence on the cross-racial continuity of insanity and, more generally, on the depth psychology possessed by Black Africans was thus his attempt to contest the widely accepted forms of scientific racism at the time.[35] Further still, the very decision to undertake a long-term psychoanalysis with a Black patient in a local context where Black/white relations were subject to legal as much as scientific regulation was an act of intended antiracist practice—one that would eventually result in his eviction from his fashionable consulting rooms for illegal interracial fraternization. Thus, even though Sachs's insistence on the fundamental similarity of white and Black psychology might seem, for a contemporary audience, to manifest one of Freudianism's most infamous sins—that of Eurocentric universalism—when understood in the local context of 1930s and 1940s South African scientific racism, his deployment of a fundamentally humanistic universalism was actually intended to contest the dominant claims of racialist psychology at the time.

Yet as *Black Hamlet* demonstrates time and again, this professed liberalism was all too often double-edged. For while it may be true that Sachs's intentions for beginning an analysis with Chavafambira were motivated by his desire to disprove naturalized claims about African psychological (and cerebral) inferiority, the fact remains that the very gesture of a white analyst taking on a Black patient for the purpose of "research" or "experiment" participates in a long and violent tradition of colonial medical experimentation. Moreover, although Sachs disagreed with some of the more contemptable claims of African ethnopsychology, he nevertheless made frequent use of the detribalization thesis for understanding what he described as Chavafambira's stymieing "Hamletism." As Sachs explains, "the circumstances of his life, the clash of his two worlds, constantly caused inner division. Every African leads a double life in the full sense of the psychological concept."[36] Rehashing the detribalization thesis as "the clash of . . . two worlds," Sachs proposed that Chavafambira's biggest psychological struggle was his inability to reconcile the competing demands of urban and *kraal* life. According to Sachs, "The black man's conflict was particularly severe in John. On the one hand he loved the white man's life, loved civilization. On the other hand, more than most natives, he was bound by his profession to his past, for he was destined to perpetuate his father, the great *nganga*."[37] For Sachs, Chavafambira's inability to resolve this conflict led him to adopt a habitually indecisive, avoidant, and irresponsible relational pattern. Drawing links between Chavafambira's decision to "avoid" conflict with his uncle, Charlie, by migrating to seek work in the city and his later resolve to "run away" from the hotel after he was wrongly accused of rape, Sachs identified what he understood to be a recurring pattern in Chavafambira's personal, professional, and political life: his titular "Hamletism."[38] Thus, while it is undoubtedly true that Sachs—by affiliating a Black African with one of the most lauded pieces of literature in the English canon and by ascribing him, as Ranjana Khanna has shown,[39] a psychic disposition (melancholia) believed only to characterize Europeans—overtly rejected much of the racist psychology then in vogue across the African continent, his psychoanalytic stylization of Chavafambira nonetheless trafficked in many of the racial tropes endemic to colonialism's paternalistic orientation.

The course of the analysis would ultimately sway Sachs's opinion about the value of any Enlightenment-style humanistic psychological practice, no matter how sympathetic its intentions. As he became more familiar with the climate of Chavafambira's daily life—which included police brutality, urban segregation, wage theft, colonial dispossession, poverty, and some remarkably poignant examples of "well-intentioned" white liberal racism, such as when Chavafambira's friend, Tembu, was invited to a white associate's house to discuss resistance to the Native bills . . . only to then be shown to the servants' latrine[40]—he increasingly came to think that the ultimate cause of much Black suffering lay in economic and political oppression, which was subsequently transformed into psychic malaise. This perspective set him apart from even the liberal psychological establishment, which still tended to see material inequity as the naturalized result of psychological capacity, adaptation, and normality. The text of *Black Hamlet* clearly evidences Sachs's toggle between these competing ideologies, particularly when it came to how he ought to narrate the origin and cause of Chavafambira's difficulties.

This tension is evident, for instance, when Sachs reflects on the abrupt death of Chavafambira's father, proposing that "this dramatic childhood experience had a retarding effect on John and on every African child in his fight for independence" before quickly changing course and asserting that "though today this important psychological factor counts little compared with the poverty and starvation, the economic exploitation, and the severe racial discrimination to which Black people are subjected in South Africa."[41] While many of Chavafambira's African friends and acquaintances in Johannesburg would make similar observations about the primary importance of racial and material forms of colonial oppression, Sachs's own adoption of this position was unusual for a European. Indeed, readers can even see in this remark some similarity to current Black and liberationist psychological reformulations of the temporality of trauma, which aim to furnish models of "continuous trauma" that take account of ongoing structural and systemic violence in racist and neocolonial settler-states, thus displacing prior singular and individualist frameworks. On the subject of Chavafambira's supposed indecisiveness, Sachs astutely observes that although "this attitude can be traced psychologically to the native method of child-rearing," there are nevertheless "other possible reasons why they refuse to make plans for the morrow. . . . Chiefly, it develops because the African is too much at the mercy of the white man's caprice to make any kind of planning for the future of value."[42] As their unconventional clinical relation developed, Sachs's appreciation of the psychosocial complexity of Chavafambira's suffering deepened.

As Dubow has persuasively shown,[43] such remarks are especially characteristic of Sachs's 1947 *Black Anger*, in which his radicalization around the intertwined issues of racism, colonialism, and capitalism in South Africa led him to a stronger emphasis on the intersection between the political economy and personal psychology—an ideological shift evidenced by the new title, which replaces a pseudodiagnostic complex with a politicized affect. The context of World War II is indispensable in understanding this increased radicalization since the rise of antisemitic global fascism and the genocidal extermination of the European Jewry would have likely heightened Sachs's own commitment to radical, coalitional, antiracist socialism. As Sachs indicatively appends in the 1947 edition, "John's greatest need was not to know his repressed unconscious, but to know the society he lived in, to recognize its ills and learn how to fight them," an observation that seems, on the surface, to pawn off clinical psychoanalysis in favor of political resistance.[44]

However, for Sachs, this transformation was less a move from psychology to politics (as in the familiar, if reductive, progression often ascribed to Fanon's work) than it was the concretization of his burgeoning conviction that psychological health, for any Black man living in colonial Johannesburg, was evidenced *by* political resistance. Inspired by Marxist inflections of psychoanalysis then flourishing throughout Europe, Sachs came to see psychic ills as derived from social inequities and, as a result, he marked therapeutic success according to the patient's willingness and ability to identify and enact appropriate "revolt."[45] Readers can see this shift in perspective in the narrative trajectory afforded by the two different texts. While the 1937 *Black Hamlet* ends sanguinely with the resolution of Chavafambira's alleged "Hamletism" through his newfound commitment to a European education for his son, Daniel, in the 1947 *Black Anger* Sachs is much more interested in Chavafambira's growing political radicalization and resistance as a metric of his psychological well-being. Sachs describes how, for some years, Chavafambira had been attending local socialist and communist meetings in Johannesburg. While the speakers at these events ran the gamut of political sensibility— calling for everything from a radical pan-Africanist revolution against white colonial oppression to an assimilationist-style uplift of Black Africans through European education—the links that each made between racial and economic forms of oppression resonated with Chavafambira. According to Sachs, he "came to feel passionately with the speakers, [and] looked for stronger protests. He attended Communist meetings in preference to others because there the speeches took on a more fiery character."[46] By 1945, Sachs plays up how Chavafambira had become a respected community leader in the struggle for racial justice in Johannesburg. He was active in the shantytown politics on the outskirts of the city and had helped to organize the Alexandra bus boycott in 1944 when transport companies hiked already exploitatively high fares for Black commuters. After nearly seven weeks of boycotting the buses and walking the eighteen-mile round trip journey from Alexandra Township to Johannesburg each day, boycotters succeeded in negotiating lower rates, a victory that Chavafambira experienced as "his own personal achievement."[47] By the case's conclusion, Sachs, anticipating Fanon's famous call for a "combined action" in psychoanalysis by at least five years, validates the success of his clinical work through the extraclinical actionalization of his patient in the service of decolonial protest.[48] "Psychoanalysis is offered here," observes Long-Innes about the case, "as a release or advance into freedom."[49] For Sachs, Chavafambira's political resistance became a sign of the analysis's clinical success.

Satisfying though this conclusion may be, it does not take much literary training to recognize that there is a spurious tidiness to the developmental arc of the story Sachs tells. According to Sachs, Chavafambira begins his journey as an intelligent and sympathetic but ultimately indecisive man marked by the "Hamletism" of his Shakespearean namesake. By the text's conclusion, Sachs reports that he had firmly resolved the hesitancy characteristic of his earlier life, and—in the revised 1947 edition especially—he emphasizes Chavafambira's pan-Africanist political radicalization as the measure of his psychological transformation. In light of this, many critics have called into question Sachs's claim to objective reportage, proposing that Sachs's "psychological biography" is at least as much an *auto*biography of the analyst's desires as it is an anatomy of the patient's defenses: a fitting diagnosis of perhaps the entire case study genre. According to Jonathan Crewe, "the racialized unconscious ultimately on display is that of the analyst rather than his subject."[50] For Long-Innes, "*Black Hamlet* is less the story of Chavafambira's evolution towards greater self-realization (though this is how Sachs presents it), than the story of his [Sachs's] own political radicalization projected onto his interpretation of Chavafambira."[51] Even Dubow observes that "Sachs himself is inscribed in the 'John' of *Black Hamlet*, a figure who is both an individual in his own right, as well as a collective or composite symbol of hope for the future."[52] Jacqueline Rose highlights how this collapse of analyst into patient, of narrator into protagonist, is largely enabled by the novelistic nature of the text, which freely employs the formal literary conventions that govern all narrative art, including plot, character, metaphor, genre, symbolism, allusion, analogy, and free indirect speech. To this, it is worth noting that Sachs's first draft of the text (titled *African Tragedy: The Life Story of a Native Doctor*) was even written in the first person, as though by Chavafambira himself: a transparent manifestation of the cross-racial identification Rose diagnoses.[53]

Through *Black Hamlet*, Sachs could thus be seen to write a revolutionary version of himself into being via Chavafambira, conjuring and securing his own self-realization through the developmental arc afforded to
his patient-qua-protagonist.

On these grounds, most scholars writing about Sachs's work and
about *Black Hamlet* have been reluctant to consider his contributions in
terms of clinical practice. Indeed, few have even described what happens
between the two men within the four walls of the consulting room as
psychoanalytic at all. As early as 1938, Sybille Yates reviewed *Black Hamlet* for the *International Journal of Psychoanalysis*, concluding that the
text was mostly useful "as a sociological study of the Negro problem in
South Africa," not a clinical case study, since "the transference situation
was hardly dealt with."[54] Sachs's trainee and colleague, Sadie Gillespie,
similarly describes it as "wholly unorthodox research . . . breaking every
analytic rule."[55] Later historians and literary critics arrive at the same
conclusion, albeit motivated by different disciplinary shibboleths: while
Dubow notes that "*Black Hamlet* is inadequate as a purely psychoanalytic
study" and should best be read as a unique historical document elucidating the social situation in interwar Johannesburg,[56] literary critic Andreas
Bertoldi avers that "there is no clinical intervention, no proper analysis,
and thus no psychological resolution."[57] Even Sachs's obituary describes
his work as exemplifying a tension between genuine psychoanalytic practice and political radicalism, a conflict that it describes as having "weak-
ened his [Sachs's] fervour as a revolutionary and blunted his perceptions
as a scientist."[58] Regardless of the social and theoretical merit critics have
readily found in the text, for both psychoanalytic and academic audiences,
it is decidedly *not* the record of a clinical encounter.

In many ways, this claim is not wrong. By virtually any contemporary standards, Sachs's enactment (rather than interpretation) of
the countertransference situation and his unrestrained involvement in
Chavafambira's life led to serious breaches of clinical technique. More
still, it is precisely these moments of clinical rupture that often find Sachs
perpetuating some of the very racial and gendered tropes produced by
the colonial order that he intended to contest. Yet I think it would be a
mistake to concede too readily to the split between legitimate and illegitimate—authentic and inauthentic—forms of clinical practice that these
accounts implicitly propose. After all, psychoanalysis was a thoroughly

heterodox endeavor from its earliest days when it came to the implementation of clinical technique. As is well known, Sigmund Freud typically knew and socialized with his clinical patients; he lent money to patients and gave time to free clinics; he conducted analyses in person and in writing, including his own iconoclastic self-analysis and the analysis of his daughter, Anna Freud. Far from being an anomaly within psychoanalysis's professional infancy, such clinical experimentations were as much a part of early practice in Vienna as they were the later transnational circulation and permutation of psychoanalysis globally. One could think, for instance, of Ashis Nandy's work on Girindrasekhar Bose, in which he discusses how Bose's early success adapting Freudian psychoanalysis for colonial India involved not only his well-known reimagining of the Oedipus complex as an unresolved desire (among his male patients) for dual sexuation but also his practical retention of some elements of hypnosis (a popular middle-class practice in Calcutta) and his alleged implementation of the "guru-*śiṣya*" paradigm in his clinical practice.[59] Or one could consider Gabriel Mendes's account of how Harlem's Lafargue Clinic (1946–1958), which was supported by literary luminaries like Richard Wright and Ralph Ellison, combined psychoanalysis with social work in an attempt to offset the mental health issues born of racism for the underserved Black citizenry.[60] Or, alternatively, one could consider Mariano Ben Plotkin's influential work on how racial ideals of whiteness and nationhood shaped the early reception of psychoanalysis in Brazil.[61] Or, again, of Aída Alejandra Golcman's discussion of the group-based therapeutic communities that were established by psychoanalysts in the Estévez Hospital of Neuropsychiatry in Buenos Aires in the 1960s.[62] As recent work by Camille Robcis has argued,[63] such (re)configurations of the clinic were perhaps most famously implemented in Southern France at Saint-Alban with the institutional psychotherapy movement which, via Fanon, would find its way to Blida-Joineville in Algeria, where Fanon creatively revised therapeutic practice with hospitalized Arab patients to include organizing day clinics, social hours, film screenings, drama clubs, and even football games.[64] More than a stable and self-evident category, then, the very claim to psychoanalytic orthodoxy—to clear boundaries between legitimate and illegitimate forms of clinical intervention—has been a powerful tool wielded to police disciplinary boundaries, secure professional authority, and ensure institutional survival through political cooperation. Psychoanalytic practice, in other words, is and has always been as varied as the numerous locales it came to inhabit.

Put in this context, it is hardly a stretch to consider that even the most unconventional aspects of Sachs's work with Chavafambira can be read as a reimagining, rather than outright refusal, of the promise of the clinic. In fact, the local and specific context of colonial Johannesburg changed the demands placed on both analyst and patient, prompting an unorthodox reconfiguration of the clinic in concert with aspirational antiracist, decolonial politics. As most, if not all, critics of this text have rightly pointed out, this was a thoroughly flawed, and even failed, clinical experiment when it came to Sachs's ability to sufficiently apprehend the repercussions of his involvement in Chavafambira's life. However, as Freud usefully pointed out in his analysis of the slips and parapraxes that constitute our collective "psychopathology" of everyday life, accidents, mistakes, and failures can also be productive. Thus, my proposal here is that it is precisely the *un*conventional and *extra* clinical nature of Sachs and Chavafambira's psychoanalytic venture that, paradoxically, constitutes its most interesting contribution to understanding the politicality of clinical practice. If one interpretation of psychoanalysis's function holds that it enables greater degrees of (psychic) freedom for the patient, then Sachs's work in colonial South Africa prompts us to consider what types of freedom a clinical analysis ought to foster when faced with a climate of political oppression.

UNCONSCIOUSNESS RAISING:
CLINIC, POLITICS, PROTEST

When Chavafambira arrived at Sachs's consulting room for his first clinical session, the racial politics of Johannesburg arrived with him. As part of his analytic practice, Sachs would typically begin each session by shaking his patient's hand upon entry—a formal, gentlemanly greeting that likely spoke to the gendered composition of his clientele. But, when Chavafambira first walked in, Sachs was brought to a crossroads. He reflected with surprising honesty on the uneasiness he felt extending this practice to a Black man. "For the first time in my life," meditated Sachs, "I had to treat a black man as my equal, and my greeting was obviously artificial."[65] Chavafambira, too, was discomfited by the greeting and he "quickly withdrew his hand," proceeding to examine the room instead. Sachs notes that, before lying down on the sofa, Chavafambira seemed especially interested in Sachs's papers and books—an interest Sachs is anxious to justify by explaining that these objects would have been "familiar to him from his work as a domestic servant in European houses."[66] Although Sachs would have likely considered this remark complimentary, it unconsciously places Chavafambira in a position of servitude before he had even so much as touched the couch. With the inverted images of "colonial sovereign" and "domestic servant" in Chavafambira's and Sachs's minds, respectively, Chavafambira's entry to the clinic was accompanied by the sociopolitical racial and labor disparities definitional to colonial domination from his inaugural session (figure 3.3).

FIGURE 3.3 Wulf Sachs and John Chavafambira.
Photographed by Ralph Bunche, 1938. Courtesy of Department of Special Collections, University Research Library, University of California, Los Angeles.

On the whole, their sessions in the consulting room proceeded according to roughly the same routine: Chavafambira would enter, shake hands, take off his coat, and assume his place on the couch. Sessions would last an hour with Sachs taking copious clinical notes. Trained as a Freudian, he operated according to a fairly standard psychoanalytic technique with the mainstays of his practice including free association and dream interpretation. After Chavafambira settled himself on the couch, he was thus "free"—insofar as he was able to articulate himself in English—to say whatever came into his mind. The subjects he discussed included his distrust of white people; his frustrations with his wife; his resentment of his avuncular father substitute, Charlie; his approach to medical practice; his ambitions for his son, Daniel; and some of his feelings about Sachs himself, whom he alternatingly disbelieved and appreciated. Over the course of the analysis, Sachs reported that he recorded some two hundred different dreams, including many transference dreams in which Sachs himself was a leading figure.[67]

As with all analyses, though, the limits of exactly how "free" Chavafambira actually was in the clinic would quickly come into view. A few months into the analysis, Sachs noticed that Chavafambira, who had been coming regularly to sessions up until this point, had become particularly withdrawn, quiet, and taciturn. Sachs connected this with escalating racial hostilities in Rooiyard, which were making Chavafambira's position there increasingly tenuous. The police had been carrying out frequent raids on the yard aimed at curtailing the illicit beer-brewing that the women relied on as part of their informal economy. The yard had also recently been placed on a list of buildings slated for demolition and the residents were actively trying to appeal this injunction. Given Chavafambira's collaboration with both Sachs and Hellmann, the other residents of the yard were growing increasingly suspicious of him, believing he might be working as a spy for the colonial authorities, either the police or the municipality. With this context in the background, Sachs assumes that Chavafambira's affective withdrawal in the clinic is race-related and he explains that he was "not surprised that he [Chavafambira] bore a grudge against me—the white man—on account of whose caprices and ill-will he and his fellows suffered so much."[68] Yet Sachs laments Chavafambira's decision to "remai[n] silent" when faced with this conflict because it seemed to Sachs yet another illustration of the "Hamletism" that Sachs hoped to dispel.[69]

When faced with this scenario, which only emerged because of the preexisting entanglement of their personal lives, Sachs makes an unconventional decision about the best course of clinical action. While orthodox Freudian or nascent Kleinian analysts may have dealt with this impasse by analyzing the (supposed) transference upon which Chavafambira's silence was based, Sachs decides to take a more interventionist approach. "It was dangerous to leave him in this resistant mood," Sachs surmised, so "I tried to induce him to talk."[70] He did this first in the clinic by returning to their mutual interest in medical practice. He shared details of his own patients and gave him various basic Western medicines as a way of trying to (re)build trust. Having succeeded, to an extent, Chavafambira returned the favor by inviting Sachs and Hellmann to accompany him while he traveled outside town to practice informally as a *nganga* (since he had not yet been formally initiated by his uncle). Following this, Sachs invited Chavafambira back to his home for lunch where, "after a good meal," Chavafambira broke his silence and talked for "a few hours at a stretch in the homely, peaceful surroundings of my private house," telling Sachs "the story of how he began to practice in Johannesburg."[71] In this way, a psychoanalytic session that began in the clinic eventually migrated to the domestic home, blurring the boundary between psychoanalytic practice and ordinary life.

It hardly needs saying that, according to virtually any contemporary clinical psychoanalytic methodology, Sachs's approach to Chavafambira's silence is anathema. Not only does Sachs determine the affective trajectory of the clinical relationship himself—deciding in advance that speech is preferable to silence; cooperation more desirable than resistance—but in order to secure his preferred outcome Sachs takes his relationship with Chavafambira from the clinic out into the city and even back into his own personal home. This is the first time in the case where Sachs intentionally dispenses with the consulting room as the scene for the analysis, but it would hardly be the last. Such movements are a common occurrence during the two and a half years of their clinical relationship. During this time, Sachs freely admits that he frequently visits Chavafambira's current residence, his family *kraal*, and his political clubs; he gets to know Chavafambira's friends, his wife, and his children. When external circumstances force Chavafambira into the hospital, into the prison, and into the asylum, Sachs brings the analysis to him, even conducting some sessions at his bedside. Although Sachs insists vigorously that he never paid Chavafambira for his time (as was common practice for colonial anthropologists and psychologists) because "it would have been disastrous to introduce money into our relationship," he nevertheless frequently gave Chavafambira money throughout their relationship, either directly or through mutual acquaintances, and one cannot help but notice how Sachs's overdetermined anxiety about analytic propriety condenses around the subject of money.[72] In both Sachs's extraclinical involvement with Chavafambira and in his directive and highly specific clinical intentionality for Chavafambira's political radicalization, Sachs inserts his own desire into what is, at least nominally, Chavafambira's analysis. As Rose observes about the case, "it is one of the ironies but also an illuminating facet of *Black Hamlet* that Sachs, wooing Chavafambira in the spirit of nonracialism," finds himself imposing his own desire in a way not dissimilar to Freud's much-admonished analysis of "Dora."[73]

Rose's comparison with Freud's "Dora" case usefully highlights the risk that Sachs runs by so explicitly taking Chavafambira's silence into his own hands. After all, the pretense of acting in the best interests of colonialized people of color has long been one of colonialism's most distinctive calling cards. In the very act, Rose suggests, of trying to secure Chavafambira's freedom to associate, Sachs ironically confines the range of his affective expression. No matter how cozy a picture he ultimately paints of the friendly, genial conclusion that results from this retreat to the domestic sphere, it does not erase the fact that Sachs's intervention is, at best, an attempt at misdirection or, at worst, a pass at bribery. On this reading, Sachs's extraclinical agenda contaminates the desired neutrality of the clinical sphere.

Rose's point is an important one since it highlights the violence inherent in a course of action that Sachs, at least, perceived to be beneficial. But what is most interesting to me about this scene is not the ways in which it diverges from orthodox psychoanalytic practice but rather its unexpected continuities with it. For although it may be true that Sachs instrumentalizes his own desire to chart the course of the analysis, making the breach of clinical boundaries coextensive with the erasure of Chavafambira's self-determination, his intervention never-theless usefully indexes the actual, lived impossibility of *any* clinical space, however orthodox and boundaried, to manifest the analytic neu-trality that is so often prized as the clinician's particular and skilled contribution. No matter how seemingly benign, the analyst's decision about how to respond to the patient—with silence or with speech, with interpretation or with affirmation, with a question or with a statement—necessarily registers the analyst's own positionality and sense of what is a normal or desirable manifestation on the patient's part. Even the curation of the physical space of the consulting room as the proper domain of analytic work is a studied construction since, as Rachel Greenspan had recently shown through Derrida's concept of the *parergon*, "the boundaries of the psychoanalytic frame have always been less stable than they might appear."[74] In other words, and as I dis-cuss more fully in chapter 5 and the epilogue, the composition of the very boundaries of the clinic itself, as much as the analyst's deliberated actions within it, constitute deliberate if plastic enactments of psycho-analysis's preferred relation to the social and political world.

Consider, for instance, the following scenarios. While one analyst might interpret a patient's anger about the analyst's lateness to a ses-sion as a transference response in need of analysis, another might take it as a justified reaction to the analyst's breach of professional respon-sibility. Equally, one analyst might interpret a Black patient's ongoing hostility, anger, and suspicion toward a white analyst as a matter of individual transference while another might see it as having to do with the inevitable social, material, and psychological benefits that accrue to the analyst's whiteness as a result of the interlocking violences of racial capitalism and mass incarceration. Recognizing this, the question of how the analyst ought to respond becomes an open issue since classical understandings of clinical phenomena like transference and projection tend to derive their unique status from the understanding that what happens in the clinic is a nonsynchronic manifestation of the personal mires of the past—not a diagnosis of present and ongoing struggles in which the analyst herself is complicit. But if the frame of analysis is expanded to encompass the structural and historical as well as the per-sonal and individual, then the supposed neutrality assumed to define the analyst's clinical presence and interpretations of the transference is complicated by her necessary embeddedness in the wider sociopolitical order. How, for instance, ought a heterosexual male analyst respond to a female patient who finds his interpretations heterosexist and paternalistic? How respond to a Black patient's rage at a white analyst's placid ignorance of white supremacy's operation through police brutality and racial capitalism? Can interpretation of the transference really take sufficient account of this?

Importantly, my point here bears on silence and interpretation equally, even if not symmetrically. Although clinically the analyst's silence is often presumed to be neutral, much activist and sociological work on race and racism has vitally called attention to the nonneutrality of silence, especially (but not exclusively) in relation to white complicity. We need think only of political slogans like the recent "White Silence Is Violence" or the earlier AIDS activism cry "Silence=Death" to understand the long historical function of silence as an operation of power. Such a diagnosis usefully highlights the fact that silence is itself an identifiable, deliberate, and habituated action whose meaning is certainly not benign, and has often been weaponized as a strategic tool of oppression. Indeed, as the clinician Natasha Stovall has recently shown, one of whiteness's special privileges, in clinical as much as sociopolitical settings, is to function as the silent, unspoken racial backdrop against which all else is rendered legible.[75] This is not to say that silence always operates the same way, as the oppressive or complicit; psychoanalysis, perhaps more than any other hermeneutic, acknowledges that silences can be as heterogenous as speech. It is just to highlight that, for the analyst, too, neither silence nor speech, action nor passivity, clinic nor street, provide any guarantee of a necessarily ethical or just form of analytic relation.

Sachs, for his part, gives readers little indication that his clinical technique was synthesizing this degree of politicized self-reflexivity. Especially at the start of the analysis, Chavafambira was, for Sachs, simply a research "specimen" whose unconscious mind he sought to dissect—"nothing more than a case of psychic vivisection"—not a patient (or person) in need of particular clinical help.[76] But as the analysis progressed, and particularly as Chavafambira's physical safety and freedom were repeatedly threatened, Sachs is brought to meditate directly on the nature and extent of his clinical responsibility to and for his patient. For if a patient can simply be abducted by the police and confined or "disappeared" without notice—as happens to Chava-fambira right after Christmas in 1933—then any analyst's insistence on maintaining appropriate "boundaries" to safeguard a fantasy of analytic neutrality would seem to be nothing but a strategic guise for complicity with state violence. This, at least, was Jacques Derrida's conclusion in his 1981 lecture "Geopsychoanalysis: . . . and the Rest of the World," when he indicted the International Psychoanalytic Association's silence on (and arguable complicity with) the state terrorism and torture being used against Argentinian citizens during the Dirty War. In writing this, Derrida may well have had in mind the public resignation, and later national expulsion, of the Austro-Argentinian analyst Marie Langer, who in 1974 quit the very Argentinian Psychoanalytic Association that she had founded as a protest to its refusal to take a stand against the escalating violence of right-wing Peronism. Although historically and geographically distinct, both Langer's and Derrida's condemnations of the ruse of psychoanalytic apoliticality have much relevance for Sachs's circumstances working in colonial South Africa given how the municipality strategically used carcerality to enforce and maintain racial subjugation. As Vaughan aptly remarks, "Sachs . . . had recognized that his whole project was coloured by the political system of South Africa, in which his subject could be arbitrarily arrested and removed from his land. The idealized relationship between analyst and subject was clearly an impossible goal in this context and the notion of 'free association' had an ironic ring."[77] It is as though Sachs is wondering, as he continually bends and reshapes the perimeters of his role as "analyst," whether free association is the best thing that psychoanalysis has to offer in conditions of unfreedom.

This quandary is brought home to Sachs quite explicitly when Chavafambira is arrested for a fourth time, following his intervention on behalf of a young Black child who was being beaten on the streets of Johannesburg by a white police officer for holding up traffic. Unsure of why Chavafambira had suddenly gone missing—again—Sachs is visited by two of their mutual acquaintances, Simon and Tembu. When he learns that Chavafambira had been imprisoned—not coincidentally, on the same day as his friend Mdlawini was charged with murder and sentenced to death by a white court—he bristles at Tembu's suggestion that he himself is responsible for Chavafambira and is thus obliged to intervene with the police on his behalf. "Tembu's last remark irritated me. There was no need to instruct me in my duties to my fellow men. I had been fulfilling them as I knew how for a long time. I had even been victimized because of it. I had been compelled to leave a consulting room in a fashionable block of flats, outwardly on some trivial pretext, but actually I suspected because John and other natives came often to visit me there."[78] Sachs's upset is due in part to the fact that he feels—justly or not—that he has already gone far beyond other European white men in his advocacy for a Black African. In this passage, Chavafambira is stripped of his particularity and becomes one of Sachs's "fellow men," one among many "other natives" whose cross-racial affiliations with Sachs had rendered him, too, a victim of racial discrimination. But in this moment, Sachs also can be seen to struggle with his own racial positioning in South Africa since, as a Jew in the increasingly antisemitic 1930s, he hardly fit comfortably under the banner of "white man." Indeed, as Sander Gilman and Celia Brickman have both persuasively shown, the ideology of anti-Blackness deployed against colonized peoples in Africa, Australia, and the Americas was also actively used in relation to the Jews of Europe, who were likewise described as "primitive," "mongrel," and "negro."[79] Such tropes were highly mobile, extending well beyond Europe where they were operationalized by even those against whom they were deployed. At various points, Sachs reports that Black acquaintances describe Jews as "jackals" preying on the South African Black majority and parrot back to him German eugenicist politics—even as indigenous Black Africans were, themselves, hardly exempted from National Socialism's genocidal agenda.[80] In a particularly well-placed retort to their companion, Dhlamini's, claim that Nazis would liberate South Africa, "free the country from the Jews and the Indians and give their shops to the Blacks," Tshakada quips, "So—our local Nazis have suddenly discovered Black Aryans?"[81]

Thus, when Tembu accuses Sachs of indifference and neglect—accuses him, in other words, of failing in his ethical duty to his patient—there is a complex racial politics at work that troubles the familiar equation of white European analyst-oppressor and Black African patient-oppressed. As Grahame Hayes has pointed out, it is likely that Sachs's initial empathy for Chavafambira came through his identification with the shared experiences of racism and deracination.

His immediate association to Tembu's accusation is that he is being put on trial, a metaphor that extends the courtroom scene with Mdlawini in which they had just participated but reverses the racial politics of judge and jury.[82]

> Try? . . . Yes—I was on trial now. The colored man, silent, lifeless, with a masked face, appeared to be the judge; Tembu, vindictive and inwardly aggressive, the prosecutor; and Simon, the simpleton, the jury. Was I to place myself in the hands of these hostile men, and protest to them my innocence? Didn't I myself, a Jew, belong to a people ceaselessly driven from pillar to post? It was useless telling them so. They would not understand me, as that morning the court had not understood Mdlawini, and would not understand John tomorrow.[83]

Sachs's fantasy of this cross-racial trial has been much commented on by critics[84] because of how the juridical discourse of the trial comes to mediate a cross-racial identification between analyst and patient, ultimately prompting the question of psychoanalysis's place in relation to the operation of colonial governmentality. The fantasy, we might say, is another permutation of the earlier question: Is the analyst king?

Yet the sequence that follows this exchange about race and justice marks a turning point for Sachs's understanding of his role as a clinician. As Sachs lies awake that night, while Chavafambira sits in jail, he reflects on his work with Chavafambira, observing that "in spite of my sympathy . . . he nevertheless had remained chiefly a psycho-anthropological specimen: the main aim had been to collect his dreams, his fantasies, and find out the workings of the primitive unconscious mind."[85] Considering that his earlier "psycho-anthropological" interest in Chavafambira as a type of research "specimen"—a "subject for study"—had been dehumanizing, Sachs is prompted by Chavafambira's arrest to articulate a new relationship between psychoanalytic practice and social justice.[86]

> Then it struck me that his self-destructive actions might be the direct result of his sudden and abrupt severance from me. I knew very well from experience that no patient could be dropped, in the state of so-called positive transference, without serious risk of

his mental health. Why had I not taken the same precaution with John? Because—I had to confess again—John had been to me only a subject of experiment, and the whole analysis nothing more than a case of psychic vivisection.

Now in the stillness of the night my main concern was for John's safety and well-being. A new man separated himself from the pages I was reading. The human: the real John.[87]

As Rose has usefully observed, there is a paradox in this meditation since, in the very moment when Sachs seems to embrace Chavafambira's full humanity and autonomy—he is more than just a "specimen" to be collected, more than "a case of psychic vivisection"—he suggests, through the language of transference, that Chavafambira is nevertheless dependent upon him. "No moment shows more strongly," remarks Rose, "the predicament or demand of the humanist, whose recognition of the other as human has, above all, to be seen. . . . Sachs remains in loco parentis. His dilemma captures the ambiguity of fostered, nurtured autonomy: 'Go forward. Take my hand.'"[88] For Rose, Sachs uses politics—that is, his decision to bail Chavafambira out of jail—to plug the hole of what she describes as "a crisis in the analytic relationship between black and white, [the] fleeting recognition by Sachs of its impossibility."[89] Although Sachs may turn first to a clinical analysis, his final resolution in favor of Chavafambira's liberation speaks, according to Rose, to his political conviction.

However, the framing of a dichotomized either/or between the clinical and the political misrepresents Sachs's verdict in this passage. On my reading, it is interestingly *through* the clinical grammar of the transference that Sachs arrives at his resolve to bail Chavafambira out of jail. That is, it is as an extension of the clinic that Sachs invests in the importance of political action. It is only by refocusing on the clinical dimension of their unconventional intimacy that Sachs is brought to reconceptualize the scope of the clinic and, more generally, the ethico-political mission of psychoanalytic practice. Put another way, it is through the clinical framework—rather than against it—that Sachs appraises Chavafambira as a full human being and pledges himself to reliable decolonial engagement. If clinical psychoanalysis is, at least according to one tradition of interpretation, about the facilitation of greater degrees of psychic freedom for the patient, then noteworthy here is how, in British colonial South Africa, psychoanalysis had to engage with freedom on both psychic *and* material planes in order to preserve its charter.

This event has significant consequences for both Sachs and Chavafambira. In the first instance, Sachs finds himself radicalized to reimagine his psychoanalytic practice in the service of an anticolonial political agenda. In the second, the violence of the colonial carceral state drives Chavafambira to action as well, albeit with a more troubling yield. After bailing Chavafambira out, Sachs decides to help him leave Johannesburg because Sachs believes that, if he were arrested again, the authorities might link him with Mdlawini's murder conviction, which could prove fatal. While in transit, Chavafambira confesses to Sachs that, before they departed, he had poisoned Maggie with a drug he had found in Sachs's medical case. Although it seemed for a moment that Chavafambira had murdered his wife, Sachs is relieved to realize that the "poisoning" had been unsuccessful since the drug Chavafambira had slipped into her tea was a harmless sleeping potion. The initial (unsuccessful) revolt against white colonial oppression is thus passed off onto the doubly oppressed Black woman, who becomes the recipient of frustrated violence against the state.

Through this sequence, Sachs reveals how the misogynistic denigration of "Woman" had tacitly functioned, throughout the analysis, as the axis of absolute difference through which the distance between white and Black forms of masculinity could articulate a relation. Sachs reports that during the period following this, he and Chavafambira, while "sharing the intimacies of family living" in Manyikaland, "had become companions. The barriers between psychoanalyst and patient, white man and Black, had broken down."[90] Buoyed by the shared symbolic murder of a woman, Sachs and Chavafambira are able to solidify their homosocial cross-racial intimacy and materialize a version of psychoanalytic relationality that Sachs, at least, lauds as a progressive evolution. The power differential of white analyst and Black patient is thus offset by the triangulated violence against Woman, which Sachs (rather perversely) reads as indexical of Chavafambira's broader willingness to engage in violence against the colonial state. With a line that has become well-known from the text, Sachs concludes from Chavafambira's attempted murder that he is now "ready for revolt."[91]

As most readers would be quick to point out, Sachs's equation of anticolonial revolutionary fervor with femicide is hardly a desirable version of decolonial politics, clinical or otherwise. Indeed, the denigration of Woman arguably functions as an efficient means of evacuating anxieties and hostilities about "the primitive" from the Black subject by attributing them instead to the feminine subject—a link Sander Gilman has similarly made in relation to Freud's writing about femininity.[92] While Maggie is positioned as dragging Chavafambira back into a primitivistic torpor, Sachs implies that his later attraction (and eventual marriage) to a light-skinned "Hametic" woman is a testament to his cosmopolitan personal and political evolution. Colonial narratives about barbarous primitivity are thus not so much overcome in Sachs's work with Chavafambira as they are relocated. Importantly, that "dark continent" in psychoanalysis is both a racialized *and* feminized figuration, a metaphoric collapse that shows how imbricated racial and sexual difference are in the colonial imaginary. To follow Anne McClintock's thinking here, we could even say that constructions of domesticity, femininity, and gender were indispensable to the way that colonialism articulated its mission and tried to secure power over its racialized subjects. Here, Woman functions primarily to pronounce or minimize racial difference.

In this way, Sachs's embrace of the revolutionary potential of the clinic is ultimately attenuated by his willingness to trade on the denigration of Woman in order to secure his ongoing homosocial intimacy with Chavafambira. In a troubling but familiar equation, Maggie becomes the disposed Oedipal third that marks the resolution of Chavafambira's ostensible "Hamletism" and the realization of his decolonial protest. Sachs thus provides a useful demonstration of the unconscious fungibility of many marginalized positions whose equation (such as the feminized Jew) allows for substitutions that carry multiple and often overdetermined meaning. Race and gender were two of the most significant of these that many analysts, in the colonies and the metropole, took up intentionally as a way of making their clinical work relevant to midcentury social reform. And, as with Sachs, the effects were often mixed.

(UN)FREE ASSOCIATIONS

Clinical psychoanalytic practice in Europe's colonies during the mid-century heyday of empire was an ambivalent undertaking. While some analysts, like Sachs, adapted their clinics liberally in an effort to better align psychoanalytic practice with social justice in conditions of manifest unfreedom, wider inequalities to do with class, race, gender, and nation nevertheless structured the clinical setting. Even for Fanon, who has been lauded as an exemplar of liberatory, decolonial clinico-political praxis, his clinical work in Blida-Joinville was marked by impasses to do with language and translation (Fanon spoke French, not Arabic, and required a translator); with culture (Fanon was French-Martinican, not Muslim or Arab, and occupied a much higher social station in midcentury France); and with gender and sexual politics (Fanon is well-known for his derogatory remarks, especially in *Black Skin, White Masks*, about both Black women and homosexuality).[93] Like Fanon and others, Sachs's clinical work struggled with the problematic of freedom and justice under colonialism, arriving at the paradoxical surmise that the best way to furnish his patient's clinical freedom was to compel him to revolt. By challenging and reshaping the orthodox boundaries of clinical practice, Sachs sought—imperfectly, fallibly—to use the clinical relation to contest forms of unfreedom, both psychic *and* material.

Far from a utopian horizon, then, Sachs and Chavafambira engaged in an interesting but flawed local experiment that looked to revise, rather than reject, the reach of the clinic for social repair. Back in the metropole, the intersection between gender and race would likewise be paramount for the ways that British analysts grappled with the effects of colonialism and the first decades of decolonization. While Sachs leaned toward an explicit socialist-liberationist view of the clinic for race-based decolonial struggle in the colonies—largely ignoring the vital role that gender played in enabling his cross-racial identificatory politics—D. W. Winnicott instead explicitly organized his clinical presence along the gendered ideals of mothering as a tacit strategy for trying to mitigate racialized, decolonial conflict at home. For Winnicott, the well-being of the nation hinged on the "good enough" efforts of women as mothers and, where they failed, his clinical work began.

CHAPTER FOUR

Dreaming of "Black Mummy"

Race, Gender, Decolonization, and D. W. Winnicott

Mothers, like analysts, can be good or not good enough.
—D. W. WINNICOTT, 1971[1]

On February 3, 1964, D. W. Winnicott held his first clinical session in London with a two-and-a-half-year-old girl nicknamed "The Piggle." In this interview, The Piggle described the nature of the persecutory dreams that had been keeping her awake at night, singling out the "babacar" and the "Black Mummy" as her nocturnal antagonists. According to The Piggle, the "babacar" and the "Black Mummy" would come and terrorize her during the night, threatening to cut off her "yams" (her breasts) or flush her down the toilet. With time, these nightmares began to bleed into The Piggle's waking thoughts, producing a disconcerting array of horrific fantasies that often featured the threat of a contaminating "Blackness" capable of turning even The Piggle herself Black. Significantly, "Black Mummy" became The Piggle's fantasy foe at the height of Britain's decolonization efforts, when the transformation from empire to Commonwealth was accompanied by a surge of Afro-Caribbean and Asian immigration that amplified racial tensions throughout the postwar British welfare state. As I explore in this chapter, through The Piggle's racially charged fears of Blackness, and accompanying idealization of whiteness, the midcentury politics of race and decolonization entered Winnicott's clinical scene.

In this chapter, I reorient feminist and political engagements with Winnicott's work, which have primarily focused on the gendered dimension of his theory of the "good enough mother," by calling attention to the intersectional racial work this theory also performs.[2] Winnicott never dealt openly with the racial and colonial tensions driving The Piggle's unconscious conflict in the clinic; rather, he surmised that "Black Mummy" was the hieroglyph of The Piggle's tenuous relationship with her mother, which had not been "good enough" to ensure her healthy development. Like many welfarist experts and policy advisers, Winnicott prioritized the psychic effects of gendered reproductive labor over those of race, racism, and decolonization, specifically designing his own clinical presence (as a white male analyst) to be a proxy for the good enough mother. In the first half of this chapter, I unpack Winnicott's construction of the mother-child relation and situate this within past feminist scholarship on his work—both that which has embraced it for a radical feminist theory of mothering and relationality and that which has demonstrated how his work helped make gendered reproductive labor central to the ideology of the postwar British welfare state.[3] Wagering that gender is central to Winnicott's theory of the good enough mother but that it necessarily performs intersectional work, I draw on critical race and postcolonial scholarship to establish how gender norms and ideologies of family formation were thoroughly racialized in postwar Britain and used strategically to secure white supremacy and British national identity during the decline of empire.[4] From this, I argue that Winnicott's theory of the good enough mother is a racialized figure who functions to codify white, middle-class British gender norms and sexual relations as a way of managing the destabilization of racial and colonial hierarchy produced during the decades of decolonization.

In the second half of this chapter, I put this argument in motion through The Piggle's case, which adds texture to the long-standing and overdetermined postwar racialization of mothering in particular. By working through The Piggle's clinical experience with Winnicott, I show how he did not just operationalize a racialized ideal of the good enough mother on an ideological level through his public lectures but also put it into practice in his clinic, where he implicitly attempted to make his clinical work relevant to and useful for the management of larger social and political breakdowns following decolonization. If Winnicott's role as a welfare expert who spent his career talking about the psychodynamics of the mother-child relation wedded him to a larger, (de)colonial conversation about the stabilization of postimperial British whiteness, then his role in the clinic, where he worked through the mother to mitigate a clearly sociopolitical anxiety about Blackness, adds complexity to the overall racial impact of his work. As I show, Winnicott's analytic role as a good enough mother in the clinic is, for better *and* for worse, an explicitly political attempt to mitigate the racial conflict splitting the entire (post)colonial British motherland.

MOTHERING A NATION: GENDER AND WINNICOTT'S POSTWAR POLITICAL PSYCHOLOGY

By the time Winnicott first saw The Piggle in early 1964, he was already three decades deep into one of the most distinguished psychoanalytic careers of the twentieth century. The most famous member of the so-called Middle Group (now known as the Independent tradition, which includes those psychoanalytic theorists who refused the postwar split in the BPS, borrowing liberally from both Anna Freud and Melanie Klein), Winnicott's theoretical innovations included the transitional object, the true and false self, the clinical holding environment, illusion and disillusionment, the squiggle game, and the good enough mother. During his years active, he twice served as the president of the BPS (1954–1959 and 1965–1968) and delivered over fifty BBC broadcasts on motherhood to the listening public. Having begun his career as a British pediatrician and early member of Klein's coterie in the 1930s and 1940s, Winnicott eventually became one of the most influential and recognizable psychoanalytic authorities for the midcentury British public, both at home and abroad.

As many historians and political theorists have established,[5] some of Winnicott's most influential ideas—both within psychoanalytic circles and in the wider public sphere—concern the mother-child relation and the psycho-political effects of maternal care. In contrast to traditionally patriarchal political thinkers (Sigmund Freud, for example) who infamously dramatized the dissemination of (political) power through an epic father-son conflict, Winnicott instead prioritized the ordinary, everyday mother-child relation as the site of political subjectivization, defining his psycho-political landscape through historically feminized experiences such as care, recognition, mutuality, and dependence.

According to Winnicott, the "self" or the "individual"—both common idioms throughout his work—could only ever emerge as a distinct and autonomous entity because the infant had first experienced a fundamental merger with the mother, whose care and environmental provision was "good enough" to enable its gradual development.[6] Such provision was indispensable because Winnicott saw the infant as a developmentally immature being, one that lacked both the cognitive processes necessary to make sense of the world and the physical capacity to satisfy its basic needs, rendering it entirely dependent on its surrounding environment for survival and health.[7] "The baby at the beginning is the opposite of sophisticated," writes Winnicott in a direct reaction against his erstwhile mentor, Melanie Klein. "Many do not find it easy to ascribe anything that could be called 'psychological' to an infant until some weeks or even months have passed."[8] Winnicott understood this early (and universal) experience of total helplessness to be a foundational—and often traumatic—event for every human being, regardless of cultural background or historical location. While the right environmental provision may ensure that the child will eventually gain selfhood, independence, and autonomy, the early experience of such sheer, unadulterated dependence and vulnerability could never fully be overcome by any straightforward developmental teleology. According to Winnicott, our experience of dependence—both how we were held and how we were dropped—informs much of our adult repertoire for social and political interaction.

Consequently, there were particularly high stakes riding on the individual economies of care provided to the nascent infant subjectivity. While other psychoanalytic theorists, including Klein, found the mother important because she served as the first internal and external "object" for the infant, Winnicott stressed that the mother's routine, empathetic care constituted for the child an entire facilitative "environment." Emphasizing the encompassing, nondifferentiated, and spatial nature of the mother's presence, Winnicott reoriented the customary (instinct-based) connection psychoanalysts were wont to make between love and food and maintained that it was "holding" that comprised the first love relation. As he explains, "The infant is held by the mother, and only understands love that is expressed in physical terms, that is to say, by live, human holding. Here is absolute dependence, and environmental failure at this very early stage cannot be defended against, except by a hold-up of the developmental process, and by infantile psychosis."[9] Winnicott termed this state of deep identificatory involvement with the infant in the first weeks and months of its life "primary maternal preoccupation," imagining it as an empathetic union so seamless that the mother—and ideally, he thought, the biological mother—meets the infant's needs before they even become articulated as needs.[10] "A woman enters into a phase," explains Winnicott, "a phase from which she ordinarily recovers in the weeks and months after the baby's birth, in which to a large extent she is the baby and the baby is her."[11]

While Winnicott is hardly the first psychologist to wax lyrical about women's naturalized maternal capacity, his belief in the possibility of an untroubled, unmediated mother-child union speaks more to his idiosyncratic appreciation of the infant's relative nonbeing than it does to the mother's potential self-effacement. This type of primary mother-child symmetry was possible because Winnicott thought that infants do not yet have a subjective "self" distinct from their environmental provision. Although there may be the appearance of a two-body relationship in early mother-child interactions—and although Winnicott did maintain that it was incumbent on mothers to reach out for an empathetic identification with their infants—because infants do not yet exist in any meaningful way as autonomous beings, either physically or emotionally, they are necessarily always apiece with their caretaker. As he famously exclaimed in a 1942 BPS meeting, "There is no such thing as a baby!" He explicated this verdict a decade later, writing, "If you show me a baby you certainly show me someone caring for the baby, or at least a pram with someone's eyes and ears glued to it. One sees a nursing couple . . . the unit is not the individual, the unit is the environment-individual set-up."[12] Winnicott's understanding of maternal holding is thus both physical and metaphorical: it names an entire psychosocial context that, if managed correctly, enables the gradual disarticulation of the infant from the mother through an intermediate space of "illusion" and the elaboration of a discrete, boundaried self; "the result is a continuity of existence that becomes a sense of existing, a sense of self, and eventually results in autonomy."[13] The normal infant's development in and through its relationship with its mother is thus characterized by an authentic continuity—a "going on being," as Winnicott often put it—that naturally contained both the possibilities for both a relatively unconflicted unity and for a sufficiently autonomous individuality.

It perhaps goes without saying that Winnicott's theory of the mother-child relation dramatically—if quietly—reshaped the psycho-dynamic landscape that most analysts (especially in the BPS) had been working with up until that point. Downgrading experiences of unconscious conflict, instinctual aggression, libidinal gratification, and societal repression, he instead put his weight behind the conceptual possibilities of mutuality, recognition, creativity, authenticity, normativity, integration, maturity, and complementarity, thinking especially about the way in which it was incumbent on the environment—that is, the mother—to adapt to the child's needs, rather than vice versa. Although Winnicott did explore the role of hate in the countertransference and the infant's fantasized destructive assaults against an object whose survival was the condition of possibility for the love relation, considered in the context of his prolific career, these papers were more the exception than the rule. As readers can see even in Winnicott's habitual reliance on the idioms of "self" and "individual," his focus tended toward externally geared appreciations of organic wholeness, unity, and relationality that invested in what he believed to be an achievable harmony between the social and the psychological. More than mere shifts in vocabulary, these reorientations register the extent to which Winnicott's expansive theorizing about the mother-child relation essentially proposed a new theory of human subjectivity driven by a more social and humanistic set of assumptions and aspirations. In contrast to thinkers like Sigmund Freud or Jacques Lacan, who sought to decenter the egoistic "self" that they believed to be a condensation of alienating constructions and misrecognitions, Winnicott's theories of the mother-child in many ways return to this conceptual center, reorienting around the felt priorities of lived experience rather than those of structural critique.[14]

For this reason, his work continues to be the object of much interest among feminist historians and political theorists, with scholars theorizing the complex implications and effects of a highly popularized psychoanalytic paradigm that places women's reproductive labor at the center of claims about psychological, social, and even political normativity. For those feminist scholars who have found refuge in his work, his theory of relationally focused mothering helps construct

an ethics of intersubjectivity that counters the long-standing patriarchal, phallocentric virtues of authority, autonomy, self-sufficiency, and
competition. Notably, the feminist psychoanalyst and sociologist Nancy
Chodorow advanced one of the first deployments of Winnicott's thinking
in this vein, arguing that the bifurcated gendering of maternal care produces hierarchical splits in subjective experience—individuality versus
intersubjectivity; autonomy versus connection; independence versus
dependence; self-interest versus mutualistic concern—which are then
lived socially as much as psychologically.[15] Chodorow thus advocates
for a more gender-fluid theory of mothering (which she finds consonant
with Winnicott's paradigm) as a way of undoing the unequal distribution, and ultimate social denigration, of the feminized experiences of
intersubjectivity, connection, and dependence. Building on Chodorow's
work, feminist theorist and Relational psychoanalyst Jessica Benjamin
used Winnicott's explication of the process of separation and individuation to envision a possible form of genuine intersubjective recognition,
one that moves beyond the subject/object binary characteristic of much
Western philosophy—which Benjamin regards as responsible for systems of gender and sexual domination—and out toward a mutualistic,
dual-subject form of recognition founded in the child's process of rap-
prochement with the mother.[16] Such thinking informs Benjamin's reappraisal of the clinical relation as well, and her attempts to democratize
the clinical space by emphasizing nonhierarchical intersubjectivity, mutuality, and recognition mirror Winnicott's own interest in (re)imagining
the familial (and clinical) sphere as more collaborative than conflicted,
where unmediated relationality with the (m)other is not only possible
but normal.

　　This initial, intersubjective feminist deployment of Winnicott's
theory of mothering has been matched by a more recent feminist and
queer revitalization of his work, which comes especially from the literary
humanities. While Michael Snediker mines Winnicott's relentlessly
optimistic diagram of subjective constitution for a queer politics of hope,
Alison Bechdel and Maggie Nelson both craft quasi-autobiograph-
ical "autotheories" that envision a gender-queer iteration of the good
enough mother at the heart of their aspirational accounts of relational
self-composition.[17] In this more recent theoretical itinerary, a feminist
recuperation of mothering becomes the basis for a nonnegativistic

exploration of sociality and relationality that deliberately counters some of queer theory's more histrionic antinormative claims.

This work usefully expands the contemporary relevance of Winnicott's most resonant concepts, demonstrating the theoretical capaciousness and flexibility of his characteristically understated way of thinking. But the very presentism that allows these theorists to make such creative use of Winnicott's oeuvre is also what occludes the historical liberalism that many (typically Marxist-feminist) historians have regarded more skeptically. For while it may be true that, read charitably, Winnicott implicitly describes the psychosocial consequences of the yoking of gender (specifically femininity) to reproductive labor and furnishes the raw materials for a gender-transitive theory of maternity and mothering, on a historical level he nevertheless collaborated, explicitly and intentionally, with the substantiation, stabilization, and expansion of the British postwar welfare state, which was virtually synonymous with a reactionary hyperinvestment in the nuclear family that circumscribed femininity and women's social function to the domestic sphere and unpaid (re)productive labor. Denise Riley famously makes this point in her landmark book, *The War in the Nursery*, where she explores the links between the postwar expansion of psychologized advice about mothering (such as that promoted by Winnicott and John Bowlby, especially) and the retrenchment of the material liberties British women had gained during World War II.[18] While state-sponsored daycares had enabled women to be working mothers during the exigencies of total war, postwar professional wisdom about children's psychological health seriously compromised such supports by corresponding maternal "deprivation" with childhood developmental issues and disorders.

The feminist historian Sally Alexander expands on this, illustrating how, even as Winnicott publicly defended day nurseries and mother-child clinics, he nevertheless insisted on the value of normative maternal care as a psychological ideal and contributed to the construction of the British welfare state. Always privileging individuation over collectivization, Winnicott actively opposed social reforms that he thought would impinge on individual creative freedom or the "good enough" middle-class home by unnecessarily expanding the managerial function of the state. As Alexander notes, "Winnicott was not a socialist but a liberal" to the extent that, for him, social welfare measures were only ever meant to supplement the individual, nuclear family and the capitalist economy; they were never intended to replace them outright.[19] Winnicott cautions that "if, however, by supplementation of those voluntary bodies by some Government department improved access to bad homes should involve the slightest degree of intrusion on the ordinary common good home, more harm than good will be done."[20] While we might initially read Winnicott's commentary as a reaction against the hypermanagerial bureaucratization of the state that accompanied the consolidation of Britain's postwar welfarism, his comments reflect his deeper commitment to the privatized nuclear family as the appropriate—and indeed desirable—basic unit of social life. For Winnicott, the family, as that fundamental first-order environmental provision, was a space more defined by harmony and self-actualization than by incestuous, unrequited longing or murderous aggression. In concert with the heyday of British welfarism and social democracy in the mid-1940s to the 1960s, Winnicott's normative, liberalistic framework lauded the importance of Britain's culturally cherished virtues (like environmental support, individuation, selfhood, maternity, relationality, and health), which were consistent with the dominant political ideology of the age. As political theorist Gal Gerson writes in his reading of Winnicott as a theorist of political liberalism, "Winnicott's psychology seems to reflect a regime that leaves the marketplace and the household alone, but surrounds them with regulations, taxes, and professional supervision: a liberal welfare state."[21] Unlike Frankfurt School thinkers, then, Winnicott never imagined that economic upheaval and radical political revolution were either natural to or necessary for psychological health. In contrast to Marxists or Foucauldian poststructuralists, Winnicott "neither condemns the marks of socialization that the person carries as oppressive branding, nor argues for dismantling individuality itself. . . . Society's incomplete and occasionally frustrating character does not provide grounds for a radical overhaul."[22] In other words, what Winnicott pursues is reform, not revolution.

Yet the implicit theory of liberalism Winnicott sets out in his work departs in distinct ways from the common doxa of the classical social contract theorists. In those models, the rational, autonomous individual has an (imaginary) a priori existence, embodying a supposedly "universal" subjectivity—one that is not only definitionally male (as Carole Pateman has established)[23] and white (as Charles W. Mills has proven)[24] but also paradigmatically adult. Insofar as Winnicott's work focuses on the child, he reimagines "the individual" as a developmental entity in process rather than as a static, dehistoricized pregiven. The child, for Winnicott, is thus not an irrational being in need of (paternal) discipline and control; nor is it an economic agent expected to contribute to the household finances. Rather, the child is a developing individual: a future political subject in the making. With this focal shift comes a rearticulation of the role that dependence and sociality play in the life of every adult subjectivity. Although Winnicott maintained that the healthy individual would eventually be able to achieve autonomy, selfhood, and a privatized "true self," the bonds of childhood forever tie that same person to her origins in dependence and sociality. The self is thus paradoxically both a private entity and a social aggregate. Because the self is always articulated in and through the mother's presence, even its most "noncommunicating elements" necessarily exist in relation to a wider social sphere.

According to Gerson, this emphasis on the fundamental sociality of the self indicates the points of collaboration between Winnicott's brand of liberalism and Britain's postwar social democracy. Incorporating specific tenets from social democracy, Winnicott's psychological theories integrate a focus on dependence and cooperative sociality with a governing appreciation of individual authenticity and unfettered creative self-expression. Such combination informs Winnicott's theory of the transitional object, for instance, in which he draws from a capitalist logic in describing this object as the child's "first possession" while simultaneously imagining this "possession" as an authentic and nonalienating fabrication of mother-child relationality. "I am not specifically studying the first object of object-relationships," explains Winnicott, in clear dispute with Klein. Rather, "I am concerned with the first possession and with the intermediate area between the subjective and that which is objectively perceived."[25] If Winnicott might be read here as mapping the child's inaugural foray into a capitalistic consumer culture that accords commodities a privileged place in the psychic landscape of the individual—a culture not dissimilar from the booming consumerism of Britain's postwar 1940s and 1950s, when mass-produced commodities achieved a new level of penetration into the homes and lives of ordinary middle-class citizens—then he nevertheless reorganizes its priorities, suggesting that individuality and sociality are mutually constituting rather than mutually exclusive. Transitional objects may be the means of constructing the self, but they are simultaneously a means of connecting and communicating with the mother; they exist in the intermediate space between two selves, facilitating their collaboration. Unlike Marx, Winnicott is thus pointedly more optimistic (indeed, arguably romantic) about the health of subject-object relations under capitalism, insisting that the transitional object never becomes subjectivized at the expense of the human subject's objectivization, as with the commodity fetish. As Gerson puts it, "Winnicott values rights and property as communicative devices rather than as private enclosures held against society"; for Winnicott, "privacy is communication; owning is sharing."[26] Rather than theorizing property and privacy as alienation, exploitation, or primitive accumulation, Winnicott revalues these traditional aspects of the capitalist political economy as the very mechanisms of sociality itself.

As is evident here, Winnicott's work often relies on a seductive both/and sensibility that, in this case, promises a softer, gentler version of capitalism seemingly accommodating of, rather than antagonistic to, human sociality and not (yet) ruthlessly sharpened by the mortifying austerities of neoliberalism. Indeed, his was a popular and influential social psychology mindset in postwar Britain that echoed the broad social and political enthusiasm for the welfare state. But, as with much in the history of liberalism, this compromise formation is double-edged in that such mollifying propositions enabled—and, indeed, were arguably designed to catalyze—the contraction of more radical political activity in the name of the better securitization and stabilization of Western capitalistic democracy. This contraction has been well-established when it came to radical feminist activity, for instance, which saw a steady decline in the postwar era, with those material advancements that were made for women resulting from a more general welfarist investment in national reconstruction and human capital than in a feminist agenda per se.[27] With great explicitness, the Beveridge Report—the 1942 policy proposal by William Beveridge that in many ways inaugurated the welfare state—tied Britain's national futurity, both cultural and demographic, to women's reproductive labor as housewives and mothers, proposing abundant "maternalist" social service policies (such as family allowances) to support the replenishment of Britain's decimated population and to secure the reproduction of its national identity as a leading liberal power.[28] These material supports were bolstered by accompanying discursive shifts that appeared to extend—rather than reverse—women's experience of wartime employment by commending the specialized nature of women's domestic labor in the home. As the feminist historian Elizabeth Wilson observes, "the theme of 'the housewife's home is her factory' was *part* of a broader theme of 'home-making as a career' so popular after the war"; by recognizing domestic work as work, "homemaking" became a legitimate career choice for women, one that seemed to make good on feminist desires for access to the public sphere while, paradoxically, reinvesting women in unpaid, reproductive labor.[29]

Like many other maternalist sages, Winnicott too trafficked in descriptions of women's reproductive labor as "work" or a "job." But he was often idiosyncratic in this regard since, unlike other social and psychological experts, he combined the grammar of domestic work with an insistence on the "ordinariness" of the maternal task, tacitly critiquing the cult(ure) of expertise that ballooned around childcare in the postwar decades by underscoring the lack of exceptionalism—and to some extent even naturalism—of the maternal role. In a radio broadcast that Winnicott gave in the autumn of 1949 titled "The Ordinary Devoted Mother," he explicitly links this experience of "ordinary" mothering with the stabilization and future expansion of the postwar British democracy, making the mother's reproductive labor central to the recreation of national identity. He explains, "We know something of the reasons why this long and exacting task, the parents' job of seeing their children through, is a job worth doing; and, in fact, we believe that it provides the only real basis for society, and the only factory for the democratic tendency in a country's social system."[30] As Gerson has shown, this specific articulation of women's work was central to the way Winnicott defined and maintained a gendered binary. Although he may refer to "the parent's job" in this passage, the radio episode from which this passage is excerpted makes clear that it is a *mother's* contribution to society that is under discussion. Gerson explains that "Winnicott perceives the distinction between men and women . . . through economic division of tasks as essential attributes of human society."[31] By imagining the home as a "factory for the democratic tendency"—a metaphor that relocates the literal factory work women performed during the war to the domestic sphere—Winnicott makes mothering central to the reproduction not just of the British population but of Britain's cultural and political identity. In doing so, he interestingly revalues the domestic sphere as a site of both labor and politics, forgoing the public/private distinction characteristic of liberalism and arguing that the organization of gender relations in the domestic sphere is foundational for the continuity of British political sensibilities in the public arena.

The consequence of this is that the careful regulation of gender—and specifically of mothering—was central to the production and reproduction of Britain's national identity during the heyday of the welfare state.[32] Insofar as the British welfare state was concerned with the provision of care, the allocation of resources, and the division between paid and unpaid labor, it had a distinct interest in and effect on the ordering of gender and sexual relations. As a National Health Service (NHS) employee and a public health adviser throughout the 1940s, 1950s, and 1960s, Winnicott helped map the gendered provisions necessary for the reproduction of the labor force, the population, and (as Winnicott thought) democratic ideology itself. Put another way: in Winnicott's thinking British welfarism was of woman born.

Although feminist critics of Winnicott's work, such as Riley, Alexander, Gerson, and Shapira,[33] have established the gendered ideology inherent in his theories of the mother-child relation and the social and political effects of this paradigm for the construction of the British welfare state, there has been a noteworthy absence of critical attention concerning how his work also contributed to national conversations about race and the decolonization of empire happening during these same decades. After the human and material devastations of World War II, Britain realized its sweeping imperial dominion was no longer economically tenable or politically defensible, especially in former colonies such as India and Jamaica where powerful anticolonial independence movements had already gained global popularity and support. It therefore began the drawn-out process of decolonization. With the postwar establishment of international regulatory bodies like the United Nations, which, in response to the racist logics that had produced the Holocaust, newly emphasized the political and ethical necessity of all-inclusive human rights, Britain slowly reshaped what had previously been an explicitly racialized justification for its dominion over its colonies. This transformation involved not only major material reorganizations (like colonial self-governance) but also significant ideological shifts as postwar Britain had to grapple with its own national identity and purpose in the absence of its long-standing raison d'être: racial empire.

The significance of this process was intensified by the fact that the transformation from empire to Commonwealth also involved a period of expanded immigration rights (1948–1962) during which time Britain encouraged emigration (primarily from the West Indies) as a way both of managing the social unrest in the Caribbean produced by Depression-era poverty and unemployment and of conscripting the cheap and abundant labor necessary for England's postwar national reconstruction.[34] Many—especially former servicemen and soldiers—took England up on this offer, and there was a consequent surge of immigration during this fourteen-year period, primarily of Black Afro-Caribbeans, many of whom resettled permanently in the United Kingdom.[35] While exact demographics vary, immigration theorist and historian James Hampshire records that, before the arrival of HMT *Empire Windrush*, "in 1948, there were just a few thousand non-white people living in the country, mostly concentrated in sea ports, but by 1968 there were over a million."[36] Synonymous now with the beginning of a multicultural Britain, the Windrush generation changed the racial composition of Britain quickly and drastically, quite literally bringing home questions of race and (de) colonization that the British public had long ignored.

In spite of this, only recently has scholarship, such as that by Jordanna Bailkin,[37] begun to address the extent to which race and decolonization were key social issues at stake in the articulation and operation of the British welfare state.[38] The first scholar to make this connection, Bailkin argues that the rise of welfarism and the decline of empire were mutually constituting; "the afterlife of Empire is imprinted in the archive of welfare," Bailkin contends.[39] Reading an archive of public policy studies from Britain's postwar decades of decolonization, Bailkin illustrates how decolonization "transformed the social relationships in Britain that have constituted our relationship of what is conventionally known as the 'postwar', and played a significant role in the reconstruction of community in 1950s and 1960s Britain."[40] In other words, Britain's postwar welfare state did not just witness, but was in fact coarticulated with, significant transformations both to the racial composition of Britain and to the ordering of global (post)colonial power.

But as Bailkin indicates, following on the foundational insights of postcolonial scholars like Ann Laura Stoler and Anne McClintock,[41] the welfare state's grappling with race and decolonization often happened through the intersectional axes of gender and sexuality. In lieu of Britain's ability to use explicitly racist tactics to secure its imperial hegemony—and in the midst of the transformation of racial demographics within England—Britain consolidated its national (racial) identity and secured its ascendency by establishing politicized and heavily moralized norms around domesticity, motherhood, childcare, gender roles, and family arrangements in general, promoting these both at home and abroad. As Caribbean cultural historian Denise Noble has shown, the intersection of the Beveridge Report, which galvanized the metropolitan welfare state, and the Moyne Report in 1945, which recommended select welfare provisions in the West Indies, particularly Jamaica, following the labor unrest of 1934–1939, reveals the way gender, sexuality, and reproductive labor served as the lynchpin between colony and metropole: while the Beveridge Report identified the importance of the woman as unwaged "housewife" in England (and thereby justified the need for welfare provisions like family allowances),[42] the Moyne Report tied the destitution of the Jamaican economy in large part to women's work outside the home and to a "lack of proper family life."[43] By pathologizing Black Afro-Caribbean family life—and by specifically targeting women and mothers as the cause of the Jamaican national crisis—Britain sutured its national identity as a leading liberal power to the racialized configurations of family life, mobilizing whiteness as a tool of ideological dominance.[44] Put another way, norms about gender, mothering, and the private sphere became a prime site for the management of racial hierarchy.

Importantly, such discourse did not just regulate racial and imperial relations in Britain's (post)colonies but also installed them at home since the postwar return of middle-class white women to the home meant that employment gaps in feminized professions (like the newly instituted NHS) were typically reliant on the labor of Afro-Caribbean immigrant women.[45] Because of their inclusion in the labor force, Black and Brown immigrant women were thus strategically rendered ineligible for the ideals of "healthy" family life newly promoted by medical and psychological experts. In other words, Britain's postwar articulation of gender norms and family life was part of, rather than separate from, its attempt to secure its national racial identity in the wake of empire. As Britain's decolonization process changed both its global power relation to its then-dominions and the racial composition of England, norms to do with gender, reproductive labor, sexuality, and the family became a pivotal source of "soft power" as Britain rearticulated an implicitly racialized national identity and colonial hierarchy.

The postwar entanglement of gender, race, and (de)colonization directly implicates Winnicott's own profuse social commentary on mothering. Even though there is virtually no social historical scholarship that deals with the part played by race and (de)colonization in Winnicott's own thinking—a lacuna likely to do with how Winnicott, like many psychoanalysts before and after him, tacitly trades in whiteness by assuming that racial identity was not the explicit backdrop against which he was working—the peak of Winnicott's career (from the late 1940s to the 1960s) coincided with some of the most heated and conflicted race talk in Britain surrounding decolonization and the Windrush generation. To this, it is worth considering a document from Winnicott's archive (figure 4.1): a yellowing newspaper clipping in which an op-ed response titled "Facing the Failure of Integration" is overlaid by Winnicott's sketch, in blue ink, of an unidentified woman—a rather ironic exemplification of the way that representations of gender were entangled with concerns about race and decolonization.

The article beneath Winnicott's doodle from November 7 (year unknown) provides a retort to an op-ed that disputed the viability of racial integration in England, speaking in particular of the "failure" of West Indian and Jamaican Black immigrants to integrate with— which is to say, assimilate to—white British culture.[46] Although the author of this rebuttal clearly means to be offering a defense of Black Afro-Caribbean immigrants, they too participate in some of the common racial stereotypes the white British constructed of Black Caribbeans. In particular, the author cites the reputedly matriarchal family structures of Jamaicans, thereby demonstrating how ideologies of

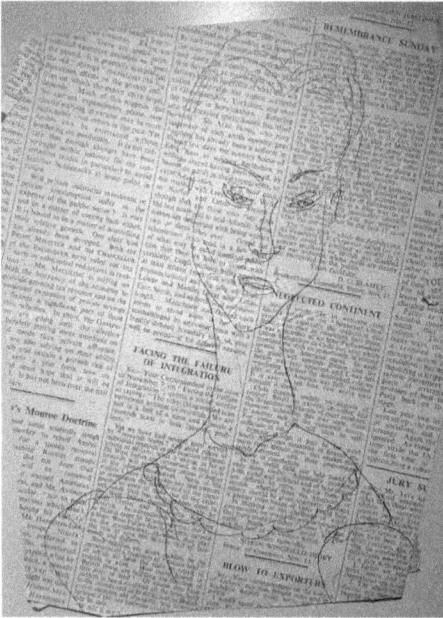

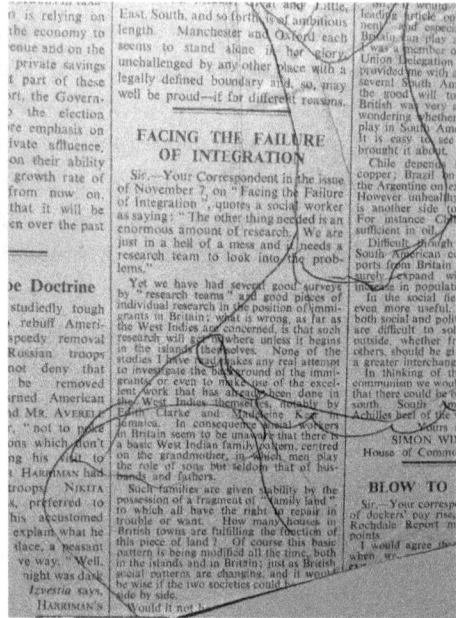

FIGURE 4.1 A AND B Archival image of Winnicott's doodle.
Winnicott Archives, Wellcome Library.

motherhood and gender performed racial work on behalf of British whiteness. In doing so, the article makes specific reference to research carried out by the colonial sociologist Edith Clarke, a white Jamaican and former student of Bronislaw Malinowski, whose anthropological research with the matrilineal Trobriand Islanders more or less inaugurated the subfield of ethnopsychoanalysis discussed in chapter 3. Carrying on Malinowski's interests, Clarke conducted research in Jamaica from 1946 to 1949 on what she described as the "dysfunctional" matriarchal family structure of Afro-Caribbeans, arriving at similar conclusions to the Moyne Report that poverty was tied to nonnuclear family life—not, for instance, to women's low wages, the global effects of the Great Depression, or centuries of colonial expropriation.[47] First known as the West Indian Social Survey, Clarke's research was eventually published in a monograph called *My Mother Who Fathered Me: A Study of the Family in Three Selected Communities in Jamaica* (1957)—a text that, in content, echoes the findings of The Moynihan Report in the United States, which was published just eight years later. Clarke's research was just one of many policy initiatives, carried out both in the motherland and in the colonies, that defined race by recourse to motherhood and kinship structures.

To the extent that Winnicott's theories focused most explicitly on the mother-child relation, documents such as this show how these newly crafted psychological conceptions of motherhood were inextricable from the postwar ideological constructions of whiteness and Blackness, which sought to manage the status, at home and abroad, of British national identity. To talk about the mother, and about normative family structure, was to speak about the consolidation of white British imperial identity against especially Black Afro-Caribbean colonial identity. Maintaining that the coarticulation of race and gender is vital to understanding Winnicott's work on the good enough mother, in the following section I take an intersectional approach to considering how race, gender, and decolonization together informed Winnicott's clinical practice. While Winnicott never explicitly racializes his understanding of the good enough mother—which becomes his template for the role of the analyst in the clinic—I unpack Winnicott's clinical sessions with The Piggle, whose fear of "Black Mummy" helps demonstrate the racial implications and effects of his clinical practice. In this way, I bring Winnicott's role as a maternal substitute in the consulting room into conversation with the political transformations in Britain wrought by decolonization, arguing that the good enough mother in the clinic embodies an attempt to mitigate and redress the national fracture in the British motherland caused by decolonization.

"THE DARK MILLIONS": RACE, DECOLONIZATION, AND "BLACK MUMMY" IN THE CLINIC

On October 7, 1956, Winnicott (who was, at the time, in his first term as president of the BPS) wrote a brief letter to his fellow BPS analyst and colleague Charles Rycroft, who was serving as the secretary of the Scientific Committee. Speaking of potential discussion topics for the Society—among which Winnicott lists the psychosoma, psychiatric consultations, and child psychoanalysis—Winnicott concludes the letter by appending the following codicil:

Also,

(4) I would like to throw a word at the [British Psychoanalytical] Society like "black" (as in the Medical Section when I was president) to see what the Society makes of it—& to bring it back-benchers. Or, perhaps, "ghost" would be better.

I might have other ideas
Yours
D. W. Winnicott[48]

The discussion that Winnicott eventually chaired on November 21, 1956, was about ghosts, not Blackness. But it is hard to ignore, in this letter, the too-clear unconscious association he makes between Blackness and a kind of spectral haunting. For however ostensibly tagged-on both the topics of "ghosts" and "Blackness" would seem to be here—cordoned off together, as they are, behind the supplemental "(4)"—it was not the pride of place psychosoma that eventually became the subject of the institutional discussion but the almost afterthought, ghosts. Much in the same way that the real kernel of an analytic session often only arrives at the very end, in a seemingly irrelevant comment, Winnicott suggests here as early as 1956 that something about Blackness had been haunting him.

As this letter indicates, the significance of Blackness was an enduring and articulated point of interest for Winnicott, especially in the latter half of his career, from the late 1940s through the 1960s.[49] While he never did have his evening discussion on this topic, he made frequent mention of it in his writings and saw a noteworthy minority of patients for whom Blackness was psychologically significant.[50] Perhaps most remarkable among these clinical encounters was his treatment of a child nicknamed "The Piggle," who suffered—among other things—from night terrors of a hallucinatory figure she called "Black Mummy." Winnicott began seeing The Piggle (who started treatment when she was two years, five months old) on February 3, 1964, and continued seeing her, over the course of sixteen "on demand" sessions, until October 28, 1966, when she had just turned five. Prior to the first consultation, her parents had corresponded with Winnicott, describing how her affect and disposition had changed following the birth of a younger sister ("Susan") seven months earlier. According to The Piggle's mother (who remains unnamed), The Piggle was listless, had "worries," was "easily bored and depressed," was unsure of her own identity, and had harassing "fantasies that ke[pt] her calling to us late at night."[51] Her nightmares were particularly concerning given how they had begun to infiltrate her waking life, blending dream with reality. As The Piggle's mother explains to Winnicott, in her fantasies:

> She has a Black Mummy and daddy. The Black Mummy comes in after her at night and says: "where are my yams?" (To yam=to eat. She pointed out her breasts, calling them yams, and pulling them to make them larger.) Sometimes she is put into the toilet by the Black Mummy. The Black Mummy, who lives in her tummy, and who can be talked to there on the telephone, is often ill, and difficult to make better.
>
> The second strand of fantasy, which started earlier, is about the "babacar." Every night she calls, again and again: "Tell me about the babacar, *all* about the babacar." The Black Mummy and daddy are often in the babacar together, or some man alone. There is very occasionally a black Piggle in evidence.[52]

Plagued by these myriad fears, The Piggle was eager for Winnicott's help. Although her parents, and occasionally Winnicott, worry that The Piggle's inability to parse fantasy from reality might indicate a step in the direction of psychosis, the family lived too far outside London to make a more regular analysis practicable and Winnicott ultimately advocated for a relatively hands-off approach, believing that The Piggle's natural developmental processes would restore her to health. In the clinical sessions they did have, Winnicott engaged with her at the level of her own fantasy as much as possible, and virtually all their clinical work featured Winnicott as a coparticipant in the child's fabricated games. Winnicott recorded each session in his notes, detailing The Piggle's play, dialogue, and physical use of the consulting room along with his own interpretations, both those given verbally during the session and those made privately and suspended as annotations in the margins. As the treatment progressed (at a rate of about one session per month, excluding summer holidays) The Piggle's fantasies morphed, including much to do with birth, death, trains, and eating. With time, she gradually became more confident in her own sense of self and most analysts who have written about the case agree that it had a salubrious effect.[53]

Given The Piggle's notable articulateness about her fears, the elaborate games she invents, and Winnicott's admirable ability to follow her lines of fantasy association (which feature many hairpin turns of cross-identification), this has been an important case for clinicians and is often taught in clinical trainings. While Teurnell bullishly reproaches Winnicott for not assuming The Piggle was sexually abused and Reeves queries the efficacy of some of Winnicott's more "conjectural" interpretations, Burgin uses the case to survey the viability of Winnicott's model of "on demand" treatment.[54] However, what is not discussed in these many clinical assessments is the extent to which The Piggle's case engages historically resonant questions about race and Blackness in the midcentury United Kingdom. Not insignificantly, The Piggle's horrific fantasies chronicle the unsavory machinations of a host of persecutory Black characters. Regarding even the bizarre "babacar"—a made-up word whose origin the mother did not know but associated with both The Piggle's doll "baba" and with her baby sister—The Piggle's mother observes that "it [too] was linked with black, black mummy, black self, and black people."[55] In fact, throughout the case The Piggle associates Blackness with all that is malevolent and hostile and perceives the "Black Mummy" as especially dangerous because she has the capacity to disseminate Blackness to all those around her, turning even The Piggle herself Black. As The Piggle tells her mother before her first consultation, "The Piga gone away, gone to the babacar. The Piga is black. Both Pigas are bad. Mummy, cry about the babacar!"[56] In each and every session, Blackness is mobilized as a signifier for what The Piggle finds harmful, threatening, and corrupt.

As most readers will swiftly recognize, there is a weighted racial significance to the particular litany of fears The Piggle associates with "Black Mummy" in 1964. As I have already discussed, the immediate postwar decades were all but synonymous with the advent of a multicultural Britain, and the rapid increase in non-white (predominantly Black and South Asian) immigrants stoked racial hostilities throughout the 1950s and 1960s. Melding together nativist sentiment with centuries of imperial white supremacy, juntas of far-right white men—like the League of Empire Loyalists, the White Defence League, and the fascist British Union—popularized slogans like "Keep Britain White" throughout the 1950s and encouraged racially motivated violence against Black citizens especially. According to Peter Fryer's lauded *Staying Power: The History of Black People in Britain*, "stimulated by fascist propaganda urging that black people be driven out of Britain, racist attacks were by 1958 a commonplace of black life in London. On weekend evenings in particular, gangs of 'teddy boys' cruised the streets looking for West Indians, Africans, or Asians."[57] By the late 1950s and early 1960s, tensions reached a boiling point with the Notting Hill and Nottingham race riots (August and September 1958), the murder of Black Antiguan carpenter Kelso Cochrane on the streets of Notting Hill (May 1959), and the Bristol Bus Boycott (April 1963).

Alongside this overt physical violence, Black and Asian immigrants were also subject to widespread employment and housing discrimination, the latter of which was a major concern given how the wartime London bombings had destroyed so much usable accommodation. In response, the British government passed the Race Relations Acts of 1965 and 1968, which recognized the amplification of racism in England and sought—however feebly and ineffectively—to make discrimination illegal.[58] But as the recent *Guardian* articles about the so-called Windrush scandal have illuminated for the public eye, the British government was itself an active conspirator in this jingoistic racism, with the Home Office wrongfully detaining and often deporting Black Afro-Caribbeans who had official leave to remain.[59] Indeed, the Conservative parliamentarian Enoch Powell made no secret of the anti-Black sentiments of the state when he made his infamous "Rivers of Blood" speech in parliament in 1968, which, although superficially decried by his peers, was extremely popular among the white British public. With the civil rights movement in full view across the Atlantic in the United States, the topic of race was thus no less at issue in midcentury Britain, particularly as it was emblemized by a growing multiethnic Black immigrant population.[60]

By the 1960s, there was a clear and identifiable "Black Britain" and a matching trend in virulent anti-Black racism.

Running parallel to Britain's long history of the material and ideological oppression of Black peoples, The Piggle's fantasies and fears reproduce some of the discursive tropes of specific midcentury anti-Black racism, suggestively associating the "Black Mummy" with aggression, violence, danger, and contamination. Metaphorizing the anti-immigration rhetoric common to much racist British discourse, The Piggle's fantasies represent Blackness as a kind of disease capable of jeopardizing the purity and health of the white mother(land). This becomes clear in the letter The Piggle's mother writes to Winnicott after The Piggle's first session:

> When she is angry, . . . [she] says urgently: "The babacar is 'taking blackness from me to you, and then I am frightened of you.'" . . . She is frightened of the Black Mummy and the black Pigga; she says: "Because they make me black."
>
> Yesterday she told me that the Black Mummy scratched my [the mother's] face, pulled off my yams, made me all dirty and killed me with "brrrrr" [feces]. I said she must be longing to have a nice clean mummy again. She told me she had one when she was a little baby.[61]

As this passage demonstrates, The Piggle's fantasy world is comprised of both highly personal, individual symbols and those that correspond with a larger sociopolitical reality. While The Piggle's idiosyncratic semantic equation of "yams" with breasts and "brrrr" with feces seems unique to her particular life experiences and subjectivity, her persistent fear of Blackness as a contamination conceptually associated with dirt, uncleanness, and indeed shit itself was anything but singular[62]—a racialized spin on what Mary Douglas has famously described as the social function of the bifurcation of "purity" and "danger."[63] As The Piggle's mother explains, "Her chief complaint about the Black Mummy is that she makes The Piggle black, and then The Piggle makes everyone, even the daddy, black."[64]

Read in connection with the racist nativist discourse in Britain, The Piggle's description of Blackness as a kind of contagious pollution that works through the mother's (reproductive) body takes on a larger political significance: it speaks to a racialized xenophobia of the pollution of a "clean" white Britain by the Black immigrant's reproductive labors. Because race was primarily a matter of immigration during this period, British racism manifested in a recognizable preoccupation with boundary management and control, where Black immigrants (especially West Indians) were affiliated with dirt, disorder, and uncleanness, an invasive affliction of the personified body politic: the "motherland."[65] Analyzing this racialized xenophobia in Britain's legislative contraction of its first postwar immigration policy, Hampshire remarks that "immigration was perceived as a 'problem' to be 'controlled', while immigrants themselves were often associated with social disorder and malady."[66] Put another way, because British racism at this time was inseparable from an acute xenophobia, Blackness was represented as a foreign, corrupting presence infecting a nation imagined as formerly pure—that is, constructed as pure only by virtue of the exclusion of the dangerous racialized "other." Racialized dog-whistle comments about cleanliness, purity, social (dis) order, and national health helped metaphorize and organize the white, anti-immigration discursive imaginary. "Black Mummy" can thus be seen to consolidate the threat that white Britain experienced immigration as posing to its sense of national identity and racial superiority. If identity is built on exclusions, then The Piggle makes clear here that her own identity—like Britain's larger national identity—was destabilized by the permeability of ostensibly secure racial categories.

Yet, as I have been arguing, gender was an equally important way that the British state and citizenry alike regulated the boundaries of race and national identity. Motherhood was a lynchpin in this regard since it was through the mother's body and reproductive labor that future generations of the national population were born and acculturated. By defining normative versus pathological forms of mothering along racial and colonial lines, postwar British discourse could effectively use the white woman-as-mother to delineate what counted as Englishness, effectively excluding those who, although formally counted as citizens, were not included as English. As Wendy Webster puts it, during the decline of empire and the racial transformation of England, "the story of nation that was told put at its centre the figure of the white woman," who, especially in her role as mother, patrolled the boundaries of white Englishness.[67]

This became a particularly important, if precarious, negotiation in the 1960s when, following the first wave of predominantly male immigrants, more Afro-Caribbean and Asian women made the journey to England. Consequently, Webster chronicles how the race discourse changed from fears about Black men and miscegenation to those focused on Black women; in England "in the early 1960s attention began to turn to black reproduction and black family life, which was represented as domestic barbarism in opposition to Englishness."[68] Although the British public had paltry access to records about immigration numbers in their own right, the media keenly followed statistics about often-sensationalized birth rates, which represented Black women as excessively fertile. "By the mid-1960s black women's visibility focused on their role as mothers, and on the need to limit their reproduction."[69] While concerns about Black mothers and family life had been a trademark anxiety in Britain's immediate postwar management of its colonies, as more Black women emigrated to Britain, managing appropriate forms of motherhood became a pivotal tool within the motherland's policing of Englishness at home as well. Given this, it seems hardly incidental that The Piggle's constellation of a boundary anxiety about contagious Blackness would be localized with the female-qua-maternal body. Echoing the demonization of Black mothers specifically, "Black Mummy"—that is, the Black maternal body—reproduces Blackness around her and, in so doing, poses a threat to white hegemony and security. As The Piggle's fantasies indicate, the mother is thus an overdetermined figure, simultaneously regulating gender, race, and nation. This fantasy constellates the common talking points of racist discourse in midcentury Britain and demonstrates how such phobias are instantiated and operationalized at the intersection between politics and psychic life.

Yet part of what is so interesting about this case is that these signifiers animate the psychic life of a two-year-old child whose fantasies register a sophisticated political unconscious far beyond her capacity for any articulate political consciousness. In an interview conducted in 2016 with the adult Piggle, now a social worker in London, she comments on the latent racial aspect of her childhood fears: "The bit that felt increasingly uncomfortable is something no one has picked up, that is, that there is a massively racist discourse going on. I don't think I meant 'black' as a racial term, but I [as The Piggle] do associate it with everything bad and frightening."[70] Whether intentional or not, The Piggle's childhood fears and fantasies testify to the racialized overdetermination of both the signifiers "Black" and "Mother" in the midcentury social imaginary. Reflecting on her first encounter with the record of this case when she was in her twenties, the adult Piggle explains that she "worr[ied] about whether I had got the bad meaning of 'black' from the racist discourse on race in the UK in the 1960s. I remember then telling myself: It's OK; it's the Queen of the Night from *The Magic Flute* who is a frightening character. And we listened to it a lot when I was little!"[71] Although an understandable discomfort, it is probably too easy to interpret The Piggle's fantasies as deriving from a single referent—even one as evocative as the Queen of the Night, which relies on the racialized bumbling of the dark-skinned North African "Moor," Monostatos, to provide comic relief in a manner similar to nineteenth-century minstrel performances. In fact, as I have been saying, what makes The Piggle's fantasies so interesting is the way they speak simultaneously to something personal and familial *and* to something social and political—that is, to something beyond The Piggle's own full consciousness or control. Thought biographically, this was a complicated (if plainly salient) intersection for The Piggle given her own multiethnic family background. While her father was a Dublin-born Irish Protestant with family ties to colonial Africa, her mother was originally a German-speaking Czech Jew from an upper-class family who fled Eastern Europe during the Holocaust, relocating as a refugee in England.[72] Even leaving aside what would have been the palpable racialization of her father's Irishness—"Those days," the adult Piggle recalls, "there were signs that said 'No dogs, Blacks or Irish'"—The Piggle's mother's racial identity would hardly count as white in midcentury England.[73] As with the racial affiliation of Irishness with Blackness, antisemitic discourse (such as that deployed, infamously, by the Nazis) frequently stoked racial hostilities by linking Jews with Blackness. As discussed in chapter 3, Jewish people were often considered "the Negroes of Europe" and Freud himself was dubbed a "Black Jew."[74] Such thinking was hardly limited to the Third Reich and was especially virulent in post-1947 England when British Army clashes with Zionist action groups over the Mandate for Palestine galvanized often violent antisemitic incidents, even figuring into the hate speech of Oswald Mosley's fascist political party, the British Union, which had been targeting Black Afro-Caribbean immigrants and was responsible for inciting the Notting Hill race riot.

The adult Piggle notes the elision of this racial legacy from the case on both discursive and visual levels: neither is race directly mentioned in the text nor does a picture of The Piggle herself appear (despite the fact that her real name, Gabrielle, remains undisguised). For readers familiar with this case, this latter erasure might come as something of a surprise since the published version of the text features an unusually memorable cover in which a photographic portrait of a blue-eyed, pale-skinned young girl, dressed in a bright red coat with vivid blue scarf, stares directly into the camera in a close-up shot. The photo, placed squarely beneath the title *The Piggle*—which is also, significantly, the patient's nickname—gives the impression of a biographical association, even as the adult Piggle records having "no idea who that child is, nor how the photo was chosen."[75] Thus, there is a complicated play of racial visibility and invisibility in her case as she implicitly insists, at the level of her own fantasy, on the centrality (and instability) of racial boundaries at stake in her personal sense of self while both Winnicott and the publishers omit potentially pertinent details of family history in a classic embrace of color-blind thinking that, implicitly but effectively, whitens the case.[76]

When it comes to the legacy of psychoanalytic theory and treatment, this is a far from uncommon phenomenon. As psychoanalytic scholars of race beginning with Fanon and continuing through Jean Walton, Kalpana Seshadri-Crooks, and Christopher Lane have rightly shown, race is often either ignored outright or positioned as a secondary appurtenance in much clinical and theoretical psychoanalytic work.[77] As I mentioned in the introduction to this book, psychoanalysis's historical silence on—and violence against—Blackness in particular has even been the subject of an entire documentary, *Black Psychoanalysts Speak*, in which contemporary Black American and Black British psychoanalysts reflect on the role of race and racism in psychoanalysis, both in regard to the (undertheorized) impact that racialization has on psychic life and in regard to the enduring legacy of racism within clinical psychoanalysis's own training bodies and institutions.[78] As is common among even contemporary psychoanalysts who, in not speaking about race in the clinic, cling to the fantasy of an analytic neutrality—as though silence itself is not an act, and a racialized one at that—Winnicott did not pursue the racial content of this fantasy—just as, when he introduced the potential discussion topic "black" for the BPS, he did not specify any awareness of his selection's racial implications.

To be sure, Winnicott likely did have race somewhere in mind in attending so often to "black" as a research interest, especially given that he made casual but not infrequent mentions of race throughout his more socially and politically minded papers.[79] But, much like his clinical encounter with The Piggle, these nods to race served primarily to gainsay its importance as a structuring fact of mental life. Readers of his work can see a good example of this in his relatively obscure 1962 paper, "Morals and Education," where he begins by arguing for the cross-cultural immutability of human nature, explaining that "what is true about human nature in London today is also true in Tokyo, in Accra, in Amsterdam and Timbuktu. It is true from whites and blacks, for giants and pygmies, for the children of the Harwell or the Cape Canaveral scientist and for the children of the Australian Aboriginal."[80] Given that much of the scientific racism prior to World War II and the Holocaust, which effectively recast racial science as epistemologically unsound and morally dangerous, was interested in substantiating claims about biological racial difference and the inferiority of nonwhite people, Winnicott's bid for a universalizing psychology—although much maligned today for its cultural and historical blindness—read in its particular historical context as a direct attempt to challenge racist logics by emphasizing the social constructedness of racial difference.

Such a move is typical in his work, where any mention of race is characteristically followed by a disavowal of its impact on, relevance to, or importance for the consideration at hand. For instance, in his troublingly misogynistic essay on birth control, "The Pill and the Moon," Winnicott reports almost in passing that a young white female patient of his was "absolutely torn with the disappointment that he [her date] hadn't raped her," only to note, at the end of the paragraph, that "incidentally, he was a very black African" but that his race "wasn't the heart of the problem."[81] Given how white supremacy has historically managed Black masculinity's threat to racial hegemony by conjuring up fantasies of hypersexualized Black men raping white women—a "white peril" trope powerfully emblazoned in cultural artifacts from films *Birth of a Nation*

(1915), *Gone with the Wind* (1939), and *To Kill a Mockingbird* (1960) to its popular revitalizations in U.S. political discourse about Latinx immigrants—the fact of her date's Blackness, and her own whiteness, seems more than merely "incidental" to the constellation of this patient's rape fantasy.[82] Although well-intentioned, such comments demonstrate the widely avowed shortcomings of liberal color-blind thinking, which, in pretending not to "see" race, remains blind to—and thus risks repeating—the keynote conceits of racism.

Yet Winnicott's more common response to race and racialization was not a repudiation of it per se but a localization of it as a matter of individual psychological, rather than structural and political, difference. In a lecture he delivered at Assembly Hall in Westminster in February 1965 on the importance of psychoanalytic research, he followed up on his earlier letter to Rycroft about why "black" was a worthwhile research topic. "What is the price of ignoring this piece of research that could so easily be done?" asks Winnicott rhetorically of his audience of mental health professionals. "One price," Winnicott answers, "is a serious one in terms of continuing misunderstanding on the part of white-skinned people in relation to black, and of the dark millions in relation to whites."[83] Juxtaposing "white-skinned people" against the undifferentiated "dark millions," Winnicott notably offers these remarks in the middle of his treatment of The Piggle, between her thirteenth and fourteenth sessions. Its shortcomings aside, such commentary registers his awareness of the racial import of the research interest he was advancing and indeed arguably even of The Piggle's fantasies. To this, it is interesting to note that of the 208 mentions of "Black" or "Blackness" in The Piggle's case, only fifteen are directly attributable to her own unprompted remarks;[84] the rest are introduced by Winnicott's clinical interpretations, his post-session notes, or the intersession letters The Piggle's mother's writes to Winnicott. Thus, while Winnicott did have an articulate interest in Blackness and an awareness of the racial import of this interest, like many psychologists and psychoanalysts he ultimately invested in the proposition that the broader social constellation of racialized categories and the forms of lived relationality attendant upon them yielded from individually accrued unconscious meaning. Put another way, for Winnicott racial hierarchies did not so much organize individual psychological experience as (an ostensibly pre-racial form of) individual psychological experience shaped and governed the sociopolitical life of race and racism.

This style of thought meant that, as much as Winnicott contributed to the postwar boom of expert interest in mothering, he (unlike many of his colleagues) never participated in any overt pathologization of Black maternity or Black family life. Readers can see this in Winnicott's only explicit discussion of race and motherhood in *Playing and Reality*: "It might turn out that the difference between the white citizen of the United States and the black-skinned citizen of that country is not so much a matter of skin color as of breastfeeding. Incalculable is the envy of the white bottle-fed population of the black people who are mostly, I believe, breast-fed."[85] Although Winnicott begins by disclaiming the importance of skin color as the key determinant of racial difference—a move that codes as a somewhat facile gesture toward a "post-racial" reasoning that gainsays the importance of the visual for structuring hierarchies of power and privilege—he does not deny racial difference altogether but instead makes it "a matter . . . of breast feeding," which is to say: a matter of maternal care. Although his particular claim about breastfeeding seems more like a figment of his own fetishized racial fantasy life than an empirical reality in the 1960s in either the United States or Britain—indeed, that Winnicott would idealize the nurturing capacity of Black breasts seems hardly separable from sentimentalized U.S. histories of slavery and wet-nursing—what is interesting is that in explaining racial difference Winnicott finds fault not with Black formations of maternal care but with the relative paucity of them among white people, that anemic "bottle-fed population." What he pathologizes, in other words, is the racial aggression of whiteness, its affective envy, which he implies constitutes the primary node of racial difference. In a critical reversal of standard racial narratives, Winnicott locates whiteness, not Blackness, as the site of racialized otherness.

Keeping in mind Winnicott's work as a public sage on maternal care, readers can see that one of the effects of this kind of statement is the idealization of breastfeeding. By locating "incalculable" envy with those deprived white children raised on bottles not breasts, he implicitly disciplines white mothers into breastfeeding, even as he disrupts the tendency to critique Black motherhood. This task, as Winnicott outlines it here, ought to be undertaken not just because bottle-fed children will feel individually envious but because this seemingly small decision about maternal care is actually the foundation of the larger social construction of race and racism. Racism, in other words, is built not on political and economic structures of disadvantage born of histories of slavery and colonialism but on the individual disadvantages of racialized maternal care. It is a matter of personal envy, not structural inequality, capitalist exploitation, or colonial expropriation. While this is a problematic surmise for how it elides the British Empire's production of and reliance on anti-Black racism as a condition of possibility for its imperial conquest and economic flourishing, what it does make clear is the extent to which Winnicott saw his work on mothering as contributing to the production of an antiracist culture. If anti-Blackness was a matter of white mothering, then by helping white mothers be "good enough" Winnicott implicitly sought to divest anti-Blackness from the envious white imaginary.

Tracking this insight back to the clinic, we can begin to appreciate the complex, even contradictory, racial work in which Winnicott was engaged. As with these two previous examples, Winnicott understood The Piggle's phobic obsession with "Black Mummy" to be indexing her internal splitting processes, which were intensified by her thwarted Oedipal desire. The Piggle felt a great love for her father, but the arrival of her sister provoked her hatred for her mother who she felt had duplicitously produced another child with her father. Unable to tolerate her own ambivalence toward her mother, The Piggle split her image into good and bad representations—white and Black, respectively—and projected them into externalized fantasy characters who then act out all the hostility and aggression she herself fears to unleash. As Winnicott surmised in the first session, "black here meant that hate had come in."[86] Unlike Klein, who would have interpreted such splitting as a trademark of the paranoid-schizoid position, Winnicott thought that this symptomatology meant that The Piggle had been spurred into a "premature ego development" because she was forced to accept her mother as a separate object prematurely. "Presumably," surmised Winnicott, "the 'Black Mummy' is a relic of her subjective preconceived notion about the mother."[87]

Or so Winnicott's story goes.

In tandem with this assessment—which selectively gives priority to the "Mummy" portion of the dual descriptor "Black Mummy" and invests in a relatively self-authored vision of social life and subjectivity not externally determined by broader symbolic, sociopolitical structures, such as race—Winnicott tried to foster what he described throughout his career as a good enough maternal holding environment in the consulting room. As I have already described, he originally developed the concept of good enough mother to outline the work performed by mothers for their infants. But, as his work progressed, he increasingly used the term to delineate what he also imagined to be the ideal function of the psychoanalyst. "Mothers, like analysts," Winnicott quips in the epigraph for this chapter, "can be good or not good enough."[88] The good enough mother thus constituted one of his most influential clinical modifications, as well as one of his most significant theoretical contributions. According to Jan Abram's psychoanalytic dictionary, *The Language of Winnicott*, "by the 1950s, Winnicott's use of the good-enough mother-infant paradigm as a way of understanding what could be provided in the analytic relationship had become the foundation of his theory of holding, and his focus was on the emotional holding-the-baby-in-mind in combination with the physical feeding, bathing and dressing."[89] More than perhaps any other analyst, then, he embraced a clinical comparison between the analyst and the mother, one that he claimed the patient experienced as not merely symbolic but as actual mothering throughout sessions.[90] For Winnicott, the emphasis on the clinic as a "holding environment"—including all parts of the analytic setting, such as the physical space and decor, the analyst's reliable presence, her individual personality, mood, liveliness, and attention—was meant to counterbalance what he felt was Klein's overzealous reliance on interpretation. Famously, Winnicott posed that "I interpret mainly to let the patient know the limits of my understanding."[91] He felt that such a rearticulation of the clinic downgraded the potential omnipotence of the analyst, relying instead on the patient to creatively produce their own meaning in the same way that the child, according to Winnicott, could inventively elaborate its own self—an idea, again, premised on a conviction about the possibility of a benign, nonintrusive environment. For the most part Winnicott intended this "holding" to be metaphorical, yet on more than one occasion he did quite literally engage in acts of physical contact and holding, using his own body as an anchoring maternal environment for a patient that he understood to be regressed to infancy.[92]

Winnicott employed this clinical technique throughout The Piggle's analysis. He aimed to curate and sustain an environment in which she could freely and securely play, acting out her fantasies through her physical use, and abuse, of objects. Breaking with analytic orthodoxy, Winnicott regularly participated in these games, taking on different characters including both The Piggle (when she was in flight from her own identity) and her mother. Indeed, the maternal function of Winnicott's clinic becomes quite literal when, in a game with The Piggle during the second session of the analysis, on March 11, 1964, she reenacts her own birth. Bringing her father into the consulting room as a mother-substitute, The Piggle inaugurates a game she names "being born": "'I'm a baby too,' she announced, as she came out head first onto the floor between her father's legs."[93] This game is an important one for The Piggle and she repeats it many times in this session and, later, in her fourth session (May 26, 1964), likewise "using a man as a woman to be born out of."[94] "Every time she was the baby being born between her father's legs and onto the floor."[95] In both instances, a discussion of Blackness, either in regards to the mother or to some other element of the scene, followed The Piggle's game. On Winnicott's interpretation, The Piggle's repetition of "being born" was a regression to an earlier, infantile stage of dependency, one in which she is simultaneously acting out an identification with her newborn sister and using her father to stage, for herself, a more perfect birth. By regressing to a developmental moment prior to her sister's birth—and thus prior to her fear of Black Mummy, that split-off representation of her mother embodying her own projected hate—Winnicott wagered that The Piggle's phobia of Black Mummy would abate.[96]

And, in fact, it did. Although The Piggle has a bout of intense "illness" following the first of these games in her second session, over the course of the analysis her anxiety about Black Mummy lessened. Considered socially and politically, this clinical result is significant for how it registers the potentially progressive racial impact of the clinic. Without doubt, Winnicott's analytic role worked in the direction of dephobicizing the Black mother. If Winnicott made clear that he understood race as a matter of mother-child relationality, then by designing his clinical presence on that very relational template he implicitly suggested that his clinic was a site for the redress of racial fracture. In this way, his clinical work was not simply socially and politically relevant but effectively aimed to offer some remedy to the (post)colonial racism that had newly engulfed the British motherland. His clinical work, in other words, goes some way toward showing that no clinical interaction is racially neutral, either with regard to the individuals involved or to its impact on the larger social sphere.

Yet this reputedly salutary clinical result tells us little about the nuance of the employed methodology in which a white male analyst strives to enact a good enough maternal environment for a half-Czech-Jewish, half-Irish girl persecuted by racialized phobias. Winnicott does not interrogate the complex racial and gender cross-identifications at work in this clinical scene; but it is nevertheless worth asking, for ourselves, what the implications and effects are of a clinical technique based on an idea of good enough mothering at a time when motherhood was such an intensely racialized category. When it comes to gender alone, Winnicott's function in the clinic has been read both as paternalistic interloper[97] and as gender-fluid exemplification of male mothering.[98] But I am ultimately less interested in thinking within that parsing than I am in understanding how the good enough mother—both as theoretical construction and clinical presence—also functions as a racialized tableau.

With regard to clinical technique, Winnicott's own physical embodiment as a white analyst was not neutral. For a child plagued by racialized fears in which whiteness and masculinity were explicitly aligned with an unambivalent idealized love, while Blackness and femininity were soldered to an externalized representation of hate, Winnicott's racial and gender identity corresponded with The Piggle's already extant good objects. Indeed, his role as an ego-syntonic good object is evident in the largely positive transference he solicited from The Piggle, meaning that it is highly likely that race—and specifically an uninterrogated love of whiteness—was a condition of possibility for the success of the clinical result. Left unanalyzed, the danger of not considering either the racialization of The Piggle's fantasies or the racialization of

Winnicott's own clinical mothering is that Winnicott risked "redress-ing" the symptoms of racial fracture by implicitly encouraging The Pig-gle's identification with whiteness. Famously, Lacan was adamant that one of the clinical consequences of courting a positive transference is the patient's ultimate identification with the ego of the analyst, which does not so much shift the patient's sticking points within the symbolic as it does smoothly replace one misrecognition for another. From this perspective, the effect of Winnicott's clinical function as a good enough maternal substitute was not nearly as straightforward as it might seem. Although Winnicott did mitigate a simultaneously personal and political fear of the gendered and racialized figure, Black Mummy, he did so not by challenging The Piggle's association of Blackness with fear and contamination but instead by reaffirming and reinstalling an investment in whiteness as tantamount to the good. By not analyzing the effect of his own whiteness in the clinic—which was likely instru-mental in The Piggle's identificatory cooperation with Winnicott and the resolution of her fears—he missed the opportunity to disarticulate the conceptual split (white/Black as equivalent to good/bad) on which her phobia was founded.

It is here that we come up against the vital shortcomings of Winn-icott's tacit conviction that the splits elaborated in personal psychology precede and determine those wider racial and colonial fractures. For, in reading white and Black as naturalized matter of love and hate—binaries unmoored, in Winnicott's approach, from the persistent and pervasive historical regulation and distribution of affect along privileged racial lines—Winnicott understands his clinical task to be the mitigation of the split through the articulation of the origin of the fear of Blackness in the mother's body. He does not, in other words, press the origin of why Black and white had taken on the affective associations they had, just as he does not aim to reorder these associations, either with regard to the idealization of whiteness or to the denigration of Blackness. This critique ultimately goes to the root of psychoanalysis's thinking about the figure of the mother given how Winnicott's unflinching acceptance of the naturalness of a split maternal representation—good and bad; white and Black—emerges from Klein's core claim that a bifurcation of the breast-qua-mother was the child's first psychological and affec-tive object-orientation. Yet as Emily Green has helpfully shown in her historical interrogation of the impact of the "Mammy" stereotype on psychoanalytic (specifically Kleinian) thinking, positing the mother as split itself participates in a well-established racial history.

> Here it is important to remember that the "maternal" had long been a composite idea, since middle-class children often had both a nurse and a mother and so "in a very real sense . . . children grew up with two mothers . . . two powerful figures."

> It was the nurse who was generally responsible for infant care, and . . . this split in the mother was a racialized one. In films such as *Gone with the Wind* and *Imitation of Life* motherhood is clearly divided along racial lines, so that the white mother is a business-woman or absent mistress while the mammy is the domestic mother. As such, the mammy is etymologically tied to breast.[99]

Green here echoes Webster's conviction that mothering is a racialized ideology and, further, contends that insofar as (especially British psychoanalysis) came to invest in a theory of the mother as the most determinative figure in psychic life, this postulation was necessarily informed by historically grounded racial archetypes. The good versus bad mother, the white versus Black mother, mirrors the historical outsourcing of mothering along racial lines and the lived racial valuations and bifurcations produced by that split.

While Winnicott's articulation of the good enough mother is clearly meant to unsettle the racialized binary Klein posits, my own concluding point here is that it does not, by virtue of that motivation alone, then become racially neutral. With regard to The Piggle, Green's insight about psychoanalysis's naturalization of what are fundamentally racial (and classed) tropes of motherhood makes meaningful The Piggle's mother's passing references to the fact that the family employed two in-home aides. The first was an au pair named Renata who, given the mother's original Czech citizenship, was likely herself also a Czech immigrant. The other was "an elderly woman" only referred to as "the Wattie," a nickname contrived by The Piggle, who she was apparently "very attached to."[100] Aside from this, the only other detail readers are given about "the Wattie" is the description that she was "the help"—two words that, even before the release of the grossly romanticized cinematic materialization of Hollywood feel-goodery about race relations in the Jim Crow South, carried a powerful racial significance.[101] Although we never learn the racial identities of either of these maternal substitutes, what Green's analysis helps clarify is the historical importance that race (and, as I discuss more thoroughly in chapter 6, class) has long played in schematizing motherhood and in adjudicating who can count, in the first place, as the good—or "the good enough"—mother. The final lesson might thus be that if there is a clearly racial haunting in Winnicott's work—both when it comes to "Black Mummy" in the clinic and "Blackness" outside of it—then, in the spirit of psychoanalysis, the ghosts might best be encouraged to speak.

Far from a universal template, then, the concept of the good enough mother is a fraught particularization embroiled with the racial and gender politics of midcentury Britain. By relying on his own embodied self to personify the good enough mother in the clinic, Winnicott used his clinical work to reconceptualize and potentially redress the political fractures produced by the process of decolonizing the motherland. Not far from Winnicott in London, during the same decades, Thomas Main would similarly use his development of a new type of clinic—the therapeutic community—as a form of social redress. Like Winnicott, Main made questions of sociality, family, and normative health central to his fundamentally welfarist social agenda. But, by transforming the conventionally privatized, couple-based clinic into a communal, residential setting, Main also used his therapeutic community as an experimental foray into the political promise of communalism during the Cold War. Toggling between the residential structures of the welfarist heterosexual nuclear family and the anti-Oedipal, anti-capitalist Leftist Communist clinic (such as those created by Jean Oury and Félix Guattari), Main's work at the Cassel Hospital dramatically redefined the social scope and capacity of the Cold War clinic.

From the Couch to the Iron Curtain

Psychoanalysis During the Cold War

CHAPTER FIVE

The Communal Clinic

Therapeutic Communities, Heteronormativity, and the Cold War

In February 1962, "Mr. Adams," a twenty-six-year-old patient, was referred by his general practitioner to the marital clinic at the Cassel Hospital. Described in remarkably unflattering terms by the hospital director and supervising psychoanalyst, Thomas Main, as "a small man in every way—dejected, inadequate-looking, simple, stupid, confused and embarrassed," he came to Cassel complaining of persistent sexual impotence, which had rendered him unable to "consummate" his marriage for the past three years.[1] Before his visit to the hospital, Adams believed that his erectile dysfunction was a wholly physiological malady, the last vestiges of a venereal disease supposedly contracted from a prostitute in the Middle East some years before. But, with his GP's referral to Cassel, his symptoms were rebranded psychosomatic, and he (and his wife) received once-a-week outpatient psychoanalytic treatment at the hospital. A total of three analysts were involved in this unique clinical approach, which consisted of two parallel individual analyses accompanied by group supervisory sessions with Main. After some six months of treatment, the analysis was dubbed a success: the couple's sex life was improved, their marriage repaired, and they returned to their everyday lives. Although they were likely unaware of it, Mr. and Mrs. Adams had participated in one of the most innovative and influential adaptations of clinical psychoanalytic practice in Britain: the therapeutic community.

In this chapter, I follow the clinical innovations in psychoanalytic practice from the private, individual consulting room to the collectivized therapeutic community, focusing particularly on the unique clinical techniques developed at the Cassel Hospital. Therapeutic communities like Cassel were a distinctly postwar phenomenon in Britain, wherein psychoanalytic praxis melded with inpatient institutional care, thereby redefining the traditional psychiatric hospital as a participatory community. From John Rickman, Wilfred Bion, and S. H. Foulkes's early wartime experiments at Northfield Military Hospital; to the social psychologist Maxwell Jones's postwar Henderson Hospital; to Denis Martin and John Pippard's larger and more squarely psychiatric Claybury Hospital in the 1950s; to David Cooper's radical countercultural attempt at "antipsychiatry" in the early 1960s at Villa 21, numerous therapeutic communities flourished in Britain between 1945 and 1970. These communities were part of a wider global movement that, in the wake of World War II, used the historically custodial and hierarchical space of the inpatient psychiatric institution for the experimental reordering of sociality, sexuality, and governmentality. In France, for instance, the Catalan psychiatrist François Tosquelles established the institutional psychotherapy movement at Saint-Alban while Félix Guattari experimented with a Marxist-Lacanian form of "schizo-analysis" at La Borde Clinic; in the United States, psychiatrist Fredric Wertham and novelist Richard Wright tackled midcentury issues around racial justice and segregation through their work with underserved Black communities at Harlem's Lafargue Clinic; and, in Algeria, Fanon famously implemented his own form of "sociotherapy" at Blida-Joinville in an effort to decolonize both the hospital and the nation.[2] Clinicians from multiple countries and traditions were thus actively embracing various forms of hospital-based sociality and communalism as an experimental antidote to many pernicious sociopolitical institutions, including colonialism, racism, authoritarianism, and the capitalistic patriarchal family form. Therapeutic communities in Britain were one piece of this wider legacy, and the Cassel Hospital is still perhaps the best known of these institutions.

Throughout this chapter, I explore Cassel's unique approach to the psychoanalytic clinic-qua-community, situating it within the larger therapeutic community movement in Britain in the postwar decades.

I discuss how, under Main, who served as Cassel's director from 1946 to 1976, therapeutic communities like Cassel redefined traditional hospital power structures, building a residential, egalitarian "communal clinic" that emphasized the importance of sociality, collectivity, and communalism for mental well-being. As I show, these clinical experimentations with communal sociality were part of a larger Cold War interest in exploring the political promise of the commune as a new social and institutional horizon. But, unlike other radical Leftist iterations that used a combination of psychoanalysis and Marxist anti-imperialism to challenge the naturalized twinned ascendency of capitalistic liberalism and bourgeois sexual normativity, I argue that Cassel's unique vision of therapeutic collectivity was wedded to a distinctly welfarist ideology of the middle-class, heterosexual nuclear family as the seat of British social democracy. By combining insights from psychoanalytic historiography and queer theory, I show how, although collectivity at Cassel was taken as the basis of both psychological and institutional life, Main's particular psychoanalytic technique ultimately routed all communalism back through the heteronormative married couple and nuclear family as *the* naturalized socioeconomic unit. Set against the backdrop of British Cold War anxieties about the spread of global communism and the decline of the British patriarchal state and family, Cassel's clinic experimented with radical political ideals of collectivity and communalism but ultimately contained them within a familiar—and familial—liberal form. I therefore consider how Cassel did not so much reject the communalism socially definitional to Cold War communism; rather, it used gender and sexual norms to retool it for the economic fortification of the capitalistic British welfare state.

"THE TOTAL INSTITUTION": PSYCHOANALYSIS AND THERAPEUTIC COMMUNITY AT THE CASSEL HOSPITAL

In a southwest suburb of London, nestled between Richmond's stately city park and Horace Walpole's surreal Gothic villa, Strawberry Hill, sits the Cassel Hospital. Originally founded and endowed in 1919 by Edmund Cassel for the treatment of shell shock, the hospital underwent several physical relocations during the wars before settling in its current location in 1948. Unlike the typically grim institutional settings of most hospitals, Cassel occupies a large, fully detached, Georgian-era building, complete with pillared front entrance and sloping, unenclosed rear gardens. Prior to its establishment, the property had been the personal home of the nineteenth-century writer and Christian philanthropist John Minter Morgan and thereafter served as both a hotel and girls' school. Today, Cassel operates as one of the few surviving NHS-affiliated psychoanalytic therapeutic communities founded in the heyday of the postwar therapeutic community movement. As Lesley Caldwell rightly puts it, "The Cassel hospital in Richmond is Britain's most famous attempt to organise treatment of in-patients with the psychoanalytic method originally developed for use in private consulting rooms."[3]

Although not many beyond the British psychoanalytic community may know its name—or be familiar with therapeutic communities, for that matter—Cassel enjoys a renowned place in the history of psychoanalytic practice. It has been home to some of the field's most prominent contemporary figures—including R. D. Hinshelwood, who served for a time as its director, and David Bell, former president of the BPS—and it is esteemed as the site of some of the most inventive reimaginings of clinical psychoanalytic practice in the twentieth century. This legacy is due in large part to the work and directorship of the Johannesburg-born and London-trained psychiatrist and psychoanalyst Thomas Main, who served as its director for thirty years. Main, who is largely credited with coining and popularizing the term "therapeutic community" in reference to Cassel, sought to radically redefine the procedures for and organization of inpatient psychiatric facilities according to more psychoanalytic principles.[4] He was a vocal critic of the carceral nature of orthodox psychiatric hospitals and proposed that the organizational defaults of the hospital itself formed a key part of the social genesis of mental illness. For Main, the passivity traditionally required of the hospitalized patient—confined, bound, and sedated—was not only a deterrent to recovery but a cause of psychological and sociological illness: a psychological outcome he termed "desocialization."[5] As Main puts it in the opening to his well-known 1946 paper, "The Hospital as a Therapeutic Institution," "By tradition, a hospital is a place wherein sick people may receive shelter from the stormy blasts of life. . . . The concept of a hospital as a refuge too often means, however, that patients are robbed of their status as responsible human beings. Too often they are called 'good' or 'bad' according only to the degree of their passivity in the face of the hospital demand for their obedience, dependency and gratitude."[6]

At Cassel, individual patients were thus treated not as dependent conscripts in need of constant care but as members of a whole social unit, where they retained autonomy over and responsibility for themselves, their environment, and their community during their stay. This reorganization of the protocols and precepts of inpatient treatment was driven by Main's psychoanalytic training; he argued that genuine psychological change would only be possible through a transformation of the entire psychic economy—not the "retirement from life" facilitated by the traditional hospital.[7] Indeed, Main interpreted even the patient's request for hospitalization as itself a potential symptom since it signaled what he viewed to be an unhealthy desire to withdraw from the demands of daily life and enter a regressive state of dependency.[8] Main's emphasis on a more participatory and egalitarian hospital structure, where staff and patients shared collective responsibility for the management of the ward, was thus his attempt at using a form of prosocial communalism to combat the hospital's collusion with what he saw to be an antisocial regression. As a result, Cassel was the only major hospital in Britain to consistently practice clinical psychoanalysis in an inpatient, communal setting.[9]

Organizationally, this philosophy meant a major structural overhaul to the spatial and social arrangement of the hospital. Initially, Main divided Cassel into two primary inpatient units called "firms" and a small outpatient unit, together totaling 104 beds.[10] But as his skepticism about inpatient treatment grew, he shrunk the inpatient firms to about fifty beds, adding a larger outpatient facility and, eventually, the marital unit that Mr. Adams would visit.[11] Each inpatient firm was assigned a staff consultant to help with daily management, but patients themselves were responsible for much of the maintenance of their everyday lives and environments. Cooking, cleaning, meal planning, budgeting, childcare, ironing, minor repairs, and even landscaping all fell within the purview of collective patient management.[12] Patients decided their own waking and sleeping hours, with some even maintaining paid employment outside of the hospital.[13] A process of democratic voting was instituted to help decide larger institutional issues and, although staff retained their uniforms and some aspects of their conventional roles, doctors were required to divest themselves of their ingrained sense of autonomy and authority. Main advises, "The anarchical rights of the doctor in the traditional hospital society have to be exchanged for the more sincere role of member in a real community, responsible not only to himself and his superiors, but to the community as a whole."[14] All staff and patients thus participated together in community discussion groups and self-reflection activities and were routinely invited to revise the nature of their roles in accordance with community need. According to the Menninger Clinic psychologist David Rapoport, who regularly visited the therapeutic community at the Henderson Hospital run by Jones for four years (1953–1957), these were places where "everyone [was] expected to make some contribution towards the shared goals of creating a social organization that will have healing properties."[15] As BPS psychoanalyst Eric Rayner put it when reflecting on his years at Cassel, it was "a very verbose process, but no one fe[lt] they [were] half-heartedly existing at the Cassel."[16] In this way, a new form of psychoanalytic practice—one that put communalism at the center of its clinical technique—was born.

As might already be evident, the psychoanalytic tenets governing Main's clinical practice at Cassel were openly iconoclastic. After having initially qualified as a psychiatrist in the 1930s, Main became increasingly interested in psychoanalysis and underwent a year's analysis with Susan Issacs during the war. He then spent the immediate postwar years formally retraining at the BPS with Michael Balint, under the joint supervision of Anna Freud, Melanie Klein, and Paula Heimann.[17] Given this diverse range of supervisors, it is hardly surprising that Main was no psychoanalytic purist. He argued, in no uncertain terms, for the importance of adapting and modifying psychoanalytic practice for new settings and scenes, making special note of the limited applicability of the Freudian-style consulting room. He cautions,

No matter how expert we may be in our own classic psychoanalytic setting we must be clear that in other settings the classical psychoanalytic *techniques* of our clinical work will not be useful. . . . For each fresh setting we have to confess major ignorance about how much or little can be attempted. We shall need to study the effect of the circumstances in which we shall meet the patient—such as whether we go to him or tell him to come to us, whether we tell him ourselves or through an intermediary; and we need to study in each session how to pace the work—whether or not to arrange special sessions, or simply use ordinary workaday contacts. . . . How long a consultation should be, whether we should decide the length or let the patient decide it, how long treatment should last and who should decide that, how it should end—these are the kind of problems that need to be solved variously in various settings.[18]

Believing that psychoanalysis was freely adjustable, Main had few qualms modifying it to meet the needs of an inpatient residential facility. In this regard, he echoed the sentiments of many postwar psychoanalysts who were less beholden to the defense of "orthodoxy" than previous generations and thus more willing to adapt clinical work for new settings and objectives.

In fact, his embrace of a collectivized group setting was especially indicative here since groups became a particular object of postwar psychoanalytic interest and innovation. From Balint groups to the Tavistock Clinic—from group psychoanalysis, democratic therapeutic communities, and family therapy to the Institute of Group Analysis—the group was a new postwar horizon for many psychoanalytic practitioners. This burgeoning interest can easily be traced to the precipitous spread of multiple "mass psychologies" (including genocidal fascism) throughout the midcentury, which brought the potentially cataclysmic affective power of the group out on the world stage. But unlike the crowd theorists of the century past—Le Bon, Trotter, Tarde—who pathologized the group as inherently regressive and threatening to the bourgeois individualism assumed to be the basis of democratic liberalism, postwar psychoanalysts instead emphasized the primary and participatory potential of sociality. As affect theorists such as Teresa Brennan have shown, their version of the self did not aspire toward totalized self-containment as the normative psychopolitical ideal, and their clinical experiments with groups and collectives can be seen as various experiments with the promise of collectivized sociality and subjectivity.[19] Far from threat or pathology, then, the postwar social group was taken up as the best potential safeguard for a democratic future. Main's instrumentalization of psychoanalysis within therapeutic communities was just one of the ways in which multiple analysts reinvented psychoanalytic theory and practice to answer changing political imaginaries. By combining a midcentury psychoanalytic interest in group processes and psychotic anxieties with a welfarist commitment to social democracy and public health, therapeutic communities like Cassel expanded the clinical norms and practices of the British psychoanalytic establishment.

Main crafted this new clinical technique by combining elements of "classical" psychoanalytic treatment with a unique form of community-based, residential living, which he argued was central to the therapeutic mission of the hospital. Per Main's stipulations, individual clinical analysis formed the basis of each patient's treatment, and every patient was provisioned with two hours of weekly analysis with a paired member staff—all of whom, before the 1960s, were required to be psychoanalytically trained through the training program at the London-based Institute of Psychoanalysis.[20] Analytic sessions throughout the week were either thirty or sixty minutes long, depending on patient need.[21] Alongside individual sessions, Main also incorporated a limited amount of group psychoanalysis, which was just being developed by S. H. Foulkes and Malcolm Pines (in the Anglophone world) as a collectivized approach to clinical practice.[22] A version of this would eventually become the cornerstone of the Tavistock Institute of Human Relations' training program, via Wilfred Bion.[23] Outpatient day clinics (such as the Adams' marital clinic) served as a nonresidential option for those near enough and well enough to return home. The daily lives of both patients and staff were therefore pervaded by multiple psychoanalytic and psychodynamic modalities. As Rayner casually notes, nearly a quarter of all psychoanalysts affiliated with the BPS in the 1980s would have worked at Cassel at some point in their careers.[24] Put another way: Cassel was a major gravitational center for midcentury British psychoanalysis.

Despite the lofty roster of BPS affiliates, many of psychoanalysis's more conventional mainstays had to be altered to accommodate Cassel's inpatient, residential setting. To begin with, although Main originally intended to provision five-times-a-week intensive psychoanalysis to all patients, the staffing and logistics of this arrangement quickly became impractical and a more limited program of twice-weekly sessions was put in place.[25] Additionally, as Cassel's practices and procedures morphed and transformed into the mid-1950s, he realized that patients in any institutional setting would necessarily encounter their analysts outside of the individualized consulting room. After some early attempts at creating entirely separate systems, Main concluded by the close of 1953 that there was no practical way of maintaining such insulation.[26] Patients would inevitably come to know their analyst's personal and professional preferences, their flaws and foibles, their habits and interests, thereby complicating the transferential relationship. Clinical boundaries would inevitably be blurred. Because of this, each analyst's work with their own countertransference would also have to be taken up differently given the multiple types of encounters between patient and analyst outside of individual sessions. Main encouraged analysts to be on the lookout for how "patients . . . weave their knowledge of staff relationships and their knowledge of other patients' relationships into their systems of feeling."[27] Indeed, the entire environment of the hospital would, in effect, become an extension of and supplement to the one-on-one analytic relationship as wider patient-patient and patient-staff relationships were laminated onto and into weekly sessions.

Rather than think of these complications as in any way jeopardizing the psychoanalytic capacity of Cassel, Main instead embraced them as the therapeutic community's most original and essential offering. He held that the total environment—the nature of the therapeutic *community* itself—was an active part of the therapeutic process, and he never wavered in his conviction that the communal aspect of Cassel was indispensable for patients' psychic well-being. Weighing the relative benefits of traditional psychoanalytic methods against therapeutic communities, Main writes:

> It is true that radical individual treatment can free the inner drives of the patient, and make him capable of a full and stable social life, but it fails to give him an assured technique for full social participation—he can learn this only from the impact of society itself. Treatment of the neurotic patient, who suffers from a disturbance of social relationships, cannot therefore be regarded as satisfactory unless it is undertaken within a framework of social reality that can provide him with opportunities for attaining fuller

social insight and for expressing and modifying his emotional drives according to the demands of real life.[28]

According to Main—and for most, if not all, therapeutic community practitioners since—the singular doctor-patient relationship, devoid of social context, was not itself sufficient for many patients. What was needed was the production of an entire social environment—a community—where the wider social setting would have as much (if not more) effect than privatized sessions in a consulting room. According to the Maudsley psychotherapist Frederick Kräupl Taylor, "in therapeutic communities it is the social atmosphere itself that is regarded as the main therapeutic measure."[29] "Therapeutic community" was thus more than just a description of a residential setting; it was a proposal for *community itself* to be understood as an active psychotherapeutic agent.

Arguably, this was Main's most significant technical contribution, and it impacted how he treated the entire community and institution of Cassel as an expressive and potentially symptomatic entity. One of the basic tenets of Main's approach to therapeutic communities was his conviction that the individual and the social group were not fundamentally separable and so disease in one had direct ties to disorder in the other. Any issues in the functioning of a firm—including patient ailment, worker dissatisfaction, and even, in one especially memorable case, the sudden appearance of a stray cat—were taken as symptomatic expressions of larger community disfunction. For instance, in the case of the cat, Main began by flagging the cat's arrival during a group session. From this, Main learned that the cat was the consequence of a recent increase in mice; the mice were then found to be the result of patients in one particular block of the hospital throwing food out of their windows; and, eventually, the food throwing was traced back to the patients' frustration with a particular analyst. Upon this revelation, the analyst adjusted their practice, the food throwing stopped, the mice dwindled, and the cat moved on.[30] The term "therapeutic community" was thus a specific way of implicating the functioning of the whole social institution in the ostensibly individual neurosis of the patient. In Main's words, "the *whole* community, all staff as well as patients, needed to be viewed as a troubled, larger system which needed treatment. Could all people in it move to a consideration of each other's plight and benefit from opportunities to examine the conscious and unconscious uses each was making of others? Could the total institution become therapeutic for all?"[31] The psychoanalytic work of a therapeutic community was ideally therefore reciprocal: as the containing effect of the community and institution helped transform patients, so too the patients transformed their institution. In this way, community itself became both a vehicle for—and an object of—psychoanalytic practice.

THE COMMUNALIST INTERNATIONAL: THE COLD WAR AND THE GLOBAL COMMUNE-CLINIC

Main's experimentation at Cassel with communal forms of psycho-analysis lasted from 1946 until his retirement in 1970, a tenure that paralleled the peak decades of British Cold War social life. This was a volatile and even contradictory time within the United Kingdom: on the one hand, it was a period marked historically by the mythology of postwar political and economic consensus, where the stability provided by middle-class expansion, welfare security, and coalitional govern-ment meant that normative ideals of domesticity, consumerism, gen-dered divisions of labor, heterosexuality, and the nuclear family were consolidated and elevated as markers of capitalistic liberal democracy, in Britain as much as in the United States. But this was also a time of global protest and resistance—from decolonization and the women's liberation movement, to civil rights and counterculturalism, to antiwar and students' rights protests, to wide scale industrial action and lesbian and gay rights—as millions of citizens contested the injustices of both authoritarian communism and liberal democracy and called for more utopian arrangements in living, working, and loving. Although so-called welfare consensus may have been the order of the day in Whitehall, on the streets and around the world optimistic experiments in new ways of being were insurgent.

Psychoanalysts, psychologists, and psychiatrists were hardly immune to this zeitgeist, and multiple practitioners around the world experi-mented with communalistic and collectivist forms of clinical practice as a new horizon for utopian political engagement. In France, for instance, the Cold War yielded a surge of various regional Leftist experiments with political and social communalism as an aspirational antidote to (neo)liberal capitalism's violent ascendency. Famously, Tosquelles, Jean Oury, Félix Guattari, and the wider French institutional psychotherapy movement combined Marxist theories of communism with specifically Lacanian psychoanalysis, creating renowned commune-clinics at Saint-Alban-sur-Limagnole and La Borde. For both these institutions, the residential environments of the hospitals were taken as the scene of radical forays into anticapitalist collectivized living, non-Oedipal sexuality, and psychological "disalientation" where the social environment was just as important a psychopolitical intervention as the more squarely psychoanalytic sessions.[32] A thousand miles away in French colonial Algeria, Fanon was implementing a similar innovation he dubbed "sociotherapy" at Blida-Joinville Psychiatric Hospital. Throughout the 1950s and into the early 1960s, Fanon incorporated culturally specific activities, clubs, sports teams, cafés, and hospital newsletters into the patients' daily activities in an effort to use the psychopolitical setting of the clinic to decolonize both his patients and the nation. According to Fanon, who had newly been charged with treating a ward of Muslim men, the colonial Eurocentrism of classical psychiatric practice could only be offset by the reintroduction of the patients' wider social environment within the hospital in the service of disalienation.[33] In these clinics, the collectivized residential psychotherapeutic setting was a key space for communist-affiliated resistances to authoritarianism, bureaucratization, colonialism, and heteronormative Oedipalization.

Similar radical ventures were likewise afoot back in Britain. Throughout the 1960s, so-called antipsychiatrists launched comparable attempts at combining anti-imperial communism and psychoanalysis via communalized clinics. The two most famous of these experiments were David Cooper's early 1960s experimental hospital ward, Villa 21, in Shenley Hospital, Hertfordshire, and his and R. D. Laing's (in)famous Kingsley Hall in London, which ran from 1965 to 1970. In Villa 21, the South-African born psychiatrist and communist Cooper oversaw a small autonomous ward of nineteen patients, all young men, who were treated primarily with group and community therapy. As with all therapeutic communities, medicalized sedations and restraints were largely eliminated.[34] Although Cooper would not publish *The Death of the Family* until 1971—the text that launched his well-known condemnation of the heterosexual nuclear family as the origin of both individual psychological and sociopolitical malady—Villa 21 constituted an early clinical experiment in the abolition of the family and the liberation from what Cooper saw as the constraining effect of all institutions. Patients were thus given free rein to act (or not) as they chose; experimental hallucinogenics were available in lieu of traditional pharmaceuticals;[35] and staff and patient roles were substantially blurred in an effort to resist the infantile-paternal dynamic central to most postwar hospital operation.[36]

Following the closure of this experiment, Cooper joined forces with the Tavistock-trained Scottish psychoanalyst Laing to found the famous Kingsley Hall in London in 1965. This was an intentional residential community where psychoses, regressions, and other forms of psychical enactment were not just tolerated but encouraged as a beneficial form of self-expression and self-becoming.[37] Unlike Villa 21, which fell more squarely within the progressive psychiatry movement, Kingsley Hall was particularly informed by psychoanalytic practice and, through Laing, had the regular participation of some of psychoanalysis's leading lights, including Marion Milner and D. W. Winnicott.[38] Although Laing and Cooper were by no means interchangeable in their professional and political visions—Laing never identified with the label "antipsychiatry" (which Cooper coined) and remained committed, throughout his career, to the treatment of individual mental illness—they shared the view that even severe forms of mental illness (like psychosis and schizophrenia) were best understood as indexing failures in the "mad" social and political order rather than constituting symptoms of an individual disease.[39] They maintained that mental illness was, as the antipsychiatry historian Oisín Wall has put it, "not only intelligible but actually a reasonable, if not always rational, reaction to an impossible social situation."[40] As such, both Villa 21 and Kingsley Hall were intentional communities meant to constitute "revolutionary centres for transforming consciousness" through their communal and egalitarian commitment to the clinical principles of demedicalization, democratization, and community participation.[41]

From even this brief survey, it is easy to see how essential the Cold War and Western counterculturalism were for the emergence and vitality of these various Leftist clinics. While experimental communal living arrangements are long-standing and diverse, motivated by multiple religious, political, and economic ideologies spanning centuries, the creation of intentional *clinical* communities governed by combined psychoanalytic and Marxist principles is perhaps unique to the Cold War moment. Without a doubt, this trend was part of the wider global "third revolution" in progressive psychiatry, begun by Philippe Pinel, which pushed for the "deinstitutionalization" of many mental hospitals and asylums. But historians such as Robcis and Wall have rightly shown how these commune-clinics also had specific political aspirations tied to the lived failures of both capitalism and communism in the twentieth century.[42] As Robcis explains with regard to the clinics at Saint-Alban and La Borde,

> The founders of institutional psychotherapy conceived of their project against the two dominant political frameworks of their time: liberalism and State Marxism in its bureaucratic Cold War version. By foregrounding the decisive role of drives, affect, and desire, institutional psychotherapy challenged the liberal ideal—inherited from the Enlightenment—of a bound, individualized, and rational self. However, it also refused the crude Marxist vision according to which the libidinal and the fantasmatic were simply displacements of a more accurate material reality, whether it be class interest, capitalist hegemony, or social structure. For institutional psychotherapy, the unconscious was not simply important to politics . . . [it] was constitutive of the political.[43]

Although by no means conflatable with institutional psychotherapists, antipsychiatrists were likewise responding to the brew of Cold War geopolitics in their indictment of the compulsory heterosexual nuclear family and consumer capitalism as the intertwined causes of the growing social experience of madness, specifically schizophrenia. For instance, Wall's book, *The British Anti-Psychiatrists: From Institutional Psychiatry to the Counter-Culture, 1960–1971*, locates the efforts of antipsychiatrists amid the larger British countercultural movements of the 1960s, which similarly advocated for antiauthoritarianism and anti-institutionalism against the backdrop of postwar coalitional British welfarism and bureaucratic Soviet authoritarian communism. While Wall does not extend his argument this far, antipsychiatry in Britain could even be seen as a response to the supposedly totalizing and manipulative function of the fields of psychology and psychoanalysis themselves since, as Daniel Pick has recently been documenting, it was only in the historical crucible of the Cold War that these disciplines became the suspect tools of mass political persuasion, supposedly amenable to the control of furtive "hidden persuaders" bent on "brainwashing" citizens, both at home and abroad.[44] In this context, the clinic emerged as a significant, if contested, space for political action as many antiauthoritarian Marxists, communists, and Leftists sought to reclaim the political promise of collectivism, both psychically and socially conceived.

What Main shared with these radical and avowedly Leftist experiments in commune-based psychoanalytic practice was a willingness to affirm the role social and institutional structures played in the genesis of seemingly individual maladies. Not only did he insist on the pernicious effects of hospital conscription and dispossession, thus affiliating with many of the anti-institutional critiques du jour. But, by imagining the therapeutic community as itself an impactful force in patient well-being, he also made communalism central to Cassel's psychopolitical mission, implicitly rejecting the individualism (post-Freudian Anglophone) psychoanalysis is often charged with perpetuating. For Main, mental illness was best understood as both socially caused and socially cured. His work at Cassel was thus his engagement with a mode of social revision and reform.

There were, however, significant differences between these more radical, explicitly anti-Oedipal Marxist commune-clinics and Main's own aspirations at Cassel. To begin with, the clinics developed by antipsychiatrists, institutional psychotherapists, and their ilk were intentional communities whose residential component was an indispensable part of what Robcis has deliberately characterized as the "permanent revolution" they were trying to affect.[45] They were constructed as durable and deliberate alternatives to the failures of the two dominant political economies of the day. Main, in contrast, approached Cassel as a principally rehabilitative facility where his final aspiration was always the swift reintegration of the patient into British civil society. He was less concerned with transforming the British social order as it currently existed than with helping his fellow citizens be better adjusted to and productive within it—a rather unequivocal example of biopolitical psychiatric management in the service of nationalistic capitalist expansion. Main even developed his own idiosyncratic term for this quality, referring often in his case studies to a patient's potential "disposability"—that is, their likelihood of being successfully discharged from the hospital and reintegrated into society. Indeed, "disposability" was a key criterion for Main's determination about whether to even recommend a patient for hospital admission. For instance, in the case of a forty-six-year-old woman who sought admission to Cassel for many neurotic bodily symptoms that her GP was unsuccessful in treating, Main initially denied her entry because "it was ominously plain that, once admitted, there would be considerable problems of disposal."[46] It was only after her brother guaranteed her a place in his own home after the treatment concluded that Main agreed to admit her. As he bluntly stated, inpatient therapeutic communities "should not be countenanced as a sound method of living, nor as an unremarkable way of life."[47] The purpose of Cassel was thus not to construct a revolution—permanent or otherwise—in patients' everyday structures of living and feeling through long-term, commune-based residential experience; it was, rather, to use select models of collectivization in the service of patient "disposal"—a nomenclature that, to borrow Main's stylization, "ominously" forecasts British social democracy's necropolitical proclivity to dehumanize and discard life at the margins.

While this difference in residential philosophy might seem insignificant at first, it indicates a much deeper political divide between Cassel and its Leftist cousins, a divide that can be traced back to the very origins of the therapeutic community movement. As is well known within therapeutic community history, Cassel and other therapeutic communities like it originated from a form of psychosocial British military experimentation known as the Northfield Experiments, which took place at Northfield Military Hospital (previously Hollymoor Hospital) in Birmingham from 1942 to 1945.[48] Famously, the so-called First Northfield Experiment was conducted over six weeks by the British psychoanalyst Wilfred Bion and his former training analyst, John Rickman. After being put in charge of a rehabilitative facility for discharged soldiers, Bion and Rickman identified similar problems as Main when it came to the dependency fostered by psychiatric institutions. Like Main, they upended the traditional custodial and pharmacological nature of the hospital, trying to encourage group self-reliance and responsibility among the patients. Yet, as a decorated major, Bion's work was unabashedly guided by the exigencies of war and by his own military affiliation. His key objective when transforming the hospital was to rehabilitate soldier-patients for active service as quickly as possible, making the hospital an unmistakable machine of war. Adapting his prior experiments in "leaderless group tests," which he developed for the British military as a more efficient means of officer selection, Bion sought to introduce the dynamics of military life within Northfield, believing that such structure would revive the group morale and esprit de corps.[49] As Bion put it in the 1943 article he and Rickman published about their experience:

> I became convinced that what was required was the sort of discipline achieved in a theatre of war by an experienced officer in command of a rather scallywag battalion. . . . [The] task is to produce self-respecting men socially adjusted to the community and therefore willing to accept its responsibilities whether in peace or war.[50]

Making a virtue of necessity, Bion openly expressed his view that the forms of group socialization and community responsibility found in war were consistent not just with military service but with mental health. He thus aimed to replicate these conditions within the ward. To achieve this, he proposed that two things were necessary: an officer and enemy. The enemy was easily supplied by neurosis itself and Bion confidently adopted the role of officer. Over the course of six weeks—with debatable degrees of success—Bion braided national interest with group psychology in an effort to achieve total unit rehabilitation.[51] As Tom Harrison notes in an otherwise worshipful study of the experiment, "This was no libertarian democracy, but an opportunity for them [the patients] to face up to their responsibilities."[52] In Bion's hands, war itself became a form of group therapy.

Accounts differ as to why the experiment was terminated, but following Bion and Rickman's departure Northfield was placed under the directorship of Foulkes, Harold Bridger, and (later) Main, who together implemented a much more psychoanalytically minded interpretation of the hospital.[53] Patients were given control over some elements of hospital organization and function (including a patient-organized social club called "The Hospital Club"); different forms of therapy (including psychoanalysis) were conducted individually and in groups; and patients contributed to the publication of a collective hospital newspaper.[54] Each of the three primary psychologists engaged with a different realm of practical innovation: while Bridger was the catalyst behind "The Hospital Club" and German émigré and Frankfurt School affiliate Foulkes was one of the pioneers of group psychoanalysis, Main became the primary proponent of a hospital-wide "community" approach, which he subsequently branded a "therapeutic community." Because of its explicit commitment to a democratic form of governance and more positive relations with J. R. Rees (the hospital's Tavistock-based administrative oversight), the "Second Northfield Experiment" lasted some eighteen months before the end of the war shuffled priorities and personnel.[55] Through their work together, Foulkes, Bridger, and Main created what is generally agreed to be the first recognizable instance of a therapeutic community in Britain.[56]

To be sure, Cassel was no military hospital, and Main was openly critical of Bion's militaristic approach.[57] But he nevertheless brought many of the practices and lessons learned at Northfield to bear on this new context. As with Northfield, Main designed Cassel with the explicit intention of preparing patients-qua-citizens for their fuller participation in the British democratic social order. For Main, patients were citizens first and foremost and illness was socially relevant because it could be nationally detrimental. As much as Main might have emphasized the social aspects of mental illness, he never departed from his sense that it was ultimately incumbent on the individual to assimilate to preexisting society. In health there was, he assumed, a relatively nonconflictual relationship between self and society—a claim that marked a stark conceptual departure from the bedrock of Freudian conflict theory. Consequently, he understood the role of any psychoanalytic institution (Cassel included) to be the better social adaptation of otherwise maladjusted individuals. The aim of the Cassel was thus "the socialization of neurotic drives, their modification by social demands within a real setting, the ego-strengthening, the increased capacity for sincere and easy social relationships, and the socialization of superego demands, [thereby] provid[ing] the individual with a capacity and a technique for stable life in a real role in the real world."[58]

Echoing some of the rhetorical touchstones of the ego psychologists that preceded him—ego-strengthening, adaptation, reality, stability—Main made clear that the role of the "social" was far from a liberatory, utopian horizon. Rather than communalism and sociality functioning as an aspirational antidote to the individualizing and privatizing protocols of capitalistic (neo)liberalism—as recent work in the humanities and qualitative social sciences has been exploring under the aegis of "the commons"—Main heralded them as the necessary and pragmatic virtues of British civic service, putting an unapologetically utilitarian spin on the clinic's politics. "The daily life of the community must be related to real tasks," advises Main in 1946, ones that are "truly relevant both to the needs and aspirations of the small society of the hospital, and to the larger society in which it is set; there must be no barriers between the hospital and the rest of society; full opportunity must be available for identifying and analyzing the interpersonal barriers that stand in the way of participation in a full community life."[59] Instead of using Cassel to intentionally call into being utopian social and political arrangements not yet in existence, Main modeled many of its practices, structures, and technical innovations on his understanding of postwar British life as it already existed, seeking to reproduce in the hospital as many of the norms of public life as possible. In this way, his comments call attention to the power that Cassel exercised to construct and define what a "real role in the real world" would be. Sociality and community participation were thus, for Main, a normative demand rather than a wish, more akin to the pragmatism of Freud's discontented "civilization" than the utopianism of liberationist communism. Main may have embraced a form of communalism similarly employed by Leftist experiments with commune-clinics, but his political mission at Cassel was a far cry from the radical futures they meant to inaugurate.

"AN AGENT OF THE HOME AND FAMILY":
GENDER, HETERONORMATIVITY,
AND BRITISH SOCIAL DEMOCRACY

Over the course of Main's thirty-year directorship, Cassel became a leading name throughout Britain in the specialized psychosocial treatment of sexual, marital, and family issues, with a particular focus on the mother-child relation. During that time, Main increasingly used the ideological grammar of the heterosexual nuclear family and the domestic home to define his political vision at Cassel. The private domestic home was, for Main, both the ideal "community" environment that Cassel sought to mirror and the naturalized unit of healthy sociality that the hospital tried to buttress and revitalize in the wider social sphere. As Britain's Cold War society fervently tried to shore up these cultural forms as the safeguard of capitalistic stability at home, Main sutured heteronormative "family values" into the otherwise unconventional communalism at Cassel. In this way, heteronormativity became the condition of possibility for the particular prosocial approach to the clinic that he devised.

Main incorporated these values both practically and ideologically, intentionally modeling Cassel's everyday operations off of the template provided by the private, middle-class, domestic home. While other therapeutic communities like Jones's democratic therapeutic community or Cooper's Villa 21 prioritized egalitarianism, direct democracy, and self-determination as the basis of their practices of communal living, Main instead turned to the domestic sphere, with its vast tallies of uncompensated reproductive labor, its patriarchal gendered hierarchies, and its dimorphic sexual norms, as his template at Cassel. As I have already mentioned, patients planned collective menus, cooked meals, balanced budgets, organized crafts, cleaned rooms, washed laundry, welcomed new patients, cared for children, and darned socks.[60] Reputed therapeutic advantages aside, this arrangement had decided financial benefits since it allowed the state-funded hospital to dramatically reduce its staff, sometimes by more than half, as it capitalized on the naturalization of reproductive labor by transforming waged institutional care work into unwaged pseudo-housework.[61] Indeed, there was a clear gendered ideology at stake in the selection of these particular tasks given that—even before the outpatient marital unit opened—Cassel catered to a high percentage of female patients. Over two-thirds of the inpatients at the hospital were women, and most were between the ages of twenty-one and thirty-five.[62] Many were mothers whose children were admitted alongside them.[63] While Main notes that "male patients by now were accustomed to seek work outside hospital," he states that the everyday household chores orchestrated by each firm were important because they "helped to give dignity and purpose to the domestic skills of the women."[64] "In this culture," Main adds, "it is commonplace for baby-care to take its place among the other domestic activities of patients who help each other to cook or wash dishes, make beds, darn socks, sew curtains, decorate rooms, shop for hospital groceries, plan hospital menus, etc."[65] According to Main, these tasks were not just practical necessities of community functioning; patients' willingness and ability to carry out the chores of daily domesticity were strong indicators of overall mental well-being. While many feminists, both now and in the 1960s, would likely have no objection to the valuing and collectivization of otherwise invisible and individualized reproductive labor—this, after all, was the lead up to the 1972 International Wages for Housework Campaign, begun originally in Manchester and London—Main's suggestion that women's willingness and eagerness to accomplish such tasks was an index of mental well-being was undoubtedly more controversial. During his time at Cassel, he made unremunerated "women's work" and the reification of the classed and gendered private sphere/public sphere split central to the hospital's social and political mission.

This gendered itinerary was not subtle, and it pervaded everything from patient diagnoses to staffing arrangements. In stark contrast to the anti-Oedipal antiauthoritarianism that was the prevailing post-war Left ideology, Main insisted on the importance of retaining select authority figures at Cassel. He himself remained the sole director of the hospital for three decades and developed a reputation as a (sometimes polarizing) charismatic leader. Firm staffing arrangements were similarly paternalistic, with pairs created between psychotherapeutic consultants (typically male) and matron nurses (typically female). Caldwell explains, "The hospital [was based] on the model of the family, of two parents with related but different functions, symbolically and actually, and a division of labour into somewhat transparently conceived maternal and paternal functions. . . . The tendency to utilise this model as a sort of short hand can still produce a perturbingly straightforward, societally normative account of men and women, of mothers, and of families."[66] Main claimed that such arrangements were a natural structure for both the public and private spheres and that eliminating them entirely would handicap patients' ability to work through negative transferences—a small holdover from Freud's insistence that the analytic situation ought to replicate the frustrating and unequitable

parent/child dynamic. As he records in an illuminating 1958 govern-
mental report on the hospital's five-year performance, "The patients
have offered help with staff problems and have involved each other in
the running of each Firm area in the same way as various members of
a family are involved in the running of a home."[67] Mapping the nuclear
family—with its hierarchical, gendered triangulation of power—onto
the experimental therapeutic community, Main replicated and reinstalled
at Cassel the very conventions of privacy, domesticity, and gendered
family formation that were (as I discuss at greater length in chapter 6)
central to Britain's Cold War capitalistic imaginary.

As time passed, this idea became a more and more literal part of
Cassel's clinical program, as Main sought increasingly not just to mimic
the conditions of heteronormative family life but also to directly incor-
porate them. This trend was first inaugurated in 1948 when a woman
seeking inpatient admission asked to bring her child with her. Gradually,
what began as an individual exception became common practice and
eventually, by 1955, was the rule. "From then on," explains Main, "we
made it a condition of admission that mothers bring their babies and
young children with them."[68] This policy meant that at any given time
there were typically between fifteen to thirty-five children staying with
their mothers in the hospital. In certain circumstances, Main would
even allow the admission of entire families in cases where only one person (typically the mother) was seeking treatment. To accommodate this,
the hospital staff expanded to include a teacher, a pediatrician, and a
child psychoanalyst, the first of whom was one of Anna Freud's trainees, Lydia Tischler.[69] Women with children were assigned individual
rooms, which Main describes as "arranged to live in an atmosphere of
domestic comfort and even homely disorder."[70] The setting was intentionally designed "to create conditions which each mother could recog-
nise as similar to those in her own home and which she could use with
a sense of domestic familiarity."[71] At all turns, Main thus tried to make
the hospital "an agent of the home and family," narrowing the scope of
Cassel's experimental "community" to the privatized domestic sphere.
As Main himself puts it, "It is remarkable how many mothers, who in
a more orthodox hospital context would be very ill, passive and dependent, are able to carry on fairly actively, supported by each other and by
their psychotherapy. The hospital tries to possess neither mother nor

child, but to offer independence and to provide support only when it is necessary, to be, in other words, the agent of the home and family rather than to replace these as the centre of the patient's life."[72]

From one angle, Main's embrace of these inclusions was part of a wider revision to hospital admission practice, such as that helmed by Thesi Bergmann, Anna Freud, Dorothy Burlingham, René Spitz, John Bowlby, and others who highlighted the unnecessary distress among hospitalized children separated from their primary caretakers. Before the interventions of these postwar analysts, hospitalized or institutionalized children were treated wholly physiologically, without consideration of the emotional distress such processes and procedures might induce. Their anguish was captured vividly by the British psychoanalyst and affiliate of Bowlby, James Robertson, in his short 1952 documentary *A Two-Year-Old Goes to Hospital*, which publicized for perhaps the first time the trauma experienced by hospitalized children who were given little or no contact with their parents. Now a classic, Robertson's film had a substantial impact on the state revision of numerous institutional policies concerning children's welfare, including visitation allowances throughout the new NHS hospital system. Part of the British welfare state's agenda for public health thus involved the incorporation of psychological and psychoanalytic insights into institutional bureaucracy in an effort to prioritize mental as much as physical health.

However, unlike these analysts, Main argued not that the separation introduced by hospitalization was detrimental to children but rather that it was a "collusion" with the escapism of the mother. He explains, "Thus we became aware of the fact that to hospitalize and separate her from her children was unwittingly to compel a divorce from her job of mothering, and from the children who made it. . . . Increasing experience had led us to suspect that admitting a mother by herself was sometimes to collude with her hostility towards her children, or at least with her wish to be separated from them."[73] In the postwar context where so much concern with national deterioration was attributed to rising divorce rates, Main's rhetorical use of "divorce" here is telling. By arguing that the hospital runs the risk of "compel[ing] a divorce" from the "job of mothering" if it "collude[s]" with a mother's wish to be admitted alone, Main clearly demonstrates his understanding of Cassel's role in safeguarding the future of the nuclear family in Britain. His conviction is that the therapeutic community must exist on a continuum with midcentury gendered and sexual norms lest—as his fear seems to be—women use the institution en masse as an escape route from their duties as wives and mothers. As is the case with much essentializing discourse, the paradox of Main's unconscious logic here is that what is imagined to be most natural must also be institutionally compelled.

Yet Main's rationale was more than mere gender essentialism. As the historian Teri Chettiar has importantly argued, Main believed that the provision of such stable domestic and familial environments was the crucible of the therapeutic community's—and Britain's—larger social democracy.[74] Like many British psychoanalysts of his era, Main interpreted the political field through the lens of individual (and group) psychology, tracing the populism undergirding both democratic and fascist political affiliations back to an Adornian-style analysis of the nuclear family. Amidst soaring divorce rates and seismic shifts in Britain's cultural landscape—including decolonization, the countercultural movement, the rise of the New Left, the feminist movement, antiwar protest, lesbian and gay rights, and the decline of British global hegemony— the reification of the nuclear family became a key way for a bevy of newly politicized psychologists (Winnicott and Bowlby among them) to contribute to the national agenda. As Chettiar aptly puts it, "Postwar British psychiatrists focused upon the healing of fracturing families as a crucial basis for ensuring collective and individual emotional well-being, as well as for curbing the rising incidence of both 'neurotic' illness and crime."[75] Chettiar further explains, "At the Cassel, mental health was equated with mature and socially responsible adulthood, and increasingly over the course of the decade following the war, both were understood to be forged within the emotional environment of the stable nuclear family. Not only was the entire family urged to participate in the therapeutic process, but, in placing mental illness directly within the ambit of the familial environment, Main's psychosocial hospital project sought to remake the family into a healthy emotional space which ensured the cultivation of responsible democratic social actors."[76] Thus, when Main replicated the private nuclear family home within the hospital, he was doing more than simply economizing or fostering an avant-garde experimental community: he was, rather, producing a concrete cultural and political landscape tied to Britain's socialized, but still fundamentally capitalistic, version of democracy. With welfare democracy imagined to be the consequence of the properly managed domestic sphere, Cassel was a tangible example of how clinical innovation constituted a form of political engineering.

In many ways, such thinking was the direct consequence of the world wars since it was only due to the pervasive experience of shell shock that previously dichotomized physiological distinctions between organic health and mental illness broke down. No longer considered to be the result of an organic lesion in certain, predisposed individuals—the so-called disease model—mental illness was, in the postwar period, widely regarded as a functional issue to which any person, when subject to the right environmental stressors, could succumb. As Rhodri Hayward has observed, with old neurological distinctions in psychiatry and psychology between organic illness and health collapsed, this shift "created a situation in which the whole population became the target for therapeutic intervention."[77] According to Michal Shapira, it was during this period that psychoanalysis became a leading political authority, contributing to "new socially democratic forms of welfare," through its distinctive universalization of psychic conflict narratives, which made ordinary citizens' mental health the prerogative of social democracy.[78] There was thus a palpable midcentury uptick in national and state interest in the psychological sciences (broadly construed) as they became newly ordained biopolitical tools for managing the efficacy and resilience of the average subject-qua-citizen.[79]

Yet framing Cassel's political mission only through the coordinates of Britain's local postwar climate—as virtually all historical scholarship on therapeutic communities does—misses the global significance of Main's innovation.[80] As I have been discussing, therapeutic communities' distinctive turn toward a prosocial communalism was part of a larger experimentation with the communal clinic that was inseparable from the global political economic struggle of the Cold War. In this context, much of Britain's (like the United States's) contest for geopolitical capitalistic superiority was affected through a cultural war at home, including what Elaine Tyler May has described as the "domestic containment" provided by the frenzied glorification of the heteronormative nuclear family form.[81] As I discuss more fully in chapter 6, sexual and gender norms were central to the project of national self-fashioning and imperial expansion, becoming vital cultural signifiers and stabilizers in a climate of amplified globalization and heightened political turmoil. Along with middle-class affluence, jingoistic nationalism, capitalist consumerism, and welfare consensus, Cold War Britain was defined by a cultural idealization of the middle-class heterosexual nuclear family in which a welfarist "family wage" ensured clear gendered divisions between public and private spheres, productive and reproductive labor, as a counteraction against the Soviet promotion of women-as-workers. Insofar as Main likewise made the domestic family the irreducible unit of clinical intervention at Cassel, he was thus (re)producing in the clinic the very kinds of gendered domestic arrangements that Britain writ large was fervently trying to shore up as part of its commitment to welfare capitalism and wider nativist British national identity (as discussed previously, in chapter 4). Put another way, Main's clinic was a site through which he could experiment with the (re)production of British cultural values within the hospital itself. For Main and others, the domestic home and nuclear family were the origin of—and the best defenses for—Cold War British social democracy.

To this end, when Main began working with Mr. and Mrs. Adams through Cassel's outpatient marital clinic, he leveraged the heteronormative couple form with an understanding of its larger political significance. As an outpatient clinic, this facility allowed married couples to continue to reside in their own domestic homes while undergoing parallel psychoanalytic and psychodynamic clinical treatments that strove to establish marital complementarity and domestic harmony, bringing the couple to a purportedly more congruous and amicable union. When it came to the Adams's treatment, for instance, Main's conviction—as well as that of the two other analysts involved, Jean Pasmore and Geoffry Orton—was that Mr. Adams's presenting complaint of sexual dysfunction was actually the symptom of a psychodynamic marital disunion. On their initial consultations, Pasmore noted the "bitter, icy atmosphere between them," calling special attention to Mr. Adams's passivity and Mrs. Adams's domineering nature.[82] Not taking Mr. Adams's complaint of erectile dysfunction at face value, the analysts used their own perceptions of each partner's personality as their diagnostic guide. These assessments were at times ruthless and can seem, to the contemporary reader, to be unambiguously based on normative expectations of proper gender roles in a heterosexual marriage. While Pasmore experienced Mr. Adams as a "useless, dim-witted nonentity" and made special and repeated note of his "downing" of work tools and his submissiveness to his father, Orton highlighted Mrs. Adams's strength, aggressiveness, contemptuousness, and "general castrativeness."[83] Main reports after the initial group consultation, "Already we had had a fair but superficial picture of a marital pair—a henpecked man and a masterful woman— and at conference it was decided to see what further exploration would show. Treatment of both partners began a month later."[84]

The treatment that followed lasted roughly six months (including summer holidays) and consisted of no more than sixteen individual once-weekly sessions for both Mr. and Mrs. Adams. These sessions were conducted by Pasmore and Orton respectively, both of whom would then meet each week with Main for supervisory sessions. During these group supervisory sessions, each analyst would report on the progress with their patient and, together, they would endeavor to understand the couple as a unit, bringing to light their (mis)uses of one another in an effort to produce symmetrical sexual complementarity. As with the therapeutic community ethos writ large, the clinical priority was cooperative sociality, both as a method of collaboration among the analysts and as an aspirational ideal for the Adamses. As Main annotates, "This conference, the third element in the treatment of the Adams couple, is our method of marrying two individual treatments so that they can remain focused on the marital interaction."[85] With the conspicuous use of the term "marrying" making Main's sexual agenda plain, the aspirational outcome of this clinical program was unequivocally marital restoration.

In the couple's case—which Main first presented as a lecture some years before publication under the title of "Mutual Projection in a Marriage"—the analytic team agreed that the Adamses were caught up in a process of mutual unconscious projective identification wherein Mr. Adams disavowed the "strong" parts of himself, which he then projected onto his wife, while Mrs. Adams did the same with the "weak" portions of herself.[86] Main's chosen descriptors—"strong" and "weak"— are hardly insignificant since they indicate the centrality of gender for the analysts' perceptions of psychic functioning. Indeed, Mr. Adams's "passivity," especially in the context of sexual roles and positions, was frequently mentioned as a symptomatic component of his larger reluctance to adopt a traditionally masculine attitude. With the treatment focused squarely on the reversal of these traits, each analyst focused their interpretation not on the transferences made between patient and analyst (as might be conventional in a more Freudian analysis) but on those undergirding each patients' relationship to their spouse. For instance, in one session, Mr. Adams began by apologizing to Pasmore for his squeaky shoes. Pasmore, who was herself wearing "disreputable" shoes that day, interpreted that he was splitting off the aggression and criticism that he actually felt for her shoes and projecting it onto her so that he could adopt a position of fearful self-criticism in relation to an imagined assailant.[87] Mr. Adams associated that his wife's shoes were often "disreputable" as well and that his whole family had always been "particular about shoes."[88] From this, he and Pasmore discussed how he often projected the aggressive and "strong" portions of himself onto his wife, while she did the same with the "weak" portions of herself, thus creating a complementary but dissatisfying marital system. "It was impressive," reflects Main, "how he understood how he projected aggressive aspects of himself into his wife and how he then hated and feared them there."[89] Session by session, Mr. and Mrs. Adams each worked to more fully inhabit the previously disavowed portions of themselves and achieve a more ostensibly harmonious union.

Now, it hardly takes a reader steeped in Lacanian critiques of the fantasy of sexual complementarity or the queer antisocial thesis to diagnose the powerful sway of gendered and sexual normativity at work in this scene of compulsory heterosexuality. In no uncertain terms, Main, Pasmore, and Orton promoted conventional dimorphic gender roles as the index of marital—and mental—health. In this regard, they were less the exception than the rule when it came to midcentury Anglophone psychoanalysis, which has retrospectively become infamous for its homophobic contraction of Freud's more radical and nonnormative claims about sexual instincts and object choice. As Dagmar Herzog succinctly puts it, "While British analysts conflicted constantly with one another over theories and methods, all developed negative views on homosexuality."[90] Analysts on both sides of the Atlantic encoded heterosexuality as a form of psychological well-being, helping transform (as Foucault established) previously criminalized behaviours into the newly internalized emplotments of identitarian formations of pathological sexuality and desire. As Herzog explains, psychoanalysis's popularization throughout the Cold War decades was due to how it offered "a mixed, at once secular and religious, 'moral sensibility' that reinforced conservative family values under the sign of 'health,' one that was expressly contemptuous of homosexuality and of any expression of female sexuality outside of marriage."[91] Hence, Cassel was one iteration of the larger psychoanalytic production of midcentury heteronormative sexuality, a testament to its distinctive prosocial reduction of the communal to the conjugal.

Importantly, this production of a normative form of "hetero-sociality," in which the heterosexual Malthusian couple was sanctified and ordained not just because of its supposed naturalism but also because of its social and economic utility, was as much about shaping and ordering public sociality as about disciplining private sexuality. As Foucault influentially argued, the nineteenth and twentieth century production of "species" sexual identity was part and parcel of the middle-class self-management endemic to capitalistic liberal democracy; emergent sexual identities (including heterosexuality) were one aspect of those notorious "techniques for maximizing life" so central to the biopolitical anatomy and flourishing of late capitalism.[92] Thus, heterosexuality—a hegemonic yet by no means necessary sexual form resulting from the inter-section of patriarchal power and patrilineal private property unique to modern Western epistemes—was reinvented throughout the twentieth century as the supposedly naturalized expression of desire and love, an affectional bond that was imagined to be both psychologically and physiologically intuitive and yet also in constant need of instruction, supplementation, and supervision.[93] In the postwar decades especially, heterosexuality and the heteronormative couple form were thereby transmogrified from the basic unit of economic production and consumption in liberal capitalism to a moralized, normative standard of sociality and subjectivity, a romanticized sexual organization of dimorphic gendered complementarity. In this regard, not only did Cassel's marital clinic contribute to the wider Cold War pathologization of gender variance and the production of what the late Christopher Chitty recently termed "sexual hegemony" through its implementation of heterosexual mythologies but it also helped underscore how wider welfare narratives about prosocial behavior, health, and well-being catered to a distinctly heteronormative articulation of public life and sociality since community itself was being defined by and reduced to the couple form. From this, one does not have to travel far to understand the importance of more recent theories of queer negativity, including those developed by Leo Bersani, Tim Dean, and Lee Edelman, whose work collectively identifies the extent to which contemporary normative political constructions of sociality and socio-political well-being are still tethered to and extend explicitly heteronormative fantasies of what Edelman calls "reproductive futurity," binding figurations of the future itself to heterosexual reproductive formations and thus positioning queerness as that which negates and opposes the larger social order.[94] While Edelman, Dean, Bersani, and others were responding to the brew of genocidal "health" programs, panics, and phobias produced by neoliberal 1980s and 1990s U.S. public policy concerning the HIV/Aids epidemic, their wider diagnosis of how saturated twentieth-century social and political discourse is with heteronormative values rings true across the midcentury transatlantic.

Read from this perspective, Cassel's role producing and instituting normative hetero-sociality constitutes one piece of a larger narrative concerning the entanglement of political, economic, and sexual forms in the Cold War. The curation of a highly stylized and discernably "performative" (to borrow Judith Butler's locution) form of sexual identity and relationality was not separable from Cassel's broader rebranding of the commune-clinic as compatible with British capitalism. For his part, Main was not shy about the social and sexual eugenics that he intended. He reported that, after roughly sixty hours of collective work, not only did Mr. Adams's sexual impotence resolve, but both he and his wife adopted more normative gender identities, achieved "mutual loving orgasm," moved to their own private domestic home, and conceived a child.[95] Using almost parodic language, Pasmore even observed after her second to last session with Mr. Adams that "He looked quite different, somehow larger, holding himself straight. He said they had tried 'sexual behaviour' and the last 3 times it had worked. He had had a proper orgasm and was on top of his wife."[96] Meanwhile, Mrs. Adams "regularly assumed in intercourse the position of being underneath" and felt a "new legitimacy of herself and her femininity."[97] In this way,

Main's work laboriously constructing hetero-sociality and heteronormativity at Cassel is almost ironic since, in its frenzied insistence on normality, it actually calls attention to the pastiche at the heart of all gendered and sexual scripts, particularly those which have been most effortfully naturalized. To trope on Butler, Cassel's reengineering of the commune-clinic through the rigid template of hetero-sociality ends up revealing the inauthenticity of gendered and sexual norms themselves, "exposing heterosexuality as an incessant and *panicked* imitation of its own naturalized idealization"—"An imitation," as she has famously written, "for which there is no original."[98]

Through Cassel's marital clinic, the heterosexual couple thus became a living embodiment of Main's clinical effort to actively construct and produce the "normal" domestic home and ostensibly natural gender-differentiated Cold War nuclear family. Indeed, Main even concluded by suggesting, in an extremely sentimentalized bit of speculation, that heterosexual marriage *itself* constituted a form of therapy with benefits that not even the best therapeutic community could produce.

> We have found—and the Adams case illustrates—that the therapist using classical post-Oedipal theory or technique can aid the mental ego, and free the marital relations from collusive mutual projective systems. . . . But the next steps towards cure and development—the acceptance of these feelings by another, and their gratification after long years of postponement—cannot be carried out by the therapist. Only the marital partner can do this and so heal the splits between mental and body ego . . . with nakedness and caresses and soothing and exciting trustworthy body behaviour.[99]

With the heterosexual couple elevated to the status of sanctified therapeutic dyad, this passage is a stark testament to the ways in which the communalism that Main implemented at Cassel was defined by and ultimately made subservient to the heteronormative domestic sphere, which by virtue of being so insistently naturalized constantly betrayed its own constructedness.

Communal clinics, such as that at Cassel, are thus a compelling reminder of the polyvalent political promise afforded by more prosocial forms of psychoanalysis. Without doubt, the sequestered therapeutic "couple" has been the recipient of numerous well-founded critiques—from diagnoses of its subtending fantasy of complementary sexual coupledom to denunciations of its affordance as a privatized, middle-class luxury. From this, the appeal of a form of psychoanalytic collectivization that acknowledges the fundamentally social sphere of subjectivity is compelling. Indeed, in the context of COVID-19 and the brutal forms of isolation and social distancing experienced by many, it is easy to see a similar wave of prosocial political theorizing and acting, visible in everything from the revitalization of discourses around care to the resignification (if not material revaluation) of "essential workers." Similar changes can be seen in the clinical sphere as well, with new calls for community psychoanalysis audible everywhere from training institutes to grassroots organizing.[100] In the contemporary moment, the promise of sociality, collectivity, and communalism have been resurrected in a way perhaps not dissimilar to the climate surrounding Main's postwar work at Cassel.

Yet the lesson Cassel offers by manufacturing so overtly the norms of heterosexuality definitional to the nuclear family is that sociality itself cannot be taken as an a priori good. There is a fantasy of community at work in Main, as in our contemporary moment, where the abstract communalism aspired to is somehow purified of the very social ills that have constituted it to begin with. Would sociality be sociality, we might wonder, without, as Lauren Berlant puts it, the "inconvenience of other people"?[101] There are important differences of scale and harm at stake in seeing these social ills manifest as forms of racism, sexism, heterosexism, and class-based dispossession, as is so clearly evident in Main. But this potentially more cynical approach to "community" allows us to interrogate the political limits of clinical communalism valued *for its own sake*. Significantly, the contemporary community-based psychoanalytic practices undertaken by clinicians such as Neil Altman, Patricia Gherovici, or Francisco González, which, like the Lafargue Clinic or the free clinics of Red Vienna, mean to broaden the frame of the consulting room by using psychoanalysis to combat racism, sexual violence, or economic dispossession, operate off a substantially different constitution of "community" than Main's work in therapeutic communities. Rather than helping a sequestered community adapt to the normative arrangement of the larger neoliberal social order—even if that order exists only at the level of fantasy—these clinicians instead transform clinical practice to try to meet the needs of those most disenfranchised. Of course, one could not say in advance how successful even these initiatives might be; as I discuss more thoroughly in the epilogue, such assessments are dependent on many local considerations, including the work of the clinician(s), the feelings of those they have treated, and various narratives about patient outcomes, which are always highly contestable (and to some extent artificial) constructions. Indeed, what might feel like a clinical success to one patient might, for a different patient with the same analyst, feel like a traumatic failure. Or, differently, these assessments can and do change within one person over time. The point worth recognizing here is that in constituting any "community" we are always and necessarily manifesting both a preexisting political form and imposing a desired political fantasy. The "social" does not preexist our imaginary of it, and this is never more evident than in the clinic. Thus, communal clinics present a unique opportunity to constitute and experiment with sociality differently and more utopically.

• • •

Sociality and various forms of communalism became key virtues for a range of Cold War psychologists, psychiatrists, and psychoanalysts. While some used experimental forms of communalized clinics to fashion Leftist alternatives to both liberal capitalism and authoritarian communism, others (like Main) implemented a form of communalism that ultimately helped reify postwar welfare social democracy. By defining communalism, collectivity, and sociality through the domestic home and the heteronormative family form, Main used therapeutic communities like Cassel to revitalize patients' interest in and attachment to their own homes and return to them as more willing and gratified citizens. Although Main never wavered in his commitment to the importance of therapeutic communities, he always understood their function as secondary and supplementary to the sacrosanct and autonomous domestic home. As he clearly explains in his 1958 report on the Cassel, "The effect on the communal life of patients has been an increased regard for home life as a part of the ordinary culture of the hospital. To some extent the hospital has ceased to be an alternative to home; it has become, rather, a supplement to the home's limited resources for handling neurotic disturbance."[102] Thus, the communalism and sociality that Main prized as the indispensable agents of therapeutic change were only ever a temporary substitute for what he saw as the ideal "communalism" of the private, domestic family home. For Main, therapeutic community was a practical and conceptual means of experimenting with ideals of communalism while ultimately reifying the cultural ideals of Cold War British capitalism.

These values would be especially important for other Cold War psychoanalysts as well. In the next and final chapter, I take up the influential psychoanalytic work of John Bowlby, who has been heavily censured within academic circles for his conservative characterizations of gender, mothering, and infantile "emotional security." Considering Bowlby's transatlantic work on motherhood and emotional security alongside the burgeoning discourse of national security, I explore how he popularized psychoanalytic theorizing for everyday consumption, making the woman's provision of "domestic security" at home coincident with the protection of national security abroad. Through Bowlby, security became the routine vernacular for our interlaced personal psychologies and political priorities.

CHAPTER SIX

Communists, Astronauts, and "Extreme Feminists"

John Bowlby and the Pursuit of (National) Security

On May 11, 1954, D. W. Winnicott wrote a letter to his friend and colleague, John Bowlby, expressing—in his characteristically matter-of-fact way—his concern that Bowlby's work was being put to far more politically nefarious uses than Bowlby had originally intended. "In my contacts," begins Winnicott,

> I come up against quite a lot of people who are worried about the way your work has been used by those who want to close down day nurseries. . . . You will probably agree with me, and I would very much like to be able to say in public discussion that you agree, that there is a deplorable shortage of Day Nurseries accommodation. . . . This is a vital problem and I am afraid that at the moment your having been quoted in connection with the closing down of the Day Nurseries is doing harm to the very valuable tendency of your argument. I wonder if there is anything you can do about this.[1]

Never one to mince words, Winnicott refers to Bowlby's immensely popular 1951 report for the World Health Organization (WHO), *Maternal Care and Mental Health.*[2] After World War II, Bowlby was commissioned to write this report on the state of homeless children's mental health and emotional well-being. In light of the massive urban air raids throughout the war and the consequent exodus of children to the countryside—not to mention the *Kindertransport* that ferried Jewish children from Eastern Europe to England—many children were left either orphaned or permanently separated from their families. Children's institutions such as the Bulldogs Bank Home, the Tavistock Clinic, and the Hampstead Nurseries expanded throughout the United Kingdom to answer this postwar need. Although Bowlby worked in some of these institutions, his appraisal of them was hardly favorable. Bowlby's report announced, in no uncertain terms, that it was *maternal* care that was pivotal to children's mental health. In his opinion, neither state welfare nor group homes were sufficient. Even the best group home was but a meager substitute for the incomparable effects of a mother's love.

Winnicott's letter echoes a much broader concern among British psychoanalysts (and later feminists) that Bowlby's insistence on the irreplaceability of the mother effectively curtailed state-provided social supports designed to help working mothers manage their childcare obligations. While Winnicott could be seen as pawning off an accusation that had also been leveled at him, Bowlby's oeuvre, far more than Winnicott's, testifies to the far-reaching public effects of postwar psychological research, effects that importantly pervaded the ideological work of the West throughout the Cold War. If Winnicott entered the homes of ordinary citizens through the BBC airwaves, Bowlby arrived on bookshelves and coffee tables. As a childcare advice book, *Maternal Care and Mental Health* (republished two years later by Penguin as *Child Care and the Growth of Love*) sold over 450,000 copies in English alone and was translated into six different languages in Bowlby's lifetime. After its initial publication, it became a staple for experts and laypeople alike, inspiring countless self-help parenting books in the decades to come, including the touchstone text in attachment parenting by the American Christian parenting duo, William and Martha Sears. It contributed hugely to the growing conviction that not only was the psychological development of children the most important component for determining their future political predilections but also that it was the white, middle-class woman-as-mother who, through her correct or incorrect forms of care, was responsible for constructing these vulnerable citizens in the making. Through his bestselling books, Bowlby had a transatlantic influence on Cold War maternal practices in the West, especially insofar as they collaborated ideologically with state policy.

While the previous chapters in this book have tackled the political work performed by and in the clinic, in this final chapter I move beyond the ambit of the clinic, focusing rather more broadly on the political climate of the Cold War Anglophone West, the hothouse within which Bowlby's claims about infantile attachment germinated. As scholars like Denise Riley, Nikolas Rose, Sally Alexander, Eli Zaretsky, Michal Shapira, Matt ffytche, Dagmar Herzog, and Daniel Pick have all importantly shown, psychologists and psychoanalysts participated both wittingly and unwittingly in the consolidation of political norms, values, and institutions through the twentieth century.[3] Chronicling the ascent of "security" logics at both individual and national levels, I contend that Bowlby's idealization of emotional security participated in the attempted consolidation and stabilization of the larger, transatlantic Cold War discourse of national security. For Bowlby, not only was the experience of emotional security the keynote virtue of psychological well-being, but its stable provision was the paramount function of the woman-as-mother. As I show, Bowlby's psychological attachment theories helped make gendered and racialized reproductive labor in the metropole vital to the West's ideological project of securing capitalism and liberal democracy against that "specter" of communism haunting not just Europe but the world. By making "domestic security" the purview of women and mothers, Bowlby implicitly nationalized women's unwaged reproductive labors, investing in the mother as the guardian of white middle-class national identity against an increasingly globalized anticolonialist and communist movement. Combining scientific ethology, psychology, and psychoanalysis, Bowlby's theories provided a psychologized, empirical touchstone for fomenting Cold War anxieties about the very real geopolitical (in)security of the Western capitalistic nation-state.

Importantly, part of my contention throughout this chapter is that, through its scientification of psychoanalysis, Bowlby's attachment theory found broad public appeal because it promised an insular, privatized form of psychological security for the individual at the precise moment when that security *could not* be fully guaranteed by and for the Western, capitalist nation-state. In other words, I read the popularity of Bowlby's security-minded attachment theory as a useful index of the actual *instability* of national security discourses during the height of the Cold War and decolonization. Read as a kind of compensatory mechanism, the wide embrace of Bowlby's work registers the fundamental impossibility of the Western nation-state's efforts to fully secure its form of liberal capitalism in a postwar atmosphere defined by globalization, state decolonization, accelerated technological advancement, and anticolonial and Black communist liberation struggle. Thus, while Bowlby's work might seem to be a straightforward recapitulation of Cold War national security discourses that helped to shore up the state, my contention here is that by making the provision of security a project first and foremost of individual psychology, Bowlby's attachment theory lays the groundwork for the advent of neoliberalism and the galvanization of what Inderpal Grewal has called "exceptional citizens," who mobilize individually on behalf of state security.[4] My most ambitious suggestion is thus that, in spite of major economic, social, and political upheavals in the last seventy years, there is actually a line of historical continuity to be tracked from Bowlby's work—one that, when charted, places racialized, gendered, and classed claims about mother-child relationality and emotional security at the center of the (re)production of the contemporary neoliberal security state.

CREATURE COMFORTS: PSYCHOANALYSIS, ETHOLOGY, ATTACHMENT

In *Maternal Care and Mental Health*, Bowlby makes a bold assertion: "Mother-love in infancy and childhood is as important for mental health as are vitamins and proteins for physical health."[5] As Bowlby routinely asserts throughout this text, maternal care is not just one component of infantile mental health; it is its indispensable foundation, the basis upon which health, well-being, and emotional security are built. Relying on a characteristic equation of physical health with emotional well-being, Bowlby, more than any other postwar psychoanalyst, positions the mother's care as the exclusive bulwark against what he would come to describe as "insecure attachments." For Bowlby, a "secure attachment" was the unequivocal proof of both a child's health and a mother's sufficient care.

Bowlby's career as a child psychologist and psychoanalyst spanned the roughly four decades of the Cold War, beginning in the mid-1940s and continuing up until his death in 1990.[6] During this time, he worked to develop, refine, and support his early claims about the determinative importance of maternal care for childhood well-being. In so doing, he crafted a unique theory of childhood psychology known as attachment theory, culling research from psychologists such as Mary Ainsworth and ethologists such as Harry Harlow and Konrad Lorenz. From this material, he proposed that the attachment bonds that children form with their primary caregiver—a figure that Bowlby unflinchingly argued ought to be the biological mother—were determinative of the child's future capacity for secure or insecure relationality. In Bowlby's understanding, children were preprogrammed with the capacity for satisfying and secure relationality and it was the failures of maternal care that sent the child barreling toward a life of insecure attachments. By 1988, with the publication of Bowlby's final major text, *A Secure Base: Parent-Child Attachment and Healthy Human Development*, he had distilled this focus on security even further, suggesting that childhood attachments were the cornerstone of all future secure psychologies, adult and child alike.[7]

Now, in a contemporary context saturated by so-called attachment parenting and by self-help literature dedicated to managing the multiple insecurities incited by postmodernism, neoliberalism, and late-stage capitalism, Bowlby's claims might seem normal, perhaps even natural. Yet syntonic as his position might be with current parenting narratives, in the context of postwar psychoanalysis it constituted a significant departure from professional orthodoxy. His conviction that there was a direct, causal relation between maternal care and secure attachments in childhood broke radically with the Object Relational psychoanalytic approach that was dominant in London.[8] Despite training with Joan Riviere, one of Klein's closest colleagues, Bowlby quickly became a vocal and rather aggressive critic of Object Relations psychoanalysis, which he described as "cultish." He positioned himself as the progenitor of a saner—and, to his mind, scientifically sounder—theory of infant mentality. In a retrospective interview with Karl Figlio and Robert Young in 1986, Bowlby rather condescendingly explained what he considered the deficiencies in previous psychoanalytic research: "Unfortunately some of the leading people in psychoanalysis have had no scientific training. Neither Melanie Klein nor Anna Freud knew the first thing about scientific method. They were totally ignorant."[9] "I've read all the [psychoanalytic] literature but I'm unimpressed. . . . I'm very unimpressed by the way in which the evidence is recorded, or rather isn't recorded."[10]

Throughout his career, Bowlby maintained that psychoanalysis's often quite deliberate refusal of an empirical scientific epistemology jeopardized the validity of its claims. While prior leading lights in British psychoanalysis, such as Melanie Klein, Karen Horney, Wilfred Bion, Michael Balint, Joan Riviere, and Ronald Fairbairn, attributed to human subjectivity a complex interiority pervaded by conflicting instincts and phantasies in which the child's own internal processes and nascent subjectivity uniquely organized its metabolization of what is conventionally called "reality," Bowlby instead proposed that the child is an almost mimetic recorder of the external experiences it encounters throughout its first months and years of life. "My view is this," Bowlby states in the same interview: "Most of what goes on in the internal world is a more or less accurate reflection of what an individual has experienced recently or long ago in the external world. . . . If a child sees his mother as a very loving person, the chances are that his mother is a loving person. If he sees her as a very rejecting person, the chances are she is a very rejecting person."[11] Not one for theories of elaborate unconscious phantasy or metapsychological structure, Bowlby exemplifies here the kind of stark realism that was characteristic of his work by arguing that the child has an unmediated, and likely accurate, perception of external reality, which becomes the basis for its internal self-constitution. His work shifted focus away from the complex psychodynamics of the inner world and instead concentrated on external observable behavior, which he wagered was the most significant and objective metric of subjective experience. But while coeval developmental psychologists such as Urie Bronfenbrenner were progressively expanding their understanding of the multiple interlocking "ecological systems" of influence simultaneously at play in that illimitable externality, Bowlby's quick slide in this passage from "external world" to "mother" demonstrates his committed reduction of the child's world to the mother's care. For Bowlby, the child's internality *was* the mother's external behavior.

Bowlby substantiated these claims about the indispensability of maternal care for childhood psychological well-being by bringing mid-century ethology together with psychoanalysis in order to produce what he believed was a truly scientific psychology.[12] He incorporated the research of leading ethologists like Konrad Lorenz (who studied imprinting in goslings) and Harry Harlow (who performed attachment experiments with rhesus monkeys).[13] For Bowlby, the appeal of their research was that it furnished him with a theory of instinctual attachment that was *not* fundamentally derivative, where attachment was itself a primary instinctual need rather than an ancillary consequence of feeding. For Bowlby, the child—and, by extension, the human being—was a creature preprogrammed with the capacity for satisfying and secure relationality. He explains, "The infant-caregiver relationship involve[es] protection and security regulation. Within this theoretic framework, attachment is conceptualized as an intense and enduring affectional bond that the infant develops with the mother figure, a bond that is biologically rooted in the function of protection from danger."[14] Imbued with the instinctual inclination to find security by seeking attachments—much like goslings imprinting on the first object they encounter—Bowlby imagined that the primary threats to childhood psychological health were not repressed desires or unconscious phantasies but lurking, external "dangers." He referred often to the evolutionary need for attachment security as a protection against "predators." The child's instincts, in other words, were not the problem since they inclined it to find ever-greater degrees of "security" in and through maternal attachments.[15] The fact that, even from the most flexible evolutionary perspective, goslings are a far cry from human infants—importantly, a human being is born and has to contend with, as Hannah Arendt has eloquently put it, "the fact of natality"—did not disrupt his conviction about the instinctual similarity of all animals.[16] He insisted that "despite the introduction of new features, there are all the signs of an evolutionary continuum."[17] The attachment behaviors of the "lower species" were "analogous, and perhaps sometimes even homologous, with much of what concerns us clinically."[18]

In this logic, human infants, as members of a species, all have universal species needs for healthy development; these include things like the mother's continuous physical proximity, the timing and responsiveness of her attention, and her own emotional disposition to the infant.

"It is a characteristic of a mother whose infant will develop securely," writes Bowlby, "that she is continuously monitoring her infant's state and, as and when he signals wanting attention, she registers his signals and acts accordingly."[19] For Bowlby, the mother thus became virtually synonymous with this experience of secure or insecure attachment; her care was the answer to the child's every instinctual need. In this way, "security" moved center stage as a major postwar psychological virtue.

As was clear to many public commentators, psychoanalysts, sociologists, and feminist critics immediately following the publication of Bowlby's report for the WHO, his theory of family life, attachment instincts, and emotional security had serious political implications for the role of women and mothers in society. While psychoanalysts like Klein, Winnicott, Susan Isaacs, and Wilfred Bion all participated in what Shaul Bar-Haim has recently described as the emergent postwar "maternalist" discourse by making the mother the central figure in the child's psychic drama,[20] Bowlby went further by rather plainly stating throughout his work that the mother's role in the child's life was not simply significant but utterly determinative of future emotional health. In one of the most cited passages from the report, Bowlby writes, "The provision of constant attention day and night, seven days a weeks and 365 days in the year, is possible only for a woman who derives profound satisfaction from seeing her child grow from babyhood, through the many phases of childhood, to become an independent man or woman, and knows that it is her care which has made this possible."[21] This is an infamous passage, in large part, because of the way it rather unforgivingly positions the mother as the infant's full-time servant. Not only must the mother be on the clock 24/7, 365 days a year, satisfying the infant's needs and desires, but she must also get "profound satisfaction" from tasks that are both often physically arduous and emotionally attenuating. Any maternal ambivalence, frustration, extradomestic ambition, or nonnormative sexual desire is all too often, within Bowlby's work, rendered symptomatic of pathological psychology or even (as I discuss in the final section of this chapter) political subversion.[22]

By incorporating ethology, Bowlby therefore also (re)defined "Woman" as a being instinctually inclined toward infant care, describing maternal instincts—much like infant attachment behavior—as "preprogrammed." "Parenting behavior, as I see it, has strong biological roots";

"like attachment behavior, [it] is in some degree preprogrammed and therefore ready to develop along certain lines when conditions elicit it."[23] Unlike psychologists such as Robert Stoller, who, in spite of his disreputable work with intersex children, was nevertheless beginning to disarticulate "sex" from "gender" by the 1950s,[24] or even psychoanalysts like Winnicott who (as discussed in chapter 4) presented a more permissive and socially oriented theory of motherhood, Bowlby maintained a fundamentally binary, biological understanding of sex, sexuality, and maternity. In the same interview with Figlio and Young, Bowlby insists that "mothers treat children differently from the way fathers do; they are complementary. There's a big overlap but there's a good deal of difference. The differences make perfectly good biological sense and to suppose that they are interchangeable is probably just wrong."[25] In response to such a biologically essentializing claim, Figlio pushed Bowlby on his argument, agreeing that gender roles are currently differentiated but pointing out that if one accepts the importance of the environment for organizing individual development (as Bowlby was wont to do), then such differentiation would be neither necessary nor universal. But Bowlby remained committed to the importance of an anatomically grounded binary sexual difference, which he maintained served a valuable evolutionary function. If Bowlby was known for having two major gripes with psychoanalysis—the first about its lack of scientism and the second about its relative indifference to the formative effects of environmental experience—then his position on gender roles and reproductive labor reveals how his emphasis on the environment was, if nothing else, highly selective. Indeed, on more than one occasion, he even went so far as to describe the mother as a "slave" to the infant or as "enslaved" by the infant's various charms and guiles.[26] "It is fortunate for their survival that babies are so designed by Nature that they beguile and enslave mothers."[27] While Sigmund Freud rather darkly joked about "His Majesty the Baby," Bowlby extends this political metaphor by configuring the mother-child relation through the historically racialized and sexualized exploitations of slavery. In a world where the male infant is king, there seems always to be an accompanying fantasy that enslaved women perform their reproductive labors for pleasure alone.

Unsurprisingly, Bowlby's work has been the object of more-or-less constant feminist censure, both in his own lifetime and in the decades since his death. Scholars from Margaret Mead to Denise Riley, Ann Oakley to Donna Haraway, and Nancy Chodorow to Élisabeth Badinter have leveled important critiques at his reduction of woman to mother; at his curtailment of the mother to the domestic sphere; at his naturalization of femininity and "maternal instincts"; at his glorification of heterosexual reproduction as tantamount to psychological health; and at his retrenchment of socialized childcare supports.[28] As Marga Viçedo observes in her study of attachment theory in the United States, "Attachment theorists claimed maternal love plays a key role in a child's development. Yet by turning mother love into an evolutionary programmed behavior and emotion, proponents of attachment theory left maternal sentiments outside the realm of moral value and praise."[29] Viçedo rightly points out that one of the consequences of Bowlby's embrace of evolutionary biologism is that it shifted debate about volitional behaviors in any given community away from their ethical merits and effectively repositioned them as a priori, natural, and universal. To this, I would also add that by naturalizing women's reproductive labors, Bowlby's claims not only returned "women's work" to the home but disguised the extent to which such labors counted as work in the first place. In making this observation, I take inspiration from much Marxist-feminist scholarship, which shows how elided, unwaged reproductive labor (performed largely by women) is the condition of possibility for waged, productive labor and is thus a key sphere for the generation of surplus value. Not insignificantly, Marxist-feminist activism, such as the 1970s Wages for Housework movement, directly politicized the domestic sphere as a site of exploitation and domination at the same time as Bowlby insistently naturalized maternal instincts and secure attachments. While his first influential texts were published in the 1950s, his landmark trilogy (*Attachment, Loss,* and *Separation*) came out in 1969, 1972, and 1980, respectively. Arriving just a few years after Betty Friedan's 1963 bestseller, *The Feminine Mystique,*[30] Bowlby's work thus seemed nothing if not a picture-perfect confirmation of the gendering of domestic reproductive labor that midcentury liberal, radical, and Marxist feminists all decried. Read in this context, Bowlby's psychological idealization of maternal domesticity struck an unequivocally political chord.

For his own part, Bowlby was well aware of the vocal feminist resistance to his research. In the same interview with Figlio and Young,

Young explicitly asked Bowlby to speculate on why he thought there was such an "antipathy" between him and feminists.[31] Showing no small measure of his own "antipathy," Bowlby stated that it was only "extreme feminists" who took issue with his work and that these women were the ones who were "very averse to believing that the way they treat their children has an enormous effect on the way those children develop."[32] Doubling down on the stereotype of uncaring feminist mothers, Bowlby added that these "extreme feminists" were not, in fact, the same women lobbying for progressive reforms for children's welfare. Rather, they were calculating careerists who deliberately "put their own careers first and the children third or fourth."[33] In other words, Bowlby presented extreme feminism as emblemizing an either/or logic between women and children rather than positioning it as a progressive (and diverse) set of movements aimed at reconfiguring social and ideological norms injurious to many minoritized and domesticated subjects, children among them. When Young pushed back on Bowlby's reduction of feminism to child-averse careerism, calling it an unfair "caricature" of feminism and pointing out the limitations of traditional gendered childcare arrangements, Bowlby rejoined that he referred only to "extreme feminists" and it was actually these feminists who caricatured *his* position.[34] Verging into the realm of conspiracy, Bowlby had even speculated, nearly two decades earlier, that much of the twentieth-century feminist movement was actually the surreptitious enactment of men, who pushed women out of the house to satisfy a thwarted Oedipal fantasy. "Men are often hell-bent on getting women out of the home," explains Bowlby in response to the largely heterosexual, middle-class feminist critiques of women's domestic confinement, such as Friedan's. "Jealousy of the baby may be one reason. Many are reliving an old sibling rivalry through their wives and children."[35] Employing some stunning kettle logic between these two interviews—feminism is somehow both a campaign organized by cold careerist women and a conceit motivated by men's unresolved unconscious resentments—what Bowlby does make clear through this commentary is that he was no friend to feminism, "extreme" or otherwise. By speaking always on the side of the ostensibly objective needs of the child, Bowlby categorically dismissed the gender politics of the claims he advanced about motherhood.

Because of this palpable political conservativism, many critical theorists have not returned to Bowlby's work since the initial feminist critiques of it. Despite its unflagging popularity in contemporary clinical psychology and, to some extent, even psychoanalysis where influential clinicians like Peter Fonagy have attempted to cull from attachment theory a point of convergence with psychoanalytic theory, there has been little academic scholarship within the humanities or critical social sciences that rereads Bowlby as a valuable resource in the struggle against multiple intersecting forms of white, cis-heteropatriarchal, capitalistic dominance.[36] Yet my own agenda here pursues attachment theory and its effects precisely *because* of the way it sutures white, middle-class women's gendered labor to the domestic sphere and the reproduction of the heterosexual family form. On my reading, a would-be "return" to Bowlby is useful not only because of a transnational political climate where processes of global migration, displacement, and technological distancing have attenuated many forms of attachment but also—and more pertinently—because his psychologies of infantile attachment and maternally provided security starkly articulate a historical shift to the very neoliberal state security logics that have come to dominate contemporary Western state policies and transatlantic nationalist agendas. If, as Grewal argues,[37] the way contemporary state securitization is enacted is through the vigilante mobilization of the private citizen for the production of state security—we might think, for instance, of the post-9/11 injunctive in the United States to surveil family, friends, and neighbors for latent terrorist elements; the unrelenting mimetic refrain in the United Kingdom of "See something, say something" or "see it, say it, sorted"; or even the classic 1950s U.S. Operations Security military billboard from Hanford Site, Nevada (see figure 6.1), which proleptically joins silence to security, making the domestic home both the source of security and the site of greatest risk—then Bowlby's work constitutes an invaluable piece of genealogy that traces the Cold War collaboration between domestic and national security, between psychology and the state. When charted, this genealogy suggests that, in a climate of ascendant neoliberalism, state policy is (as Nikolas Rose has argued)[38] apiece with and lived through psychological knowledge and the production of historically particular subjectivities. In other words, my suggestion here is that Bowlby's promotion of secure attachments—a psychological

FIGURE 6.1 Cold War "OPSEC" billboard from Hanford Site.
Hanford DDRS (N1D0023596).

grammar popular still—was not just parroting a preexisting state discourse. Rather, in shifting the provision of security from the state to
the individual, the language of emotional, interpersonal security actively
contributed to the construction and stabilization of Cold War policies
and priorities about "security" that would only increase in prominence
and significance under consolidated Reagan–Thatcher neoliberalism,
becoming codified as what we now know as the distinct security state.
Through attachment theory, the mother-child couple became a central
figure in the political project of securing the nation, beginning with the
Cold War and continuing through to the contemporary security state.

DOMESTIC SECURITY: MOTHERHOOD
AND THE COLD WAR

Although the Cold War is typically framed as a bipolar conflict between
two national superpowers—the United States and the USSR—promoting
two different political economies—capitalism and communism—it was
at its core a global standoff that engaged most of the world, Britain not
least of all. At the close of World War II, Britain was allied with the
United States in its growing perception that, after the defeat of fascism,
so-called Eastern communism was the major threat to liberal, capitalistic
democracy. Since the United States was armed with the nuclear (and
monetary) capacity to pose the greatest threat to the USSR, Britain was
forced to occupy a more ancillary position as the United States stepped
forward as the most dominant global actor in the second half of the
twentieth century.

Yet Britain remained a key player in the production of Cold War politics, providing, on the one hand, discursive support through its global BBC broadcasts that promoted the capitalist West and, on the other hand, material support through its proxy wars, Commonwealth imperial ties, and worldwide trade connections.[39] Together with decolonization, the Cold War pervaded all aspects of British policymaking in the postwar period and was catalyzed as much by the nation's economic, material interests as by its political anticommunist ideology.[40] As Michael Kandiah argues, the Cold War had a vital role in the construction of the British welfare state and the rise of a coalitional "new conservatism" in the postwar years.[41] Adding nuance to the historical claim that the immediate postwar years found British politics in a broad epistemological consensus, Kandiah explores how the conservative party's support of the welfare state—organized as it was within a strict capitalistic framework—was part of a specifically Cold War electoral strategy to regain and retain power by becoming a populist party organized around basic capitalist values: individual freedom, commerce, private ownership, enterprise, and profit. In order to safeguard the appeal of capitalism at home, this new conservative party simply agreed to extend its benefits to more citizens through a welfare state model—a strategy that arguably paid off given the long-standing Conservative majority between 1951 and 1964.

During these years, national security was a paramount priority and Britain, like the United States, felt acutely that Eastern European, Asian, and Global South communism posed a double threat to the West's global capitalistic expansion and global military peace. "Security," after all, has the dual connotation of freedom from the threat of violence *and* monetary surety, a proof of investment capital. It is thus a combined military and monetary discourse. Linking these forms of material "security," a UK Foreign Office Planning Staff paper from 1959–60 reports in no uncertain terms that "the ultimate aim of any Government in the United Kingdom must always remain the security of these islands from foreign domination and attack, the prosperity of the British people and the protection of our individual freedom and liberty."[42] Britain's national security was thus understood as an intertwining of its military, ideological, and economic agendas—its independence, liberty, and prosperity. While a concern with security has been a part of political discourse going back at least to social contract theorists like Thomas Hobbes, its particular configuration as a preventive economic policy of the modern nation-state emerged in the postwar stalemate between NATO allies and the Communist Bloc.[43] As James Der Derian explains, "As distance, oceans and borders became less of a protective barrier to alien identities, and a new international economy required penetration into other worlds, *national interest* became too weak a semantic guide. We found a stronger one in *national security*."[44] Put another way, only during the Cold War, with its combined military and political-economic crises, did the discourse of "national security" truly find its footing.[45]

It was in this historical shift that Bowlby's work on individual, infantile emotional security emerged and found an audience, on both sides of the Atlantic. Because the threat of a turn from "Cold" to "Hot" war was tantamount not just to vast military casualties but to nuclear species extinction—a situation of "mutually assured destruction"— there were catastrophic stakes attached to any perceived bellicosity. Such intensified unpredictability made the psychological impulses and neuroses of the individual tremendously important for narrating politics since even a rogue scientist could start a nuclear war. This was, after all, the cinematic era of villainous scientists like Dr. Strangelove and Dr. No, where personal mania met political mayhem.

Answering this anxiety, psychologists like Bowlby soldered their developing theories of the mind to geopolitical concerns. For Bowlby, social and political events—including war, fascism, democracy, communism, and revolution—were best understood through individual psychological idioms such as aggression or affection. Indeed, some of Bowlby's first psychological publications—written before he would come to unify his work under the moniker attachment theory—addressed the psychic status of world events, including his coauthored book *Personal Aggressiveness and War* in 1939 and his 1946 article "Psychology and Democracy."[46] Explicitly citing the proliferation of nuclear weapons as the justification for a more rigorous scientific psychology, Bowlby argues in 1946 that "with the advent of the atomic bomb . . . the hope for the future lies in a far more profound understanding of the nature of the emotional forces involved and the development of scientific social techniques for modifying them."[47] Writing in the immediate wake of the evisceration of Hiroshima and Nagasaki, Bowlby makes the ultimate claim for the importance of psychology by suggesting that the survival of the human species would only be possible with the help of more sophisticated individual psychological knowledge and disciplinary apparatuses. The best way to understand and regulate technological advancements and weapons of mass destruction was not through newly formed world councils and regulatory bodies (like the United Nations or NATO, formed in 1945 and 1949, respectively); nor was it through international treaties (like 1970's Treaty on the Non-Proliferation of Nuclear Weapons); rather, Bowlby posits that a deeper understanding of the dynamics of individual psychology, and more technologized approaches to "modifying them," was the best avenue for safeguarding humanity. For a contemporary reader, this argument is far from unfamiliar seeing as how our own political present, this "Second Cold War," has been saturated with multiple news stories about Donald Trump's possible narcissistic disorders and Vladimir Putin's megalomania. In these narratives, the best way to understand—and ensure—national security is through a psychologization of the individual citizen or politician.

Not insignificantly, these postwar psychological and psychoanalytic narratives gave special pride of place to the mother, who was imagined as both the fundamental guarantor of political security and its biggest potential threat. For better and for worse, the middle-class postwar mother emerged as the most important subject of political psychology, the most powerful agent of national security or insecurity. In her capacity to reproduce the next generation of citizens and raise them as psychologically healthy—that is, democratic—subjectivities, motherhood accrued a tremendous political agency and responsibility in the Cold War West. As I noted in chapter 4, Winnicott once described the mother's reproductive labor in the domestic sphere as "that factory for the democratic tendency," a striking catchphrase that transforms women's waged wartime factory work into postwar, unwaged reproductive labor, all the while reimagining the private domestic home as the origin of politics. According to Elaine Tyler May's groundbreaking study of Cold War family life, this ideology of domesticity was a central way that foreign policies of national security established themselves.[48] As the Cold War escalated, the mother ensured "domestic security" on all fronts.

Thus, when Bowlby described maternal care as central to the child's psychological health, he was contributing to a broader Cold War narrative in which mother-child relationality was the crucible of political subjectivity and futurity. The quality of mothering a child received had, for Bowlby, a direct and proportional effect on the kind of political subject the child would become. According to one of his biographers, Suzan van Dijken, "Bowlby realized that his research had a social impact. He saw the problem of deprived children as a social problem; deprived children could become delinquent or become a burden to society in another way. . . . By breaking this vicious circle, Bowlby believed society would become better."[49] Although what counts as a "better" society was the very cynosure of Cold War capitalist versus communist debate, van Dijken's remarks nonetheless speak to the sociopolitical character and aim of Bowlby's interventions. While his work certainly naturalized women's reproductive labor, returned women to the domestic sphere, and tethered femininity to maternity, in doing so it did not reify a tidy split between public and private, political and apolitical. Rather it extended a politicization of the mother as engineer of (national) security—and of the clinical psychoanalyst as its necessary adviser. If a child's mind mirrored the care it received, then it only followed for Bowlby that secure mothering in secure homes would produce secure children and a secure nation. In the nuclear age, the stable, nuclear family ensconced in the domestic home was an integral part of Britain's Cold War security endeavor. In this way, Bowlby's social psychology worked to justify women's relegation to the home by rendering her role there coextensive with the protection and reproduction of state ideology. Far from passive domestic props, mothers operating exclusively within the domestic sphere were represented as responsible for the welfare of a whole community, of a nation, of a world. By fostering secure attachments in her children, the mother could construct productive, liberal, capitalistic citizen-subjects for the future. The child was that template for a potentially secure geopolitical horizon, that fantasized figuration of reproductive futurity, that answer to pronatalist national anxieties, that liberal citizen-in-the-making.[50]

As one might expect, though, such templates of socially sanctioned motherhood were only truly available to a select group of women, namely those who were white, heterosexual, and middle class. Not only did Bowlby's claims about the normality and health of what was essentially a single-income home supported by the postwar husband's "family wage" implicitly exclude the working class, but insofar as the 1960s, especially, saw the influx of many Black Afro-Caribbean women who immigrated to England precisely to fill the "pink collar" service-sector jobs from which white women were discouraged, Bowlby's normative templates also implicitly excluded many recent Black immigrants.[51] His hierarchical valuation of different psychological qualities thus echoed this wider sexual, classed, and raced stratification: while characteristics like alliance, attachment, resilience, cooperation, and security were prized as the epitome of mental health, traits like antisociality, delinquency, emotional insularity, and helplessness were indicative of disordered attachment, which he linked with illegal or socially stigmatized practices, such as crime, prostitution, and single motherhood.[52] At a time when social discourses of antisociality and delinquency functioned as dog whistle messages about working-class white youth and when reportage about crime and cultural insularity were used rhetorically to justify the reputed "failure" of racial integration and multiculturalism following the Windrush generation, Bowlby's psychological values recapitulate two key midcentury moral panic discourses. In Bowlby's work, there was a highly permeable line between social mores and the so-called natural order.

Moreover, given the midcentury British pathologization of Black immigrant motherhood (which I discussed in chapter 4) and the prior colonial critiques of Caribbean family structure (such as the major social hygiene program in Jamaica known as the Mass Marriage Movement in 1944–45), it is hardly a stretch to hear the racialized chastisement of unwed mothers at play in Bowlby's discussion of single mothers and "illegitimate" children in the United States: "Studies carried out in America make clear . . . that the girl who has a socially unacceptable illegitimate baby often comes from an unsatisfactory family background and has developed a neurotic character, the illegitimate baby being born in the nature of a symptom of her neurosis. . . . With many girls[,] becoming an unmarried mother is neurotic and not just accidental. In other cases the girls are psychopathic or defective."[53] In this passage, Bowlby enters into a long history of criminology going back to Cesare Lombroso's *La Donna Delinquente: La Prostituta e la Donna Normale* (translated as *Criminal Woman*), which represents racialized and working-class women, especially, as threats to the social order best contained by the discourses of either criminality or psychopathology. Tying single motherhood to neurosis, psychopathy, moral defect—and, at one point, insanity and promiscuity—Bowlby suggests that the institution of heterosexual marriage and the nuclear family, themselves constructs of modern European capitalist whiteness, are inseparable from the normative standards of mental health. This was a surmise similarly arrived at by the Moynihan Report in 1965, which castigated Black American mothers along extremely similar lines. Even leaving aside the fact that Bowlby, in his WHO report, is disproportionately and inexplicably interested in discussing prostitutes and the potentially deleterious effects they have on children, his work quite plainly contributes to an established social hygiene discourse by regulating maternal comportment.

To this, it is worth remembering that Bowlby's early development of attachment theory in the 1950s and early 1960s relied on and was developed through colonial psychological research conducted outside of the British metropole, specifically in colonial British East Africa. As Bowlby was beginning work on maternal attachment, before he officially codified attachment theory, his research assistant at the Tavistock, Mary Ainsworth (née Salter), moved to the then-British Protectorate of Uganda to carry out mother-child interviews and observations in various villages near Kampala in 1954. Working with twenty-six local mothers and their twenty-eight children, Ainsworth specifically observed the weaning rituals of the mother-child dyads, which involved the child's physical separation from the mother, and conducted interviews with the mothers via a translator. Aside from Bowlby's observations of the psychological damage produced by the many separated and orphaned children during World War II and his reliance on the ethological animal research carried out by Lorenz and Harlow, Ainsworth's work in Uganda was the first real empirical trial of Bowlby's theories with human subjects. Her explicit aim in carrying out this research was to lend support to Bowlby's speculations about the universality of the negative psychological effects of maternal deprivation and attachment, shoring him up against his many detractors.[54] Combining her observations of mother-child pairs in 1950s Uganda with the methodologically similar—but culturally quite different—ones she carried out later in 1960s Baltimore, Maryland, Ainsworth eventually published her research in 1967 as *Infancy in Uganda: Infant Care and the Growth of Love*—a text that, despite the diversity of evidence recorded (such as polygamous households and community caretaking arrangements), affirmed Bowlby's claims about the indispensability of monotropic attachment.[55] Ainsworth's work made sense of the vast cultural differences between her research subjects by arguing that while infantile attachment needs are universal, it was ultimately later Ugandan weaning practices that explained the ostensibly unique African character—a style of distinctly colonial psychological reasoning that Erik Linstrum describes as "reviving an old idea of colonial psychology: the theory of traumatic weaning" to account for difference.[56] This research in Uganda provided the basis of the now well-known "strange situation" test and the tripart personality typology of attachment—"secure," "anxious-avoidant," and "anxious-resistant"—which would become Bowlby's most famous intellectual legacy.[57]

The fact that, via Ainsworth, the research Bowlby relied on to substantiate his claims was carried out in colonial East Africa is hardly incidental to the style of thought in which he engaged. Indeed, in turning to Africa as a testing ground for ideas derived from the ethological study of animals, Bowlby's work implicitly traded on gendered, colonial imaginaries of "primitivity" that represented the non-Western world and its inhabitations less contorted by the developments of "civilization" consequently closer to nature. The glorification of the nonwhite "primitive" woman-as-mother is given undeniable visual purchase in the striking selection of cover art for volume 1 of his Attachment and Loss trilogy, which features a bare-breasted Amazonian woman staring directly into the camera against a shrubby, outdoor background while holding a toddler on her hip. Over the photograph is the title, *Attachment*, which both names the text and mediates the viewer's encounter with the image, organizing the viewer's interpretation of the image's content and composition. Contextualized as the first installment of the series, this cover is made more noteworthy by the fact that the two subsequent texts—*Separation* and *Loss*—although designed in exactly the same style, both feature cover photos of singular white Western children in indoor, domestic spaces looking despondent and forlorn. Although not remarked upon in the scholarship on Bowlby, such reliance on the visual and anecdotal currency of the non-European woman as the exemplar of secure, natural attachment extends the racial ideology of Britain's colonial empire in which the "primitive" was idealized for her supposed naturalness and simultaneously subjugated for this very same reason since, within this logic, the colonized lack a civilizing culture. As Wendy Webster notes, "The emphasis on the natural in literature on motherhood sometimes meant that the 'primitive woman' was offered as a role model to teach the 'civilized' woman how to behave and to revert to the natural state from which civilization had distracted her."[58] While such comments might seem to reverse the racial hierarchy on which the postwar British state still depended by suggesting to white, middle-class British women that their absence from the home was unnatural and the potential cause of community decline, they actually index how nostalgic racial narratives of a declining colonial order helped organize metropolitan white women's ideological investment in motherhood during the Cold War as a project of national securitization.

This small example from Bowlby's work shows how important race and the effects of decolonization were for both the United Kingdom's and the United States's construction and regulation of their national identity during the Cold War. This, after all, was the context in the United States within which the fantasied link between Jewishness and communism sealed the fate of the Rosenbergs and where centuries of state-sanctioned anti-Blackness found the cover necessary to criminalize Angela Davis, Assata Shakur, and Huey P. Newton while orchestrating the covert assassinations of Fred Hampton and Malcolm X. Then FBI director, J. Edgar Hoover, even described the Black Panther Party as "the greatest threat to the internal security of the country"—a comment that directly soldered Blackness to subversive political activity—and organized extensive counterintelligence operations that mirrored the Soviet Union's own authoritarian surveillance and policing strategies to monitor and disrupt the group.[59] Internationally, this was also the context of the Suez Canal Crisis (1956), the Bay of Pigs Invasion (1961), and the Cuban Missile Crisis (1962), three keynote events, all but synonymous with the Cold War, that engaged the United Kingdom and the United States in a standoff with communist-aligned former European colonies (Egypt and Cuba) whose anticolonial agendas insisted on making plain the link between capitalism and imperialism. Add to this the many international proxy wars catalyzed, funded, or otherwise supported by the leading Cold War powers; the consolidation of the

Anglophone West's global, neocolonial capitalist dominance through the neoliberal financial compliance leveraged by Bretton Woods's predatory structural adjustment programs; and both communist and capitalist leaders' scramble to curry favor with newly liberated nations in Africa, South Asia, and the Caribbean, and the Cold War can be seen to play out its global political economic battle through the management of insecure racial categories at home and the reorganization of (post) colonial legacies abroad.

Thus, Bowlby's theories served to govern what Rose has called the "private self" at home, through the mother, because of mounting political anxiety about the intertwined expansion of communism and anticolonialism abroad.[60] Readers can see something of this logical extension in Bowlby's *Maternal Care and Mental Health*, where he explains the public consequences of private life.

> The proper care of children deprived of a normal home life can now be seen to be not merely an act of common humanity, but to be essential for the mental and social welfare of a community. For, when their care is neglected, as happens in every country in the Western world today, they grow up to reproduce themselves. Deprived children, whether in their own homes of out of them, are a source of social infection as real and serious as are carriers of diphtheria and typhoid. And just as preventative measures have reduced these diseases to negligible proportions, so can determined action greatly reduce the number of deprived children in our midst and the growth of adults liable to produce more of them.[61]

Mobilizing the language of "social infection" in a way that extends the social hygiene discourses so popular before the war, Bowlby positions bad mothering and insufficient domesticity as an epidemic that jeopardizes broader social and national welfare. By listing diphtheria and typhoid as analogous dangers—two diseases associated principally with poor sanitation—his description of "normal home life" and the consequences of its absence traffics in a common enough imputation of the urban working class, such as that found a century earlier in Edwin Chadwick's 1842 report on the sanitary conditions of the London working class or Thomas Mayhew's 1851 report on the urban poor. As with these reports, Bowlby tied the fate of the broader British nation to those most deprived. But where Chadwick and Mayhew found filth, squalor, overcrowding, and poverty in Britain's metropole, Bowlby found emotional sterility and affective deprivation. The danger—and this is where a characteristically Cold War anxiety becomes visible—is that those who he alternately describes as "insecure," "deprived," "delinquent," or "antisocial" will, without proper professional intervention, cyclically "reproduce" themselves, thereby catalyzing an uncontrollable corruption of the West from within. As Bowlby explains a few pages earlier, "neglected children grow up to become neglectful parents," a potential spiral of moral delinquency that, given the direct link between private psychology and public political affiliation, could rupture the West's insular Cold War "containment" strategy.[62]

In this context, women's secure location within the domestic sphere was a crucial way that Britain constructed its national identity through its contrast with the Soviet Union (and many other communist nations, for that matter), which specifically glorified the mother *as* worker.[63] Like many others during these postwar years, Bowlby's support of a highly particularized maternal domestic ideal was at least in part a defense against a communist lifestyle by and through the reification of specific gendered practices. In other words, national identity was being produced and maintained by the gendering of labor, or more accurately by the elision of Western women's reproductive labor *as labor*. This implicit wedding of the private to the public, of the domestic to the foreign, of the scientific to the political, is perhaps nowhere clearer than in Bowlby's description of the ideal, healthy mother-child relationship:

> In healthy development it is towards [the mother] that each of the [infant's] several responses becomes directed, much as each of the subjects of the realm comes to direct his loyalty towards the Queen; and it is in relation to the mother that the several responses become integrated into the complex behavior which I have termed 'attachment behavior', much as it is in relation to the Sovereign that the components of our constitution become integrated into a working whole.[64]

In this fascinating passage, Bowlby articulates the psychological attachment behavior of the infant through the political organization of

Britain's monarchy in 1958. As goes the Queen-mother and her national subjects, so goes the individual mother and her infant. Such an analogy has a double effect. In the first instance, this rhetorical flourish politicizes maternal care, putting domestic maternity on the "right" side of Cold War politics. But, at the same time, by using the vocabulary of psychological health to talk about the organization of political power and government, it simultaneously naturalizes the Commonwealth of Nations and makes clear that UK liberal democracy is tantamount to psychological well-being. Read in the context of decolonization, where so many regional anticolonialist struggles were supported both ideologically and materially by Leninist, anti-imperialist communism, Bowlby's genuflection to the Queen even codes as an implicit reproach of colonial liberation struggles, such as Egypt's revolution and the Suez Canal crisis, which sealed the UK's fate as an empire in decline just a few years before. In his narration of the child's attachments, Bowlby effectively makes a case for how attachment to the mother—the Queen-mother—is the naturalized state of security both for the individual child and for the entire (post)colonial Commonwealth.

Yet if the white, heterosexual, middle-class mother was the potential producer and protector of security, then she was also, by virtue of this power, its biggest potential threat. With two announced "motherlands" attempting to secure and expand their respective political economies in part through contrasted domestic ideologies, the Cold War mother was an intensely overdetermined figure. In addition to contracting the socially sanctioned templates for women's role in society—and making them available only to a select group of white, heterosexual, middle-class women allied with the state's ideological agenda—the Cold War fixation on the near-omnipotent power of the mother had a flip side that only too easily reversed into her demonization. As can be seen in anticommunist Cold War Hollywood cinema like *My Son John* (1952) or, more explicitly, *The Manchurian Candidate* (1962), the mother as a representative of the domestic family was the cornerstone upon which political affiliation rested, a powerful but for this reason dangerous and suspect entity. Indeed, it might not even be too much to say that in Bowlby's articulation of the mother as all-powerful agent and the child as passive tabula rasa there is a clear echo of Cold War anxieties about propaganda and brainwashing, where the imagined psychological malleability of the citizen-qua-subject becomes one of the biggest points of vulnerability in the state's attempt to ensure security.[65] Since they had such unmediated access to inchoate subjectivities, mothers were imbued with the power to shape security—but therefore also to subvert it. If securely attached citizens were the mark of a mother's success, then insecure, delinquent, or even subversive individuals were the unequivocal proof of a broken home. This line of thought not only justified co-opting many psychologists and psychoanalysts into direct state service, a collaboration that Knuth Müller has explored with regard to the American CIA's experimental consort with psychoanalysts and which Pick is currently exploring in his Wellcome-funded "Hidden Persuaders" project.[66] Further, they justified the entry of psychologically minded surveillance techniques into the home, where professionals and private citizens alike were encouraged to vigilantly guard against the latent communist within.

Although Bowlby remained staunchly committed to an understanding of his work as objective—an ideological investment in a masculinist, European notion of scientific objectivity likely appealing because it distinguished him from the recent (and typically violent) experiments in politicized psychology found in both German National Socialism[67] and Soviet Communism[68]—he nevertheless also contributed to this paranoia about communist infiltration through his research. Carefully reversing the accusations of political conservativism regularly leveled at him, Bowlby read any politically minded criticism of his work as not only scientifically unsound but also tacitly motivated by what he called "vested interests."

> Whenever I hear the issue of maternal deprivation being discussed, I find two groups with a vested interest in shooting down the theory. The Communists are one, for the obvious reason that they need their women at work and thus their children must be cared for by others. The professional women are the second group. They have, in fact, neglected their families. But it's the last thing they want to admit.[69]

At the height of the Cold War, the proximity Bowlby establishes between "the communists" and "professional women" is extremely effective: by placing "professional women" so close to the much-maligned communists, Bowlby effectively discredits feminist claims to gender parity and women's role in public life. Such claims, he suggests, are just the fodder of dangerous political radicals. In fact, at a time when Britain was actively looking for "Red" infiltration within the motherland, such rhetoric even implies that *all* professional women might be latent communists.

But, at the same time, by pairing communists and professional women together, Bowlby implicitly reminds the reader how important the domestic sphere is for the production of foreign policy. With Senator McCarthy's arrests and interrogations on transatlantic airwaves and television screens, paranoia about communism constellated, as I have been suggesting, around gender nonconformity and homosexuality, but also around Jewishness, Blackness, and Hispanicity; the working class and left-leaning intellectualism; and Asian and Global South national identity. Together, these aspects of personal identity and the private sphere functioned as the variegated political symptoms of the communist sympathizer. Thus, Bowlby's link between communists and professional women slyly shades working women "Red," effectively promoting maternal domesticity as the proof of Cold War allegiance. Subtle claims like this participated in a cultural rhetoric that aligned the domestic sphere with security, depicting women's domesticity as both the crucible of their children's psychological normality *and* the evidence of their own Western capitalist allegiance. To borrow May's analytic, this was the political ethos of "containment," which trafficked in continuities between the home and the homeland, domestic security and foreign relations, producing the white, middle-class nuclear family as "the best bulwark against the dangers of the cold war."[70] What Bowlby makes clear here is that mothering—and mothering well—is a display of patriotism for the British motherland.

Exceptional as such language might seem, this is far from the only time that Bowlby uses the political climate of the Cold War to help him substantiate his psychological arguments. In a lecture in the United States in 1970, Bowlby continues to elaborate on how he defines the psychological normality born of responsible mothering by giving a very noteworthy example of those he sees as paragons of attachment security.

> Astronauts rank high as self-reliant men capable of living and working effectively in conditions of great potential danger and stress. . . . The performance of the crew of Apollo 13, which met

with a mishap *en route* to the moon, is testimony to their capacity in this respect. Not only did they maintain their own efficiency in conditions of great danger but they continued to cooperate trustingly and efficiently with their companions at the base on earth.

Turning to their life histories we find that these men grew up in relatively small well-organized communities, with considerable family solidarity and strong identification with the father. . . . During childhood, they said, they had felt with mother above everything else secure.[71]

With Apollo 13's technological crisis fresh in the minds and hearts of millions of Americans, Bowlby praises U.S. astronauts not just for their bravery, patriotism, and skill—that is, not just for their willingness to advance the West's economic and ideological agenda in the Cold War—but interestingly for their psychological stability and emotional maturity. He traces their success as astronauts back to their childhood. It should perhaps come as no surprise that, for Cold War psychologists, national heroes also become psychological exemplars. The fact that Bowlby's discussion of emotional security in this passage revolves around a group of men in a profession that advanced the West's international standing in a "space race" that emblemized the Cold War is hardly insignificant. By making their willingness to engage in physical exploration, and their comfort doing so, central to its account of normative psychological health and well-being, attachment theory can be seen to naturalize historical narratives of Western imperial exploration (and, implicitly, conquest) and extend them into present desires for space travel—that new frontier. Unlike those suspect "professional women," the professional success of the male astronauts on Apollo 13 is testament to their dual psychological *and* political integrity. And it was, Bowlby notes, these men's experiences of maternal security that, "above everything else," formed the bedrock of their exceptional contributions to national security.

What all of these examples—from suspect communist women to hale and hearty American astronauts—make clear is that the "security" of one's emotional attachments is anything but separable from a global climate of *insecurity* experienced throughout the Cold War. Such thinking has an impact not only on the legitimation of the catapulting neo-imperial space explorations that resulted in the planting of the

American flag on an entirely new planetary body but, by (re)articulating the experience of security as something born and fostered in the domestic home, Bowlby's attachment theory also anticipated the reorganization of state security logics following the end of the Cold War, where the twin forces of globalization and neoliberalism both heightened the everyday experience of material and affective insecurity for many, if not most, citizens while continuing to transform security into a matter of individual authorship and guardianship. Through Bowlby's articulation of the mother-child relation as a site of individualized, realizable secure attachments, his child-focused psychology helped to shore up the global insecurities introduced by the Cold War and extended into the contemporary, neoliberal security state.

STATES OF SECURITY: NEOLIBERALISM, FEMINISM, AND THE SECURITY STATE

In Grewal's *Saving the Security State*, she considers how the prototypically white masculine vigilante commitment to national security in the contemporary U.S. neoliberal security state has also been taken up by two types of women: "security moms" and "security feminists." As she puts it, "These two female figures, the security mom and the security feminist, the one protecting the home and the other protecting the security state, are important in their attempts to maintain the division between public and private even while transgressing the boundaries of civilian and military, home and work, domestic and international. Their work in securitizing the security state makes them exceptional citizens, even as their sovereignty is more insecure than that of their male counterparts."[72] Her overall argument in this text is that what particularizes the security endeavors definitional to the contemporary U.S. neoliberal security state is that a more diffuse form of state power, which collapses the boundaries between private and public as imagined by social contract theorists, nominates and operates through so-called exceptional citizens, or typically white, middle-class pronationalist men who are incited individually to American national protectionism as a result of the atrophy of state-provided welfare. With the galvanization of neoliberalism in 1970s Latin America (notably Chile) through the International Monetary Fund's recall of U.S. loans and neoliberalism's consequent spread, throughout the transatlantic Anglophone West, in the austerity eras of Reagan and Thatcher, the security itineraries that had shaped Cold War national security policy were significantly reformed. Perpetual war, the increased privatization of the commons, the reformation of U.S. global (neo)imperialism through international aid and humanitarianism, the explosion of the racist and sexist carceral state, the depletion or outright elimination of welfare support and social services, the rise of authoritarianism worldwide, the militarization and technologization of everyday surveillance and policing, and the unbridled hyperconcentration of capital (and power) in the hands of a new oligarch global elite were just some of the accelerated transformations that reoriented national security in the age of globalization. Yet as the securitization of virtually every aspect of contemporary post-9/11 American life has expanded and intensified, the right to and experience of the security ostensibly provisioned by these state measures has only been afforded to a small group of elite (typically white, middle-class, hetero- or homonationalist Christian) citizens. Given the decline of state welfare support, actual material and affective insecurity has been on the rise, leading to the production of exceptionalized private citizens who individually attempt to make good on the state's long-standing promises of security.

Drawing from Rose's influential claim that, in addition to economic policies, neoliberalism also produces a distinct "entrepreneurial subjectivity" pursuant of self-fashioning as a panacea for the lack of state provision, Grewal charts how "in response to these insecurities of the new century, private individuals who see themselves as normative citizens become empowered to take responsibility for maintaining the imperial security state."[73] Reconfiguring the well-established triangulated relationship between state, citizen, and sovereignty, the exceptional citizen—both "soft power" humanitarian aid worker and militant, avowedly racist and xenophobic vigilante—is born. Among these exceptional figures who enact an individualized form of securitization on behalf of a decentralized (if no less dominant) state are two typologies of implicitly raced and classed pronationalist women— the "security mom" and "security feminist." Each in her own way, these political subjectivities maintain that it is by virtue of their gendered and domestic location that they are able to contribute to the security state.

When it comes to "security moms," it is primarily through their position as mothers that they insert their contribution to national security. Grewal shows how, by cultivating security in their children, by managing their children with the same kind of doubled security-and-surveillance techniques key to the state's policies, and then by applying the paternalistic protocols of parenting to global populations and peoples as a way of ostensibly safeguarding security, "security moms" rely on the coextensiveness of domestic security with state security, a move that Grewal argues is central to the unique way that women engage themselves as political actors today.

While this chapter's main focus is not the consolidation of security discourses within present-day U.S. neoliberalism, I think it worthwhile to conclude with the provocation that, in spite of these significant changes, the persistence of state security logics implicates Bowlby's thinking about mother-child emotional security in the contemporary neoliberal state. Certainly, Bowlby was not dealing with a national security climate as nebulous, technologized, or global as today's. As many political theorists have documented, after the Soviet Union ended, the nature of national security discourse had to change profoundly to address and specularize different kinds of enemy "threats."[74] Yet the Cold War established the priorities and protocols of the national security state that remain with us today, however transformed. Even as neoliberalism has changed the relationship between the state and the marketplace, redefining who (or what!) gets to count as a "person" deserving of its aegis, in post-9/11 Anglophone society, concerns about state security—along with the raced, classed, religious, sexual, and gendered moral panics that accompany them—continue to be some of the most influential national and global discourses. What Grewal's analysis helpfully shows is that insofar as the panic to guarantee national security persists, it persists precisely through an individualized entrepreneurial subjectivity, one that continues to include the figure of the mother in the domestic sphere as a key contributor to the security state. By providing a template through which security is imagined and furnished, emotionally and psychologically (rather than materially and physically) through the mother-child relation, Bowlby's work continues to impact how we orient ourselves to the intersection between security and the state. If we have witnessed an amplification of security discourses in Trump's fervor for his border wall or in the realization of Brexit, then we have also witnessed a not-unrelated boom of attachment parenting that strives for security in, through, and for the domestic family form. My most ambitious suggestion is thus that, in spite of major economic, social, and political changes in the past seventy years, there is actually a line of historical continuity to be followed here, one that (when charted) suggests that the desecuritization of the contemporary neoliberal security state is tightly bound up with the urgent work of rethinking the mother-child relation—and by extension the whole of human subjectivity, as conceived by psychoanalytic orthodoxy—outside the vocabulary of safety and in/security.

Epilogue

Here, There, and Everywhere—Now

On October 29, 2021, the American Psychological Association (APA) issued what was, for many, a memorable statement on the status of race and racism within the psychological establishment. Framed as an "apology to people of color," the statement began by bluntly acknowledging that it had "failed" as an institutional leader through its direct complicity with racism and had "hurt many through racism, racial discrimination, and denigration of people of color, thereby falling short on its mission to benefit society and improve lives." It apologized for its "actions and inactions" and affirmed its commitment to antiracist work in the future.[1]

This document was one of many such progressively minded institutional declarations publicized in the wake of George Floyd's murder in May 2020. Psychological and psychoanalytic institutions aplenty—from the American Psychoanalytic Association (June 2, 2020), to the British Psychoanalytical Society (June 10, 2020), the British Psychoanalytic Council (June 20, 2020), and the International Psychoanalytic Association (August 2021)—issued a variety of statements on antiracism that ranged from cursory denunciations (such as the IPA's) to more thorough self-examinations and apologies (like the American Psychoanalytic Association's).[2] What made the APA's statement unique, however, was the depth of the research detailed in its unflinching account of how psychology (broadly) and the APA (specifically) have upheld white supremacy within their discipline. Over the course of five thousand words, and with a reference list two pages long, the APA outlined four "levels" of racism—structural, institutional, interpersonal, and internalized—and documented everything from its role in overt forms of extermination and exclusion to the cultural biases baked into its founding theories. From this, the APA pledged ongoing work on both institutional and clinical levels to reimagine psychological care along more progressive lines.

Statements such as these, and the calls to action they include, speak to a broader trend among contemporary psychological and psychoanalytic practitioners wherein clinical practice is being reimagined as inseparably intertwined with political action. Although the documents do not state it explicitly, these apologies acknowledge the political nature of the praxis that institutions such as the BPS disseminate and legitimate. In a 2020s world saturated with apocalyptic narratives about climate change, reproductive justice, genocide, gun violence, pandemics, social media, racism, AI, poverty, transphobia, education, LGBTQ rights, and resurgent multinational Christo-fascism, there has been a growing public demand among many psychoanalytic patients and practitioners to account for the embeddedness of the clinic in culture and politics. At the same time, academics who had previously embraced psychoanalysis primarily as a paradigm for the analysis of art and culture are newly taking up the clinic as a site of potentially progressive theorizing and acting—a movement that I hailed in the introduction as a new "clinical turn" in humanistic social theorizing. For both fields, a politicized clinic is ascendant.

As with the institutional apologies, much of this recent work draws its imperative from the scene of antiracist activism, where, for instance, the subtle but powerful role of whiteness is identified as an unconscious backdrop for many clinical encounters. As Natasha Stovall writes in her recent think piece, "Whiteness on the Couch," "Despite the outsize drama that whiteness brings to the public scene, it is still not much more than a cognitive wisp in most white Americans' daily brainscape, including those of most, but not all, white therapists. The silence about whiteness in most therapies is deafening." "Whiteness," she appends, "is nothing if not unconscious."[3] For Stovall and many others like her, contesting white supremacy means putting whiteness itself on the couch:

both reframing as "culture bound syndromes" particular to whiteness what have long been billed as social epidemics (mass school shootings; anorexia; malignant narcissism) while also reconsidering the extent to which clinical practice itself is structured by racialized norms. In fact, there has been a recent efflorescence of therapeutic and psychoanalytic writing about race, racism, and the clinic, with frequent calls for revised practice in the name, specifically, of antiracism.[4]

But whiteness and (anti)racism more generally are just one aspect of a wider trend. Over the past eight years, especially, there has been a boom in clinical practices that position themselves as extensions of social justice movements. In 2016, for instance, the Psychoanalytic Institute of Northern California inaugurated a new training track on Community Psychoanalysis that "challenges the formal definition and scope of psychoanalysis . . . by broadening how psychoanalysis is defined, who benefits from it, and what is deemed teachable at a psychoanalytic institute."[5] With clinical work directed toward refugees and asylum seekers, the incarcerated, and first responders, the CPT&C foregoes any understanding of the clinic as dyadic, privatized, or apolitical.[6] Similarly, The Red Clinic, a transnational collective of analysts working to combine communist politics with psychotherapeutic and psychoanalytic practice, promises a low-fee and politically progressive alternative to what it implicitly diagnoses as the capitalist and neocolonialist design of much psychotherapy. By offering a "sustainable provision of psychotherapy for the working-class and the oppressed in the broadest senses of the terms," The Red Clinic addresses the psychic aspect of social organization and explicitly reimagines the clinic as part of a political project for the more just redistribution of wealth.[7] In São Paulo, three major psychoanalytic free clinics have been established since 2016: the Public Clinic of Vila Itororó and two Open Psychoanalysis Clinics on Casa de Povo and Praça Roosevelt, respectively. A major hub for revisionist psychoanalytic practice, Brazil is home to numerous clinical innovations like these, a swelling movement that has been dubbed "psychoanalysis in the streets"/"*psicanálise na rua*." Where once the idea of the clinic as a site of neutrality felt like a promise that embodied one of psychoanalysis's most unique ideals—that of a realm of nonjudgmental free association—increasingly it has been reframed as a peril, a practical impossibility whose function masks hegemonic normative values as incontestable truth.

These are just a few examples of the varieties of practice being inno-
vated in multinational locations. Yet, as I discussed in the introduction,
many of the lessons taken from these recent clinical programs have long
been at play within psychoanalytic practice, especially when understood
globally. Not only, as Elizabeth Danto showed, were the first generation
of psychoanalysts across Europe some of the practitioners least wedded
to the orthodoxies of the fee, the dyadic consulting room, or the analytic hour.[8] But, as psychoanalysis disseminated globally, practitioners
throughout the Global South especially adapted their practices freely
in order to address the different sociopolitical demands produced by
the intersection of colonialism, racism, and capitalism. Rejecting the
racist and colonialist split in the distribution of suffering—psychic, if
white and from the Global North; physical, if Black, Brown, or from the
Global South—decolonial clinicians throughout the Global South have
long sought to mobilize the clinic as a sphere through which to contest
oppression. This legacy is the subject of Raluca Soreanu's UKRI-funded
research project, "Free Clinics and a Psychoanalysis for the People: Progressive Histories, Collective Practices, Implications for Our Times,"
where she consolidates the revitalized interest in the clinic to track the
many contemporary initiatives around the world that experiment with
and from the model of the free clinic.[9] More than simple treatment sites,
these clinics "have set up alternative points of accumulation, principles
of circulation and modes of redistribution, grounding an alternative
economy of care" that takes "steps toward a psychosocial theory of
value" where currency itself is reimagined through the clinical frame.[10]
As Ankhi Mukherjee discusses at length in her own study of free clinics
in London, Bangalore, and New York, psychoanalytic free clinics can
even be thought of as addressing mental health gaps resultant from
global poverty given the much higher recorded instances of psychological diagnoses like depression and anxiety among the economically dispossessed.[11] Whether through the model of the free clinic or through an
ever expanding range of adapted clinical techniques, the clinic is one of
the leading sites for envisioning a humanistic mental health service that
furthers the itinerary of contemporary justice movements.

One way to understand the value of these clinical projects—
beyond their potential for on-the-ground help to individual people
and communities—is that they explicitly reject the spurious separation

between practice and politics that has long haunted the Anglophone psychoanalytic tradition, especially. As I detail throughout this book, even clinical techniques that deny the political and position themselves as the height of orthodoxy (Kleinian reparation, Winnicottian good enough mothering, Bowlbian emotional security, etc.) take on necessarily political work—however much disavowal may mask and mystify that function. Ironically, psychoanalysis itself is perhaps the best cartographer of the dangers of disavowal since, through the perverse operation of simultaneous knowledge and denial, disavowal has an unparalleled power to bind potential transformation to conscious recognition, refusing change on the basis that knowledge is already both known and unknown and therefore not available for conscious assimilation. Ignorance is not a passive but an active epistemological stance. In the clinic, this can mean that the reputedly "apolitical" does its dirtiest—and most effective—work shoring up contingent and contestable values through the malleable practice of analytic interpretation. For instance, do we read a trans woman's persecutory dreams of penises as a phobic reaction to her own "unresolved" sexual differentiation? Or as a traumatic symptom indexing the patriarchal hypervaluation of this particular part of her anatomy? Does a woman's repeated engagement in so-called risky sex signify her openness to new experience and her autonomy over her own sexuality? Or is it attention-seeking behavior that points to long-standing abuse? Why is it that the diagnostic language of patient "seduction" accrues so asymmetrically to women? How respond to a student patient who says they can no longer afford the analytic fee? How decide which resistances require adjustment of the analyst's technique and which represent an unconscious defense of the patient? How treat—as in Fanon's famous case—a Black patient's dream of turning white?

To some extent, these hypotheticals are falsely posed. Many clinicians working today would likely say that their work involves holding numerous possible interpretive truths in mind at once and that it seeks to broaden rather than narrow the range of narrative possibilities available to patients. "Reality" for psychoanalysis is as much psychical as sociological, meaning that in an ideal situation it would always be the patient's narrative and perception that is given precedence. After all, one way of understanding many analysts' thoroughgoing commitment to an ideal like neutrality is to recall that it is typically intended as a safeguard *for the patient*, as a method for keeping the clinical space free from the analyst's own values or judgments. To differing degrees depending on one's analytic orientation or school, then, the clinic and the analyst's interpretations and punctuations would all address the patient's unique constellation of unconscious signifiers. In this regard, it would be difficult (if not outright impossible) to imagine any possible interpretive range for the previous scenarios without the nuanced personal history afforded by the analysis itself. Very little can be done with a psychoanalytic interpretation imagined in the abstract.

Yet for however much we might laud this ideal, one of the points I have maintained throughout this book is that there is still an unavoidable negotiation at play in any clinical situation when it comes to arbitrating between the analyst's interpretive epistemology and that of the patient. As Adam Phillips aptly queries, "Who, for example, decides what constitutes a problem for the patient? And by what criteria?"[12] As Phillips points out, interpretation is one of the most ethically and politically fraught aspects of the analytic situation since the process of determining *what* counts as a problem for the patient is always bound up with deciding *who* has the authority to adjudicate it. Any disavowal of this authority—or any refusal to acknowledge the politicality (which is to say, the contingency and contestability) of the values subtending it—runs the risk of simply exercising the analyst's own ideology rather than exorcising the patient's unconscious. By casting subjective priorities as uncontested analytic truth, claims to the apolitical or politically neutral clinic exert a conformist demand all their own.

Take the concept of clinical boundaries, for instance, which I discussed in chapter 3 and which many practicing analysts today still treat as one of the most necessary aspects of any professional treatment. As an especially sacrosanct buzzword of 2020s "therapy speak," it can feel difficult to contest the appeal to maintaining proper boundaries, particularly when they implicitly promise the alignment of psychological health with ethical professional conduct. Yet as the recent case of Jonah Hill has demonstrated with startling transparency, no "boundary"—personal or professional—is naturalized fact separable from questions of power and politics. In Hill's case, the demand for appropriate boundaries was leveraged as a rebranded form of patriarchal control and masculine sex right in relation to women. "Surfing with men," "modeling," "sexual pictures," and "friendships with women . . . in unstable places" were all, for Hill, boundary violations perpetrated by his ex-girlfriend. Although many clinical psychologists and therapists would testify that Hill misused (or even "weaponized") the concept of boundaries, contorting a framework for self-governance into a means for controlling others, I think the case actually provides a much deeper object lesson about the protean nature of boundaries themselves. Lily Scherlis has recently written on the subject and has described how boundaries "have a seductive moral authority as the dominant metaphor for how human relationships should work"; derived from a recognizably capitalistic property relation in an economy of scarcity, they provide a persuasive strategy for safeguarding precious resources and autonomy, encouraging you to relate "to yourself like a plot of land you own." Yet, writes Scherlis, there is no "deeper plane of existence where boundaries live . . . no substratum beneath the appearances of things where lines between people are etched: boundaries are just a wildly influential story about how people work."[13]

For Scherlis, our current cultural fetish with boundaries emerges from decades of distilled self-help literature propagated during the Cold War, not from the "pure gold" of psychoanalysis proper, which she preserves as the one psychological realm committed to "muck[ing] up people's boundaries, to trouble[ing] their placement, their firmness, their brittleness."[14] This is a version of psychoanalysis that I too value and hope to see realized. However, I think this idealized characterization ultimately oversells the field's purity when it comes to many of these normative psychological shibboleths. Although Sigmund Freud and perhaps even Jacques Lacan may not have held much store by "good boundaries," psychoanalytic orientations today are incredibly diverse and varied with many trainings and practitioners keenly vested in defining and maintaining boundaries, particularly in the clinic. Beyond the routine pathologization of various forms of metapsychological and interpersonal boundary transgression and/or eroticization—something I have personally experienced in even Lacanian clinics, which typically imagine themselves as unbeholden to the more normative covenants of their object- and ego-oriented kin—there are very few analysts today who would not, for instance, see an analyst showing up at a patient's house as a significant violation of boundaries, with this judgement likely made regardless of the effect it had on the patient. Indeed, it is primarily due to incidents like this that the significance of maverick analysts (such as Pakistani-British psychoanalyst Masud Khan) has been minimized or suppressed within the BPS.[15] Our difficulty in even imagining this scenario as anything other than damaging for the patient speaks to how ingrained many norms around professional boundaries are, and how allied they have come to be with a normative ethico-psychological notion of the good. Indeed, boundaries accrue their professional authority from the implicit moral claim that they stand on the side of patient welfare. But what if the analyst's arrival at the patient's house could be shown (leaving aside: How? By what criteria?) to be for the patient's own good? How respond if or when a boundary introduces harm?

My advocacy here is not for doing away with clinical boundaries as though such an erasure would produce a situation any less arbitrary, conflicted, or potentially violent than that found in instances of their self-serving instantiation. Rather, I just want to identify that any aspect of a clinical situation, even one as seemingly self-evident as professional boundaries, is a consequence of interpretive judgement about and contestation over the nature of the good, which is often taken, through various degrees of interpretive alchemy, to mean the patient's good. Ivan Ward, in his comments about social clinics, puts this well when he asks us to continually reflect on the power asserted in the process of creating, maintaining, and enforcing boundaries, both clinically and institutionally.

> We should question the way that psychoanalysts and others employ the notion of boundaries as if they were making universal and value-free claims. To my mind, the term is often used as a kind of fetish, and the 'boundary' is put in place not for rational reasons but in order to establish certain patterns of relationships which put the person drawing the boundary in a position of dominance. Psychotherapists may be discombobulated if you violate any of these precious—one might say sacred—boundaries, despite the fact that they are often arbitrarily chosen.[16]

Such questioning is vital, for Ward and others, because the retooling of some of psychoanalysis's self-legitimating orthodoxies enables a greater diversity of practice, particularly when it comes to situations where psychoanalytic orthodoxy can be seen as its own form of boundary keeping: a professional gatekeeping designed to secure the reproduction of like-for-like. To put a deconstructive spin on it, boundaries are a subtle yet effective means for reproducing social exclusion since only by delimiting the exterior, the "not-me," can internal self-identity be maintained.

I have therefore tried throughout this book to unpick the often surreptitious political work performed in twentieth-century clinics, both orthodox and heterodox, in the hopes of dispelling any refuge in the mythology of a neutral, apolitical, or benign clinic. Refusing any reading of the clinic as having a singular, consolidated, and predetermined effect—either for better or for worse—I consider instead how the clinic is a prime site for the elaboration of what Michel Foucault, in his discussion of ethics, has described as "pessimistic activism."

> My point is not that everything is bad, but that everything is dangerous, which is not exactly the same as bad. If everything is dangerous, then we always have something to do. So my position leads not to apathy but to a hyper- and pessimistic activism. I think that the ethico-political choice we have to make every day is to determine which is the main danger.[17]

Thought in terms of the clinic, which Foucault famously (if uncharitably) censured for its "confessional" imperative, this cautionary activism captures something of the historical variability that is necessarily at play when, each and every day, we must determine anew what constitutes the "main danger." Foucault's point here is that danger circulates because of the changeability of history itself; no clinic nor technique can be treated as an a priori good devoid of context. To embrace this uniquely pessimistic call to activism as an alternative ethos for the clinic is therefore to release any certainty we might hold about the universal value or efficacy of work that, however frequently or recently, met its intention.

In this spirit, I want to close with my own final note of "pessimistic activism" concerning the polyvalent political capacity of those clinics that embrace an expressly social justice mission, fashioning themselves as bastions of progressive practice. We might easily be forgiven for a wholesale endorsement of these visions—not only because they seem to answer psychoanalysis's long-standing rhetorical foe ("But how is it political?") but also because they make a promise that many, in our era of intersecting crises, have felt is badly needed: that the amelioration of individual misery (even if just to Freud's famous "ordinary unhappiness") would contribute to political transformation. The fantasy here is an alignment of wills: as goes the clinic, so goes the patient—and, ideally, the larger social order. This is a fantasy I too find appealing, even if there are significant qualifications to consider when it comes to the highly particular arrangement of each individual practice.

As I stated in the introduction, to acknowledge that the clinic is political is not to advocate for a politicized wave of analytic persuasion, which would likely be as just as structurally ineffective as it would be individually harmful. Moreover, as I have recognized time and again, there is much in clinical practice that operates under the capacious sign of social justice that itself bears further scrutiny. I would not be the first, for instance, to highlight the flatness of the "multicultural competency" trainings found in many clinical institutes, which embrace a familiar liberal celebration of "identity" and "diversity," presenting minoritized racial and ethnic groups as homogenous subfields for (implicitly white) specialization.[18] The assumed audience of such trainings (white, cis-gender, heterosexual, North American or European) is relevant if predictable, and it repeats a common trope in much of the literature on this topic wherein work intended to challenge racial, sexual, colonial, and gender hierarchy is implicitly addressed to those in privileged positions, thus offering the narrowest possible imaginary for change as a form of paternalist recognition while simultaneously reifying in the field's formative but implicit whiteness. This is what Tomiwa Owolade has recently described as the "narcissism of anti-racist therapy," a designation that speaks to both the popularity of this type of literature and its signature motifs.[19] Here, the problem is not the political-economic structures that support and enforce cisheteropatriarchal white supremacy—neoliberal capitalism, policing, mass incarceration, compulsory heterosexuality, the devaluation of reproductive labor, and sexual domination—but the individual consciousness and emotional economies of (white) analysts who are positioned (and position themselves) as both problem and solution. Take this passage from Helen Morgan's recent book, *The Work of Whiteness: A Psychoanalytic Perspective*:

> The existence of those who publicly avow white supremacy and engage in overtly racist language and acts can allow "white liberals" to perpetuate the illusion that, being not like them, we are therefore not racist. Meanwhile our racism, which has the same roots as that of the white supremacist, goes underground to operate at the more invisible level of white privilege and white solipsism.[20]

The rhetorical first person plural is difficult to ignore here—"we racists," "our racism"—given the performative, confessional, and invitational work it enacts, making absolutely clear that this is a book *about* whiteness *for* white readers. But so too is the status of "the liberal" conspicuous given how it is presented as both a position with which the reader is imagined to identify and as the only seeming alternative to the (white) supremacist. In this narrowing, not only do long and powerful histories of Leftist activism and critique, including those by Black radicals like Fanon (who is cited only five times throughout the entire text), disappear. But the scope of liberalism itself becomes unwieldy and difficult to define since it is used primarily to designate a nebulous constellation of individual affects and values, not a set of policies or party affiliations.

Clinically, this absorption with the paradoxes of liberal consciousness under white supremacy produces mixed results. Morgan narrates the case of her patient, "Janet," who brought racist associations into the analysis only to then quickly pronounce them resolved, inviting Morgan to ignore them and move on in what she describes as an act of conspiratorial collusion and disavowal. While Morgan astutely refuses this invitation, providing an instructive case study of clinical anti-racism motored primarily by the analyst's own political commitments, she nevertheless presents the ubiquity of internal racism (both Janet's and her own) as in conflict with their liberalism—rather than as what many scholars, including Charles W. Mills, have shown to be the basis of liberalism itself.[21] This is a tension throughout Morgan's work, which could be characterized as both a dissection of the contradictions inherent in the psychic life of liberalism (silence, colorblind thinking, self-reliance, etc) and a faith in its capacity to be reformed through individual consciousness, analysis, and intention.

Part of what I am trying to draw out of this example is the wide variety of ways that contemporary clinicians position the work of social justice in the clinic. Although not all will share Morgan's fascination with liberalism, there is a broad preference among many justice-oriented clinical practices for the embrace of a humanistic epistemological schema that prioritizes conceptual frameworks of trauma, repair, critical consciousness/*conscientização*, mental health, and even liberation. This corresponds with what I see as a larger contemporary turn toward relational and interpersonal interpretive styles across the humanities and critical social sciences and away from the self-undoing protocols of much poststructuralist thinking, including Jacques Lacan's. But such practices often entail implicit fantasies about psychic wholeness, well-being, and self-sovereignty that reproduce a quasi-adaptational or "curable" subject who is imagined to be both thoroughly self-conscious and potentially remedied of the mollifying injuries of late neoliberal, neoimperial capitalism. Even when it comes to the free clinic movement these concerns manifest since, if we take psychoanalysis's insights about the unconscious and internal conflict seriously, then it is difficult to understand in advance what the personal (or political) outcomes of even the most Left-leaning clinical projects might be. Although I do not subscribe to the view that the only way to secure the patient's investment in an analysis is through the instantiation of a fee—after all, the "cost" of an analysis can be variously located—it is nevertheless important to consider how such alternative economies of exchange sit within larger structures and institutions, where the free clinic could become nothing more than a paternalistic arm of the psychoanalytic institution's requisite charity capitalism. Or, where the free clinic functions as a panacea for the increasingly privatized, neoliberal health care system, supplementing and buttressing one of the most easily identifiable causes of social harm. Indeed, as Jordan Osserman has recently noted in conversation, it is typically the most institutionally precarious clinicians (including trainees, immigrants, genderqueer folks, and people of color) who take on the low-paid labor of free clinic work, meaning that the labor practices of clinicians themselves are implicated in the structural inequities they seek to redress.

Thus, even as I find it vital to take up the clinic as a political space, I also think there is danger in treating psychoanalysis and the clinic as if they constitute predictable, primary, or sufficient political action. As with my analysis of the historical case studies throughout this book, the political promise of the clinic as a site for revolutionary action and engagement is genuinely mixed. When I first began to think seriously about the clinic, I remember being inspired by Leo Bersani's exchange with Adam Phillips in their coauthored *Intimacies*. In response to Phillips's creative rethinking about the purpose of clinical psychoanalysis— where, in lieu of "normative health" or "personal growth," he instead proposes that the clinic, with its unique relational structure, might be one of the best places for the experimental realization of the "new relational modes" that Foucault was apt to call for in the latter years of his work—Bersani wonders if the clinic's most radical promise might only be realizable outside or beyond the clinic itself. He writes, "I will be considering psychoanalysis as an inspiration for modes of exchange that can only take place outside of psychoanalysis."[22]

As I finish this book, my thinking has returned to this provocative speculation as encapsulating something enigmatic about the appeal of the clinic today. Given Foucault's call to pessimistic activism, I can offer no ready-made or surefire practices that allow the clinic to transcend danger or to realize any particular political mission assuredly. All I have are new ways to think about the peril—and promise—it affords.

Notes

INTRODUCTION: ON NEUTRALITY AND OTHER CLINICAL FICTIONS

1. Tim Dean and Christopher Lane, eds., *Homosexuality and Psychoanalysis* (Chicago: University of Chicago Press, 2001), 5.
2. Elizabeth Danto, *Freud's Free Clinics: Psychoanalysis and Social Justice, 1918–1938* (New York: Columbia University Press, 2005), 3.
3. A full account of Fanon's biography and of the expansive field of Fanon studies is beyond the scope of this book, but for further introductory reading see David Macey, *Frantz Fanon: A Biography* (New York: Verso, 2012); Nigel C. Gibson, *Fanon: The Postcolonial Imagination* (Cambridge: Polity, 2003); and Achille Mbembe, "Frantz Fanon's Oeuvres: A Metaphoric Thought," *Journal of Contemporary African Art* 32 (2013): 8–17.
4. For a fuller account of Saint-Alban and the brand of institutional psychotherapy developed there, see Camille Robcis, *Disalienation: Politics, Philosophy, and Radical Psychiatry in Postwar France* (Chicago: Chicago University Press, 2021).
5. Jean Khalfa notes that the original title of *Black Skin, White Masks*, which Fanon published in 1952 but likely began writing before his doctoral studies, was *Essay on the Disalienation of the Black*. In her own commentary on this, Robcis describes how "in *Black Skin, White Masks*, as in his medical thesis and in his article 'The North African Syndrome,' Fanon turned to a wide array of texts and disciplines to study the phenomenon of racial alienation. He referred

to his book as a 'clinical study,' and in that sense, we can read it in line with these two other works, as a complementary text—one of three attempts to explore the question of causality in mental illness and to elaborate a theory of subjectivity that drew on psychiatry, psychoanalysis, phenomenology, and politics" (Robcis, *Disalienation*, 56). For further discussion of Fanon's early psychiatric work, including his dissertation's relationship to *Black Skin, White Masks*, see Jean Khalfa, "Fanon, Revolutionary, Psychiatrist," in *Alienation and Freedom*, ed. Jean Khalfa and Robert C. Young, trans. Steven Corcoran (London: Bloomsbury, 2018), 167–202.

6. Given his social and scientific context, Fanon's interpretation of North African "madness" was especially noteworthy. At the time, the reigning consensus among psychiatrists of the "Algiers School" was that African-Islamic men, especially, had an inherent inclination toward madness that resulted from Muslim cultural practices, such as child marriages. By positioning colonialism itself as the cause of this psychic suffering, Fanon not only resisted the racist and essentialized claims of this dominant school but also effectively "provincialized" psychiatry itself by insisting that clinical treatments were culturally relative. For an excellent overview of the Algiers school's colonial psychology to which Fanon was responding, see Richard C. Keller, *Colonial Madness: Psychiatry in French North Africa* (Chicago: University of Chicago Press, 2007). For Fanon's direct response to this body of work, see his essay "The North African Syndrome," originally published in 1952 and collected in *Toward the African Revolution*, trans. Haakon Chevalier (New York: Grove, 1967).

7. Jean Khalfa notes that Fanon borrowed this phrase from one of Jacques Lacan's early affiliates, Henri Ey. See Jean Khalfa, "Fanon and Psychiatry," *Nottingham French Studies* 54, no. 1 (2015): 52–71.

8. For a fuller account of Fanon's theory of action, see Erica Burman, *Fanon, Education, Action: Child as Method* (London: Routledge, 2018).

9. Robcis, *Disalienation*.

10. Frantz Fanon, "Social Therapy in a Ward of Muslim Men: Methodological Difficulties," in *Alienation and Freedom*, ed. Jean Khalfa and Robert C. Young, trans. Steven Corcoran (London: Bloomsbury, 2018), 362.

11. For the collected works of Fanon's previously unpublished clinical writings, see "Part II: Psychiatric Writings," in *Alienation and Freedom*, 165–530. For excellent accounts of his clinical work, see Richard C. Keller, "Clinician and Revolutionary: Frantz Fanon, Biography, and the History of Colonial Medicine," *Bulletin of the History of Medicine* 81, no. 4 (2007): 823–41; Azeen Khan, "The Subaltern Clinic," *boundary 2* 46, no. 4 (2019): 181–217; and Robcis, *Disalienation*. Also relevant are Lou Turner and Hannah Neville, *Frantz Fanon's Psychotherapeutic Approaches to Clinical Work: Practicing Internationally*

with Marginalized Communities (London: Routledge, 2020); David Marriott, "The Clinic as Praxis," in *Whither Fanon* (Stanford, CA: Stanford University Press, 2018); Lewis R. Gordon, "Revolutionary Therapy," in *What Fanon Said: A Philosophical Introduction to His Life and Thought* (New York: Fordham University Press, 2015), 75–105; Jean Khalfa, "Fanon, Revolutionary, Psychiatrist"; Françoise Vergès, "To Cure and to Free: The Fanonian Project of 'Decolonized Psychiatry,'" in *Fanon: A Critical Reader*, ed. Lewis R. Gordon, T. Denean Sharpley-Whiting, and Renée T. White (Oxford: Blackwell, 1996), 85–99; Jock McCulloch, *Black Soul, White Artifact: Fanon's Clinical Psychology and Social Theory* (Cambridge: Cambridge University Press, 1983); Hussein Abdilahi Bulhan, "Frantz Fanon: The Revolutionary Psychiatrist," *Race & Class* 21 (1980): 251–71; and Paul L. Adams, "The Social Psychiatry of Frantz Fanon," *American Journal of Psychiatry* 127, no. 6 (1970): 809–14.

12. Fanon, *Toward the African Revolution*, 53. In her chapter on Fanon and institutional psychotherapy, Robcis observes the double meaning of Fanon's use of the French *aliéné* to describe the Arab under colonialism. "By choosing the adjective *aliéné* to describe the colonized Algerians, Fanon was playing with the double-meaning of the term in French: estranged and foreign— even in their own land—but also mentally unstable, crazy, insane" (Robcis, *Disalienation*, 48).

13. Daniel Gaztambide, *A People's History of Psychoanalysis: From Freud to Liberation Psychology* (Lexington, KY: Lexington Books, 2019), 122.

14. Nathan Hale, *Freud and the Americans: The Beginnings of Psychoanalysis in the United States, 1876–1917* (Oxford: Oxford University Press, 1971); Nathan Hale, *The Rise and Crisis of Psychoanalysis in the United States, 1917–1985: Freud and the Americans*, vol. 2 (Oxford: Oxford University Press, 1995).

15. Christiane Hartnack, "Vishnu on Freud's Desk: Psychoanalysis in Colonial India," *Social Research: An International Quarterly* 57 (1990): 921–49; Nancy Caro Hollander, "Psychoanalysis Confronts the Politics of Repression: The Case of Argentina," *Social Science & Medicine* 28, no. 7 (1989): 751–58; Nancy Caro Hollander, *Love in a Time of Hate: Liberation Psychology in Latin America* (New Brunswick, NJ: Rutgers University Press, 1997); Hale, *Freud and the Americans*; Hale, *The Rise and Crisis of Psychoanalysis in the United States*; Ashis Nandy, "The Savage Freud: The First Non-Western Psychoanalyst in Colonial India," in *The Savage Freud and Other Essays on Possible and Retrievable Selves* (Princeton, NJ: Princeton University Press, 1995), 81–144; Mariano Ben Plotkin, *Freud in the Pampas: The Formation of a Psychoanalytic Culture in Argentina, 1910–1983* (Stanford, CA: Stanford University Press, 2001); Joy Damousi, *Freud in the Antipodes: A Cultural History of Psychoanalysis in Australia* (Sydney: University of New South Wales, 2005); Joy Damousi and Mariano Ben Plotkin,

eds., *The Transnational Unconscious: Essays in the History of Psychoanalysis and Transnationalism* (New York: Palgrave Macmillan, 2009); Joy Damousi and Mariano Ben Plotkin, *Psychoanalysis and Politics: Histories of Psychoanalysis Under Conditions of Restricted Political Freedom* (Oxford: Oxford University Press, 2012); Warwick Anderson, Deborah Jenson, and Richard C. Keller, eds., *Unconscious Dominions: Psychoanalysis, Colonial Trauma, and Global Sovereignties* (Durham, NC: Duke University Press, 2011); John C. Burnham, ed., *After Freud Left: A Century of Psychoanalysis in America* (Chicago: University of Chicago Press, 2012); Matt ffytche and Daniel Pick, eds., *Psychoanalysis and the Age of Totalitarianism* (London: Routledge, 2016); Omina El Shakry, *The Arabic Freud: Psychoanalysis and Islam in Modern Egypt* (Princeton, NJ: Princeton University Press, 2017); Dagmar Herzog, *Cold War Freud: Psychoanalysis in an Age of Catastrophes* (Cambridge: Cambridge University Press, 2017); and Robcis, *Disalienation*.

16. In 1951, Langer published *Maternidad y sexo*, which was translated by Nancy Caro Hollander as *Motherhood and Sexuality* in 1992. A complicated book, the text both argues for economic and labor reforms to enable women's greater participation in the workforce and suggests that women's unresolved conflicts are the origin of infertility.

17. For further reading about the history of psychoanalysis in Argentina, see the numerous writings of Mariano Ben Plotkin (especially *Freud in the Pampas*) and Nancy Caro Hollander, "Psychoanalysis Confronts the Politics of Repression." Also relevant is Hollander, *Love in a Time of Hate*, and the 2021 documentary on Langer, *Chasing the Revolution: Marie Langer, Revolution, and Society*, directed by Lily Ford, which was produced as part of Daniel Pick's *Hidden Persuaders* project.

18. For a fuller account of this scandalous episode, see Helena Besserman Vianna, "The Lobo-Cabernite Affair," *Journal of the American Psychoanalytic Association* 48, no. 3 (2000): 1023–29 and Julia Borossa, "Psychoanalysis and Taking Sides: Two Moments in the History of the Psychoanalytic Movement," in *Psychology and Politics: Intersections of Science and Ideology in the History of the Psy-Sciences*, ed. Anna Borgos, Ferenc Erős, and Júlia Gyimesci (Budapest: Central European University Press, 2019). Besserman Vianna has written her own extensive account of this event—*Não Conte a Ninguém . . .: Contribuição à História das Sociedades Psicanalíticas do Rio de Janeiro* (1994)—but it is still only available in Portuguese, Spanish, and French.

19. Sander Gilman, *Freud, Race, and Gender* (Princeton, NJ: Princeton University Press, 1994).

20. John C. Burnham, "The 'New Freud Studies': A Historiographical Shift," *Journal of the Historical Society* 6, no. 2 (2006): 213–33.

21. As Matt ffytche, editor of *Psychoanalysis and History*, notes in his inaugural editorial introduction to the journal following John Forrester's death, "psychoanalytic history may begin with Freud and his colleagues, or thereabouts, but that was simply the opening chapter. What has become increasingly fascinating, for historians and psychoanalysts alike, are the multiple sequels beyond Vienna—in the 1930s, the 1950s, the 1980s, and now the 2000s—during which psychoanalysis has reached across various geographical and cultural boundaries, and embedded itself in many other fields, including modern psychology, philosophy, literature, politics and the social sciences and humanities more broadly." Matt ffytche, "Introduction," *Psychoanalysis & History* 18, no. 1 (2016): 1.

22. George Makari, *Revolution in Mind: The Creation of Psychoanalysis* (New York: Harper, 2008); Burnham, *After Freud Left*. For the use of "Dollaria," see Sigmund Freud, "Letter from Sigmund Freud to Oskar Pfister, August 20, 1930," in *Psychoanalysis and Faith: The Letters of Sigmund Freud and Oskar Pfister* (London: Forgotten Books, 2018), 135. For the second quotation, see the letter from Sigmund Freud to Otto Rank, May 23, 1924, in E. James Lieberman, *Acts of Will: The Life and Work of Otto Rank* (New York: Free Press, 1998), 228.

23. Damousi and Plotkin, *Psychoanalysis and Politics*; ffytche and Pick, *Psychoanalysis and the Age of Totalitarianism*.

24. Erik Linstrum, *Ruling Minds: Psychology and the British Empire* (Cambridge, MA: Harvard University Press, 2016); Herzog, *Cold War Freud*; Anderson, Jenson, and Keller, *Unconscious Dominions*.

25. Also noteworthy in this trend are Sherry Turkle, *Psychoanalytic Politics: Freud's French Revolution* (New York: Basic Books, 1978); Denise Riley, *The War in the Nursery: Theories of the Child and Mother* (London: Virago, 1983); Hale, *The Rise and Crisis of Psychoanalysis in the United States, 1917–1985*; Plotkin, *Freud in the Pampas*; Celia Brickman, *Aboriginal Populations in the Mind: Race and Primitivity in Psychoanalysis* (New York: Columbia University Press, 2003); Eli Zaretsky, *Secrets of the Soul: A Social and Cultural History of Psychoanalysis* (New York: Knopf, 2004) and *Political Freud: A History* (New York: Columbia University Press, 2015); Damousi and Plotkin, *The Transnational Unconscious*; Veronika Fuechtner, *Berlin Psychoanalytic: Psychoanalysis and Culture in Weimar Republic Germany and Beyond* (Los Angeles: University of California Press, 2011); Daniel Pick, *The Pursuit of the Nazi Mind: Hitler, Hess, and the Analysts* (Oxford: Oxford University Press, 2014); Lewis Aron and Karen Starr, *A Psychotherapy for the People: Toward a Progressive Psychoanalysis* (London: Routledge, 2013); Sally Alexander and Barbara Taylor, eds., *History and Psyche: Culture, Psychoanalysis, and the Past* (London: Palgrave Macmillan, 2012); Michal Shapira, *The War Inside:*

Psychoanalysis, Total War, and the Making of the Democratic Self in Postwar Britain (Cambridge: Cambridge University Press, 2013); El Shakry, *The Arabic Freud*; John Forrester and Laura Cameron, *Freud in Cambridge* (Cambridge: Cambridge University Press, 2017); Patricia Gherovici and Christopher Christian, *Psychoanalysis in the Barrios: Race, Class, and the Unconscious* (New York: Routledge, 2018); Gaztambide, *A People's History of Psychoanalysis*; Shaul Bar-Haim, *The Maternalists: Psychoanalysis, Motherhood, and the British Welfare State* (Philadelphia: University of Pennsylvania Press, 2021); Robcis, *Disalienation*; Ankhi Mukherjee, *Unseen City: The Psychic Lives of the Urban Poor* (Cambridge: Cambridge University Press, 2022); and Michelle Rada, ed., "Psychoanalysis and Solidarity," special issue, *differences* 33, no. 2–3 (2022).

26. This list of fields is by no means comprehensive. Psychoanalytic theory has also been a major resource for film theory, political theory, and literary theory more broadly. Within film theory, see the works of Christian Metz, Laura Mulvey, Kaja Silverman, Todd McGowan, and Mary Ann Doane. Within political theory, scholars such as Axel Honneth, C. Fred Alford, Amy Allen, Noëlle McAfee, Gal Gerson, David McIvor, Matthew Bowker, and Amy Buzby have drawn on Object Relations psychoanalysis in their theorizations of contemporary democracy. Such work continues the tradition of psychoanalytically informed political theorizing popularized from the 1970s to the 1990s by figures such as Slavoj Žižek, Ernesto Laclau, and Yannis Stavrakakis but deliberately moves beyond a Lacanian discourse analysis framework to consider the importance of affect, phantasy, ethics, embodiment, aesthetics, and the terrain of the interpersonal in the body politic. Within literary theory, figures such as Harold Bloom, Sandra Gilbert, and Susan Gubar first popularized Freudian readings of fiction in the 1970s. Following the rise of semiotics and deconstruction ushered in by Lacan and Derrida in the 1980s, critics such as Barbara Johnson, Shoshana Felman, Diana Fuss, Jacqueline Rose, and Jane Gallop continued this legacy but furnished new psychoanalytic readings that were less concerned with biographical and characterological psychology and more interested in language, desire, and form. Chronicling the psychoanalytic contributions to all these fields would be a book in its own right, so this curtailed overview is simply a representative sample.

27. Juliet Mitchell, *Psychoanalysis and Feminism: A Radical Reassessment of Freudian Psychoanalysis* (New York: Basic Books, [1974] 2000).

28. Noreen O'Connor and Joanna Ryan, *Wild Desires and Mistaken Identities: Lesbianism and Psychoanalysis* (New York: Columbia University Press, 1993).

29. Adam Phillips, "Keeping It Moving: Commentary on Judith Butler's 'Melancholy Gender/Refused Identification,'" in Judith Butler, *The Psychic Life*

of Power: Theories in Subjection (Stanford, CA: Stanford University Press, 1997), 157.

30. Sigmund Freud, *Three Essays on the Theory of Sexuality*, ed. and trans. James Strachey (New York: Basic Books, [1905] 1962), 10–12.

31. Diana Fuss, "Pink Freud," *GLQ* 2, nos. 1–2 (1995): 1–9.

32. Ranjana Khanna, *Dark Continents: Psychoanalysis and Colonialism* (Durham, NC: Duke University Press, 2003).

33. Brickman, *Aboriginal Populations in the Mind*.

34. Gohar Homayounpour, *Doing Psychoanalysis in Tehran* (Cambridge, MA: MIT Press, 2012); Robert K. Beshara, *Decolonial Psychoanalysis: Towards Critical Islamophobia Studies* (New York: Routledge, 2019); Gaztambide, *A People's History of Psychoanalysis*; Lara Sheehi and Stephen Sheehi, *Psychoanalysis Under Occupation: Practicing Resistance in Palestine* (London: Routledge, 2022); Mukherjee, *Unseen City*; Stefania Pandolfo, *Knot of the Soul: Madness, Psychoanalysis, Islam* (Chicago: University of Chicago Press, 2018); Karima Lazali, *Colonial Trauma: A Study of the Psychic and Political Consequences of Colonial Oppression in Algeria*, trans. Matthew B. Smith (Cambridge: Polity, 2021); Gherovici and Christian, *Psychoanalysis in the Barrios*.

35. Anne Anlin Cheng, *The Melancholy of Race: Psychoanalysis, Assimilation, and Hidden Grief* (Oxford: Oxford University Press, 2001).

36. Judith Butler, *The Psychic Life of Power: Theories in Subjection* (Stanford, CA: Stanford University Press, 1997).

37. David Eng and David Kazanjian, *Loss: The Politics of Mourning* (Los Angeles: University of California Press, 2003); David Eng and Shinhee Han, *Racial Melancholia, Racial Dissociation: On the Social and Psychic Lives of Asian Americans* (Durham, NC: Duke University Press, 2019); Antonio Viego, "The Clinical, the Speculative, and What Must be Made Up in the Space Between Them," in *Dead Subjects: Toward a Politics of Loss in Latino Studies* (Durham, NC: Duke University Press, 2007).

38. Kalpana Seshadri-Crooks, *Desiring Whiteness: A Lacanian Analysis of Race* (New York: Routledge, 2000).

39. David Marriott, *Haunted Life: Visual Culture and Black Modernity* (New York: Rutgers University Press, 2007); David Marriott, *Lacan Noir: Lacan and Afro-Pessimism* (London: Palgrave Macmillan, 2021); Sheldon George and Derek Hook, eds., *Lacan and Race: Racism, Identity and Psychoanalytic Theory* (New York: Routledge, 2021); Sheldon George, *Trauma and Race: A Lacanian Study of African American Racial Identity* (Waco, TX: Baylor University Press, 2016); Orlando Patterson, *Slavery and Social Death: A Comparative Study* (Cambridge, MA: Harvard University Press, 1982). For further work on race and psychoanalysis outside of the Afropessimist school, see

Hortense Spillers, "Mama's Baby, Papa's Maybe: An American Grammar Book," *Diacritics* 17, no. 2 (1987): 65–81 and "'All the Things You Could Be by Now If Sigmund Freud's Wife Was Your Mother': Psychoanalysis and Race," *Critical Inquiry* 22 (1996): 710–34; Elizabeth Abel, "Race, Class, and Psychoanalysis? Opening Questions," in *Conflicts in Feminism*, ed. Marianne Hirsch and Evelyn Fox Keller (London: Routledge, 1990), 184–204; Mary Ann Doane, "Dark Continents: Epistemologies of Racial and Sexual Difference in Psychoanalysis and the Cinema," in *Femmes Fatales: Feminism, Film Theory, Psychoanalysis* (New York: Routledge, 1991), 209–48; Diana Fuss, "Interior Colonies: Frantz Fanon and the Politics of Identification," in *Identification Papers* (London: Routledge, 1995), 141–65; Barbara Johnson, *The Feminist Difference: Literature, Psychoanalysis, Race, and Gender* (Cambridge, MA: Harvard University Press, 1998); Elizabeth Abel, Barbara Christian, and Helene Moglen, eds., *Female Subjects in Black and White: Race, Psychoanalysis, Feminism* (Los Angeles: University of California Press, 1997); Claudia Tate, *Psychoanalysis and Black Novels: Desire and the Protocols of Race* (Oxford: Oxford University Press, 1998); Christopher Lane, ed., *The Psychoanalysis of Race* (New York: Columbia University Press, 1998); Seshadri-Crooks, *Desiring Whiteness*; Jean Walton, *Fair Sex, Savage Dreams: Race, Psychoanalysis, Sexual Difference* (Durham, NC: Duke University Press, 2001); and Stephen Frosh, "Psychoanalysis, Colonialism, and Racism," *Journal of Theoretical and Philosophical Psychology* 33, no. 3 (2013): 141–54.

40. Inderpal Grewal, *Saving the Security State: Exceptional Citizens in Twenty-First Century America* (Durham, NC: Duke University Press, 2017).

41. Zaretsky, *Secrets of the Soul.*

42. For the purpose of this book, I am focusing rather narrowly on clinicians who theorize the space of the clinic itself. However, there is a large body of scholarship by clinicians using social theory to provide nuance and elaborate on psychoanalytic accounts of subjectivity. On gender theory, for instance, see the work of Jessica Benjamin, Susie Orbach, Adrienne Harris, Alessandra Lemma, Carol Gilligan, Lynne Layton, Ken Corbett, or Avgi Saketopoulou. On transgender theory, see Patricia Gherovici, Alessandra Lemma, Shanna Carlson, Eve Watson, Oren Gozlan, or Avgi Saketopoulou. On critical race theory, see Fakhry Davids, Neil Altman, Farhad Dalal, Helen Morgan, or Derek Hook. On LGBTQ theory, see Joanna Ryan, Noreen Giffney, Eve Watson, or Ken Corbett.

43. Lynne Layton, Nancy Caro Hollander, and Susan Gutwill, *Psychoanalysis, Class and Politics: Encounters in the Clinical Setting* (New York: Routledge, 2006), 5–6.

44. For further clinical critiques of neutrality, many from the Relational school, see Owen Renik, "The Ideal of the Anonymous Analyst and the Problem

of Self-Disclosure," *Psychoanalytic Quarterly* 64 (1995): 466–95 and "The Perils of Neutrality," *Psychoanalytic Quarterly* 65 (1996): 495–517; Samuel Gerson, "Neutrality, Resistance, and Self-Disclosure in an Intersubjective Psychoanalysis," *Psychoanalytic Dialogues* 6 (1996): 623–45; Irwin Z. Hoffman, "The Intimate and Ironic Authority of the Psychoanalyst's Presence," *Psychoanalytic Quarterly* 65 (1996): 102–36; Stephen H. Portuges, "The Politics of Psychoanalytic Neutrality," *International Journal of Applied Psychoanalytic Studies* 6 (2009): 61–73 and "Psychoanalytic Neutrality, Race, and Racism," *Journal of the American Psychoanalytic Association* 70, no. 2 (2022): 323–34; Matthew Bowker, "Analytical and Political Neutrality: Change, Privilege, and Responsibility," *Free Associations: Psychoanalysis and Culture, Media, Groups, Politics* 71 (2017): 1–17; and Fakhry Davids, "Race and Analytic Neutrality: Clinical and Theoretical Considerations," *Psychoanalytic Quarterly* 91 (2022): 371–93.

45. Layton, Hollander, and Gutwill, *Psychoanalysis, Class and Politics*, 2.
46. Basia Winograd, dir., *Black Psychoanalysts Speak*, 2014.
47. For a clinical think piece about the structural and affective force of whiteness in the clinic, see Natasha Stovall, "Whiteness on the Couch," *Longreads*, August 12, 2019, https://longreads.com/2019/08/12/whiteness-on-the-couch/.
48. Adam Phillips and Devorah Baum, "Politics in the Consulting Room," *Granta*, February 14, 2019, https://granta.com/politics-in-the-consulting-room/.
49. Suzanne Stewart-Steinberg, *Impious Fidelity: Anna Freud, Psychoanalysis, and Politics* (Ithaca, NY: Cornell University Press, 2011); Shapira, *The War Inside.*
50. Melanie Klein, *Narrative of a Child Analysis: The Conduct of the Psycho-Analysis of Children as Seen in the Treatment of a Ten-Year-Old Boy* (London: Random House, [1961] 1998).
51. Damousi and Plotkin, *The Transnational Unconscious*; Linstrum, *Ruling Minds*; Herzog, *Cold War Freud.*
52. Megan Vaughan, "The Madman and the Medicine Man: Colonial Psychiatry and the Theory of Deculturation," in *Curing Their Ills: Colonial Power and African Illness* (Cambridge: Cambridge University Press, 1991), 100–28; Nikolas Rose, *Inventing Ourselves: Psychology, Power, and Personhood* (Cambridge: Cambridge University Press, 1998); Khanna, *Dark Continents.*
53. D. W. Winnicott, *The Piggle: An Account of the Psychoanalytic Treatment of a Little Girl*, ed. Ishak Ramzy (London: Penguin, [1971] 1977).
54. Riley, *The War in the Nursery*; Nancy Chodorow, *The Reproduction of Mothering: Psychoanalysis and the Sociology of Gender* (Los Angeles: University of California Press, 1978); Alexander and Taylor, *History and Psyche.*
55. Grewal, *Saving the Security State.*

1. ON GOOD AUTHORITY: ANNA FREUD, CHILD ANALYSIS, AND THE POLITICS OF AUTHORITY

Portions of this chapter have been published in Carolyn Laubender, "On Good Authority: Anna Freud and the Politics of Child Analysis," *Psychoanalysis and History* 19, no. 3 (2017): 297–322.

1. Adam Phillips, *Promises, Promises: Essays on Psychoanalysis and Literature* (New York: Basic Books, 2001), 5.

2. Sigmund Freud, "Foreword," in August Aichhorn, *Wayward Youth* (New York: Penguin, 1965), v.

3. Freud, "Foreword," vii. The original German term, *Nacherziehung*, is first translated throughout Freud's work as "re-education"; however, the editors of the Standard Edition note that this is a substantial mistranslation since "nachr" conveys a temporal element, an "after"-ness, rather than a repetition.

4. Born in 1895, Anna Freud's birth coincided with Sigmund Freud and Joseph Breuer's publication of *Case Studies in Hysteria*. For a detailed biography of Anna Freud's early life and her description of herself as psychoanalysis's twin, see Elisabeth Young-Bruehl, *Anna Freud: A Biography* (New Haven, CT: Yale University Press, 2008).

5. Suzanne Stewart-Steinberg, *Impious Fidelity: Anna Freud, Psychoanalysis, and Politics* (Ithaca, NY: Cornell University Press, 2011); Michal Shapira, *The War Inside: Psychoanalysis, Total War, and the Making of the Democratic Self in Postwar Britain* (Cambridge: Cambridge University Press, 2013).

6. For a detailed biography of her life, see Young-Bruehl, *Anna Freud*. For other studies (many by clinicians) on Anna Freud that provide substantial biographical detail, see Robert Coles, *Anna Freud* (Reading, MA: Addison-Wesley, 1992); Joseph Sandler, Hansi Kennedy, and Robert L. Tyson, *Techniques of Child Analysis: Discussions with Anna Freud* (Cambridge, MA: Harvard University Press, 1986); Nick Midgley, *Reading Anna Freud* (London: Routledge, 2013); Rose Edgcumbe, *Anna Freud: A View of Development, Disturbance and Therapeutic Techniques* (London: Routledge, 2000); and Claudine Geissmann and Pierre Geissmann, *A History of Child Psychoanalysis* (London: Routledge, 1998).

7. Hermine Hug-Hellmuth was the first child psychoanalyst and her pedagogical aspirations were not dissimilar to Anna Freud's. However, Hug-Hellmuth's early death (she was murdered by her nephew in 1924) meant that most of her papers were destroyed per the specifications of her will. Consequently, much less has been written about her compared to Anna Freud and Melanie Klein. For further reading see "Introduction" and "The Origins of Child Analysis" in Alex Holder, *Anna Freud, Melanie Klein, and the Psychoanalysis of Children and Adolescents* (London: Karnac, 2005); and "Hermine Hug-Hellmuth: Pioneer and Most

Obstinate of Freud's Disciples" in Geissmann and Geissmann, *A History of Child Psychoanalysis.*

8. This statement is perhaps truer of academic rather than clinical scholarship, but British clinical work still reflects the dominance of the Object Relations tradition. For the few critical academic treatments of Anna Freud's work, see Janet Sayers, *Mothering Psychoanalysis: Helene Deutsch, Karen Horney, Anna Freud, and Melanie Klein* (New York: Norton, 1991); Kurt Jacobsen, "Escape from the Treadmill: Education, Politics, and the Mainsprings of Child Analysis," in *Vienna: World of Yesterday, 1885–1914*, ed. Stephen Bronner and Peter Wagner (Atlantic Highlands, NJ: Humanities, 1994); Lynda Hart, "Knights in Shining Armor and Other Relations," *Between the Body and the Flesh: Performing Sadomasochism* (New York: Columbia University Press, 1998), 11–35; Deborah Britzman, *After-Education: Anna Freud, Melanie Klein, and Psychoanalytic Histories of Learning* (New York: New York State University Press, 2003); Stewart-Steinberg, *Impious Fidelity*; Shapira, *The War Inside*; Lyndsey Stonebridge, *The Destructive Element: British Psychoanalysis and Modernism* (New York: Routledge, 1998); and Shaul Bar-Haim, "The Child's Position: The Concept of Childhood in Interwar Psychoanalysis," in *Childhood, Literature, and Science: Fragile Subjects*, ed. Jutta Ahlbeck, Päivi Lappalainen, Kati Launis, and Kirsi Tuohela (London: Routledge, 2017). For a recuperative reading of Anna Freud's account of the ego, see Jacqueline Rose, *Why War? Psychoanalysis, Politics, and the Return to Melanie Klein* (Oxford: Blackwell University Press, 1993).

9. Anna Freud, "On Beating Fantasies and Daydreams," in *The Writings of Anna Freud*, vol. 1 (New York: International Universities Press, [1922] 1974), 137–57.

10. Sigmund Freud, "Analysis of a Phobia in a Five-Year-Old Boy ['Little Hans']," in *The "Wolfman" and Other Cases*, ed. Adam Phillips, trans. Adey Huish (New York: Penguin, [1909] 2003), 1–122.

11. Freud, "Analysis of a Phobia in a Five-Year-Old Boy ['Little Hans']," 4. Sigmund Freud, *Three Essays on the Theory of Sexuality*, ed. and trans. James Strachey (New York: Basic Books, [1905] 1962).

12. Although in many ways the professional conflict between Freud and Klein culminated in the so-called Controversial Discussions (1941–1946) held by the BPS, their disagreements with one another spanned decades. As early as 1927, Klein and other notable British analysts were already leveling substantial (and often vitriolic) critiques of Freud's first book at a symposium organized by Ernest Jones. Freud responded with biting dismissals of her own, and the intractable differences between their interpretations of Freudian theory ("drive" versus "object relational") eventually resulted in an ironically named "gentleman's agreement" between the two women that split the BPS definitively into two different professional training tracks (with a third

"independent" stream pulling from both groups). While Freud and Klein were collegial professionally, they never arrived at anything like theoretical or personal resolution and the fundamental differences between their approaches still shape (especially British) psychoanalytic institutes today. For further reading on this conflict, see Pearl King and Riccardo Steiner, eds., *The Freud-Klein Controversies: 1941–45* (London: Routledge, 1991). For an excellent social analysis, see the chapter "The War in the Nursery" in Rose, *Why War?* and Adam Phillips's 2001 response essay, "Bombs Away." Deborah Britzman's *After-Education* also has a relevant analysis of the role that education played in these debates.

13. For information about Freud's political affiliations, see Young-Bruehl, *Anna Freud*, 177–78.

14. For further reading on Red Vienna, see Helmut Gruber, *Red Vienna: An Experiment in Working Class Culture, 1919–1934* (New York: Oxford University Press, 1991).

15. For further reading about the Hietzing School, see Elizabeth Danto and Alexandra Steiner-Strauss, eds., *Freud/Tiffany: Anna Freud, Dorothy Tiffany Burlingham and "The Best Possible School"* (London: Routledge, 2019).

16. For a historical analysis of the Matchbox School, see Midgley, *Reading Anna Freud*; Nick Midgley, "The Matchbox School: Anna Freud and the Idea of a Psychoanalytically Informed Education," *Journal of Child Psychotherapy* 34, no. 1 (2018); Danto and Steiner-Strauss, *Freud/Tiffany*, 2019.

17. Midgley, *Reading Anna Freud*, 35.

18. Elizabeth Danto, *Freud's Free Clinics: Psychoanalysis and Social Justice, 1918–1938* (New York: Columbia University Press, 2005).

19. Anna Freud, "Child Analysis as a Subspecialty," in *The Writings of Anna Freud*, vol. 7 (New York: International Universities Press, [1970] 1971), 209.

20. Quoted in Coles, *Anna Freud*, 152.

21. Danto, *Freud's Free Clinics*, 110–12.

22. Eli Zaretsky, *Secrets of the Soul: A Social and Cultural History of Psychoanalysis* (New York: Knopf, 2004), 244.

23. Whereas Sigmund Freud had referred to the three entities in his structural model of mind—the id, the ego, and the superego—as "agencies" (*instanz*), Anna Freud interestingly refers to them as "institutions" throughout her writings, both in English and in German. This is a noteworthy modification since it corresponds to her principally institutional role in psychoanalysis: not only did she herself run a number of children's institutes, but after her father's death she was also responsible for much of the institutionalization of psychoanalysis itself, both in Britain and in the United States.

24. Danto, *Freud's Free Clinics*; Stewart-Steinberg, *Impious Fidelity*; Shapira, *The War Inside*.

25. For clinicians, one of Anna Freud's most important theories is her reconfiguration of Sigmund Freud's psychosexual stages as "developmental lines." For further reading on this, see Anna Freud, *The Ego and the Mechanisms of Defence*, in *The Writings of Anna Freud*, vol. 2 (New York: International Universities Press, [1936] 1966), 59–82; Holder, *Anna Freud, Melanie Klein, and the Psychoanalysis of Children and Adolescents*, 326–46; Midgley, *Reading Anna Freud*, 130–44; and Edgcumbe, *Anna Freud*, 114–59.

26. Anna Freud, *Four Lectures on Child Analysis*, in *The Writings of Anna Freud*, vol. 1 (New York: International Universities Press, [1926] 1974), 58.

27. For a further discussion of Anna Freud's metapsychological theorization of the ego and the superego in relation to the child, see Carolyn Laubender, "On Good Authority: Anna Freud and the Politics of Child Analysis," *Psychoanalysis and History* 19, no. 3 (2017): 303–6.

28. Freud, *Four Lectures on Child Analysis*, 45.

29. Freud, *Four Lectures on Child Analysis*, 40.

30. Freud, *Four Lectures on Child Analysis*, 7.

31. Freud, *Four Lectures on Child Analysis*, 41.

32. Freud, *Four Lectures on Child Analysis*, 11.

33. Freud, *Four Lectures on Child Analysis*, 12.

34. Freud, *Four Lectures on Child Analysis*, 13–14.

35. Freud, *Four Lectures on Child Analysis*, 22–23.

36. Freud, "On Beating Fantasies and Daydreams," 145–46.

37. Freud, "On Beating Fantasies and Daydreams," 148.

38. Freud, "On Beating Fantasies and Daydreams," 146.

39. Freud, *Four Lectures on Child Analysis*, 45.

40. Freud, *Four Lectures on Child Analysis*, 61.

41. Freud, *Four Lectures on Child Analysis*, 62.

42. Freud, *Four Lectures on Child Analysis*, 63.

43. Freud, *Four Lectures on Child Analysis*, 19.

44. Freud, *Four Lectures on Child Analysis*, 60.

45. Freud, *Four Lectures on Child Analysis*, 65. Emphasis added.

46. Freud, *Four Lectures on Child Analysis*, 46.

47. Quoted in Young-Bruehl, *Anna Freud*, 215.

48. Freud, *Four Lectures on Child Analysis*, 60. Emphasis added.

49. Sandler, Kennedy, and Tyson, *Techniques of Child Analysis*, 6.

50. Danto, *Freud's Free Clinics*; Stewart-Steinberg, *Impious Fidelity*; Shapira, *The War Inside*.

51. Freud, *The Ego and the Mechanisms of Defence*, 6.

52. This historical scholarship on the child was famously inaugurated by Philippe Ariès in *Centuries of Childhood: A Social History of Family Life* (New York:

Vintage, 1965). Ariès gained notoriety because of his contentious claim that the category of "the child" did not exist in the medieval period and is an "invention" of modernity. His argument provoked much debate and arguably helped inaugurate the trend in social and cultural history that would especially take hold in the 1970s. For other general histories of "the child" and childhood, see Margaret Hewitt and Ivy Pinchbeck, *Children in English Society*, vol. 1 (London: Routledge, 1969); C. John Sommerville, *The Rise and Fall of Childhood* (New York: Vintage, 1990); Hugh Cunningham, Children and Childhood in Western Society Since 1500 (New York: Longman, 1995); Carolyn Steedman, *Strange Dislocations: Childhood and the Idea of Human Interiority, 1780–1930* (London: Virago, 1995); Harry Hendrick, *Children, Childhood, and English Society, 1880–1990* (Cambridge: Cambridge University Press, 1997); Colin Heywood, *A History of Childhood: Children and Childhood in the West from Medieval to Modern Times* (Cambridge: Polity, 2001) and *Childhood in Modern Europe* (Cambridge: Cambridge University Press, 2018); Sally Shuttleworth, *The Mind of the Child: Child Development in Literature, Science, and Medicine, 1840–1900* (Oxford: Oxford University Press, 2010); Peter Sterns, *Childhood in World History* (New York: Routledge, 2006). For more specific analyses, see Elliot West, *Growing Up in Twentieth-Century America: A History and Reference Guide* (Westport, CT: Greenwood, 1996); R. Danielle Egan and Gail Hawkes, *Theorizing the Sexual Child in Modernity* (New York: Palgrave Macmillan, 2010); Amy F. Ogata, *Designing the Creative Child: Playthings and Places in Midcentury America* (Minneapolis: University of Minnesota Press, 2013); Marta Gutman and Ning de Corninck-Smith, *Designing Modern Childhoods: History, Space, and the Material Culture of Children* (New Brunswick, NJ: Rutgers University Press, 2008); and Nikolas Rose, *Governing the Soul: The Shaping of the Private Self* (London: Free Association, 1989).

53. Viviana Zelizer, *Pricing the Priceless Child: The Changing Social Value of Children* (Princeton, NJ: Princeton University Press, 1985).

54. Rose, *Governing the Soul*; Zelizer, *Pricing the Priceless Child*; and Kate Cregan and Denise Cuthbert, *Global Childhoods: Issues and Debates* (Thousand Oaks, CA: SAGE, 2014).

55. Lee Edelman, *No Future: Queer Theory and the Death Drive* (Durham, NC: Duke University Press, 2004).

56. Ellen Key published her landmark text, *The Century of the Child* (London: Forgotten, [1900] 2015), quite dramatically on New Year's Eve in 1900, hoping it would help to usher in a set of political transformations that would improve the amount and quality of attention given to childhood for the next hundred years. And, as most historians of childhood would now agree, the twentieth century was indeed the century of the child.

57. Frank Furedi, *Authority: A Sociological History* (Cambridge: Cambridge University Press, 2013), 362.

58. See Theodor Adorno et al., *The Authoritarian Personality* (New York: Harper & Row, 1950) for an exemplary instance of how psychoanalysis provided a vocabulary for linking domestic and familial authority to the rise of national authoritarianism.

59. Midgley, *Reading Anna Freud*, 48.

60. Peter C. Caldwell effectively describes the paradox undergirding the authority of constitutional democracies when he notes the logical fractures in the Austrian Constitution, which made its claim to legitimacy always a bit spurious. "The 1920 Austrian Constitution, for example, was created according to the norm regulating the formation of a constitutive national assembly in 1918. When a legal scientist followed the rule for creating a new constitution back to the rules creating those rules, eventually a break appeared in the continuity of legal development. Viewed in terms of legal norms, the Austro-Hungarian emperor's agreement in 1918 to recognize any decision by the National Council on the state's form was illegal according to existing law, since it was not approved by the Austro-Hungarian Imperial Council (*Reichsrat*). That revolutionary break in legal continuity raised the question of how to explain why a constitution was valid." Peter C. Caldwell, *Popular Sovereignty and the Crisis of German Constitutional Law: The Theory and Practice of Weimar Constitutionalism* (Durham, NC: Duke University Press, 1997), 92. For a similar debate in neighboring Germany, see Furedi, *Authority*, 352.

61. Barbara Jelavich, *Modern Austria: Empire & Republic, 1800–1986* (Cambridge: Cambridge University Press, 1987), 170.

62. Furedi, *Authority*, 351.

63. In an interesting layer on the general skepticism about democracy, the rise of authoritarian governments throughout Europe was often cited as an additional proof of democracy's failures. The Hungarian sociologist Karl Mannheim elaborates this position in 1933 when he writes in "The Democratization of Culture" that "dictatorships can only arise in democracies. . . . Dictatorship is not the antithesis of democracy; it represents one of the possible ways in which a democratic society may try to resolve its problems" (quoted in Furedi, *Authority*, 353). Democracy, ironically, suffered both from too little authority and the tendency to generate too much authoritarianism.

64. Furedi, *Authority*, 351.

65. Walter Lippmann, *Public Opinion* (New York: Macmillan, [1922] 1956), 75.

66. Max Weber, "Politics as a Vocation," in *Max Weber: Essays in Sociology*, ed. and trans. H. H. Gerth and C. Wright Mills (New York: Oxford University Press, [1919] 1946), 78.

67. Andreas Anter, *Max Weber's Theory of the Modern State: Origin, Structure, Significance* (London: Palgrave Macmillan, 2014), 48.

68. Furedi, *Authority*, 357.

69. For further reading on the Bulldogs Bank Home, see Stewart-Steinberg, *Impious Fidelity*.

2. BEYOND REPAIR: WAR, REPARATION, AND JUSTICE IN MELANIE KLEIN'S CLINIC

Portions of this chapter have already been published. See Carolyn Laubender, "Beyond Repair: Interpretation, Reparation, and Melanie Klein's Clinical Play Technique," *Studies in Gender and Sexuality* 20, no. 1 (2019): 51–67.

1. Quoted in Phyllis Grosskurth, *Melanie Klein: Her World and Her Work* (London: Jason Aronson, 1986), 262.

2. Klein's published case study of this analysis, *Narrative of a Child Analysis*, includes ninety-three sessions, but her diary lists ninety-six. Melanie Klein, *Narrative of a Child Analysis: The Conduct of the Psycho-Analysis of Children as Seen in the Treatment of a Ten-Year-Old Boy* (London: Random House, [1961] 1998).

3. Klein, *Narrative of a Child Analysis*, 19–20.

4. For a reading of the role of empire in this archive of images, see Carolyn Laubender, "Empires of Mind: Postcolonial Cartographies of 'The Empire' in *Narrative of a Child Analysis*," *Psychoanalysis, Culture, and Society* 26 (2021): 223–44.

5. Throughout her work, Klein spells "unconscious *ph*antasy" with a "ph" to distinguish it from more conscious, individual fantasies, such as those detailed in Sigmund Freud's writings on beating fantasies and Anna Freud's writings on daydreams. In her thinking, unconscious phantasy is a universal aspect of human experience, true of infants, children, and adults alike.

6. Eli Zaretsky, "Melanie Klein and the Emergence of Modern Personal Life," in *Reading Melanie Klein*, ed. John Phillips and Lyndsey Stonebridge (London: Routledge, 1998); Adam Phillips, *Promises, Promises: Essays on Psychoanalysis and Literature* (New York: Basic Books, 2001); Michal Shapira, *The War Inside: Psychoanalysis, Total War, and the Making of the Democratic Self in Postwar Britain* (Cambridge: Cambridge University Press, 2013); Michael Roper, "From the Shell-Shocked Soldier to the Nervous Child: Psychoanalysis in the Aftermath of the First World War," *Psychoanalysis and History* 18, no. 1 (2016): 39–69.

7. C. Fred Alford, *Melanie Klein and Critical Social Theory* (New Haven, CT: Yale University Press, 1989); Gal Gerson, "Winnicott, Participation, and Gender," *Feminism & Psychology* 14, no. 4 (2004): 561–81; David McIvor, "The Cunning of Recognition: Melanie Klein and Contemporary Critical Theory,"

Contemporary Critical Theory 15, no. 3 (2016): 243–63; Amy Allen, *Critique on the Couch: Why Critical Theory Needs Psychoanalysis* (New York: Columbia University Press, 2019).

8. For a comprehensive biography of Melanie Klein's life and work, see Grosskurth, *Melanie Klein*. For other biographical writings, see Hanna Segal, *Introduction to the Work of Melanie Klein* (London: Karnac, 1988); Janet Sayers, *Mothering Psychoanalysis: Helene Deutsch, Karen Horney, Anna Freud, and Melanie Klein* (New York: Norton, 1991); Julia Segal, *Melanie Klein* (London: SAGE, 1992); Claudine Geissmann and Pierre Geissmann, *A History of Child Psychoanalysis* (London: Routledge, 1998); Julia Kristeva, *Melanie Klein*, trans. Ross Guberman (New York: Columbia University Press, 2001); and Deborah Britzman, *Melanie Klein: Early Analysis, Play, and the Question of Freedom* (London: Springer, 2016).

9. I specify this period because although Klein certainly published in the 1920s, her early approach to child analysis was educative in nature and emphasized the importance of sexual enlightenment. See, for example, Melanie Klein, "The Development of a Child" (1921) and "The Rôle of School in the Libidinal Development of a Child" (1922), both published in *Love, Guilt, and Reparation and Other Works, 1921-1945* (New York: Free Press, 1975). This analytic approach began to change toward the end of the 1920s. Not insignificantly, this change occurred almost exactly when Anna Freud popularized her own analytic technique that took pedagogy as its hallmark. By 1932, with the publication of her first monograph, Melanie Klein, *The Psycho-Analysis of Children* (London: Vintage, [1932] 1975), Klein had abandoned her early enlightenment models and thoroughly established her phantasy-focused "play-technique" as a stark contrast to Freud's more pedagogical method.

10. For a full accounting of these discussions, see Pearl King and Ricardo Steiner, eds., *The Freud-Klein Controversies: 1941–45* (London: Routledge, 1991). For astute cultural histories and more theoretical analyses of them, see Jacqueline Rose, *Why War? Psychoanalysis, Politics, and the Return to Melanie Klein* (Oxford: Blackwell University Press, 1993); Phillips, *Promises, Promises*; Deborah Britzman, *After-Education: Anna Freud, Melanie Klein, and Psychoanalytic Histories of Learning* (New York: New York State University Press, 2003); and George Makari, *Revolution in Mind: The Creation of Psychoanalysis* (New York: Harper, 2008).

11. Jones made the first remark in a letter to Melanie Klein in 1942 (quoted in Elisabeth Young-Bruehl, *Anna Freud: A Biography* [New Haven, CT: Yale University Press, 2008], 259) and the second is from a mutually snippy exchange between Sigmund Freud and Jones in 1927, surrounding the publication of Anna Freud's first book in English (quoted in Makari, *Revolution in Mind*, 429).

12. J. B. Pontalis, "The Question Child," in *Reading Melanie Klein*, ed. John Phillips and Lyndsey Stonebridge (London: Routledge, 1998), 83.

13. Melanie Klein, "The Psychological Principles of Early Analysis," in *Love, Guilt, and Reparation and Other Works, 1921-1945* (New York: Free Press, [1926] 1975), 135.

14. Klein, "The Psychological Principles of Early Analysis," 137.

15. Klein, "The Psychological Principles of Early Analysis," 138.

16. Klein, *The Psycho-Analysis of Children*, 16.

17. Although children were allowed to bring their own toys, Klein also provided a curated selection of objects. The array of small, simple toys included figures of cars, people, houses, animals, trees, and carts. To the extent that play operates as symbolic language in Klein's play technique, the provision of toys is roughly equivalent to the provision of the words the child can use throughout the sessions. Explains Klein, "Their smallness, their number and their great variety give the child a wide range of representational play, while their very simplicity enables them to be put to the most varied uses. Thus, toys like these are well suited for the expression of phantasies and experiences in all kinds of ways and in great detail" (Klein, *The Psycho-Analysis of Children*, 32–33). Klein's choice of objects—small or large, geometric or organic, neutral or brightly colored, damaged or fully functioning—already determines the symbolic capacity of the child's play. For instance, driven by her sense of which phantasies predominate in the child's mind, Klein repeatedly asserts that the child should also have access to running water specifically because many oral and urethral phantasies are represented through this medium.

18. Klein, *The Psycho-Analysis of Children*, 20–21.

19. For a more thorough discussion of Klein's interpretive technique and a detailed consideration of the ethical issues it raises in clinical practice, see Carolyn Laubender, "Beyond Repair: Interpretation, Reparation, and Melanie Klein's Clinical Play Technique," *Studies in Gender and Sexuality* 20, no. 1 (2019): 51–67.

20. Anna Freud, *Four Lectures on Child Analysis*, in *The Writings of Anna Freud*, vol. 1 (New York: International Universities Press, [1926] 1974), 37.

21. Critiques such as these were common, even among Klein's main supporters and acolytes. For instance, in a review of Klein's *Narrative of a Child Analysis*, Elisabeth Geleerd, in "Evaluation of Melanie Klein's 'Narrative of a Child Analysis,'" *International Journal of Psychoanalysis* 44 (1963): 506, charges rather forcefully that "Klein's random way of interpreting does not reflect the material but, rather, her preconceived theoretical assumptions regarding child development." For other such points, see Hanna Segal and Donald Meltzer, "Narrative of a Child Analysis," *International Journal of Psychoanalysis* 44 (1963): 507–13; and Donald Meltzer, *The Kleinian Development* (London: Karnac, 1978).

22. For a deeper consideration of the different models of temporality in Anna Freud's and Klein's respective theories of the child, see Shaul Bar-Haim,

"The Child's Position: The Concept of Childhood in Interwar Psychoanalysis,"
in *Childhood, Literature, and Science: Fragile Subjects*, ed. Jutta Ahlbeck,
Päivi Lappalainen, Kati Launis, and Kirsi Tuohela (London: Routledge, 2017).

23. Melanie Klein, "Criminal Tendencies in Normal Children," in *Love, Guilt,
and Reparation and Other Works, 1921–1945* (New York: Free Press, [1927]
1975), 173.

24. Klein draws much of her thinking about unconscious phantasy from a biological understanding of phylogenesis and narrates the unconscious phantasies
of the child (and adult) according to the instinctual inheritance of the past.
Endowed with this unconscious instinctual knowledge, children "represent
symbolically phantasies, wishes and experiences [in their play]. Here they
are employing the same phylogenetically acquired mode of expression as we
are familiar with from dreams" (Klein, "The Psychological Principles of Early
Analysis," 134). For further reading on the role of instinct in Klein's theory
of unconscious phantasy, see Susan Isaacs, "On the Nature and Function of
Phantasy," *International Journal of Psychoanalysis* 29 ([1943] 1948): 73–97;
and Robert D. Hinshelwood, *A Dictionary of Kleinian Thought* (London: Free
Association, 1998), 34.

25. While there has been substantial debate about the differences of meaning
in Sigmund Freud's use of the German "trieb" versus "instinkt" (and about
the Stracheys's translation of both these terms), when it comes to Klein this
debate is less relevant since almost all of her post-1920s writing is in English,
where she almost exclusively uses the language of "instinct."

26. Juliet Mitchell, "Introduction," in *The Selected Melanie Klein*, ed. Juliet Mitchell
(New York: Free Press, 1986), 24.

27. Nancy Chodorow, *The Reproduction of Mothering: Psychoanalysis and the
Sociology of Gender* (Los Angeles: University of California Press, 1978).

28. Denise Riley, *The War in the Nursery: Theories of the Child and Mother*
(London: Virago, 1983).

29. Jacqueline Rose, *Why War? Psychoanalysis, Politics, and the Return to Melanie
Klein* (Oxford: Blackwell University Press, 1993); Lyndsey Stonebridge, *The
Destructive Element: British Psychoanalysis and Modernism* (New York:
Routledge, 1998); Julia Kristeva, *Melanie Klein*, trans. Ross Guberman (New
York: Columbia University Press, 2001); Ramón Soto-Crespo, "Heterosexuality
Terminable or Interminable? Kleinian Fantasies of Reparation and Mourning,"
in *Homosexuality and Psychoanalysis*, ed. Tim Dean and Christopher Lane
(Chicago: University of Chicago Press, 2001), 190-209.

30. For a compelling analysis of the elision of Klein's biologism from feminist
readings of her work, see Elizabeth A. Wilson, *Gut Feminism* (Durham, NC:
Duke University Press, 2015).

31. For a fuller elaboration of the role of the death instinct in Klein's work (especially vis-à-vis literary and aesthetic modernism), see Leo Bersani, *The Culture of Redemption* (Cambridge, MA: Harvard University Press, 1990); Stonebridge, *The Destructive Element*; and Esther Sánchez-Pardo, *Cultures of the Death Drive: Melanie Klein and Modernist Melancholia* (Durham, NC: Duke University Press, 2003).

32. Departing from both Sigmund and Anna Freud, who held that the superego was a precipitate of the Oedipus complex and solidified in the child somewhere around the fifth year of life, Klein argues that the superego is introjected much earlier in the child's life, at the beginning of Oedipalization, when the child's unbridled oral-sadistic instincts are at their height. Klein dramatically predated the Oedipal scenario, imagining children as young as one in the thick of an Oedipal crisis. Consequently, the formation of the superego, for Klein, was more bound up with instinctual conflict than with the child's actual perception of its parents. Claudine and Pierre Geissmann write, "For Klein, the child's superego is more marked by the child's instincts than by its real parents" (*A History of Child Psychoanalysis*, 129). In the process of expurgating the death instinct, the child introjects a superego. In 1933, Klein writes,

> In order to escape from being destroyed by its own death instinct, the organism employs its narcissistic, or self-regarding libido to force the former outward, and direct it against its objects. . . .
>
> This apparently earliest measure of defence on the part of the ego constitutes, I think, the foundation of the development of the superego, whose excessive violence at this early stage would thus be accounted for by the fact that it is an offshoot of very intense destructive instincts. (Melanie Klein, "The Early Development of Conscience in the Child," in *Love, Guilt, and Reparation and Other Works, 1921–1945* [New York: Free Press, (1933) 1975], 250.)

Because of this, the child (especially the female child, a point I have argued elsewhere [Laubender, "Beyond Repair"]) internalizes an overly strong superego that wreaks havoc on the child's relatively weak and defenseless ego. Continues Klein: "Since the first imagos it [the child] thus forms are endowed with all the attributes of the intense sadism belonging to this stage of its development . . . the small child becomes dominated by the fear of suffering unimaginable cruel attacks, both from its real objects and from its superego" (Klein, "The Early Development of Conscience in the Child," 251). Klein discusses this further in her 1932 *The Psycho-Analysis of Children*, but, in addition to an understanding of the superego as a persecutory force, one of the yields of acknowledging Klein's predating of the Oedipal complex is the recognition that her work is not really pre-Oedipal in the way many social commentators suggest.

33. In their foundational text in childhood studies, James, Jenks, and Prout identify five key "presociological discourses" that pertain to the contemporary ideology of childhood in the Global North, including among these the "immanent" and the "innocent" child, as derived from Locke and Rousseau, respectively. Allison James, Chris Jenks, and Alan Prout, *Theorizing Childhood* (Cambridge: Polity, 1998), 3–21.

34. Phillips, *Promises, Promises*, 41.

35. Klein, *Narrative of a Child Analysis*, 15.

36. Klein, *Narrative of a Child Analysis*, 28.

37. Throughout Klein's oeuvre, she maintains that "mental health" is demonstrated by a normative genital heterosexuality. While she acknowledges that homosexual energies and attachments are constantly present in every individual's mental life, she nevertheless argues that the "unsuccessful" sublimation of these libidinal investments can itself be a cause for psychoanalytic intervention. For examples of this, see cases like "Mr. B," "Erna," "Rita," "Little Dick," and "Richard." For a creative rereading of her work that challenges her heteronormativity, see Soto-Crespo, "Heterosexuality Terminable or Interminable?"

38. Shapira, *The War Inside*.

39. Daniel Pick does not explore the coincidence of "asylum" that was motoring Hess's escape, but his desire for political refuge through an appeal to psychological malady is certainly noteworthy. Daniel Pick, *The Pursuit of the Nazi Mind: Hitler, Hess, and the Analysts* (Oxford: Oxford University Press, 2014).

40. Phillips, *Promises, Promises*; Shapira, *The War Inside*; and Roper, "From the Shell-Shocked Soldier to the Nervous Child."

41. Shapira, *The War Inside*, 90.

42. Zaretsky, "Melanie Klein and the Emergence of Modern Personal Life," 32.

43. Roper, "From the Shell-Shocked Soldier to the Nervous Child."

44. Klein, *Narrative of a Child Analysis*, 466.

45. To this, Klein notes at an earlier point in Richard's analysis, "It is an essential part of psycho-analytic therapy (and this applies to children and adults) that the patient should be enabled by the analyst's interpretations to integrate the split-off and contrasting aspects of self" (Klein, *Narrative of a Child Analysis*, 77).

46. Klein, *Narrative of a Child Analysis*, 66–67.

47. Quoted in Grosskurth, *Melanie Klein*, 262.

48. Klein, *Narrative of a Child Analysis*, 56.

49. Klein, *Narrative of a Child Analysis*, 57.

50. Klein, *Narrative of a Child Analysis*, 114.

51. Hinshelwood, *A Dictionary of Kleinian Thought*, 378.

52. Melanie Klein, "A Contribution to the Psychogenesis of Manic Depressive States," in *Love, Guilt, and Reparation and Other Works, 1921–1945* (New York: Free Press, [1935] 1975), 264.

53. Melanie Klein, "Love, Guilt and Reparation," in *Love, Guilt, and Reparation and Other Works, 1921–1945* (New York: Free Press, [1937] 1975), 308–9.

54. Klein, "Love, Guilt and Reparation," 313.

55. Klein, *Narrative of a Child Analysis*, 366–67.

56. Klein, *Narrative of a Child Analysis*, 16.

57. Klein, *Narrative of a Child Analysis*, 44.

58. Klein, *Narrative of a Child Analysis*, 51.

59. Klein, *Narrative of a Child Analysis*, 61.

60. Klein, *Narrative of a Child Analysis*, 125.

61. Klein, *Narrative of a Child Analysis*, 277.

62. Klein, *Narrative of a Child Analysis*, 341.

63. Klein, *Narrative of a Child Analysis*, 367.

64. Klein, *Narrative of a Child Analysis*, 434.

65. Klein, *Narrative of a Child Analysis*, 434.

66. Karl Figlio, *Remembering as Reparation: Psychoanalysis and Historical Memory* (London: Palgrave Macmillan, 2017).

67. Alford, *Melanie Klein and Critical Social Theory*; C. Fred Alford, *Psychology and the Natural Law of Reparation* (New York: Cambridge University Press, 2006).

68. In addition to Alford, notable critics in this trend include Axel Honneth, *The Struggle for Recognition: The Moral Grammar of Social Conflicts* (Cambridge: Polity, 1992); Gerson, "Winnicott, Participation, and Gender"; McIvor, "The Cunning of Recognition"; Matthew H. Bowker and Amy Buzby, eds., *D. W. Winnicott and Political Theory: Recentering the Subject* (London: Palgrave Macmillan, 2017); Noëlle McAfee, *Fear of a Breakdown: Psychoanalysis and Politics* (New York: Columbia University Press, 2019); and Allen, *Critique on the Couch*. As Allen notes, there is an implicit division within this work regarding assumptions about the fundamentality of aggression and destruction to the human condition, with those who downgrade this element (Honneth; Bowker and Buzby) preferring the work of post-Kleinian Object Relations theorists, notably D. W. Winnicott.

69. Sedgwick's methodological proposition has been a generative one for queer theory, feminist theory, affect theory, and literary studies generally, with scholars taking up the "reparative turn" both as a stylistic for reading and as an object in and of itself. José Muñoz, "The Vulnerability Artist: Nao Bustamante and the Sad Beauty of Reparation," *Women & Performance: A Journal of Feminist Theory* 16 (2006): 191–200; Heather Love, *Feeling Backward: Loss and the Politics of Queer History* (Boston, MA: Harvard University Press, 2007); Elizabeth Freeman, *Time Binds: Queer Temporalities, Queer Histories* (Durham, NC: Duke University Press, 2010); Ellis Hanson, "The Future's Eve: Reparative Reading After Sedgwick," *South Atlantic Quarterly* 110, no. 1 (2011): 101–19;

Ann Cvetkovitch, *Depression: A Public Feeling* (Durham, NC: Duke University Press, 2012); Robyn Wiegman, "The Times We're In," *Feminist Theory* 15, no. 1 (2014): 4–25; Clare Hemmings, "The Materials of Reparation," *Feminist Theory* 15, no. 1 (2014): 27–30; Gail Lewis, "Not by Criticality Alone," *Feminist Theory* 15, no. 1 (2014): 31–38; Jackie Stacey, "Wishing Away Ambivalence," *Feminist Theory* 15, no. 1 (2014): 39–49; and David Eng, "Colonial Object Relations," *Social Text* 34, no. 1 (2016): 1–19 have all participated in the conversation about reparative reading, sometimes enacting and sometimes critiquing it. Other key contributors to the debates about a "post-critique" critical method, beyond the scope of "reparative reading" specifically, include Steven Marcus and Sharon Best, Rita Felski, Ellen Rooney, Franco Moretti, and Toril Moi, as well as a number of special issues of journals such as *Novel* (2009), *Representations* (2009), *differences* (2010), *SAQ* (2011), *GLQ* (2011), *M/C Journal* (2012), and *Feminist Theory* (2014), among others. Rita Felski, "Introduction," *New Literary History* 45, no. 2 (2014): v–xi.

70. Bersani, *The Culture of Redemption*; Rose, *Why War?*; Stonebridge, *The Destructive Element*; and Sánchez-Pardo, *Cultures of the Death Drive*.

71. Public discussion about reparations began in Britain after the publication of Norman Angell's influential *The Great Illusion* (first published in 1909 as *Europe's Optical Illusion*, and republished in 1910 under its new title). Norman Angell, *The Great Illusion: A Study of the Relation of Military Power to National Advantage* (New York: G. P. Putnam, [1909] 1913). A general critique of war between industrialized countries, Angell's text presciently argued that major military excursions would never yield the material gain that they sought given how codependent modern nations were because of increasingly global flows of exchange. As part of this point, Angell was sharply critical of monetary reparations as compensation for the losses of war. While his work was disputed, the historian Robert E. Bunselmeyer states, "Angell's theory and the criticisms around it must nevertheless be considered the first origin of British thinking about reparation and indemnity" (Robert E. Bunselmeyer, *The Cost of War, 1914–1919: British Economic War Aims and the Origins of Reparation* [Hamden, CT: Shoe String, 1975], 63). Angell's work set the stage for a decades-long conversation throughout Europe about reparative justice.

72. John Maynard Keynes, *The Economic Consequences of the Peace* (New York: Skyhorse, [1919] 2007).

73. For further case-study analyses of different national reparations programs throughout the twentieth century, see Pablo de Grieff's edited collection, *The Handbook of Reparations* (Oxford: Oxford University Press, 2006). See Ta-Nehisi Coates, "The Case for Reparations," *The Atlantic*, June 2014, for his much-publicized defense of reparations.

74. Ruth Rubio-Marìn, *The Gender of Reparations: Unsettling Sexual Hierarchies While Redressing Human Rights Violations* (Cambridge: Cambridge University Press, 2009), 7.

75. Klein, *Narrative of a Child Analysis*, 466.

76. Klein, "Love, Guilt and Reparation," 311.

77. Hinshelwood, *A Dictionary of Kleinian Thought*, 414.

78. Klein, "Love, Guilt and Reparation," 334.

79. Eng, "Colonial Object Relations," 14.

80. Melanie Klein, "Infantile Anxiety-Situations Reflected in a Work of Art and in the Creative Impulse," in *Love, Guilt, and Reparation and Other Works, 1921–1945* (New York: Free Press, [1929] 1975), 217.

81. For a consideration of the painter's identity, see A. O. Olsen, "Depression and Reparation as Themes in Melanie Klein's Analysis of the Painter Ruth Weber," *Scandinavian Psychoanalytic Review* 27, no. 1 (2004).

82. Jean Walton, "Re-Placing Race in (White) Psychoanalytic Discourse: Founding Narratives of Feminism," *Critical Inquiry* 21, no. 4 (1995): 799.

3. TRAVELING ANALYSIS: WULF SACHS, RACIAL JUSTICE, AND THE (DE)COLONIAL CLINIC IN SOUTH AFRICA

1. "Chavafambira" is the name Sachs uses throughout *Black Hamlet*, but historical records are not able to verify whether Sachs in any way modified the name for this publication. While it was not uncommon for Black Africans to adopt Anglicized first names, especially those who worked for white employers in urban centers, none of the other documents that refer to Chavafambira (such as Ellen Hellmann's *Rooiyard: A Sociological Study of an Urban Native Slum Yard*, Rhodes-Livingstone Papers No. 13 [Oxford: Oxford University Press, 1948] or Ralph Bunche's diary from the period, which has been published as a travelogue entitled *An African American in South Africa: The Travel Notes of Ralph J. Bunche 28 September 1937–1 January 1938* [Athens: Ohio University Press, 1992]) do so by name. The South African historian Saul Dubow speculates that John's surname was most likely spelled "Chawafambira" (Saul Dubow, "Wulf Sachs' 'Black Hamlet': A Case of Psychic Vivisection?," *African Affairs* 92, no. 369 [1993]: 3).

2. Mariano Ben Plotkin, *Freud in the Pampas: The Formation of a Psychoanalytic Culture in Argentina, 1910–1983* (Stanford, CA: Stanford University Press, 2001); Joy Damousi, *Freud in the Antipodes: A Cultural History of Psychoanalysis in Australia* (Sydney: University of New South Wales, 2005); Warwick

Anderson, Deborah Jenson, and Richard C. Keller, eds., *Unconscious Dominions: Psychoanalysis, Colonial Trauma, and Global Sovereignties* (Durham, NC: Duke University Press, 2011); Erik Linstrum, *Ruling Minds: Psychology and the British Empire* (Cambridge, MA: Harvard University Press, 2016); Ross Trusscott and Derek Hook, "The Vicissitudes of Anger: Psychoanalysis in the Time of Apartheid," in *Psychoanalysis and the Age of Totalitarianism*, ed. Matt ffytche and Daniel Pick (London: Routledge, 2016), 193–204; Dagmar Herzog, *Cold War Freud: Psychoanalysis in an Age of Catastrophes* (Cambridge: Cambridge University Press, 2017); and Aline Rubin, Belinda Mandelbaum, and Stephen Frosh, "No Memory, No Desire: Psychoanalysis in Brazil During Repressive Times," *Psychoanalysis and History* 18, no. 1 (2016): 93–118.

3. Wulf Sachs, *Black Hamlet* (Boston: Little, Brown, 1947).

4. Jacqueline Rose, "Black Hamlet," in *States of Fantasy* (Oxford: Oxford University Press, 1996), 38–55; Dubow, "Wulf Sachs' 'Black Hamlet'"; Chesca Long-Innes, "Wulf Sachs' Black Hamlet: Constructing the 'Native Mind,'" *Issues in English Studies in Southern Africa* 5, no. 2 (2000): 78–85; Ranjana Khanna, *Dark Continents: Psychoanalysis and Colonialism* (Durham, NC: Duke University Press, 2003); Andreas Bertoldi, "Shakespeare, Psychoanalysis, and the Colonial Encounter: The Case of Wulf Sachs' Black Hamlet," in *Post-Colonial Shakespeares*, ed. Ania Loomba and Martin Orkin (New York: Routledge, 2003), 235–58.

5. Sachs, *Black Hamlet*, 125–26.

6. Sachs, *Black Hamlet*, 125–26.

7. Sachs, *Black Hamlet*, 125–26.

8. Gilles Deleuze and Félix Guattari, "Psychoanalysis and Ethnology," *SubStance* 4, nos. 11–12 (1975): 173.

9. Michael Molnar, ed., *The Diary of Sigmund Freud, 1929–1939: A Record of the Final Decade* (London: Hogarth, 1992), 173.

10. Although Sachs established a South African Psychoanalytic Society in the 1930s—something Freud himself notes in the 1935 postscript of his "Autobiographical Study"—the quick succession of apartheid's implementation in 1948 and Wulf Sachs's death in 1949 extinguished the nascent training regime. See Mark Solms, "The Establishment of an Accredited Training Institute in South Africa," *Psycho-Analytic Psychotherapy in South Africa* 18, no. 1 (2010).

11. Rickman, J. "Wulf Sachs, 1893–1949," *International Journal of Psychoanalysis* 31 (1950): 288–89.

12. Sachs, *Black Hamlet*, 24–25.

13. Sachs, *Black Hamlet*, xi.

14. Sachs, *Black Hamlet*, 7.
15. Dubow, "Wulf Sachs' 'Black Hamlet,'" 6.
16. For further reading on the Native Bills, see Saul Dubow, *Racial Segregation and the Origins of Apartheid in Twentieth Century South Africa, 1919–36* (London: Palgrave Macmillan, 1989).
17. Quoted in Dubow, "Wulf Sachs' 'Black Hamlet,'" 8.
18. While scholars of South African history generally agree that pre-apartheid segregation was inextricable from the period of accelerated industrialization that followed on the heels of the formation of the Union of South Africa, there is debate about the relationship between industrialization, segregation, and capitalist expansion. For accounts of how capitalism relied on segregation for its instantiation, see Harold Wolpe, "Capitalism and Cheap Labor-Power in South Africa: From Segregation to Apartheid," *Economy and Society* 1, no. 4 (1972): 425–56; Martin Legassick, "South Africa: Capital Accumulation and Violence," *Economy and Society* 3, no. 3 (1974): 253–91; Frederick A. Johnstone, *Class, Race, and Gold: A Study of Class Relations and Racial Discrimination in South Africa* (London: Routledge and Kegan Paul, 1976); and Martin Lacey, *Working for Boroko: The Origins of a Coercive Labor System in South Africa* (Johannesburg: Ravan, 1981). For the argument that segregation was a more autonomous ideological racial system with only a "weak" relation to capitalist development, see Dubow, *Racial Segregation and the Origins of Apartheid in Twentieth Century South Africa*. For an overview of these debates within the field of South African Scholarship, also see Dubow, *Racial Segregation and the Origins of Apartheid in Twentieth Century South Africa*, and Zachary Levenson and Marcel Paret, "The South African Tradition of Racial Capitalism," *Ethnic and Racial Studies* 46, no. 16 (2023): 3403–24.
19. Dubow, "Wulf Sachs' 'Black Hamlet,'" 1.
20. Dubow, "Wulf Sachs' 'Black Hamlet,'" 3.
21. Barbara Celarent, *"Rooiyard: A Sociological Survey of an Urban Native Slum Yard* by Ellen Hellmann," *American Journal of Sociology* 118, no. 1 (July 2012): 275.
22. Hellmann, *Rooiyard*, 17.
23. Hellmann, *Rooiyard*, 10.
24. Maynard W. Swanson, "The Sanitation Syndrome: Bubonic Plague and Urban Native Policy in the Cape Colony, 1900–1909," *Journal of African History* 18, no. 3 (1977): 387–410; Wulf Sachs, with a new introduction by Saul Dubow and Jacqueline Rose, *Black Hamlet* (Baltimore, MD: John Hopkins University Press, 1996).
25. Dubow, "Wulf Sachs' 'Black Hamlet,'" 2.
26. Sachs, *Black Hamlet*, 160.

27. For further reading on Carothers and East African ethnopsychology, see Chloe Campbell, "Kenyan Medical Discourse and Eugenics," in *Race and Empire: Eugenics in Colonial Kenya*, ed. Chloe Campbell, Andrew Thompson, and John Mackenzie (Manchester: Manchester University Press, 2007), 39–76; Jock McCulloch, *Colonial Psychiatry and the African Mind* (Cambridge: Cambridge University Press, 1995); Sloan Mahone, "East African Psychiatry and the Practical Problems of Empire," in *Psychiatry and Empire*, ed. Sloan Mahone and Megan Vaughan (London: Palgrave Macmillan, 2007), 41–67; and Megan Vaughan, "The Madman and the Medicine Man: Colonial Psychiatry and the Theory of Deculturation," in *Curing Their Ills: Colonial Power and African Illness* (Cambridge: Cambridge University Press, 1991), 100–128. While British East African (ethno)psychologists were some of the most well-known and prolific on the continent, their general interest in using the intersection of culture and anatomy to define racial difference was common across Africa. For research on French North Africa, see Richard C. Keller, "Madness and Colonization: Psychiatry in the British and French Empires, 1800–1962," *Journal of Social History* 35, no. 2 (2001): 295–326; and Richard C. Keller, *Colonial Madness: Psychiatry in French North Africa* (Chicago: University of Chicago Press, 2007). For West Africa, see Jonathan Sadowsky, *Imperial Bedlam: Institutions of Madness in Colonial Southwest Nigeria* (Los Angeles: University of California Press, 1999).

28. Although Carothers nominally attributed this cerebral deficiency to East African "culture" rather than biological "race," his conception of culture shared little with the flexible and plastic anthropological uses of this concept. While earlier non-African ethnopsychological research by the anthropologists Bronislaw Malinowski and Margaret Mead tended to emphasize the horizontal and contingent variegations of culture, arguing that the cultural norms and psychological rubrics of the Anglophone West were local and contingent rather than global and universal, African ethnopsychologists like Carothers took a wholly different tack, promulgating more intransigent accounts that supposedly substantiated African inferiority. According to McCulloch in his thorough history of the East African colonial psychiatry, "Carothers was careful to attribute these [cerebral] qualities to their culture rather than to their race, but he did characterize Africans as, in effect, delinquent children," neurologically and psychologically unsuited to the developmental standards of European civilization (McCulloch, *Colonial Psychiatry and the African Mind*, 52). Ultimately, his writing confirmed the immutability of African inferiority. As Megan Vaughan adroitly explains, colonial ethnopsychology in Africa was thus much less concerned with the etiology of madness per se than it was with locating and circumscribing Black "Africanness" through the creation of specific psychological rubrics that used

culture to preserve previous ideas of racial difference and hierarchy (Vaughan, "The Madman and the Medicine Man," 119). For fuller accounts of Carothers's claims and influence, see McCulloch, *Colonial Psychiatry and the African Mind*; and Vaughan, "The Madman and the Medicine Man." For further reading on Carothers's predecessors, including H. L. Gordon and the pathologist F. W. Vint, see Campbell, "Kenyan Medical Discourse and Eugenics"; and Mahone, "East African Psychiatry and the Practical Problems of Empire."

29. Carothers's work garnered him much international attention throughout the midcentury, both laudatory and critical. In 1952, for instance, he was commissioned by the WHO to write a report on the status of mental health in Africa. This report, titled *The African Mind in Health and Disease: A Study in Ethnopsychiatry*, was one of many such surveys commissioned by the WHO in the immediate aftermath of World War II that specifically targeted social psychology as a crucible of postwar recovery. This research was widely recognized and Carothers was subsequently invited to the WHO conferences in Geneva, Switzerland, where he presented his work and rubbed shoulders with intellectual luminaries like Konrad Lorenz and Margaret Mead (McCulloch, *Colonial Psychiatry and the African Mind*, 58). Shortly thereafter, the British government also asked Carothers to provide an analysis of the Mau Mau rebellion, a request that itself showcases Carothers's willing collaboration—and African ethnopsychology's overall compatibility—with the British state's colonial agenda. In *The Psychology of Mau Mau*, published in 1954, Carothers assessed the anticolonial action and ideology of the Mau Mau. Basing his conclusions on the conviction that their resistance was fundamentally a matter of psychology and not oppression, expropriation, or dispossession, he argued that this political movement resulted from the conflict between the psychological collectivity engendered by traditional African tribal lifestyles and the independent individualism galvanized by European modernization. Mau Mau, he explains, is "an anxious conflictual situation [resulting] in people who, from contact with the alien culture, had lost the supportive and constraining influences of their own culture, yet had not lost their 'magic' modes of thinking" (John Colin Carothers, *The Psychology of Mau Mau* [Nairobi: Printed by the Govt. printer, 1954], 15). Styled here as a "clash of cultures" rather than "deculturation" or "detribalization," Carothers's psychologization of politics was well-received and clearly visible as a major influence on the 1960 Cornfield Report, the official British colonial doctrine on the Mau Mau uprising. As McCulloch states, Carothers's publications "from 1940 until 1960 eventually made him the most frequently quoted psychiatrist of the colonial era. Carothers' influence was such that [even] Frantz Fanon was moved to include an attack upon him in *The Wretched of the Earth*" (McCulloch, *Colonial Psychiatry and the African Mind*, 51).

But by the time Fanon levelled this critique in 1961—in tandem with the growing African independence movements—the tide had already begun to turn and Carothers's research, particularly, was becoming the object of rigorous postcolonial and antiracist censure. For further reading, see John Lonsdale, "Mau Maus of the Mind: Making Mau Mau and Remaking Kenya," *Journal of African History* 31, no. 3 (1990): 393–421.

30. Part of the reason for the popularity of this theory (which was also known as the "deculturation" or "acculturation" thesis, as various reports put it) was that it purported to explain the fact that a disproportionate number of the recorded cases of institutionalized, "mad" Africans were drawn from those living in Europeanized, urban centers (rather than on rural reserves). Such statistics led colonial physicians and psychiatrists to conclude that European education and culture itself was to blame for the spikes in asylum populations. Accordingly, Vaughan states that, from the 1930s to the 1950s, the deculturation thesis "remained virtually hegemonic in both professional and popular writings on African psychology" (Vaughan, "The Madman and the Medicine Man," 113). Flawed in many ways, this interpretation took no notice of the role that migration played in the lives of urban Africans, both as a psychological stressor and as a physical barrier that disconnected many from established informal networks of familial and community care. Moreover, as Vaughan points out, the focus on European education, specifically, as posing the greatest threat to the African mind clearly extends colonial anxieties about the role formal education could play in facilitating colonial assimilation—and potentially even galvanizing anticolonial resistance (Vaughan, "The Madman and the Medicine Man," 110). This familiar paradox was part and parcel of the "civilizing mission" that was British colonialism's raison d'être.

31. Carothers's postwar contribution to ethnopsychology was, in many ways, the distillation of much earlier, interwar scientific and psychological claim-making in the East African context. Decades prior to Carothers's celebrity in the 1950s, Gordon was already publishing and presenting research in the 1930s on the supposed cerebral deficiency of East Africans, which (he argued) made them poor candidates for European education and acculturation. Gordon insisted that atrophied frontal lobes were a fixed racial difference and, as such, he advanced an insistently structural, rather than functional, theory of African neurological deficiency. A great advocate of eugenics, he presented papers to the Eugenics Society in London in the 1930s and continued to defend Nazi eugenicists for their unflinching commitment to what he saw as racial refinement well into the 1940s. Gordon's claims were strongly bolstered by the findings of his collaborator, F. W. Vint, a government-appointed pathologist stationed at the Pathological Research Laboratory in Nairobi who had a strong

reputation for scientific rigor (see Campbell, "Kenyan Medical Discourse and Eugenics," 41; Mahone, "East African Psychiatry and the Practical Problems of Empire," 47). Throughout the 1930s, Vint carried out mass autopsies on Africans, specifically weighing their brain matter and measuring the size of the prefrontal cortex. Although Vint generally drew far fewer racial conclusions from his work, the raw data he collected was used by Gordon to substantiate his claims. While Gordon's research undoubtedly invested in a much stronger interpretation of constitutional racial difference than Carothers—indeed, Gordon has since become one of the most often cited exemplars of scientific racism in East Africa—all three thinkers concurred throughout their careers on the relative intransigence of supposed African inferiority. For further reading on East African psychology, see Mahone, "East African Psychiatry and the Practical Problems of Empire." For further reading specifically about eugenics in Kenya, see Campbell, "Kenyan Medical Discourse and Eugenics."

32. Wulf Sachs, "The Insane Native: An Introduction to a Psychological Study," *South African Journal of Science* 30 (1933): 710.
33. Sachs, *Black Hamlet*, 4.
34. Sachs, *Black Hamlet*, 3.
35. See Rose, "Black Hamlet"; Khanna, *Dark Continents*; and Bertoldi, "Shakespeare, Psychoanalysis, and the Colonial Encounter."
36. Sachs, *Black Hamlet*, 168.
37. Sachs, *Black Hamlet*, 169.
38. Sachs, *Black Hamlet*, 63–68.
39. Khanna, "Hamlet in the Colonial Archive," *Dark Continents*, 231–68.
40. Sachs, *Black Hamlet*, 223.
41. Sachs, *Black Hamlet*, 51.
42. Sachs, *Black Hamlet*, 317.
43. Dubow, "Wulf Sachs' 'Black Hamlet.'"
44. Sachs, *Black Hamlet*, 275.
45. For an excellent analysis of how "alienation" functions as the lynchpin of the case by joining colonial labor exploitation with psychological self-division, see Wahbie Long, "Alienation: A New Orienting Principle for Psychotherapists in South Africa," *Psychoanalytic Psychotherapy in South Africa* 25, no. 1 (2017): 67–90.
46. Sachs, *Black Hamlet*, 164.
47. Sachs, *Black Hamlet*, 323.
48. Frantz Fanon, *Black Skin, White Masks* (New York: Grove, [1952] 2008), 80.
49. Long-Innes, "Wulf Sachs' *Black Hamlet*," 82.
50. Jonathan V. Crewe, "Black Hamlet: Psychoanalysis on Trial in South Africa," *Poetics Today* 22, no. 2 (2001): 413.
51. Long-Innes, "Wulf Sachs' *Black Hamlet*," 82.

52. Dubow, "Wulf Sachs' 'Black Hamlet,'" 14.
53. Sachs's original draft manuscript is still in existence. See the University of the Witwatersrand Historical Papers Research Archive, A2120.
54. Sybille Yates, "Review: Black Hamlet," *International Journal of Psychoanalysis* 19, no. 2 (1938): 251–52.
55. Sadie Gillespie, "Historical Notes on the First South African Psychoanalytic Society," *Psychoanalytic Psychotherapy in South Africa* 1 (1992): 4.
56. Dubow, "Wulf Sachs' 'Black Hamlet,'" 14.
57. Bertoldi, "Shakespeare, Psychoanalysis, and the Colonial Encounter," 245.
58. Rickman, "Wulf Sachs, 1893–1949," 288–89.
59. Ashis Nandy, "The Savage Freud: The First Non-Western Psychoanalyst in Colonial India," in *The Savage Freud and Other Essays on Possible and Retrievable Selves* (Princeton, NJ: Princeton University Press, 1995), 81–144.
60. Gabriel N. Mendes, *Under the Strain of Color: Harlem's Lafargue Clinic and the Promise of an Antiracist Psychiatry* (Ithaca, NY: Cornell University Press, 2015).
61. Mariano Ben Plotkin, "Psychoanalysis, Race, and National Identity: The Reception of Psychoanalysis in Brazil, 1910–1940," in *Unconscious Dominions: Psychoanalysis, Colonial Trauma, and Global Sovereignties*, ed. Warwick Anderson, Deborah Jenson, and Richard C. Keller (Durham, NC: Duke University Press, 2011), 113–40.
62. Aída Alejandra Golcman, "The Experiment of the Therapeutic Communities in Argentina: The Case of the Hospital Estévez," *Psychoanalysis and History* 14, no. 2 (2021): 269–84.
63. Camille Robcis, *Disalienation: Politics, Philosophy, and Radical Psychiatry in Postwar France* (Chicago: Chicago University Press, 2021).
64. See the recently translated collection of Fanon's early writings, Frantz Fanon, *Alienation and Freedom*, ed. Jean Khalfa and Robert C. Young, trans. Steven Corcoran (London: Bloomsbury, 2018).
65. Sachs, *Black Hamlet*, 9.
66. Sachs, *Black Hamlet*, 9.
67. Sachs, *Black Hamlet*, 98.
68. Sachs, *Black Hamlet*, 84.
69. Sachs, *Black Hamlet*, 84.
70. Sachs, *Black Hamlet*, 84.
71. Sachs, *Black Hamlet*, 85.
72. Sachs, *Black Hamlet*, 6–7.
73. Sachs, Dubow, and Rose, *Black Hamlet*, 45.
74. Rachel Greenspan, "Framing Psychoanalysis in the Context of the World," *Differences* 33, nos. 2–3 (2022): 93.

75. Natasha Stovall, "Whiteness on the Couch," *Longreads*, August 12, 2019, https://longreads.com/2019/08/12/whiteness-on-the-couch/.

76. Sachs, *Black Hamlet*, 221, 222.

77. Vaughan, "The Madman and the Medicine Man," 119.

78. Sachs, *Black Hamlet*, 218.

79. Sander Gilman, *Freud, Race, and Gender* (Princeton, NJ: Princeton University Press, 1994); Celia Brickman, *Aboriginal Populations in the Mind: Race and Primitivity in Psychoanalysis* (New York: Columbia University Press, 2003), 163.

80. Sachs, *Black Hamlet*, 220.

81. Sachs, *Black Hamlet*, 302.

82. Grahame Hayes, "Sachs, Chavafambira, Maggie: Prurience or the Pathology of Social Relations?," *South African Journal of Psychology* 32, no. 2 (2002): 43–48.

83. Sachs, *Black Hamlet*, 220.

84. Rose, "Black Hamlet"; Crewe, "Black Hamlet"; Adam Sitze, "Treating Life Literally," *Law Critique* 18 (2007): 55–89.

85. Sachs, *Black Hamlet*, 221.

86. Sachs, *Black Hamlet*, 9, 221.

87. Sachs, *Black Hamlet*, 222.

88. Rose, "Black Hamlet," 49–50.

89. Rose, "Black Hamlet," 49–50.

90. Sachs, *Black Hamlet*, 275.

91. Sachs, *Black Hamlet*, 232.

92. Gilman, *Freud, Race, and Gender*.

93. Fanon, *Black Skin, White Masks*.

4. DREAMING OF "BLACK MUMMY": RACE, GENDER, DECOLONIZATION, AND D. W. WINNICOTT

1. D. W. Winnicott, *Playing and Reality* (London: Routledge, [1971] 1991), 119.

2. See Nancy Chodorow, *The Reproduction of Mothering: Psychoanalysis and the Sociology of Gender* (Los Angeles: University of California Press, 1978); Denise Riley, *The War in the Nursery: Theories of the Child and Mother* (London: Virago, 1983); Janice Doane and Devon Hodges, *From Klein to Kristeva: Psychoanalytic Feminism and the Search for the "Good Enough" Mother* (Ann Arbor: University of Michigan Press, 1993); Gal Gerson, "Winnicott, Participation, and Gender," *Feminism & Psychology* 14, no. 4 (2004): 561–81; Sally Alexander, "D. W. Winnicott and the Social Democratic Vision," in *Psychoanalysis in the Age of Totalitarianism*, ed. Matt ffytche and Daniel Pick (London: Routledge, 2016);

Sally Alexander and Barbara Taylor, eds., *History and Psyche: Culture, Psychoanalysis, and the Past* (London: Palgrave Macmillan, 2012).

3. For scholarship on the theory of mothering and relationality, see Chodorow, *The Reproduction of Mothering*; Jessica Benjamin, *The Bonds of Love: Psychoanalysis, Feminism, and the Problem of Domination* (New York: Pantheon, 1988); Alison Bechdel, *Are You My Mother? A Comic Drama* (New York: Mariner, 2012); and Maggie Nelson, *The Argonauts* (Minneapolis, MN: Greywolf, 2015). For scholarship on the ideology of the postwar British welfare state, see Riley, *The War in the Nursery*; Gerson, "Winnicott, Participation, and Gender"; Michal Shapira, *The War Inside: Psychoanalysis, Total War, and the Making of the Democratic Self in Postwar Britain* (Cambridge: Cambridge University Press, 2013); Alexander, "D. W. Winnicott and the Social Democratic Vision"; Alexander and Taylor, *History and Psyche*.

4. See Anne McClintock, *Imperial Leather: Race, Gender and Sexuality in the Colonial Contest* (New York: Routledge, 1995); Ann Laura Stoler, *Carnal Knowledge and Imperial Power: Race and the Intimate in Colonial Rule* (Los Angeles: University of California Press, 2002); Wendy Webster, *Englishness and Empire, 1939–1965* (Oxford: Oxford University Press, 2005); Jordanna Bailkin, *The Afterlife of Empire* (Berkeley: University of California Press, 2012); Denise Noble, "Decolonizing Britain and Domesticating Women: Race, Gender, and Women's Work in Post-1945 British Decolonial and Metropolitan Liberal Reform Discourses," *Meridians: Feminism, Race, Transnationalism* 13, no. 1 (2015): 53–77.

5. Riley, *The War in the Nursery*; Nikolas Rose, *Governing the Soul: The Shaping of the Private Self* (London: Free Association, 1989); Gerson, "Winnicott, Participation, and Gender"; Alexander, "D. W. Winnicott and the Social Democratic Vision"; Alexander and Taylor, *History and Psyche*; Shapira, *The War Inside*.

6. Winnicott's vocabulary differs notably from much previous standard psychoanalytic vernacular. Although Winnicott will sometimes employ ready-made psychoanalytic argot like "the ego," he more frequently speaks in terms of the "self," "infant," or "individual," making so-called ordinary language key to his personal and professional ethos. As he explains in a letter to David Rapoport in 1953, "I am one of those people who feel compelled to work in my own way and to express myself in my own language first; by a struggle I sometimes come around to rewording what I am saying to bring it in line with other work, in which case I usually find that my own 'original' ideas were not so original" (D. W. Winnicott, *The Spontaneous Gesture: Selected Letters of D. W. Winnicott*, ed. F. Robert Rodman [Cambridge, MA: Harvard University Press, 1987], 53–54). A few months later, in a much more self-effacing letter to Anna Freud, he follows this up by stating, "I have an irritating way of saying

things in my own language instead of learning how to use the terms of psycho-analytic metapsychology" (Winnicott, *The Spontaneous Gesture*, 57–58). While this deprioritization of technical language undoubtedly made Winnicott's work more publicly accessible, it also downgraded the prominence of the unconscious, reimagining primary relational fault lines as between self/other rather than conscious/unconscious.

7. For further discussion of Winnicott's view of dependence, see D. W. Winnicott, *Babies and Their Mothers*, ed. Clare Winnicott, Ray Shepherd, and Madeleine Davis (Reading, MA: Addison-Wesley, 1987), 83.

8. See Winnicott, *Babies and Their Mothers*, 37. Winnicott would even say, in a clear shot at Klein, that infants did not yet even have a distinct division between conscious and unconscious. "For the baby there is not yet a conscious and an unconscious in the area that I wish to examine. What is there is an armful of anatomy and physiology" (Winnicott, *The Spontaneous Gesture*, 89).

9. D. W. Winnicott, *The Family and Individual Development* (London: Routledge, [1965] 2006), 216.

10. As Abram notes in his entry for "Holding," "Generally speaking he [Winnicott] believed that it is best if there is one main carer at the beginning of the baby's life, and in optimum circumstances this person should be the biological mother. However, Winnicott's contention through his work is that an adoptive mother who is able to go into a state of primary maternal preoccupation will also be able to offer the necessary ingredients of the holding environment" (Jan Abram, *The Language of Winnicott: A Dictionary of Winnicott's Use of Words* [London: Karnac, 2007], 194–95).

11. Winnicott, *Babies and Their Mothers*, 6.

12. D. W. Winnicott, *Through Pediatrics to Psychoanalysis: Collected Papers* (New York: Brunner/Mazel, [1958] 1992), 99.

13. D. W. Winnicott, *Home Is Where We Start From: Essays by a Psychoanalyst* (London: Norton, [1986] 1990), 28.

14. For an exemplification of this recentering of selfhood, as applied to political theory, see Matthew H. Bowker and Amy Buzby, eds., *D. W. Winnicott and Political Theory: Recentering the Subject* (London: Palgrave Macmillan, 2017).

15. Chodorow, *The Reproduction of Mothering*.

16. Benjamin, *The Bonds of Love*; Jessica Benjamin, *Like Subjects, Love Objects: Essays on Recognition and Sexual Difference* (New Haven, CT: Yale University Press, 1995).

17. Michael Snediker, *Queer Optimism: Lyric Personhood and Other Felicitous Persuasions* (Minneapolis: University of Minnesota Press, 2008); Bechdel, *Are You My Mother?*; Nelson, *The Argonauts*. Although not explicitly feminist, a number of recent political theorists have mobilized Winnicott's work,

beginning famously with Axel Honneth's reclamation of intersubjective recognition as the basis of political subjectivity and social justice: Axel Honneth, *The Struggle for Recognition: The Moral Grammar of Social Conflicts* (Cambridge: Polity, 1992). For continuing work in this trend in normative political theory, see Bonnie Honig, *Public Things: Democracy in Disrepair* (New York: Fordham University Press, 2017); Bowker and Buzby, *D. W. Winnicott and Political Theory*; David McIvor, "In Transition, But to Where? Winnicott, Integration, and Democratic Associations," in *D. W. Winnicott and Political Theory*, ed. Amy Buzby and Matthew Bowker (London: Palgrave Macmillan, 2017), 205–27; Noëlle McAfee, *Fear of a Breakdown: Psychoanalysis and Politics* (New York: Columbia University Press, 2019); and Joanna Kellond, *Donald Winnicott and the Politics of Care* (London: Palgrave Macmillan, 2022).

18. Riley, *The War in the Nursery*.
19. Alexander and Taylor, *History and Psyche*, 154.
20. Winnicott, *The Spontaneous Gesture*, 21.
21. Gal Gerson, "Individuality, Deliberation, and Welfare in Donald Winnicott," *History of the Human Sciences* 18, no. 1 (2005): 120.
22. Gerson, "Individuality, Deliberation, and Welfare in Donald Winnicott," 116.
23. Carole Pateman, *The Sexual Contract* (Stanford, CA: Stanford University Press, 1988).
24. Charles W. Mills, *The Racial Contract* (Ithaca, NY: Cornell University Press, 1997).
25. Winnicott, *Playing and Reality*, 4.
26. Gerson, "Individuality, Deliberation, and Welfare in Donald Winnicott," 107, 117.
27. For further analysis of the relationship between feminism and gender gains during the welfare state, see Ann Taylor Allen, *Feminism and Motherhood in Western Europe, 1890–1970: The Maternal Dilemma* (London: Palgrave Macmillan, 2005), 209–34; and Elizabeth Wilson, *Only Halfway to Paradise: Women in Postwar Britain, 1945–1968* (New York: Routledge, 1990). For a more theoretical consideration of the way that policy initiatives born of the idea of gender (like parental leave and state-sponsored child care)—which would seem, on the face of it, to be feminist windfalls—were actually more interested in population management and pronatalist national advancement than in gender equity, see Jemima Repo, *The Biopolitics of Gender* (Oxford: Oxford University Press, 2015).
28. For more on the role of gender in the Beveridge Report, see Noble, "Decolonizing Britain and Domesticating Women." For an analysis of how psychoanalysts contributed to the construction of a "maternalist" British state, see Shaul Bar-Haim, *The Maternalists: Psychoanalysis, Motherhood, and the British Welfare State* (Philadelphia: University of Pennsylvania Press, 2021).

29. Wilson, *Only Halfway to Paradise*, 22.
30. Winnicott, *Home Is Where We Start From*, 124.
31. Gerson, "Winnicott, Participation, and Gender," 566.
32. The archive on gender in the British welfare state is expansive, but for introductory reading see Ann Orloff, "Gender in the Welfare State," *Annual Review in Sociology* 22 (1996): 51–78; Mary Daly, *The Gender Division of Welfare: The Impact of the British and German Welfare States* (Cambridge: Cambridge University Press, 2000); Mary Daly and Katherine Rake, *Gender and the Welfare State: Care, Work and Welfare in Europe and the USA* (Cambridge: Polity, 2003); Gerson, "Winnicott, Participation, and Gender"; Noble, "Decolonizing Britain and Domesticating Women"; and Nancy Fraser, *Fortunes of Feminism: From State-Managed Capitalism to Neoliberal Crisis* (New York: Verso, 2013).
33. Riley, *The War in the Nursery*; Alexander and Taylor, *History and Psyche*; Gerson, "Winnicott, Participation, and Gender"; Shapira, *The War Inside*.
34. For more on Caribbean Depression-era poverty and the consequent labor unrest, see Joan French, "Colonial Policy Towards Women After the 1938 Uprising: The Case of Jamaica," *Caribbean Quarterly* (1988): 38–61; and Barbara Bush, "Colonial Research and the Social Sciences at the End of Empire: The West Indian Social Survey, 1944–57," *Journal of Imperial and Commonwealth History* 41, no. 3 (2013): 451–74. According to The Report of the Royal Commission on Population (published in 1949), Britain would need 140,000 new workers each year in order to recover from the losses of the war. The report strongly encouraged reliance on immigration to meet this need, even as it anxiously managed racial concerns about miscegenation (cited in Noble, "Decolonizing Britain and Domesticating Women," 71).
35. The British Nationality Act of 1948 gave citizenship and the right of UK settlement to any resident of the British Empire. Such an open policy to immigration was contested almost immediately following the docking of HMT *Empire Windrush*, with Clement Attlee's Labor government receiving complaints from numerous members of Parliament about the number of Brown and Black immigrants. This open immigration and citizenship policy was then revised by the Commonwealth Immigrants Act of 1962—a clearly discriminatory piece of legislation—which imposed immigration quotas only on "New Commonwealth" countries (such as India and Jamaica). This act was swiftly followed by two further, equally discriminatory immigrations acts (of 1968 and 1971, respectively) that effectively foreclosed immigration for the majority of the formerly colonized, except where there were preexisting family or labor ties to the UK. Although Labor had generally supported more open immigration policies through the early 1960s, by the time the party was reelected in 1964 under Prime Minister Harold Wilson, it was in broad consensus with the

Conservatives (and the wider white public) on the need for greater Common-wealth immigration restriction. Immigration policy was revised yet again in 1973 when Britain ascended to the European Union but with no major changes applied to its (post)colonies.

36. James Hampshire, *Citizenship and Belonging: Immigration and the Politics of Demographic Governance in Postwar Britain* (London: Palgrave Macmillan, 2005), 10; Rosie Wild, "'Black Was the Colour of Our Fight': The Transna-tional Roots of British Black Power," in *The Other Special Relationship: Race, Rights, and Riots in Britain and the United States*, ed. Robin C. G. Kelley and Stephen Tuck (London: Palgrave Macmillan, 2015), 25–46, puts the rela-tive population size of non-white British citizens as 2 percent of the overall English population.

37. Bailkin, *The Afterlife of Empire*.

38. For further research on decolonization and the welfare state, see Kennetta Hammond Perry, "Black Britain and the Politics of Race in the 20th Century," *History Compass* 12, no. 8 (2014): 651–63; Noble, "Decolonizing Britain and Domesticating Women"; and Nadja Durbach, "One British Thing: A Bottle of Welfare Orange Juice, c. 1961–1971," *Journal of British Studies* 57 (2018): 564–67.

39. Bailkin, *The Afterlife of Empire*, 15.

40. Bailkin, *The Afterlife of Empire*, 2.

41. Stoler, *Carnal Knowledge and Imperial Power*; McClintock, *Imperial Leather*.

42. Noble, "Decolonizing Britain and Domesticating Women," 58–64.

43. Noble, "Decolonizing Britain and Domesticating Women," 64–72; for further reading on the role of gender in the Moyne Report, see French, "Colonial Pol-icy Towards Women After the 1938 Uprising"; and Bush, "Colonial Research and the Social Sciences at the End of Empire." As Bush puts it, "The West India Royal Commission Report [i.e., The Moyne Report] attributed the social problems impeding progress in the Caribbean to three major factors, the low status of women, the lack of family life and the absence of a well-defined programme of welfare and recommended an 'organized campaign' against 'the social, moral and economic evils of promiscuity'" (Bush, "Colonial Research and the Social Sciences at the End of Empire," 453). Following that report, the welfare policies in Jamaica aimed to produce "proper" families (for middle-class women, primarily) with married, monogamous heterosexual couples com-prised of a housewife and male breadwinner (French, "Colonial Policy Towards Women After the 1938 Uprising," 39–40). As with the welfare provisions in England, then, the welfare in Jamaica operated through the gendered organiza-tion of the family unit, constituting a kind of ideological, rather than material, dominance.

44. See Noble, "Decolonizing Britain and Domesticating Women"; and Barbara Bush, "Feminising Empire? British Women's Activist Networks in Defending and Challenging Empire from 1918 to Decolonisation," *Women's History Review* 25, no. 4 (2016): 511.

45. Webster, *Englishness and Empire, 1939–1965.*

46. The article was necessarily post-1957 but was likely between 1958 and the early 1960s given that the Notting Hill and Nottingham race riots in 1958 sparked much public debate about race, immigration, and integration, newly licensing a public outcry against commonwealth immigration (Wild, "'Black Was the Colour of Our Fight'").

47. The noteworthy difference between Clarke's work and the Moyne Report is that Clarke never advocated for the greater institutionalization of marriage among Jamaicans—a key objective of the Moyne Report's welfare provisions. For further readings on her work, see Mindie Lazarus-Black, "My Mother Never Fathered Me: Rethinking Kinship and the Governing of Families," *Social and Economic Studies* 44, no. 1 (1995): 49–71; Christine Barrow, "Edith Clarke: Jamaican Social Reformer and Anthropologist," *Caribbean Quarterly* 44, no. 3/4 (1998): 15–34; and Bush, "Colonial Research and the Social Sciences at the End of Empire."

48. D. W. Winnicott, *The Collected Works of D. W. Winnicott: Volume 5, 1955– 1959*, ed. Lesley Caldwell and Helen Taylor Robinson (New York: Oxford, 2016), 173.

49. For a reading of the role of "Black" in Winnicott's work, see P. C. Hogan, "The Politics of Otherness in Clinical Psychoanalysis: Racism as Pathogen in a Case of D. W. Winnicott," *Literature and Psychology* 38, no. 4 (1992): 36–43; and Lesley Caldwell, "Symbolic and Anticipated: Winnicott's Attention to the Use of Black in the Consulting Room," *British Journal of Psychotherapy* 32, no. 3 (2016): 376–91. Hogan's and Caldwell's are the only scholarship to my knowledge that considers at all the role of race in Winnicott's work, albeit from a more squarely clinical perspective.

50. See D. W. Winnicott, "Hallucination and Dehallucination," in *The Collected Works of D. W. Winnicott: Volume 5, 1955–1959*, ed. Lesley Caldwell and Helen Taylor Robinson (New York: Oxford, [1957] 2016); D. W. Winnicott, "The Price of Disregarding Psychoanalytic Research," in *The Collected Works of D. W. Winnicott: Volume 5, 1955–1959*, ed. Lesley Caldwell and Helen Taylor Robinson (New York: Oxford, [1965] 2016); and D. W. Winnicott, "Use of Two, Use of Black," in *The Collected Works of D. W. Winnicott: Volume 5, 1955–1959*, ed. Lesley Caldwell and Helen Taylor Robinson (New York: Oxford, [1965] 2016).

51. D. W. Winnicott, *The Piggle: An Account of the Psychoanalytic Treatment of a Little Girl*, ed. Ishak Ramzy (London: Penguin, [1971] 1977), 5–6.

52. Winnicott, *The Piggle*, 6–7.

53. See Lena Teurnell, "An Alternative Reading in Winnicott: The Piggle—A Sexually Abused Girl?," *International Forum of Psychoanalysis* 2, no. 3 (1993): 139–44; Christopher Reeves, "Reappraising Winnicott's *The Piggle*: A Critical Commentary, Part I," *British Journal of Psychotherapy* 31, no. 2 (2015): 156–90; Dieter Burgin, "Analysis on Demand," *British Journal of Psychotherapy* 32, no. 3 (2016): 347–58; and Deborah Anna Luepnitz, "The Name of the Piggle: Reconsidering Winnicott's Classic Case in Light of Some Conversations with the Adult 'Gabrielle,'" *International Journal of Psychoanalysis* 98 (2017): 343–70.

54. Teurnell, "An Alternative Reading in Winnicott"; Reeves, "Reappraising Winnicott's *The Piggle*"; Burgin, "Analysis on Demand."

55. Winnicott, *The Piggle*, 15.

56. Winnicott, *The Piggle*, 7.

57. Peter Fryer, *Staying Power: The History of Black People in Britain* (London: Pluto, 2010), 378.

58. Wild notes that, in addition to being "half-hearted," the Acts' criminalization of the incitement of racial hatred was actually used to disproportionately target and indict Black activists. "The new criminal penalty set out by the United Kingdom's first law against racial discrimination was being used against black people almost as often as it was against whites, even though they constituted only 2 percent of the UK population" (Wild, "'Black Was the Colour of Our Fight,'" 38). Both of the Acts were later revoked in 1976.

59. Kevin Rawlinson, Nadeem Badshaw, and Matthew Weaver, "Windrush Scandal: Timeline of Key Events," *The Guardian*, March 31, 2022, https://www.theguardian.com/uk-news/2018/apr/16/windrush-era-citizens-row-timeline-of-key-events.

60. Kennetta Hammond Perry argues that, following the London Solidarity March in 1963 held in support of the March on Washington, Black Britons mobilized the events, experiences, and discourses of race in the United States (and particularly Black antiracist struggle) as a kind of "discursive capital that . . . transcended the boundaries of the American nation" (Kennetta Hammond Perry, "'U.S. Negroes, Your Fight Is Our Fight': Black Britons and the 1963 March on Washington," in *The Other Special Relationship: Race, Rights, and Riots in Britain and the United States*, ed. Robin D. G. Kelley and Stephen Tuck [London: Palgrave Macmillan, 2015], 8). Although racial formation in Britain was unique, in the postwar period especially there was significant cross-pollination with the United States. For further consideration of this, see Robin D. G. Kelley and Stephen Tuck, eds., *The Other Special Relationship: Race, Rights, and Riots in Britain and the United States* (London: Palgrave Macmillan, 2015).

61. Winnicott, *The Piggle*, 21.
62. The equation of Blackness with feces had an especially ugly history that found its way into psychoanalytic theory. The former president of the New York Psychoanalytic Association and celebrity psychoanalyst Lawrence Kubie and the Michigan psychoanalyst James Hamilton both published essays (in 1965 and 1966, respectively) that used psychological and psychoanalytic thinking to validate the supposed "anality" of white prejudice, giving scientific authority to a long-standing discursive ploy of racist oppression. This argument was then quickly popularized by Joel Kovel in his 1970 *White Racism: A Psychohistory*, which, although meaning to diagnose the psychology of anti-Black racism as an identifiable psychic malady, further doubled down on the racist reduction of Black people to "certain raw manifestations of anal fantasies" (Joel Kovel, *White Racism: A Psychohistory* [New York: Columbia University Press, 1970], 88); "black people have come to be represented as the personification of dirt, an equation that stays locked in the deeper recesses of the unconscious, and so pervades the course of social action between the races beyond any need of awareness" (Kovel, *White Racism*, 89–90). The evacuation of Black psychological interiority, the reduction of Black people to a denigrated symbol of white unconscious life, and the disparagement of Blackness as a (social) contamination was thus so established a racial logic that it worked across the Atlantic, pervading, with little offense or inflammation, both overtly conservative and ostensibly liberal scientific racist thought. See Lawrence Kubie, "The Ontogeny of Racial Prejudice," *Journal of Nervous and Mental Disease* 141, no. 3 (1965): 265–73; James W. Hamilton, "Some Dynamics of Anti-Negro Prejudice," *Psychoanalytic Review* 53 (1966): 5–15; and Kovel, *White Racism*. For a contemporary analysis of this, see Fakhry Davids, *Internal Racism: A Psychoanalytic Approach to Race and Difference* (London: Red Globe, 2011), 175–81.
63. Mary Douglas, *Purity and Danger: An Analysis of the Concepts of Pollution and Taboo* (Routledge and Kegan Paul, 1966).
64. Winnicott, *The Piggle*, 34.
65. For further analysis of the way that cleanliness and racial hygiene organized categorizations of whiteness and Blackness, see Wendy Webster, *Imagining Home: Gender, "Race," and National Identity, 1945–64* (New York: Routledge, 1998), 65–67, 102–5.
66. Hampshire, *Citizenship and Belonging*, 10.
67. Webster, *Imagining Home*, 49.
68. Webster, *Imagining Home*, 47.
69. Webster, *Imagining Home*, 48.
70. Luepnitz, "The Name of the Piggle," 352.
71. Luepnitz, "The Name of the Piggle," 352.

72. Luepnitz, "The Name of the Piggle," 353–55.

73. Luepnitz, "The Name of the Piggle," 355.

74. Sander Gilman, *Freud, Race, and Gender* (Princeton, NJ: Princeton University Press, 1994), 19–21.

75. Luepnitz, "The Name of the Piggle," 352.

76. While Winnicott himself prepared the manuscript for publication, he died before it went to press. Together, his wife, Clare; his fellow analyst Ishak Ramzy; his protégée and collaborator, Masud Khan; The Piggle's mother; and the publishers were the final editors of the work and the ones who took it to press.

77. Frantz Fanon, *Black Skin, White Masks* (New York: Grove, [1952] 2008); Jean Walton, "Re-Placing Race in (White) Psychoanalytic Discourse: Founding Narratives of Feminism," *Critical Inquiry* 21, no. 4 (1995): 775–804; Kalpana Seshadri-Crooks, *Desiring Whiteness: A Lacanian Analysis of Race* (New York: Routledge, 2000); and Christopher Lane, ed., *The Psychoanalysis of Race* (New York: Columbia University Press, 1998).

78. Basia Winograd, dir., *Black Psychoanalysts Speak*, 2014.

79. See, for instance, these works by Winnicott: D. W. Winnicott, "The Discussion of War Aims," in *Home Is Where We Start From: Essays by a Psychoanalyst* (London: Norton, [1986] 1990), 215; D. W. Winnicott, *The Child, the Family, and the Outside World* (London: Penguin, 2021), 214; and D. W. Winnicott, "Morals and Education," in *The Maturational Processes and the Facilitating Environment* (London: Karnac, [1962] 1990), 93.

80. Winnicott, "Morals and Education," 93.

81. D. W. Winnicott, "The Pill and the Moon," in *The Collected Works of D. W. Winnicott: Volume 9, 1969–1971*, ed. Lesley Caldwell and Helen Taylor Robinson (New York: Oxford, [1969] 2016), 200–201.

82. For a more detailed and historically specific account of how Black male sexuality was regarded (and sensationalized) in 1950s and 1960s Britain, see Webster, *Imagining Home*, 50–54.

83. Winnicott, "The Price of Disregarding Psychoanalytic Research," 174.

84. Reeves, "Reappraising Winnicott's *The Piggle*," 168–69.

85. Winnicott, *Playing and Reality*, 192.

86. Winnicott, *The Piggle*, 15.

87. Winnicott, *The Piggle*, 16–17.

88. Winnicott, *Playing and Reality*, 119.

89. Abram, *The Language of Winnicott*, 194.

90. Winnicott believed this to be true for children in analysis just as much as it was for adults since his approach to the temporality of age suggested that adult patients ultimately "all become babies and children in the course of treatment" anyway (Winnicott, *Home Is Where We Start From*, 147).

91. D. W. Winnicott, "The Use of an Object," in *Playing and Reality* (London: Routledge, [1971] 1991), 86.
92. See D. W. Winnicott, "The Mother-Infant Experience of Mutuality," in *The Collected Works of D. W. Winnicott: Volume 9, 1969–1971*, ed. Lesley Caldwell and Helen Taylor Robinson (New York: Oxford, [1969] 2016), where he gives a short case study detailing his physical contact with a patient (Margaret Little). Also see Margaret's own separate account of her analysis with Winnicott, which included different forms of touching or holding. Margaret Little, *Psychotic Anxieties and Containment: A Personal Record of an Analysis with Winnicott* (London: Jason Aronson, 1977).
93. Winnicott, *The Piggle*, 28–29.
94. Winnicott, *The Piggle*, 59.
95. Winnicott, *The Piggle*, 28–29.
96. This unorthodox clinical technique prompted Masud Khan to reject The Piggle case from publication in the International Psychoanalytic Library he was editing. While Clare Winnicott saw Winnicott's work in this case as the most representative of his psychoanalytic contributions, Khan thought it lacked the key elements that would even make it "psychoanalytic" in the first place. For more background on the publication history of this case study, see Reeves, "Reappraising Winnicott's *The Piggle*," 156–90.
97. Riley, *The War in the Nursery*; Alexander, "D. W. Winnicott and the Social Democratic Vision"; Alexander and Taylor, *History and Psyche*.
98. Nelson, *The Argonauts*.
99. Emily Green, "Melanie Klein and the Black Mammy: An Exploration of the Influence of the Mammy Stereotype on Klein's Maternal and Its Contribution to the 'Whiteness' of Psychoanalysis," *Studies in Gender and Sexuality* 19, no. 3 (2018): 171.
100. Winnicott, *The Piggle*, 36–37.
101. Winnicott, *The Piggle*, 36.

5. THE COMMUNAL CLINIC: THERAPEUTIC COMMUNITIES, HETERONORMATIVITY, AND THE COLD WAR

1. Thomas Main, "A Theory of Marriage and Its Technical Applications," in *The Ailment and Other Psychoanalytic Essays*, ed. Jennifer Johns (London: Free Association, [1966] 1989), 79.
2. For a detailed history of institutional psychotherapy, see Camille Robcis, *Disalienation: Politics, Philosophy, and Radical Psychiatry in Postwar France* (Chicago: Chicago University Press, 2021). For a history of the Lafargue Clinic,

see Gabriel N. Mendes, *Under the Strain of Color: Harlem's Lafargue Clinic and the Promise of an Antiracist Psychiatry* (Ithaca, NY: Cornell University Press, 2015). For Fanon's clinical contributions, see Jean Khalfa, "Fanon, Revolutionary, Psychiatrist," in *Alienation and Freedom*, ed. Jean Khalfa and Robert C. Young, trans. Steven Corcoran (London: Bloomsbury, 2018), 167–202.

3. Lesley Caldwell, "Continuities and Discontinuities at the Cassel Hospital Richmond 1977–1982," *Psychoanalytic Studies* 3, no. 3/4 (2001): 363.

4. Whether Main's 1946 use of "therapeutic community" was really the first publication of the term is disputed. As Jon A. Mills and Tom Harrison show, the term was first used by Harry Sack Sullivan in 1939. However, Main was undoubtedly its popularizer and most well-known affiliate. For further discussion, see Jennifer Johns, "Thomas Forrest Main (25 February 1911–20 May 1990)," *Psychoanalytic Psychotherapy* 5 (1990): 81; and Jon A. Mills and Tom Harrison, "John Rickman, Wilfred Ruprecht Bion, and the Origins of the Therapeutic Community," *History of Psychology* 10, no. 1 (2007): 25.

5. Thomas Main, "The Hospital as a Therapeutic Institution," in *The Ailment and Other Psychoanalytic Essays*, ed. Jennifer Johns (London: Free Association, [1946] 1989), 7–8.

6. Main, "The Hospital as a Therapeutic Institution," 7.

7. Thomas Main, "In-Patient Psychotherapy of Neurosis," in *The Ailment and Other Psychoanalytic Essays*, ed. Jennifer Johns (London: Free Association, [1958] 1989), 37.

8. Main, "In-Patient Psychotherapy of Neurosis."

9. Thomas Main, "The Cassel Hospital for Functional Nervous Disorders" (1968), Wellcome Archives, MS.7913/41, 6.

10. In March 1954, this distribution was changed to ninety-four adult beds and ten children's beds to accommodate the inclusion of mothers with children. See Thomas Main, "Reports for the Five Years 1st April 1953 to 31st March 1958" (1958), Wellcome Archives, WLM28.BE5C34, 4.

11. Main's two accounts of the final inpatient bed counts disagree. The former cites fifty beds; the latter, sixty. Main, "Reports for the Five Years 1st April 1953 to 31st March 1958," 7, and Main, "The Cassel Hospital for Functional Nervous Disorders," 15.

12. Main, "Reports for the Five Years 1st April 1953 to 31st March 1958," 10–11; Caldwell, "Continuities and Discontinuities at the Cassel Hospital Richmond 1977–1982," 367.

13. Thomas Main, "Mothers with Children on a Psychiatric Unit," in *The Ailment and Other Psychoanalytic Essays*, ed. Jennifer Johns (London: Free Association, [1961] 1989), 56.

14. Main, "The Hospital as a Therapeutic Institution," 8–9.

15. David Rapoport, *Community as Doctor: New Perspectives on a Therapeutic Community* (London: Tavistock, 1960), 10.

16. Eric Rayner, "Introduction," in *The Ailment and Other Psychoanalytic Essays*, ed. Jennifer Johns (London: Free Association, 1989), xix.

17. See Johns, "Thomas Forrest Main"; T. T. Hayley, "Thomas Forrest Main (1911–1990)," *International Journal of Psychoanalysis* 72 (1991): 719–22; and Malcolm Pines, "Main, Thomas Forrest (1911–1990)," *Oxford Dictionary of National Biography* (Oxford: Oxford University Press, 2004).

18. Thomas Main, "Psychiatrists, Psychotherapies, and Psychoanalytic Training," in *The Ailment and Other Psychoanalytic Essays*, ed. Jennifer Johns (London: Free Association, [1968] 1989), 188–89.

19. Teresa Brennan, "Transmission in Groups," in *The Transmission of Affect* (Ithaca, NY: Cornell University Press, 2004), 51–73.

20. Main, "Reports for the Five Years 1st April 1953 to 31st March 1958," 7; Caldwell, "Continuities and Discontinuities at the Cassel Hospital Richmond 1977–1982," 364–65.

21. Caldwell, "Continuities and Discontinuities at the Cassel Hospital Richmond 1977–1982," 367.

22. A few years prior to Foulkes's work, a different version of group analysis was being developed in Argentina by Enrique Pichon-Rivière. See Juan Tubert-Oklander and Reyna Hernández-Tubert, *Operative Groups: The Latin-American Approach to Group Analysis* (London: Jessica Kingsley, 2003); and Juan Tubert-Oklander, *The One and the Many: Relational Psychoanalysis and Group Analysis* (Abingdon: Routledge, 2014), 15–19.

23. For a comprehensive history of the Tavistock Clinic, see H. V. Dicks, *50 Years of the Tavistock Clinic* (London: Routledge, 1970).

24. Rayner, "Introduction," xv.

25. Caldwell, "Continuities and Discontinuities at the Cassel Hospital Richmond 1977–1982," 365.

26. Main, "Reports for the Five Years 1st April 1953 to 31st March 1958," 10.

27. Main, "In-Patient Psychotherapy of Neurosis," 48.

28. Main, "The Hospital as a Therapeutic Institution," 8.

29. Frederick Kräupl Taylor, "A History of Group and Administrative Therapy in Great Britain," *British Journal of Medical Psychology* 31, nos. 3–4 (1958): 157.

30. Rayner, "Introduction," xix.

31. Thomas Main, "The Concept of the Therapeutic Community: Variations and Vicissitudes," in *The Ailment and Other Psychoanalytic Essays*, ed. Jennifer Johns (London: Free Association, [1981] 1989), 136.

32. For further detail, see Robcis, *Disalienation*.

33. For further reading on Fanon's clinical work, see note 11 of the introduction.

34. Oisín Wall, *The British Anti-Psychiatrists: From Institutional Psychiatry to the Counter-Culture, 1960–1971* (London: Routledge, 2017), 62–63.

35. Wall, *The British Anti-Psychiatrists*, 63.

36. For further reading on this, see Oisín Wall, "The Birth and Death of Villa 21," *History of Psychiatry* 24, no. 3 (2013): 326–40; Oisín Wall, "Anti-Psychiatry: David Cooper and the Villa 21 Experiment," *Contemporary Psychotherapy* 7, no. 1 (2015); Wall, *The British Anti-Psychiatrists*.

37. For the detailed account of Kingsley Hall's most famous patient—Mary Barnes— who experimented with near-infantile levels of regression, see her account of the experience (cowritten with her analyst, Joseph Berke), Mary Barnes and Joseph Berke, *Mary Barnes: Two Accounts of a Journey Through Madness* (London: Penguin, 1971), and Adrian Chapman's articles about her experience there: Adrian Chapman, "'May All Be Shattered into God': Mary Barnes and Her Journey Through Madness in Kingsley Hall," *Journal of the Medical Humanities* 41 (2020): 207–28; and Adrian Chapman, "Dwelling in Strangeness: Accounts of the Kingsley Hall Community, London (1965–1970), Established by R. D. Laing," *Journal of the Medical Humanities* 42, no. 3 (2021): 471–94.

38. Wall, *The British Anti-Psychiatrists*, 15.

39. Laing trained first as a medical doctor and psychiatrist and later as a psycho-analyst at the London Institute of Psychoanalysis, where he was analyzed by Charles Rycroft and supervised by Winnicott and Marion Milner (Wall, *The British Anti-Psychiatrists*, 9–11). Cooper, by contrast, was more radical in his contention that the best way to address individual ailments was collective rev-olution, and he was active in various communist and anti-imperialist political parties. For further reading on both, see Wall, *The British Anti-Psychiatrists*.

40. Wall, *The British Anti-Psychiatrists*, 19.

41. David Cooper, ed., *The Dialectics of Liberation* (London: Penguin, 1968), 197.

42. Robcis, *Disalienation*; Wall, *The British Anti-Psychiatrists*.

43. Robcis, *Disalienation*, 10.

44. Daniel Pick, *Brainwashed: A New History of Thought Control* (London: Wellcome Collection, 2022). See also Charlie Williams, "Public Psychology and the Cold War Brainwashing Scare," *History and Philosophy of Psychology* 21, no. 1 (2020): 21–30.

45. Camille Robcis, "Jean Oury and Clinique de La Borde: A Conversation with Camille Robcis," *Somatosphere*, June 3, 2014, http://somatosphere.net/2014 /jean-oury-and-clinique-de-la-borde-a-conversation-with-camille-robcis .html/; Camille Robcis, "Institutional Psychotherapy in France: An Interview with Camille Robcis," *Hidden Persuaders Blog*, September 28, 2017, http:// www7.bbk.ac.uk/hiddenpersuaders/blog/robcis-interview/; Robcis, *Disalien-ation*, 12, 47.

46. Main, "In-Patient Psychotherapy of Neurosis," 45.
47. Main, "In-Patient Psychotherapy of Neurosis," 45.
48. Some scholars also contend that Maxwell Jones's own military experiments at Mill Hill Hospital in 1941 constitute an additional point of origin. See Rex Haigh, "The Quintessence of a Therapeutic Environment: The Foundations for the Windsor Conference 2014," *Therapeutic Communities: The International Journal of Therapeutic Communities* 36, no. 1 (2015): 7–8; Edgar Jones, "War and the Practice of Psychotherapy: The UK Experience 1939–1960," *Medical History* 48 (2004): 494; and D. W. Millard, "Maxwell Jones and the Therapeutic Community," in *150 Years of British Psychiatry, Volume 2: The Aftermath*, ed. H. Freeman and G. E. Berrios (London: Athlone, 1996).
49. Rather than relying purely on class status or lengthy and intimidating intelligence tests, Bion's Leaderless Group Test assigned a work task to a group of recruits without any clear instruction or organizational hierarchy for its completion. His thinking was that natural leaders would emerge as the group worked to complete its task, thus giving a clear indication about which individuals showed the greatest potential. A triumph of the nascent, principally psychological form of managerialism that would dominate the neoliberal capitalist landscape, Bion's tests became the basis not just of his Northfield experiments but of many subsequent management development schemes, such as those used by Unilever Company (Peter Miller and Nikolas Rose, "The Tavistock Programme: The Government of Subjectivity and Social Life," *Sociology* 22, no. 2 [1988]: 185). Although the experiments would seem, on the surface, to embody a subversive challenge to rigid military hierarchies, their deeper effect was, as Miller and Rose have shown, the square alignment of early group therapeutics with state priorities—a precocious augur of the neoliberal self-entrepreneurialism to come.
50. Wilfred Bion and John Rickman, "Intragroup Tensions in Therapy: Their Study as the Task of the Group," *Lancet* 2 (1943): 678.
51. Details on the actual daily practices at Northfield during this time are hazy, but beyond establishing some basic regulations for the men—the requirement of one hour's physical training, participation in a least one work group, and attendance at the daily "parade"—Bion seems to have turned the majority of the ward's operations over to the patients. According to him, although little was accomplished at first, the men eventually organized themselves into effective work groups, undertook extensive cleaning of the facilities, arranged dance classes, and pressed malingerers into more active service. But a survey of the facility conducted by the War Office painted a very different picture: "The chaos in the hospital cinema hall, with newspapers and condom-strewn floors, resulted in immediate termination of the project" (quoted in Ben

Shephard, "A Tale of Two Hospitals," in *A War of Nerves: Soldiers and Psychiatrists in the Twentieth Century* [Cambridge, MA: Harvard University Press, 2003], 260).

52. Tom Harrison, *Bion, Rickman, Foulkes and the Northfield Experiments: Advancing on a Different Front* (London: J. Kingsley, 2000), 15.

53. The exact reason for Bion and Rickman's reposting is still debated. According to some, it was the direct result of the chaos of the early weeks of the experiment and the failure to inform the War Office and administrators of their unconventional tactics (Patrick de Maré, "Large Group Perspectives," *Group Analysis* 18, no. 2 [1985]: 79–92; Jones, "War and the Practice of Psychotherapy," 497); according to others, it was a more personalized punishment due to conflicts with J. R. Rees; and, according to still others, it was a routine reorganization to do with Bion's discovery and handling of financial discrepancies (Nafsika Thalassis, "Soldiers in Psychiatric Therapy: The Case of Northfield Military Hospital 1942–1946," *Social History of Medicine* 20, no. 2 [2007]: 359–60). See also Millard, *150 Years of British Psychiatry*, 588.

54. In her analysis of the two Northfield experiments, Thalassis documents patients' political and often subversive contributions to this paper. In one issue, a patient sardonically noted that the astrology section would be discontinued because "as a harmless sedative and as a cheap means of bringing comfort to the millions, astrology cannot hope to compete with behaviourist psychology" (quoted in Thalassis, "Soldiers in Psychiatric Therapy," 364). In others, Thalassis records how patients freely criticized the war, U.S. foreign policy, Winston Churchill, and even the colonial policies underwriting the British Empire.

55. Millard, *150 Years of British Psychiatry*, 588.

56. For further reading, see the original accounts of the experiment in Menninger Foundation, *The Bulletin of the Menninger Clinic* 10, no. 3 (1946). For secondary accounts and analyses of the experiments, see Rapoport, *Community as Doctor*; Robert D. Hinshelwood, "The Therapeutic Community in a Changing Cultural and Political Climate," *International Journal of Therapeutic Communities* 10, no. 1 (1989): 63–69; Millard, *150 Years of British Psychiatry*; Harrison, *Bion, Rickman, Foulkes and the Northfield Experiments*; Thalassis, "Soldiers in Psychiatric Therapy"; and Mills and Harrison, "John Rickman, Wilfred Ruprecht Bion, and the Origins of the Therapeutic Community."

57. Main, "The Concept of the Therapeutic Community."

58. Main, "The Hospital as a Therapeutic Institution," 11.

59. Main, "The Hospital as a Therapeutic Institution," 8.

60. Main, "Reports for the Five Years 1st April 1953 to 31st March 1958," 10–13.

61. Main, "Reports for the Five Years 1st April 1953 to 31st March 1958," 13.

62. Main, "Reports for the Five Years 1st April 1953 to 31st March 1958," 26.

63. Main, "Reports for the Five Years 1st April 1953 to 31st March 1958," 16.
64. Main, "Reports for the Five Years 1st April 1953 to 31st March 1958," 13.
65. Main, "Mothers with Children on a Psychiatric Unit," 57.
66. Caldwell, "Continuities and Discontinuities at the Cassel Hospital Richmond 1977–1982," 374.
67. Main, "Reports for the Five Years 1st April 1953 to 31st March 1958," 11.
68. Main, "Mothers with Children on a Psychiatric Unit," 57.
69. Main, "The Cassel Hospital for Functional Nervous Disorders," 14; Caldwell, "Continuities and Discontinuities at the Cassel Hospital Richmond 1977–1982," 375.
70. Main, "Mothers with Children on a Psychiatric Unit," 59.
71. Main, "The Cassel Hospital for Functional Nervous Disorders," 16.
72. Main, "Mothers with Children on a Psychiatric Unit," 60.
73. Main, "Mothers with Children on a Psychiatric Unit," 56.
74. Teri Chettiar, "Democratizing Mental Health: Motherhood, Therapeutic Community and the Emergence of the Psychiatric Family at the Cassel Hospital in Post-Second World War Britain," *History of the Human Sciences* 25, no. 5 (2012): 107–22.
75. Chettiar, "Democratizing Mental Health," 109.
76. Chettiar, "Democratizing Mental Health," 109–10.
77. Rhodri Hayward, *The Transformation of the Psyche in British Primary Care, 1870–1970* (London: Bloomsbury, 2014), 78.
78. Michal Shapira, *The War Inside: Psychoanalysis, Total War, and the Making of the Democratic Self in Postwar Britain* (Cambridge: Cambridge University Press, 2013), 18.
79. Main himself notes this conceptual shift as the backdrop for Cassel in his unpublished history of the hospital. See Main, "The Cassel Hospital for Functional Nervous Disorders."
80. See Rayner, "Introduction"; Chettiar, "Democratizing Mental Health"; Harrison, *Bion, Rickman, Foulkes and the Northfield Experiments*; and Thalassis, "Soldiers in Psychiatric Therapy."
81. Elaine Tyler May, *Homeward Bound: American Families in the Cold War Era* (London: Taylor & Francis, 1988).
82. Main, "A Theory of Marriage and Its Technical Applications," 79.
83. Main, "A Theory of Marriage and Its Technical Applications," 77, 81, 87.
84. Main, "A Theory of Marriage and Its Technical Applications," 80.
85. Main, "A Theory of Marriage and Its Technical Applications," 81.
86. Main, "A Theory of Marriage and Its Technical Applications," 81.
87. Main, "A Theory of Marriage and Its Technical Applications," 83.
88. Main, "A Theory of Marriage and Its Technical Applications," 83.

89. Main, "A Theory of Marriage and Its Technical Applications," 83.

90. Dagmar Herzog, *Cold War Freud: Psychoanalysis in an Age of Catastrophes* (Cambridge: Cambridge University Press, 2017), 61.

91. Herzog, *Cold War Freud*, 67.

92. Michel Foucault, *History of Sexuality: An Introduction, Vol. 1* (New York: Vintage, 1990), 43, 123. For further reading, see Christopher Chitty, *Sexual Hegemony: Statecraft, Sodomy, and Capital in the Rise of the World System*, ed. Max Fox (Durham, NC: Duke University Press, 2020).

93. For further reading on the relatively recent invention of heterosexuality, see Jonathan Katz, *The Invention of Heterosexuality* (Chicago: University of Chicago Press, 1995).

94. Lee Edelman, *No Future: Queer Theory and the Death Drive* (Durham, NC: Duke University Press, 2004).

95. Main, "A Theory of Marriage and Its Technical Applications," 97.

96. Main, "A Theory of Marriage and Its Technical Applications," 84.

97. Main, "A Theory of Marriage and Its Technical Applications," 89, 92.

98. Judith Butler, "Imitation and Gender Insubordination," in *Inside/Out: Lesbian Theories, Gay Theories*, ed. Diana Fuss (London: Routledge, 1992), 23, 21.

99. Main, "A Theory of Marriage and Its Technical Applications," 99.

100. See Stuart Twemlow, "The Broadening Vision: A Case for Community-Based Psychoanalysis in the Context of Usual Practice," *Journal of the American Psychoanalytic Association* 61, no. 4 (2013): 663–90; and Francisco J. González and Rachel Peltz, "Community Psychoanalysis: Collaborative Practice as Psychoanalysis," *Psychoanalytic Dialogues* 31, no. 4 (2021): 409–27.

101. Lauren Berlant, *On the Inconvenience of Other People* (Durham, NC: Duke University Press, 2022).

102. Main, "Reports for the Five Years 1st April 1953 to 31st March 1958," 15.

6. COMMUNISTS, ASTRONAUTS, AND "EXTREME FEMINISTS": JOHN BOWLBY AND THE PURSUIT OF (NATIONAL) SECURITY

1. D. W. Winnicott, *The Spontaneous Gesture: Selected Letters of D. W. Winnicott*, ed. F. Robert Rodman (Cambridge, MA: Harvard University Press, 1987), 65–66.

2. John Bowlby, *Maternal Care and Mental Health*, in *Maternal Care and Mental Health & Deprivation of Maternal Care* (New York: Schocken, [1951] 1966).

3. Denise Riley, *The War in the Nursery: Theories of the Child and Mother* (London: Virago, 1983); Nikolas Rose, *Governing the Soul: The Shaping of the Private Self* (London: Free Association, 1989); Sally Alexander, "D. W. Winnicott and the Social Democratic Vision," in *Psychoanalysis in the Age of Totalitarianism*, ed.

Matt ffytche and Daniel Pick (London: Routledge, 2016); Sally Alexander and Barbara Taylor, eds., *History and Psyche: Culture, Psychoanalysis, and the Past* (London: Palgrave Macmillan, 2012); Eli Zaretsky, *Secrets of the Soul: A Social and Cultural History of Psychoanalysis* (New York: Knopf, 2004); Michal Shapira, *The War Inside: Psychoanalysis, Total War, and the Making of the Democratic Self in Postwar Britain* (Cambridge: Cambridge University Press, 2013); Matt ffytche, "Introduction," *Psychoanalysis & History* 18, no. 1 (2016): 1–5; Dagmar Herzog, *Cold War Freud: Psychoanalysis in an Age of Catastrophes* (Cambridge: Cambridge University Press, 2017); and Daniel Pick, *Brainwashed: A New History of Thought Control* (London: Wellcome Collection, 2022).

4. Inderpal Grewal, *Saving the Security State: Exceptional Citizens in Twenty-First Century America* (Durham, NC: Duke University Press, 2017).

5. Bowlby, *Maternal Care and Mental Health*, 158.

6. For biographies of Bowlby's life, see Suzan van Dijken, *John Bowlby: His Early Life: A Biographical Journey into the Roots of Attachment Theory* (London: Free Association, 1998); Frank C. P. van der Horst, *John Bowlby—From Psychoanalysis to Ethology: Unraveling the Roots of Attachment Theory* (Sussex: Wiley-Blackwell, 2011); and Jeremy Holmes, *John Bowlby and Attachment Theory*, 2nd ed. (New York: Routledge, 2014).

7. John Bowlby, *A Secure Base: Parent-Child Attachment and Healthy Human Development* (New York: Basic Books, 1988).

8. When Bowlby first began his work in psychoanalysis, doing his clinical residency at the Institute of Psychoanalysis, he (like Winnicott) trained in a specifically Kleinian tradition. But as he would later acknowledge, this early alignment hardly matched his own conceptual leanings. "At that time," reflects Bowlby, "I had not realized that my interest in real-life experiences and situations was so alien to the Kleinian outlook; on the contrary, I believed my ideals were compatible with theirs" (quoted in Phyllis Grosskurth, *Melanie Klein: Her World and Her Work* [London: Jason Aronson, 1986], 402). Although he spent many years throughout the 1940s and 1950s trying to establish the compatibility of his views and Klein's, as time passed he increasingly positioned the two systems as fundamentally incompatible. For an example of Bowlby's early work in the Kleinian vein, see John Bowlby, "The Nature of the Child's Tie to His Mother," *International Journal of Psychoanalysis* 39 (1958): 350–73.

9. Karl Figlio and R. M. Young, "An Interview with John Bowlby on the Origins and Reception of His Work," *Free Associations* 1, no. 6 (1986): 45.

10. Figlio and Young, "An Interview with John Bowlby," 43.

11. Figlio and Young, "An Interview with John Bowlby," 43.

12. For an extensive analysis of the way Bowlby used—and often abused—ethological research, see Marga Viçedo, *The Nature and Nurture of Love: From*

Imprinting to Attachment in Cold War America (Chicago: University of Chicago Press, 2013).

13. For Bowlby's own description of his adoption of Lorenz's research, see Bowlby, *A Secure Base*, 25.

14. Quoted in Carol Garhart Mooney, *Theories of Attachment: An Introduction to Bowlby, Ainsworth, Gerber, Brazelton, Kennell, and Klaus* (St. Paul, MN: Redleaf, 2010), 7.

15. Because Bowlby was applying theories from ethology, his concept of the instinct was derived not from psychoanalysis (with its own complex theory of biological life) but from ethology. Differentiating his own understanding of instincts from psychoanalytic doxa, Bowlby explains, "At that time it was widely held that the reason a child develops a close tie to his mother is that she feeds him. Two kinds of drive are postulated, primary and secondary. Food is thought of as primary; the personal relationship, referred to as 'dependency', as secondary. This theory did not seem to me to fit the facts" (Bowlby, *A Secure Base*, 24). Following up, Marga Viçedo affirms that "Bowlby adopted an ethological, and specifically Lorenzian, conception of instinct. . . . [He] emphasized that he was using instinct in the ethological sense, not the psychoanalytic" (Viçedo, *The Nature and Nurture of Love*, 86).

16. Hannah Arendt, *The Human Condition* (Chicago: University of Chicago Press, [1958] 1998), 177.

17. John Bowlby, *The Making and Breaking of Affectional Bonds* (London: Routledge, 1989), 40.

18. Bowlby, *The Making and Breaking of Affectional Bonds*, 36.

19. Bowlby, *A Secure Base*, 131.

20. Shaul Bar-Haim, *The Maternalists: Psychoanalysis, Motherhood, and the British Welfare State* (Philadelphia: University of Pennsylvania Press, 2021).

21. Bowlby, *Maternal Care and Mental Health*, 67.

22. Bowlby, *A Secure Base*, 4–5.

23. Bowlby, *A Secure Base*, 4–5.

24. For a fascinating account of the origins of the disarticulation of "gender" from "sex" within the psychological community, see Jemima Repo, *The Biopolitics of Gender* (Oxford: Oxford University Press, 2015).

25. Figlio and Young, "An Interview with John Bowlby," 52.

26. Bowlby, *The Making and Breaking of Affectional Bonds*, 48.

27. Bowlby, "The Nature of the Child's Tie to His Mother," 367.

28. Margaret Mead, "Some Theoretical Considerations of the Problem of Mother-Child Separation," in *Personal Character and Cultural Milieu: A Collection of Readings*, ed. Douglas Gilbert Haring (Syracuse, NY: Syracuse University Press, 1954); Nancy Chodorow, *The Reproduction of Mothering: Psychoanalysis and*

the *Sociology of Gender* (Los Angeles: University of California Press, 1978); Ann Oakley, *Subject Women: Where Women Stand Today—Politically, Economically, Socially, Emotionally* (New York: Pantheon, 1981); Riley, *The War in the Nursery*; Donna Haraway, *Primate Visions: Gender, Race and Nature in the World of Modern Science* (New York: Routledge, 1989). Also see Susan H. Franzblau, "Historicizing Attachment Theory: Binding the Ties that Bind," *Feminism & Psychology* 19, no. 1 (1999): 22–31; Susan Contratto, "A Feminist Critique of Attachment Theory and Evolutionary Psychology," in *Rethinking Mental Health and Disorder: Feminist Perspectives*, ed. Mary Ballou and Laura S. Brown (New York: Guilford, 2002), 29–47; and Juliet Mitchell, "Attachment and Maternal Deprivation: How Did John Bowlby Miss the Siblings?," in *Siblings: Sex and Violence* (Cambridge: Polity, 2003).

29. Viçedo, *The Nature and Nurture of Love*, 810.

30. Betty Friedan, *The Feminine Mystique* (London: Norton, [1963] 2001).

31. Figlio and Young, "An Interview with John Bowlby," 50.

32. Figlio and Young, "An Interview with John Bowlby," 51.

33. Figlio and Young, "An Interview with John Bowlby," 51.

34. Figlio and Young, "An Interview with John Bowlby," 51–52.

35. Quoted in Evelyn Ringold, "Bringing Up Baby in Britain," *New York Times*, June 13, 1965.

36. For appreciations of the psychological merit of attachment theory, see Peter Fonagy and Mary Target, "The Rooting of the Mind in the Body: New Links Between Attachment Theory and Psychoanalytic Thought," *Journal of the American Psychoanalytic Association* 55, no. 2 (2007): 411–56; Peter Fonagy, "Points of Contact and Divergence Between Psychoanalytic and Attachment Theories: Is Psychoanalytic Theory Truly Different," *Psychoanalytic Inquiry* 19, no. 4 (1999): 448–80; and Peter Fonagy et al., "Why Are We Interested in Attachments?," in *The Routledge Handbook of Attachment: Theory* (New York: Routledge, 2014), 31–48. For a reading of Bowlby's claims about attachment through Deleuzian philosophy, see Robbie Duschinsky, Monica Greco, and Judith Soloman, "The Politics of Attachment: Lines of Flight with Bowlby, Deleuze and Guittari," *Theory, Culture & Society* 32, nos. 7–8 (2015): 173–95.

37. Grewal, *Saving the Security State*.

38. Rose, *Governing the Soul*.

39. For further reading on these elements of Britain's participation in the Cold War, see Sean Greenwood, *Britain and the Cold War, 1945–91* (London: Macmillan, 2000); Wayne M. Reynolds, "Whatever Happened to the Fourth British Empire? The Cold War, Empire Defence v. the USA, 1943–57," in *Cold War Britain, 1945–1964: New Perspectives*, ed. Michael Francis Hopkins, Michael Kandiah, and Gillian Staerck (New York: Palgrave Macmillan, 2003);

Matthew Grant, ed., *The British Way in Cold Warfare: Intelligence, Diplomacy, and the Bomb, 1945–1975* (London: Continuum, 2009); Alban Webb, *London Calling: Britain, the BBC World Service, and the Cold War* (London: Bloomsbury, 2014); Jim Smyth, *Cold War Culture: Intellectuals, the Media, and the Practice of History* (London: I. B. Tauris, 2016); and Nicholas J. Barnett, *Britain's Cold War: Culture, Modernity, and the Soviet Threat* (London: I. B. Tauris, 2018).

40. For the multiple ways the Cold War shaped British policy internally, see Michael F. Hopkins, Michael D. Kandiah, and Gillian Staerck, eds., *Cold War Britain, 1945–64: New Perspectives* (New York: Palgrave Macmillan, 2003).

41. Michael Kandiah, *Cold War Britain, 1945–1964: New Perspectives*, ed. Michael F. Hopkins, Michael D. Kandiah, and Gillian Staerck (London: Palgrave Macmillan, 2003).

42. Quoted in Hopkins, Kandiah, and Staerck, *Cold War Britain*, 1.

43. For a long-view conceptual genealogy of some political philosophies of "security" prior to the Cold War, see James Der Derian, "The Value of Security: Hobbes, Marx, Nietzsche, and Baudrillard," in *On Security*, ed. Ronnie D. Lipschutz (New York: Columbia University Press, 1995). For a sense of how national security, even in its contemporary neoliberal configurations, is tied to a specifically Cold War state policy, see Ronnie D. Lipschutz, ed., *On Security* (New York: Columbia University Press, 1995).

44. Der Derian, "The Value of Security," 42.

45. The National Security Act of 1947 not only constellated and codified the discourse of national security that would come to drive U.S. foreign policy for decades to come but also inaugurated what many consider to be the first official year of the Cold War. In other words, from a Western perspective Cold War politics *is* the policy of national security. For an account of the antecedents of the rise of national security discourse, see Douglas T. Stuart, *Creating the National Security State: A History of the Law that Transformed America* (Princeton, NJ: Princeton University Press, 2008). For an analysis of the status of global security discourses since the Cold War, see Lipschutz, *On Security*.

46. John Bowlby and E. F. M. Durbin, *Personal Aggressiveness and War* (New York: Columbia University Press, 1939); John Bowlby, "Psychology and Democracy," *Political Quarterly* (1946): 61–76.

47. Bowlby, "Psychology and Democracy," 76.

48. Elaine Tyler May, *Homeward Bound: American Families in the Cold War Era* (London: Taylor & Francis, 1988).

49. van Dijken, *John Bowlby: His Early Life*, 152.

50. Lee Edelman, *No Future: Queer Theory and the Death Drive* (Durham, NC: Duke University Press, 2004).

51. For further historical analysis of this immigration trend, see Denise Noble, "Decolonizing Britain and Domesticating Women: Race, Gender, and Women's Work in Post-1945 British Decolonial and Metropolitan Liberal Reform Discourses," *Meridians: Feminism, Race, Transnationalism* 13, no. 1 (2015): 53–77; Wendy Webster, *Imagining Home: Gender, "Race," and National Identity, 1945–64* (New York: Routledge, 1998); and Wendy Webster, *Englishness and Empire, 1939–1965* (Oxford: Oxford University Press, 2005).

52. Bowlby, *A Secure Base*, 127.

53. Bowlby, *Maternal Care and Mental Health*, 93–94.

54. Viçedo, *The Nature and Nurture of Love*, 194.

55. Mary D. Salter Ainsworth, *Infancy in Uganda: Infant Care and the Growth of Love* (Baltimore, MD: Johns Hopkins University Press, 1967).

56. Erik Linstrum, *Ruling Minds: Psychology and the British Empire* (Cambridge, MA: Harvard University Press, 2016), 194.

57. For a detailed description of Ainsworth's research, her theoretical biases when interpreting the data, and Bowlby's use of it, see Viçedo, *The Nature and Nurture of Love*, 183–208. However, Viçedo does not address the racial, cultural, or colonial implications of Bowlby's incorporation of this research.

58. Webster, *Imagining Home*, 93.

59. "Hoover Calls Panthers Top Threat to Security," *Washington Post*, July 16, 1969.

60. Rose, *Governing the Soul*.

61. Bowlby, *Maternal Care and Mental Health*, 157.

62. Bowlby, *Maternal Care and Mental Health*, 154.

63. Further reading on the changes in maternalist ideology and policy from the Bolshevik revolution to the postsocialist era can be found in Jenny Kaminer, "Mothers of a New World: Maternity and Culture in the Soviet Period," in *Gender in Twentieth-Century Eastern Europe and the USSR*, ed. Catherine Baker (New York: Red Globe, 2016).

64. Bowlby, "The Nature of the Child's Tie to His Mother," 370.

65. See Pick, *Brainwashed*.

66. Knuth Müller, "Psychoanalysis and American Intelligence Since 1940: Unexpected Liaisons," in *Psychoanalysis and the Age of Totalitarianism*, ed. Matt ffytche and Daniel Pick (London: Routledge, 2016); Pick, *Brainwashed*.

67. Geoffrey Cocks, *Psychotherapy in the Third Reich* (New Brunswick, NJ: Transaction, 1997); Müller, "Psychoanalysis and American Intelligence Since 1940."

68. Sarah Marks and Mat Savelli, eds., *Psychiatry in Communist Europe* (London: Palgrave Macmillan, 2015); Ana Antic, "Therapeutic Violence: Psychoanalysis and the 'Re-education' of Political Prisoners in Cold War Yugoslavia and

Eastern Europe," in *Psychoanalysis and the Age of Totalitarianism*, ed. Matt ffytche and Daniel Pick (London: Routledge, 2016).

69. Quoted in Viçedo, *The Nature and Nurture of Love*, 225.

70. May, *Homeward Bound*, 9.

71. Bowlby, *The Making and Breaking of Affectional Bonds*, 129–30.

72. Grewal, *Saving the Security State*, 122.

73. See Grewal, *Saving the Security State*, 2. For the defining account of neoliberalism that attends specifically to its imperial economic policies, see David Harvey, *A Brief History of Neoliberalism* (Oxford: Oxford University Press, 2005). For Nikolas Rose's description of the "entrepreneurial self" he sees as a result of what he calls "advanced liberalism," see Rose, *Governing the Soul*.

74. For further reading on how Cold War national security discourse has been retooled, see the chapters by Wæver, Buzan, and Lipschutz in Lipschutz, *On Security*.

EPILOGUE: HERE, THERE, AND EVERYWHERE—NOW

1. American Psychological Association, "Apology to People of Color for APA's Role in Promoting, Perpetuating, and Failing to Challenge Racism, Racial Discrimination, and Human Hierarchy in U.S.," October 29, 2021, https://www.apa.org/about/policy/racism-apology.

2. The ApsA's statement has since become the lengthy Holmes Commission on Racial Equity in the Psychoanalytic Profession, released Juneteenth 2023. At over four hundred pages, and including two hundred pages of appendices that detail original qualitative research about the role of race and racism in the field, it is now the single most thorough report on the topic.

3. Natasha Stovall, "Whiteness on the Couch," *Longreads*, August 12, 2019, https://longreads.com/2019/08/12/whiteness-on-the-couch/.

4. Recent work in this genre runs the gamut from rather facile and white-catering "therapy talk" in the tradition of Robin DiAngelo's *White Fragility* to more rigorous and critical scholarship that moves beyond an imagined self-focused white audience assiduously trying to interrogate and secure their own anti/racism. For a selection of this trend, see Michael O'Loughlin, "Whiteness and the Psychoanalytic Imagination," *Contemporary Psychoanalysis* 56, no. 4 (2020): 1–22; Alexandra Woods, "The Work Before Us: Whiteness and the Psychoanalytic Institute," *Psychoanalysis, Culture & Society* 25, no. 1 (2020): 230–49; Donald Moss, "On Having Whiteness," *Journal of the American Psychoanalytic Association* 69, no. 2 (2021): 355–71; Neil Altman, *White Privilege: Psychoanalytic Perspectives* (London: Routledge, 2020); Helen Morgan, *The Work of Whiteness: A Psychoanalytic Perspective* (London: Routledge, 2021);

Molly Merson, "The Whiteness Taboo: Interrogating Whiteness in Psychoanalysis," *Psychoanalytic Dialogues* 31, no. 1 (2021): 13–27; Fakhry Davids, "Race and Analytic Neutrality: Clinical and Theoretical Considerations," *Psychoanalytic Quarterly* 91 (2022): 371–93; Hannah Zeavin, "Unfree Associations: Parasitic Whiteness On and Off the Couch," *n+1 Magazine* 42 (2022), https://www.nplusonemag.com/issue-42/essays/unfree-associations/; Tomiwa Owolade, "The Narcissism of Anti-Racist Therapy," *New Statesman*, January 25, 2023, https://www.newstatesman.com/comment/2023/01/narcissism-anti-racist-therapy-helen-morgan-book. For older, foundational pieces, see Kimberlyn Leary, "Race, Self-Disclosure, and 'Forbidden Talk': Race and Ethnicity in Contemporary Clinical Practice," *Psychoanalytic Quarterly* 66, no. 2 (1997): 163–89; Lynne Layton, Nancy Caro Hollander, and Susan Gutwill, *Psychoanalysis, Class and Politics: Encounters in the Clinical Setting* (New York: Routledge, 2006); and Neil Altman, "Whiteness," *Psychoanalytic Quarterly* 75, no. 1 (2006): 45–72.

5. Psychoanalytic Institute of Northern California, "Overview," https://pinccptc.org/.

6. A few years later, following Floyd's murder, Tracey L. Sidesinger and Carlos Padrón founded the New York Center for Community Psychoanalysis (NYCCP), which was "developed to address longstanding systemic racial and class disparities in the provision of mental health care," https://www.youtube.com/watch?v=_2fJRg7_dNM.

7. The Red Clinic, "Mission Statement," https://www.redclinic.org/statement.

8. Elizabeth Danto, *Freud's Free Clinics: Psychoanalysis and Social Justice, 1918–1938* (New York: Columbia University Press, 2005).

9. For this project's published outputs, see this special issue: "Psychoanalysis for the People: Free Clinics and the Social Mission of Psychoanalysis," *Psychoanalysis and History* 24, no. 3 (2022).

10. Matt ffytche, Joanna Ryan, and Raluca Soreanu, "Psychoanalysis for the People: Interrogations and Innovations," *Psychoanalysis and History* 24, no. 3 (2022): 258.

11. Ankhi Mukherjee, *Unseen City: The Psychic Lives of the Urban Poor* (Cambridge: Cambridge University Press, 2022). To this, we could add the scholarship and practices of contemporary decolonial clinical-intellectuals like Patricia Gherovici, Gohar Homayounpour, Lara Sheehi, Avgi Saketopoulou, and Daniel Gaztambide, who all foreground their political commitment to justice through their clinical work.

12. Adam Phillips, "Keeping It Moving: Commentary on Judith Butler's 'Melancholy Gender/Refused Identification,'" in Judith Butler, *The Psychic Life of Power: Theories in Subjection* (Stanford, CA: Stanford University Press, 1997), 155.

13. Lily Scherlis, "Boundary Issues: How Boundaries Became the Rules for Mental Health—and Explain Everything," *Parapraxis Magazine*, https://www.parapraxismagazine.com/articles/boundary-issues.
14. Scherlis, "Boundary Issues."
15. Within mainstream clinical trainings, Khan's work is rarely discussed—or, if it is, it is typically framed as exemplifying a dereliction of duty. Indeed, his entire archive held at the IPA was surreptitiously ordered to be destroyed in 2019 by Paul Crake (executive director), Virginia Ungar (president), Sergio Nick (vice president), and Andrew Brook (treasurer) without the consultation of the IPA's board.
16. Ivan Ward, "Social Clinics and Analytic Boundaries," *Psychoanalysis and History* 24, no. 3 (2022): 372.
17. Michel Foucault, "On the Genealogy of Ethics: An Overview of Work in Progress," in *Ethics: Subjectivity and Truth*, ed. Paul Rabinow, trans. Robert Hurley (New York: New Press, 1994), 253–80.
18. For further reading on this, see the foundational piece D. W. Sue and D. Sue, "Barriers to Effective Cross-Cultural Counselling," *Journal of Counselling Psychology* 24, no. 5 (1977): 420–29.
19. Owolade, "The Narcissism of Anti-Racist Therapy."
20. Morgan, *The Work of Whiteness*, 3.
21. Charles W. Mills, *The Racial Contract* (Ithaca, NY: Cornell University Press, 1997).
22. Leo Bersani and Adam Phillips, *Intimacies* (Chicago: University of Chicago Press, 2008), 4.

Bibliography

Abel, Elizabeth. "Race, Class, and Psychoanalysis? Opening Questions." In *Conflicts in Feminism*, ed. Marianne Hirsch and Evelyn Fox Keller, 184–204. London: Routledge, 1990.

Abel, Elizabeth, Barbara Christian, and Helene Moglen, eds. *Female Subjects in Black and White: Race, Psychoanalysis, Feminism*. Los Angeles: University of California Press, 1997.

Abram, Jan. *The Language of Winnicott: A Dictionary of Winnicott's Use of Words*. London: Karnac, 2007.

Adams, Paul L. "The Social Psychiatry of Frantz Fanon." *American Journal of Psychiatry* 127, no. 6 (1970): 809–14.

Adorno, Theodor, et al. *The Authoritarian Personality*. New York: Harper & Row, 1950.

Aichhorn, August. *Wayward Youth*. New York: Penguin, 1965.

Ainsworth, Mary D. Salter. *Infancy in Uganda: Infant Care and the Growth of Love*. Baltimore, MD: Johns Hopkins University Press, 1967.

Alexander, Sally. "D. W. Winnicott and the Social Democratic Vision." In *Psychoanalysis in the Age of Totalitarianism*, ed. Matt ffytche and Daniel Pick. London: Routledge, 2016.

Alexander, Sally, and Barbara Taylor, eds. *History and Psyche: Culture, Psychoanalysis, and the Past*. London: Palgrave Macmillan, 2012.

Alford, C. Fred. *Melanie Klein and Critical Social Theory*. New Haven, CT: Yale University Press, 1989.

——. *Psychology and the Natural Law of Reparation*. New York: Cambridge University Press, 2006.

Allen, Amy. *Critique on the Couch: Why Critical Theory Needs Psychoanalysis*. New York: Columbia University Press, 2019.

Allen, Amy, and Brian O'Connor, eds. *Transitional Subjects: Critical Theory and Object Relations*. New York: Columbia University Press, 2019.

Allen, Ann Taylor. *Feminism and Motherhood in Western Europe, 1890–1970: The Maternal Dilemma*. London: Palgrave Macmillan, 2005.

——. "Too Emancipated? Women in the Soviet Union and Eastern Europe, 1945–1989." In *Women in Twentieth-Century Europe*, 97–115. London: Palgrave Macmillan, 2008.

Altman, Neil. *The Analyst in the Inner City: Race, Class and Culture Through a Psychoanalytic Lens*. New York: Analytic, 1995.

——. "Whiteness." *Psychoanalytic Quarterly* 75, no. 1 (2006): 45–72.

——. *White Privilege: Psychoanalytic Perspectives*. London: Routledge, 2020.

American Psychological Association. "Apology to People of Color for APA's Role in Promoting, Perpetuating, and Failing to Challenge Racism, Racial Discrimination, and Human Hierarchy in U.S." October 29, 2021. https://www.apa.org/about/policy/racism-apology.

Anderson, Michael. "The Emergence of the Modern Life Cycle in Britain." *Social History* 10, no. 1 (1985): 69–87.

Anderson, Warwick, Deborah Jenson, and Richard C. Keller, eds. *Unconscious Dominions: Psychoanalysis, Colonial Trauma, and Global Sovereignties*. Durham, NC: Duke University Press, 2011.

Angell, Norman. *The Great Illusion: A Study of the Relation of Military Power to National Advantage*. New York: G. P. Putnam, [1909] 1913.

Anter, Andreas. *Max Weber's Theory of the Modern State: Origin, Structure, Significance*. London: Palgrave Macmillan, 2014.

Antic, Ana. "Therapeutic Violence: Psychoanalysis and the 'Re-education' of Political Prisoners in Cold War Yugoslavia and Eastern Europe." In *Psychoanalysis and the Age of Totalitarianism*, ed. Matt ffytche and Daniel Pick. London: Routledge, 2016.

Appignanesi, Lisa, and John Forrester. *Freud's Women: Family, Patients, Followers*. New York: Basic Books, 1992.

Arendt, Hannah. *The Human Condition*. Chicago: University of Chicago Press, [1958] 1998.

Ariès, Philippe. *Centuries of Childhood: A Social History of Family Life*. New York: Vintage, 1965.

Aron, Lewis, and Karen Starr. *A Psychotherapy for the People: Toward a Progressive Psychoanalysis*. London: Routledge, 2013.

Bailkin, Jordanna. *The Afterlife of Empire*. Berkeley: University of California Press, 2012.

Baker, Catherine, ed. *Gender in Twentieth-Century Eastern Europe and the USSR*. London: Palgrave Macmillan, 2017.

Bar-Haim, Shaul. "The Child's Position: The Concept of Childhood in Interwar Psychoanalysis." In *Childhood, Literature, and Science: Fragile Subjects*, ed. Jutta Ahlbeck, Päivi Lappalainen, Kati Launis, and Kirsi Tuohela. London: Routledge, 2017.

——. *The Maternalists: Psychoanalysis, Motherhood, and the British Welfare State*. Philadelphia: University of Pennsylvania Press, 2021.

Barnes, Mary, and Joseph Berke. *Mary Barnes: Two Accounts of a Journey Through Madness*. London: Penguin, 1971.

Barnett, Nicholas J. *Britain's Cold War: Culture, Modernity, and the Soviet Threat*. London: I. B. Tauris, 2018.

Barrow, Christine. "Edith Clarke: Jamaican Social Reformer and Anthropologist." *Caribbean Quarterly* 44, no. 3/4 (1998): 15–34.

Bechdel, Alison. *Are You My Mother? A Comic Drama*. New York: Mariner, 2012.

Benjamin, Jessica. *The Bonds of Love: Psychoanalysis, Feminism, and the Problem of Domination*. New York: Pantheon, 1988.

——. *Like Subjects, Love Objects: Essays on Recognition and Sexual Difference*. New Haven, CT: Yale University Press, 1995.

——. *The Shadow of the Other: Intersubjectivity and Gender in Psychoanalysis*. London: Routledge, 1998.

Berlant, Lauren. *Cruel Optimism*. Durham, NC: Duke University Press, 2011.

——. *On the Inconvenience of Other People*. Durham, NC: Duke University Press, 2022.

Bersani, Leo. *The Culture of Redemption*. Cambridge, MA: Harvard University Press, 1990.

——. *The Freudian Body: Psychoanalysis and Art*. New York: Columbia University Press, 1986.

Bersani, Leo, and Adam Phillips. *Intimacies*. Chicago: University of Chicago Press, 2008.

Bertoldi, Andreas. "Shakespeare, Psychoanalysis, and the Colonial Encounter: The Case of Wulf Sachs' *Black Hamlet*." In *Post-Colonial Shakespeares*, ed. Ania Loomba and Martin Orkin, 235–58. New York: Routledge, 2003.

Beshara, Robert K. *Decolonial Psychoanalysis: Towards Critical Islamophobia Studies*. New York: Routledge, 2019.

Besserman Vianna, Helena. "The Lobo-Cabernite Affair." *Journal of the American Psychoanalytic Association* 48, no. 3 (2000): 1023–29.

Bion, Wilfred. "The Leaderless Group Project." *Bulletin of the Menninger Clinic* 10 (1946): 77–81.

Bion, Wilfred, and John Rickman. "Intragroup Tensions in Therapy: Their Study as the Task of the Group." *Lancet* 2 (1943): 678–81.

Bloom, Leonard. "Black Hamlet: A Psychoanalyst Destrangers a Stranger." *PINS* 30 (2004): 35–41.

——. "On Wulf Sachs' Black Hamlet," *Psychoanalysis and History* 6, no. 2 (2004): 253–64.

Borossa, Julia. "Psychoanalysis and Taking Sides: Two Moments in the History of the Psychoanalytic Movement." In *Psychology and Politics: Intersections of Science and Ideology in the History of the Psy-Sciences*, ed. Anna Borgos, Ferenc Erős, and Júlia Gyimesci. Budapest: Central European University Press, 2019.

Bowker, Matthew. "Analytical and Political Neutrality: Change, Privilege, and Responsibility." *Free Associations: Psychoanalysis and Culture, Media, Groups, Politics* 71 (2017): 1–17.

Bowker, Matthew H., and Amy Buzby, eds. *D. W. Winnicott and Political Theory: Recentering the Subject*. London: Palgrave Macmillan, 2017.

Bowlby, John. *Forty-Four Juvenile Thieves: Their Characters and Home Lives*. London: Baillère, Tindall & Cox, [1944] 1946.

——. *The Making and Breaking of Affectional Bonds*. London: Routledge, 1989.

——. *Maternal Care and Mental Health*. In *Maternal Care and Mental Health & Deprivation of Maternal Care*. New York: Schocken, [1951] 1966.

——. "The Nature of the Child's Tie to His Mother." *International Journal of Psychoanalysis* 39 (1958): 350–73.

——. "Psychology and Democracy." *Political Quarterly* (1946): 61–76.

——. *A Secure Base: Parent-Child Attachment and Healthy Human Development*. New York: Basic Books, 1988.

Bowlby, John, and E. F. M. Durbin. *Personal Aggressiveness and War*. New York: Columbia University Press, 1939.

Brennan, Teresa. "Transmission in Groups." In *The Transmission of Affect*. Ithaca, NY: Cornell University Press, 2004.

Brickman, Celia. *Aboriginal Populations in the Mind: Race and Primitivity in Psychoanalysis*. New York: Columbia University Press, 2003.

Britzman, Deborah. *After-Education: Anna Freud, Melanie Klein, and Psychoanalytic Histories of Learning*. New York: New York State University Press, 2003.

——. *Melanie Klein: Early Analysis, Play, and the Question of Freedom*. London: Springer, 2016.

Brunner, José. *Freud and the Politics of Psychoanalysis*. London: Routledge, 2001.

Bueskens, Petra, ed. *Mothering and Psychoanalysis: Clinical, Sociological and Feminist Perspectives*. Bradford, ON: Demeter, 2014.

Bulhan, Hussein Abdilahi. "Frantz Fanon: The Revolutionary Psychiatrist." *Race & Class* 21 (1980): 251–71.

Bunche, Ralph. *An African American in South Africa: The Travel Notes of Ralph J. Bunche 28 September 1937–1 January 1938*. Athens: Ohio University Press, 1992.

Bunselmeyer, Robert E. *The Cost of War, 1914–1919: British Economic War Aims and the Origins of Reparation*. Hamden, CT: Shoe String, 1975.

Burgin, Dieter. "Analysis on Demand." *British Journal of Psychotherapy* 32, no. 3 (2016): 347–58.

Burman, Erica. *Fanon, Education, Action: Child as Method*. London: Routledge, 2018.

Burnham, John C., ed. *After Freud Left: A Century of Psychoanalysis in America*. Chicago: University of Chicago Press, 2012.

——. "The 'New Freud Studies': A Historiographical Shift." *Journal of the Historical Society* 6, no. 2 (2006): 213–33.

Bush, Barbara. "Colonial Research and the Social Sciences at the End of Empire: The West Indian Social Survey, 1944–57." *Journal of Imperial and Commonwealth History* 41, no. 3 (2013): 451–74.

——. "Feminising Empire? British Women's Activist Networks in Defending and Challenging Empire from 1918 to Decolonisation." *Women's History Review* 25, no. 4 (2016): 499–519.

Butler, Judith. "Imitation and Gender Insubordination." In *Inside/Out: Lesbian Theories, Gay Theories*, ed. Diana Fuss, 13–31. London: Routledge, 1992.

——. *The Psychic Life of Power: Theories in Subjection*. Stanford, CA: Stanford University Press, 1997.

Caldwell, Lesley. "Continuities and Discontinuities at the Cassel Hospital Richmond 1977–1982." *Psychoanalytic Studies* 3, no. 3/4 (2001): 363 79.

——. "Symbolic and Anticipated: Winnicott's Attention to the Use of Black in the Consulting Room." *British Journal of Psychotherapy* 32, no. 3 (2016): 376–91.

Caldwell, Peter C. *Popular Sovereignty and the Crisis of German Constitutional Law: The Theory and Practice of Weimar Constitutionalism*. Durham, NC: Duke University Press, 1997.

Campbell, Chloe. "Kenyan Medical Discourse and Eugenics." In *Race and Empire: Eugenics in Colonial Kenya*, ed. Chloe Campbell, Andrew Thompson, and John Mackenzie, 39–76. Manchester: Manchester University Press, 2007.

Carothers, John Colin. *The Psychology of Mau Mau*. Nairobi: Printed by the Govt. printer, 1954.

Celarent, Barbara. "*Rooiyard: A Sociological Survey of an Urban Native Slum Yard* by Ellen Hellmann." *American Journal of Sociology* 118, no. 1 (July 2012): 274–80.

Chadwick, Edwin. "1842 Report on the Sanitary Condition of the Labouring Population of Great Britain." House of Commons Sessional Paper, 1842.

Chapman, Adrian. "Dwelling in Strangeness: Accounts of the Kingsley Hall Community, London (1965–1970), Established by R. D. Laing." *Journal of the Medical Humanities* 42, no. 3 (2021): 471–94.

——. "'May All Be Shattered into God': Mary Barnes and Her Journey Through Madness in Kingsley Hall." *Journal of the Medical Humanities* 41 (2020): 207–28.

Cheng, Anne Anlin. *The Melancholy of Race: Psychoanalysis, Assimilation, and Hidden Grief*. Oxford: Oxford University Press, 2001.

Chettiar, Teri. "Democratizing Mental Health: Motherhood, Therapeutic Community and the Emergence of the Psychiatric Family at the Cassel Hospital in Post-Second World War Britain." *History of the Human Sciences* 25, no. 5 (2012): 107–22.

Chitty, Christopher. *Sexual Hegemony: Statecraft, Sodomy, and Capital in the Rise of the World System*, ed. Max Fox. Durham, NC: Duke University Press, 2020.

Chodorow, Nancy. *Feminism and Psychoanalytic Theory*. New Haven, CT: Yale University Press, 1989.

——. *The Reproduction of Mothering: Psychoanalysis and the Sociology of Gender*. Los Angeles: University of California Press, 1978.

Coates, Ta-Nehisi. "The Case for Reparations." *The Atlantic*, June 2014.

Cocks, Geoffrey. *Psychotherapy in the Third Reich*. New Brunswick, NJ: Transaction, 1997.

Coles, Robert. *Anna Freud*. Reading, MA: Addison-Wesley, 1992.

Contratto, Susan. "A Feminist Critique of Attachment Theory and Evolutionary Psychology." In *Rethinking Mental Health and Disorder: Feminist Perspectives*, ed. Mary Ballou and Laura S. Brown, 29–47. New York: Guilford, 2002.

Cooper, David, ed. *The Dialectics of Liberation*. London: Penguin, 1968.

Cregan, Kate, and Denise Cuthbert, *Global Childhoods: Issues and Debates*. Thousand Oaks, CA: SAGE, 2014.

Crewe, Jonathan V. "Black Hamlet: Psychoanalysis on Trial in South Africa." *Poetics Today* 22, no. 2 (2001): 413–33.

Cunningham, Hugh. *Children and Childhood in Western Society Since 1500*. New York: Longman, 1995.

Cvetkovitch, Ann. *Depression: A Public Feeling*. Durham, NC: Duke University Press, 2012.

Daly, Mary. *The Gender Division of Welfare: The Impact of the British and German Welfare States*. Cambridge: Cambridge University Press, 2000.

Daly, Mary, and Katherine Rake. *Gender and the Welfare State: Care, Work and Welfare in Europe and the USA*. Cambridge: Polity, 2003.

Damousi, Joy. *Freud in the Antipodes: A Cultural History of Psychoanalysis in Australia*. Sydney: University of New South Wales, 2005.

Damousi, Joy, and Mariano Ben Plotkin. *Psychoanalysis and Politics: Histories of Psychoanalysis Under Conditions of Restricted Political Freedom*. Oxford: Oxford University Press, 2012.

——, eds. *The Transnational Unconscious: Essays in the History of Psychoanalysis and Transnationalism*. New York: Palgrave Macmillan, 2009.

Danto, Elizabeth. *Freud's Free Clinics: Psychoanalysis and Social Justice, 1918–1938*. New York: Columbia University Press, 2005.

Danto, Elizabeth, and Alexandra Steiner-Strauss, eds. *Freud/Tiffany: Anna Freud, Dorothy Tiffany Burlingham and "The Best Possible School"*. London: Routledge, 2019.

Davids, Fakhry. *Internal Racism: A Psychoanalytic Approach to Race and Difference*. London: Red Globe, 2011.

——. "Race and Analytic Neutrality: Clinical and Theoretical Considerations." *Psychoanalytic Quarterly* 91 (2022): 371–93.

de Grieff, Pablo. *The Handbook of Reparations*. Oxford: Oxford University Press, 2006.

de Maré, Patrick. "Large Group Perspectives." *Group Analysis* 18, no. 2 (1985): 79–92.

Dean, Tim. *Beyond Sexuality*. Chicago: Chicago University Press, 2000.

Dean, Tim, and Christopher Lane, eds. *Homosexuality and Psychoanalysis*. Chicago: University of Chicago Press, 2001.

Deleuze, Gilles, and Félix Guattari. "Psychoanalysis and Ethnology." *SubStance* 4, nos. 11–12 (1975): 170–97.

deMause, Lloyd, ed. *The History of Childhood*. Lanham, MD: Rowman and Littlefield, 1995.

Der Derian, James. "The Value of Security: Hobbes, Marx, Nietzsche, and Baudrillard." In *On Security*, ed. Ronnie D. Lipschutz. New York: Columbia University Press, 1995.

Derrida, Jacques. "Geopsychoanalysis: 'and the Rest of the World.'" In *The Psychoanalysis of Race*, ed. Christopher Lane, 65–90. New York: Columbia University Press, 1998.

Dicks, H. V. *50 Years of the Tavistock Clinic*. London: Routledge, 1970.

Dimen, Muriel, and Virginia Goldner, eds. *Gender in the Psychoanalytic Space: Between Clinic and Culture*. New York: Other Press, 2002.

Doane, Janice, and Devon Hodges. *From Klein to Kristeva: Psychoanalytic Feminism and the Search for the "Good Enough" Mother*. Ann Arbor: University of Michigan Press, 1993.

Doane, Mary Ann. "Dark Continents: Epistemologies of Racial and Sexual Difference in Psychoanalysis and the Cinema." In *Femmes Fatales: Feminism, Film Theory, Psychoanalysis*, 209–48. New York: Routledge, 1991.

Douglas, Mary. *Purity and Danger: An Analysis of the Concepts of Pollution and Taboo*. Routledge and Kegan Paul, 1966.

Dubow, Saul. *Racial Segregation and the Origins of Apartheid in Twentieth Century South Africa, 1919–36*. London: Palgrave Macmillan, 1989.

——. "Wulf Sachs' 'Black Hamlet': A Case of Psychic Vivisection?" *African Affairs* 92, no. 369 (1993): 1–16.

Durbach, Nadja. "One British Thing: A Bottle of Welfare Orange Juice, c. 1961–1971." *Journal of British Studies* 57 (2018): 564–67.

Durrheim, Kevin. "Wulf Sachs, Race Trouble, and the Will to Know." *PINS* 51 (2016): 99–104.

Duschinsky, Robbie, Monica Greco, and Judith Soloman. "The Politics of Attachment: Lines of Flight with Bowlby, Deleuze and Guittari." *Theory, Culture & Society* 32, nos. 7–8 (2015): 173–95.

Edelman, Lee. *No Future: Queer Theory and the Death Drive*. Durham, NC: Duke University Press, 2004.

Edgcumbe, Rose. *Anna Freud: A View of Development, Disturbance and Therapeutic Techniques*. London: Routledge, 2000.

Edmundson, Mark. *The Death of Sigmund Freud: Fascism, Psychoanalysis and the Rise of Fundamentalism*. London: Bloomsbury, 2008.

Egan, R. Danielle, and Gail Hawkes. *Theorizing the Sexual Child in Modernity*. New York: Palgrave Macmillan, 2010.

El Shakry, Omina. *The Arabic Freud: Psychoanalysis and Islam in Modern Egypt*. Princeton, NJ: Princeton University Press, 2017.

Eng, David. "Colonial Object Relations." *Social Text* 34, no. 1 (2016): 1–19.

Eng, David, and David Kazanjian. *Loss: The Politics of Mourning*. Los Angeles: University of California Press, 2003.

Eng, David, and Shinhee Han. *Racial Melancholia, Racial Dissociation: On the Social and Psychic Lives of Asian Americans*. Durham, NC: Duke University Press, 2019.

Fanon, Frantz. *Alienation and Freedom*, ed. Jean Khalfa and Robert C. Young, trans. Steven Corcoran. London: Bloomsbury, 2018.

——. *Black Skin, White Masks*. New York: Grove, [1952] 2008.

——. "Social Therapy in a Ward of Muslim Men: Methodological Difficulties." In *Alienation and Freedom*, ed. Jean Khalfa and Robert C. Young, trans. Steven Corcoran, 353–72. London: Bloomsbury, 2018.

——. *Toward the African Revolution*, trans. Haakon Chevalier. New York: Grove, 1967.

Felski, Rita. "Introduction." *New Literary History* 45, no. 2 (2014): v–xi.

ffytche, Matt. "Introduction." *Psychoanalysis & History* 18, no. 1 (2016): 1–5.

ffytche, Matt, and Daniel Pick, eds. *Psychoanalysis and the Age of Totalitarianism*. London: Routledge, 2016.

ffytche, Matt, Joanna Ryan, and Raluca Soreanu. "Psychoanalysis for the People: Interrogations and Innovations." *Psychoanalysis and History* 24, no. 3 (2022): 253–67.

Figlio, Karl. *Remembering as Reparation: Psychoanalysis and Historical Memory*. London: Palgrave Macmillan, 2017.

Figlio, Karl, and R. M. Young. "An Interview with John Bowlby on the Origins and Reception of His Work." *Free Associations* 1, no. 6 (1986): 36–64.

Fonagy, Peter. "Points of Contact and Divergence Between Psychoanalytic and Attachment Theories: Is Psychoanalytic Theory Truly Different." *Psychoanalytic Inquiry* 19, no. 4 (1999): 448–80.

Fonagy, Peter, and Mary Target. "The Rooting of the Mind in the Body: New Links Between Attachment Theory and Psychoanalytic Thought." *Journal of the American Psychoanalytic Association* 55, no. 2 (2007): 411–56.

Fonagy, Peter, Nicolas Lorenzini, Chloe Campbell, and Patrick Luyten. "Why Are We Interested in Attachments?" In *The Routledge Handbook of Attachment: Theory*, 31–48. New York: Routledge, 2014.

Ford, Lily, dir. *Chasing the Revolution: Marie Langer, Revolution, and Society*. Hidden Persuaders, 2021.

Forrester, John. *Dispatches from the Freud Wars: Psychoanalysis and Its Passions*. Cambridge, MA: Harvard University Press, 1998.

Forrester, John, and Laura Cameron. *Freud in Cambridge*. Cambridge: Cambridge University Press, 2017.

Foucault, Michel. "On the Genealogy of Ethics: An Overview of Work in Progress." In *Ethics: Subjectivity and Truth*, ed. Paul Rabinow, trans. Robert Hurley, 253–80. New York: New Press, 1994.

——. *History of Sexuality: An Introduction, Vol. 1*. New York: Vintage, 1990.

Franzblau, Susan H. "Historicizing Attachment Theory: Binding the Ties that Bind." *Feminism & Psychology* 19, no. 1 (1999): 22–31.

Fraser, Nancy. *Fortunes of Feminism: From State-Managed Capitalism to Neoliberal Crisis*. New York: Verso, 2013.

Freeman, Elizabeth. *Time Binds: Queer Temporalities, Queer Histories*. Durham, NC: Duke University Press, 2010.

French, Joan. "Colonial Policy Towards Women After the 1938 Uprising: The Case of Jamaica." *Caribbean Quarterly* (1988): 38–61.

Freud, Anna. "On Beating Fantasies and Daydreams." In *The Writings of Anna Freud*, vol. 1, 137–57. New York: International Universities Press, [1922] 1974.

——. "Child Analysis as a Subspecialty." In *The Writings of Anna Freud*, vol. 7, 204–22. New York: International Universities Press, [1970] 1971.

——. *The Ego and the Mechanisms of Defence*. In *The Writings of Anna Freud*, vol. 2. New York: International Universities Press, [1936] 1966.

——. *Four Lectures on Child Analysis*. In *The Writings of Anna Freud*, vol. 1, 3–72. New York: International Universities Press, [1926] 1974.

——. *Infants Without Families: Reports on the Hampstead Nurseries, 1939–1945*. In *The Writings of Anna Freud*, vol. 3. New York: International Universities Press, 1973.

——. "The Relation Between Psychoanalysis and Education," *Four Lectures on Psychoanalysis for Teachers and Parents*. In *The Writings of Anna Freud*, vol. 1, 121–36. New York: International Universities Press, [1930] 1974.

Freud, Sigmund. "Analysis of a Phobia in a Five-Year-Old Boy ['Little Hans']." In *The "Wolfman" and Other Cases*, ed. Adam Phillips, trans. Adey Huish, 1–122. New York: Penguin, [1909] 2003.

——. "Analysis Terminable and Interminable." In *Wild Analysis*, ed. Adam Phillips, trans. Alan Bance, 171–208. London: Penguin, [1937] 2002.

——. "Foreword." In August Aichhorn, *Wayward Youth*. New York: Penguin, 1965.

——. "Letter from Sigmund Freud to Oskar Pfister, August 20, 1930." In *Psychoanalysis and Faith: The Letters of Sigmund Freud and Oskar Pfister*. London: Forgotten Books, 2018.

——. *The Standard Edition of Complete Psychological Works of Sigmund Freud*. 24 vols. Ed. James Strachey in collaboration with Anna Freud, assisted by Alix Strachey and Alan Tyson. London: Hogarth Press and Institute of Psychoanalysis, 1953–74.

——. *Three Essays on the Theory of Sexuality*, ed. and trans. James Strachey. New York: Basic Books, [1905] 1962.

——. "On 'Wild' Analysis." In *Wild Analysis*, ed. Adam Phillips, trans. Alan Bance, 1–10. London: Penguin, [1910] 2002.

Friedan, Betty. *The Feminine Mystique*. London: Norton, [1963] 2001.

Frosh, Stephen. *The Politics of Psychoanalysis: An Introduction to Freudian and Post-Freudian Theory*. New York: New York University Press, [1987] 1999.

——. "Psychoanalysis, Colonialism, and Racism," *Journal of Theoretical and Philosophical Psychology* 33, no. 3 (2013): 141–54.

Fryer, Peter. *Staying Power: The History of Black People in Britain*. London: Pluto, 2010.

Fuechtner, Veronika. *Berlin Psychoanalytic: Psychoanalysis and Culture in Weimar Republic Germany and Beyond*. Los Angeles: University of California Press, 2011.

Furedi, Frank. *Authority: A Sociological History*. Cambridge: Cambridge University Press, 2013.

Fuss, Diana. "Interior Colonies: Frantz Fanon and the Politics of Identification." In *Identification Papers*, 141–65. London: Routledge, 1995.

——. "Pink Freud." *GLQ* 2, nos. 1–2 (1995): 1–9.

Gay, Peter. *Freud: A Life for Our Time*. New York: Norton, [1988] 2006.

Gaztambide, Daniel. *A People's History of Psychoanalysis: From Freud to Liberation Psychology*. Lexington, KY: Lexington Books, 2019.

Geissmann, Claudine, and Pierre Geissmann. *A History of Child Psychoanalysis*. London: Routledge, 1998.

Geleerd, Elisabeth. "Evaluation of Melanie Klein's 'Narrative of a Child Analysis.'" *International Journal of Psychoanalysis* 44 (1963): 493–506.

George, Sheldon. *Trauma and Race: A Lacanian Study of African American Racial Identity.* Waco, TX: Baylor University Press, 2016.

George, Sheldon, and Derek Hook, eds. *Lacan and Race: Racism, Identity and Psychoanalytic Theory.* New York: Routledge, 2021.

Gerson, Gal. "Individuality, Deliberation, and Welfare in Donald Winnicott." *History of the Human Sciences* 18, no. 1 (2005): 107–26.

——. "Winnicott, Participation, and Gender." *Feminism & Psychology* 14, no. 4 (2004): 561–81.

Gerson, Samuel. "Neutrality, Resistance, and Self-Disclosure in an Intersubjective Psychoanalysis." *Psychoanalytic Dialogues* 6 (1996): 623–45.

Gherovici, Patricia, and Christopher Christian. *Psychoanalysis in the Barrios: Race, Class, and the Unconscious.* New York: Routledge, 2018.

Gibson, Nigel C. *Fanon: The Postcolonial Imagination.* Cambridge: Polity, 2003.

Gillespie, Sadie. "Historical Notes on the First South African Psychoanalytic Society." *Psychoanalytic Psychotherapy in South Africa* 1 (1992): 1–6.

Gilman, Sander. *Freud, Race, and Gender.* Princeton, NJ: Princeton University Press, 1994.

Golcman, Aída Alejandra. "The Experiment of the Therapeutic Communities in Argentina: The Case of the Hospital Estévez." *Psychoanalysis and History* 14, no. 2 (2021): 269–84.

Goldman, Dobi. "Introduction." In *In One's Bones: The Clinical Genius of Winnicott,* ed. Dobi Goldman, xi–xxix. London: Jason Aronson, 1993.

González, Francisco J., and Rachel Peltz. "Community Psychoanalysis: Collaborative Practice as Psychoanalysis." *Psychoanalytic Dialogues* 31, no. 4 (2021): 409–27.

Gordon, Lewis R. "Revolutionary Therapy." In *What Fanon Said: A Philosophical Introduction to His Life and Thought,* 75–105. New York: Fordham University Press, 2015.

Grant, Matthew, ed. *The British Way in Cold Warfare: Intelligence, Diplomacy, and the Bomb, 1945–1975.* London: Continuum, 2009.

Green, Emily. "Melanie Klein and the Black Mammy: An Exploration of the Influence of the Mammy Stereotype on Klein's Maternal and Its Contribution to the 'Whiteness' of Psychoanalysis." *Studies in Gender and Sexuality* 19, no. 3 (2018): 164–82.

Greenspan, Rachel. "Framing Psychoanalysis in the Context of the World." *Differences* 33, nos. 2–3 (2022): 90–109.

Greenwood, Sean. *Britain and the Cold War, 1945–91.* London: Macmillan, 2000.

Grewal, Inderpal. *Saving the Security State: Exceptional Citizens in Twenty-First Century America.* Durham, NC: Duke University Press, 2017.

Grosskurth, Phyllis. *Melanie Klein: Her World and Her Work.* London: Jason Aronson, 1986.

Gruber, Helmut. *Red Vienna: An Experiment in Working Class Culture, 1919–1934.* New York: Oxford University Press, 1991.

Gutman, Marta, and Ning de Corninck-Smith. *Designing Modern Childhoods: History, Space, and the Material Culture of Children.* New Brunswick, NJ: Rutgers University Press, 2008.

Haigh, Rex. "The Quintessence of a Therapeutic Environment: The Foundations for the Windsor Conference 2014." *Therapeutic Communities: The International Journal of Therapeutic Communities* 36, no. 1 (2015): 1–11.

Hale, Nathan. *Freud and the Americans: The Beginnings of Psychoanalysis in the United States, 1876–1917.* Oxford: Oxford University Press, 1971.

——. *The Rise and Crisis of Psychoanalysis in the United States, 1917–1985: Freud and the Americans*, vol. 2. Oxford: Oxford University Press, 1995.

Hamilton, James W. "Some Dynamics of Anti-Negro Prejudice." *Psychoanalytic Review* 53 (1966): 5–15.

Hampshire, James. *Citizenship and Belonging: Immigration and the Politics of Demographic Governance in Postwar Britain.* London: Palgrave Macmillan, 2005.

Hanson, Ellis. "The Future's Eve: Reparative Reading After Sedgwick." *South Atlantic Quarterly* 110, no. 1 (2011): 101–19.

Haraway, Donna. *Primate Visions: Gender, Race and Nature in the World of Modern Science.* New York: Routledge, 1989.

Harris, Dominic. "Kingsley Hall: R. D. Laing's Experiment in Anti-Psychiatry." *The Guardian*, September 1, 2012.

Harrison, Tom. *Bion, Rickman, Foulkes and the Northfield Experiments: Advancing on a Different Front.* London: J. Kingsley, 2000.

Hart, Lynda. "Knights in Shining Armor and Other Relations." *Between the Body and the Flesh: Performing Sadomasochism* (New York: Columbia University Press, 1998): 11–35.

Hartmann, L. "Winnicott: Life and Work." *American Journal of Psychiatry* 160, no. 12 (2003): 2255–56.

Hartnack, Christiane. "Vishnu on Freud's Desk: Psychoanalysis in Colonial India." *Social Research: An International Quarterly* 57 (1990): 921–49.

Harvey, David. *A Brief History of Neoliberalism.* Oxford: Oxford University Press, 2005.

Hayley, T. T. "Thomas Forrest Main (1911–1990)." *International Journal of Psychoanalysis* 72 (1991): 719–22.

Hayes, Grahame. "Sachs, Chavafambira, Maggie: Prurience or the Pathology of Social Relations?" *South African Journal of Psychology* 32, no. 2 (2002): 43–48.

Hayward, Rhodri. *The Transformation of the Psyche in British Primary Care, 1870–1970*. London: Bloomsbury, 2014.

Hellmann, Ellen. *Rooiyard: A Sociological Study of an Urban Native Slum Yard*, Rhodes-Livingstone Papers No. 13. Oxford: Oxford University Press, 1948.

Hemmings, Clare. "The Materials of Reparation." *Feminist Theory* 15, no. 1 (2014): 27–30.

Hendrick, Harry. *Children, Childhood, and English Society, 1880–1990*. Cambridge: Cambridge University Press, 1997.

Herzog, Dagmar. *Cold War Freud: Psychoanalysis in an Age of Catastrophes*. Cambridge: Cambridge University Press, 2017.

Hewitt, Margaret, and Ivy Pinchbeck. *Children in English Society*, vol. 1. London: Routledge, 1969.

Heywood, Colin. *Childhood in Modern Europe*. Cambridge: Cambridge University Press, 2018.

——. *A History of Childhood: Children and Childhood in the West from Medieval to Modern Times*. Cambridge: Polity, 2001.

Hinshelwood, Robert D. *A Dictionary of Kleinian Thought*. London: Free Association, 1998.

——. "The Therapeutic Community in a Changing Cultural and Political Climate." *International Journal of Therapeutic Communities* 10, no. 1 (1989): 63–69.

Hoffman, Irwin Z. "The Intimate and Ironic Authority of the Psychoanalyst's Presence." *Psychoanalytic Quarterly* 65 (1996): 102–36.

Hogan, P. C. "The Politics of Otherness in Clinical Psychoanalysis: Racism as Pathogen in a Case of D. W. Winnicott." *Literature and Psychology* 38, no. 4 (1992): 36–43.

Holder, Alex. *Anna Freud, Melanie Klein, and the Psychoanalysis of Children and Adolescents*. London: Karnac, 2005.

Hollander, Nancy Caro. *Love in a Time of Hate: Liberation Psychology in Latin America*. New Brunswick, NJ: Rutgers University Press, 1997.

——. "Psychoanalysis Confronts the Politics of Repression: The Case of Argentina." *Social Science & Medicine* 28, no. 7 (1989): 751–58.

Holmes, Jeremy. *John Bowlby and Attachment Theory*, 2nd ed. New York: Routledge, 2014.

Homayounpour, Gohar. *Doing Psychoanalysis in Tehran*. Cambridge, MA: MIT Press, 2012.

Honig, Bonnie. *Public Things: Democracy in Disrepair*. New York: Fordham University Press, 2017.

Honneth, Axel. *The Struggle for Recognition: The Moral Grammar of Social Conflicts*. Cambridge: Polity, 1992.

"Hoover Calls Panthers Top Threat to Security." *Washington Post*, July 16, 1969.

Hopkins, Michael F., Michael D. Kandiah, and Gillian Staerck, eds. *Cold War Britain, 1945–64: New Perspectives.* New York: Palgrave Macmillan, 2003.

Isaacs, Susan. "On the Nature and Function of Phantasy." *International Journal of Psychoanalysis* 29 ([1943] 1948): 73–97.

Jacobs, Michael. *D. W. Winnicott.* London: SAGE, 1995.

Jacobsen, Kurt. "Escape from the Treadmill: Education, Politics, and the Main-springs of Child Analysis." In *Vienna: World of Yesterday, 1885–1914,* ed. Stephen Bronner and Peter Wagner. Atlantic Highlands, NJ: Humanities, 1994.

Jacobus, Mary. *First Things: Maternal Imagery in Literature, Art, and Psychoanalysis.* New York: Routledge, 1996.

Jacoby, Russell. *The Repression of Psychoanalysis: Otto Fenichel and the Political Freudians.* Chicago: Chicago University Press, 1983.

James, Allison, Chris Jenks, and Alan Prout. *Theorizing Childhood.* Cambridge: Polity, 1998.

Jelavich, Barbara. *Modern Austria: Empire & Republic, 1800–1986.* Cambridge: Cambridge University Press, 1987.

Johns, Jennifer. "Thomas Forrest Main (25 February 1911–20 May 1990)." *Psychoanalytic Psychotherapy* 5 (1990): 81.

Johnson, Barbara. *The Feminist Difference: Literature, Psychoanalysis, Race, and Gender.* Cambridge, MA: Harvard University Press, 1998.

Johnstone, Frederick A. *Class, Race, and Gold: A Study of Class Relations and Racial Discrimination in South Africa.* London: Routledge and Kegan Paul, 1976.

Jones, Edgar. "War and the Practice of Psychotherapy: The UK Experience 1939–1960." *Medical History* 48 (2004): 493–510.

Kaminer, Jenny. "Mothers of a New World: Maternity and Culture in the Soviet Period." In *Gender in Twentieth-Century Eastern Europe and the USSR,* ed. Catherine Baker. London: Red Globe, 2016.

Kandiah, Michael. *Cold War Britain, 1945–1964: New Perspectives,* ed. Michael F. Hopkins, Michael D. Kandiah, and Gillian Staerck. London: Palgrave Macmillan, 2003.

Katz, Jonathan. *The Invention of Heterosexuality.* Chicago: University of Chicago Press, 1995.

Keller, Richard C. "Clinician and Revolutionary: Frantz Fanon, Biography, and the History of Colonial Medicine." *Bulletin of the History of Medicine* 81, no. 4 (2007): 823–41.

——. *Colonial Madness: Psychiatry in French North Africa.* Chicago: University of Chicago Press, 2007.

——. "Madness and Colonization: Psychiatry in the British and French Empires, 1800–1962." *Journal of Social History* 35, no. 2 (2001): 295–326.

——. "Taking Science to the Colonies: Psychiatric Innovation in France and North Africa." In *Psychiatry and Empire*, ed. Sloan Mahone and Megan Vaughan. London: Palgrave Macmillan, 2007.

Kelley, Robin D. G., and Stephen Tuck, eds. *The Other Special Relationship: Race, Rights, and Riots in Britain and the United States*. London: Palgrave Macmillan, 2015.

Kellond, Joanna. *Donald Winnicott and the Politics of Care*. London: Palgrave Macmillan, 2022.

Kent, Bruce. *The Spoils of War: Politics, Economics and the Diplomacy of Reparations 1918–1932*. Oxford: Clarendon, 1992.

Key, Ellen. *The Century of the Child*. London: Forgotten, [1900] 2015.

Keynes, John Maynard. *The Economic Consequences of the Peace*. New York: Skyhorse, [1919] 2007.

Khalfa, Jean. "Fanon and Psychiatry." *Nottingham French Studies* 54, no. 1 (2015): 52–71.

——. "Fanon, Revolutionary, Psychiatrist." In *Alienation and Freedom*, ed. Jean Khalfa and Robert C. Young, trans. Steven Corcoran, 167–202. London: Bloomsbury, 2018.

Khan, Azeen. "The Subaltern Clinic." *boundary 2* 46, no. 4 (2019): 181–217.

Khanna, Ranjana. *Dark Continents: Psychoanalysis and Colonialism*. Durham, NC: Duke University Press, 2003.

King, Pearl, and Ricardo Steiner, eds. *The Freud-Klein Controversies: 1941–45*. London: Routledge, 1991.

Klein, Melanie. "A Contribution to the Psychogenesis of Manic Depressive States." In *Love, Guilt, and Reparation and Other Works, 1921–1945*, 262–89. New York: Free Press, [1935] 1975.

——. "Criminal Tendencies in Normal Children." In *Love, Guilt, and Reparation and Other Works, 1921–1945*, 170–85. New York: Free Press, [1927] 1975.

——. "The Development of a Child." In *Love, Guilt, and Reparation and Other Works, 1921–1945*, 1–53. New York: Free Press, [1921] 1975.

——. "The Early Development of Conscience in the Child." In *Love, Guilt, and Reparation and Other Works, 1921–1945*, 248–57. New York: Free Press, [1933] 1975.

——. "Infantile Anxiety-Situations Reflected in a Work of Art and in the Creative Impulse." In *Love, Guilt, and Reparation and Other Works, 1921–1945*, 210–18. New York: Free Press, [1929] 1975.

——. "Love, Guilt and Reparation." In *Love, Guilt, and Reparation and Other Works, 1921–1945*, 306–43. New York: Free Press, [1937] 1975.

——. *Narrative of a Child Analysis: The Conduct of the Psycho-Analysis of Children as Seen in the Treatment of a Ten-Year-Old Boy*. London: Random House, [1961] 1998.

——. *The Psycho-Analysis of Children*. London: Vintage, [1932] 1975.

——. "The Psychological Principles of Early Analysis." In *Love, Guilt, and Reparation and Other Works, 1921–1945*, 128–38. New York: Free Press, [1926] 1975.

——. "The Rôle of School in the Libidinal Development of a Child." In *Love, Guilt, and Reparation and Other Works, 1921–1945*. New York: Free Press, [1922] 1975.

——. "Symposium on Child-Analysis." In *Love, Guilt, and Reparation and Other Works, 1921–1945*, 139–69. New York: Free Press, [1927] 1975.

Kovel, Joel. *White Racism: A Psychohistory*. New York: Columbia University Press, 1970.

Kristeva, Julia. *Melanie Klein*, trans. Ross Guberman. New York: Columbia University Press, 2001.

Kubie, Lawrence. "The Ontogeny of Racial Prejudice." *Journal of Nervous and Mental Disease* 141, no. 3 (1965): 265–73.

Lacey, Martin. *Working for Boroko: The Origins of a Coercive Labor System in South Africa*. Johannesburg: Ravan, 1981.

Lane, Christopher. "Psychoanalysis and Colonialism Redux: Why Mannoni's 'Prospero Complex' Still Haunts Us." *Journal of Modern Literature* 25, no. 3/4 (2002): 127–50.

——, ed. *The Psychoanalysis of Race*. New York: Columbia University Press, 1998.

Laubender, Carolyn. "Beyond Repair: Interpretation, Reparation, and Melanie Klein's Clinical Play Technique." *Studies in Gender and Sexuality* 20, no. 1 (2019): 51–67.

——. "Empires of Mind: Postcolonial Cartographies of 'The Empire' in *Narrative of a Child Analysis*." *Psychoanalysis, Culture, and Society* 26 (2021): 223–44.

——. "On Good Authority: Anna Freud and the Politics of Child Analysis." *Psychoanalysis and History* 19, no. 3 (2017): 297–322.

Layton, Lynne, Nancy Caro Hollander, and Susan Gutwill. *Psychoanalysis, Class and Politics: Encounters in the Clinical Setting*. New York: Routledge, 2006.

Lazali, Karima. *Colonial Trauma: A Study of the Psychic and Political Consequences of Colonial Oppression in Algeria*, trans. Matthew B. Smith. Cambridge: Polity, 2021.

Lazarus-Black, Mindie. "My Mother Never Fathered Me: Rethinking Kinship and the Governing of Families." *Social and Economic Studies* 44, no. 1 (1995): 49–71.

Leary, Kimberlyn. "Race, Self-Disclosure, and 'Forbidden Talk': Race and Ethnicity in Contemporary Clinical Practice." *Psychoanalytic Quarterly* 66, no. 2 (1997): 163–89.

Legassick, Martin. "South Africa: Capital Accumulation and Violence." *Economy and Society* 3, no. 3 (1974): 253–91.

Levenson, Zachary, and Marcel Paret. "The South African Tradition of Racial Capitalism." *Ethnic and Racial Studies* 46, no. 16 (2023): 3403–24.

Lewis, Gail. "Not by Criticality Alone." *Feminist Theory* 15, no. 1 (2014): 31–38.

Lieberman, E. James. *Acts of Will: The Life and Work of Otto Rank*. New York: Free Press, 1998.

Lieberman, E. James, and Robert Kramer. *The Letters of Sigmund Freud and Otto Rank: Inside Psychoanalysis*, trans. Gregory C. Richter. Baltimore, MD: Johns Hopkins University Press, 2012.

Linstrum, Erik. *Ruling Minds: Psychology and the British Empire*. Cambridge, MA: Harvard University Press, 2016.

Lippmann, Walter. *Public Opinion*. New York: Macmillan, [1922] 1956.

Lipschutz, Ronnie D., ed. *On Security*. New York: Columbia University Press, 1995.

Little, Margaret. *Psychotic Anxieties and Containment: A Personal Record of an Analysis with Winnicott*. London: Jason Aronson, 1977.

Long, Wahbie. "Alienation: A New Orienting Principle for Psychotherapists in South Africa." *Psychoanalytic Psychotherapy in South Africa* 25, no. 1 (2017): 67–90.

Long-Innes, Chesca. "Wulf Sachs' *Black Hamlet*: Constructing the 'Native Mind.'" *Issues in English Studies in Southern Africa* 5, no. 2 (2000): 78–85.

Lonsdale, John. "Mau Maus of the Mind: Making Mau Mau and Remaking Kenya." *Journal of African History* 31, no. 3 (1990): 393–421.

Love, Heather. *Feeling Backward: Loss and the Politics of Queer History*. Boston, MA: Harvard University Press, 2007.

Luepnitz, Deborah Anna. "The Name of the Piggle: Reconsidering Winnicott's Classic Case in Light of Some Conversations with the Adult 'Gabrielle.'" *International Journal of Psychoanalysis* 98 (2017): 313–70.

Macey, David. *Frantz Fanon: A Biography*. New York: Verso, 2012.

Mahone, Sloan. "East African Psychiatry and the Practical Problems of Empire." In *Psychiatry and Empire*, ed. Sloan Mahone and Megan Vaughan, 41–67. London: Palgrave Macmillan, 2007.

Mahoney, Patrick J. "'A Child Is Being Beaten': A Clinical, Historical, and Textual Study." In *On Freud's "A Child Is Being Beaten,"* ed. Ethel Spector Person, 47–66. New Haven, CT: Yale University Press, 1997.

Main, Thomas. "The Cassel Hospital for Functional Nervous Disorders" (1968). Wellcome Archives, MS.7913/41.

——. "The Concept of the Therapeutic Community: Variations and Vicissitudes." In *The Ailment and Other Psychoanalytic Essays*, ed. Jennifer Johns, 123–44. London: Free Association, [1981] 1989.

——. "The Hospital as a Therapeutic Institution." In *The Ailment and Other Psychoanalytic Essays*, ed. Jennifer Johns, 7–11. London: Free Association, [1946] 1989.

——. "In-Patient Psychotherapy of Neurosis." In *The Ailment and Other Psychoanalytic Essays*, ed. Jennifer Johns, 36–50. London: Free Association, [1958] 1989.

——. "Mothers with Children on a Psychiatric Unit." In *The Ailment and Other Psychoanalytic Essays*, ed. Jennifer Johns, 51–65. London: Free Association, [1961] 1989.

——. "Psychiatrists, Psychotherapies, and Psychoanalytic Training," in *The Ailment and Other Psychoanalytic Essays*, ed. Jennifer Johns, 179–94. London: Free Association, [1968] 1989.

——. "Reports for the Five Years 1st April 1953 to 31st March 1958" (1958), Wellcome Archives, WLM28.BE5C34.

——. "A Theory of Marriage and Its Technical Applications." In *The Ailment and Other Psychoanalytic Essays*, ed. Jennifer Johns, 77–99. London: Free Association, [1966] 1989.

Makari, George. *Revolution in Mind: The Creation of Psychoanalysis*. New York: Harper, 2008.

Malcolm, Janet. *Psychoanalysis: The Impossible Profession*. New York: Vintage, 1982.

Marks, Sarah, and Mat Savelli, eds. *Psychiatry in Communist Europe*. London: Palgrave Macmillan, 2015.

Marriott, David. "The Clinic as Praxis." In *Whither Fanon*. Stanford, CA: Stanford University Press, 2018.

——. *Haunted Life: Visual Culture and Black Modernity*. New York: Rutgers University Press, 2007.

——. *Lacan Noir: Lacan and Afro-Pessimism*. London: Palgrave Macmillan, 2021.

May, Elaine Tyler. *Homeward Bound: American Families in the Cold War Era*. London: Taylor & Francis, 1988.

Mayhew, Henry. "London Labour and the London Poor." *Morning Chronicle*, 1840.

Mbembe, Achille. "Frantz Fanon's Oeuvres: A Metaphoric Thought." *Journal of Contemporary African Art* 32 (2013): 8–17.

McAfee, Noëlle. *Fear of a Breakdown: Psychoanalysis and Politics*. New York: Columbia University Press, 2019.

McClintock, Anne. *Imperial Leather: Race, Gender and Sexuality in the Colonial Contest*. New York: Routledge, 1995.

McCulloch, Jock. *Black Soul, White Artifact: Fanon's Clinical Psychology and Social Theory*. Cambridge: Cambridge University Press, 1983.

——. *Colonial Psychiatry and the African Mind*. Cambridge: Cambridge University Press, 1995.

McIvor, David. "The Cunning of Recognition: Melanie Klein and Contemporary Critical Theory." *Contemporary Critical Theory* 15, no. 3 (2016): 243–63.

——. "In Transition, But to Where? Winnicott, Integration, and Democratic Associations." In *D. W. Winnicott and Political Theory*, ed. Amy Buzby and Matthew Bowker, 205–27. London: Palgrave Macmillan, 2017.

Mead, Margaret. "Some Theoretical Considerations of the Problem of Mother-Child Separation." In *Personal Character and Cultural Milieu: A Collection of Readings*, ed. Douglas Gilbert Haring. Syracuse, NY: Syracuse University Press, 1954.

Meltzer, Donald. *The Kleinian Development*. London: Karnac, 1978.

Mendes, Gabriel N. *Under the Strain of Color: Harlem's Lafargue Clinic and the Promise of an Antiracist Psychiatry*. Ithaca, NY: Cornell University Press, 2015.

Menninger Foundation, *The Bulletin of the Menninger Clinic* 10, no. 3 (1946).

Merson, Molly. "The Whiteness Taboo: Interrogating Whiteness in Psychoanalysis." *Psychoanalytic Dialogues* 31, no. 1 (2021): 13–27.

Midgley, Nick. "The Matchbox School: Anna Freud and the Idea of a Psychoanalytically Informed Education." *Journal of Child Psychotherapy* 34, no. 1 (2018).

——. *Reading Anna Freud*. London: Routledge, 2013.

Millard, D. W. "Maxwell Jones and the Therapeutic Community." In *150 Years of British Psychiatry, Volume 2: The Aftermath*, ed. H. Freeman and G. E. Berrios, 81–604. London: Athlone, 1996.

Miller, Peter, and Nikolas Rose. "The Tavistock Programme: The Government of Subjectivity and Social Life." *Sociology* 22, no. 2 (1988): 171–92.

Mills, Charles W. *The Racial Contract*. Ithaca, NY: Cornell University Press, 1997.

Mills, Jon A., and Tom Harrison. "John Rickman, Wilfred Ruprecht Bion, and the Origins of the Therapeutic Community." *History of Psychology* 10, no. 1 (2007): 22–43.

Mitchell, Juliet. "Attachment and Maternal Deprivation: How Did John Bowlby Miss the Siblings?" In *Siblings: Sex and Violence*. Cambridge: Polity, 2003.

——. "Introduction." In *The Selected Melanie Klein*, ed. Juliet Mitchell, 9–34. New York: Free Press, 1986.

——. *Psychoanalysis and Feminism: A Radical Reassessment of Freudian Psychoanalysis*. New York: Basic Books, [1974] 2000.

Molnar, Michael, ed. *The Diary of Sigmund Freud, 1929–1939: A Record of the Final Decade*. London: Hogarth, 1992.

Mooney, Carol Garhart. *Theories of Attachment: An Introduction to Bowlby, Ainsworth, Gerber, Brazelton, Kennell, and Klaus*. St. Paul, MN: Redleaf, 2010.

Morgan, Helen. *The Work of Whiteness: A Psychoanalytic Perspective*. London: Routledge, 2021.

Moss, Donald. "On Having Whiteness." *Journal of the American Psychoanalytic Association* 69, no. 2 (2021): 355–71.

Muir, Brian. "Is In-Patient Psychotherapy a Valid Concept?" In *The Family as In-Patient: Working with Families and Adolescents at the Cassel Hospital*, ed. Roger Kennedy, Ann Heymans, and Lydia Tischler, 64–77. London: Free Association, 1987.

Mukherjee, Ankhi. *Unseen City: The Psychic Lives of the Urban Poor*. Cambridge: Cambridge University Press, 2022.

Müller, Knuth. "Psychoanalysis and American Intelligence Since 1940: Unexpected Liaisons." In *Psychoanalysis and the Age of Totalitarianism*, ed. Matt ffytche and Daniel Pick. London: Routledge, 2016.

Muñoz, José. "The Vulnerability Artist: Nao Bustamante and the Sad Beauty of Reparation." *Women & Performance: A Journal of Feminist Theory* 16 (2006): 191–200.

Nandy, Ashis. "The Savage Freud: The First Non-Western Psychoanalyst in Colonial India." In *The Savage Freud and Other Essays on Possible and Retrievable Selves*, 81–144. Princeton, NJ: Princeton University Press, 1995.

Nelson, Maggie. *The Argonauts*. Minneapolis, MN: Greywolf, 2015.

Noble, Denise. "Decolonizing Britain and Domesticating Women: Race, Gender, and Women's Work in Post-1945 British Decolonial and Metropolitan Liberal Reform Discourses." *Meridians: Feminism, Race, Transnationalism* 13, no. 1 (2015): 53–77.

Oakley, Ann. *Subject Women: Where Women Stand Today—Politically, Economically, Socially, Emotionally*. New York: Pantheon, 1981.

O'Connor, Noreen, and Joanna Ryan. *Wild Desires and Mistaken Identities: Lesbianism and Psychoanalysis*. New York: Columbia University Press, 1993.

Ogata, Amy F. *Designing the Creative Child: Playthings and Places in Midcentury America*. Minneapolis: University of Minnesota Press, 2013.

O'Loughlin, Michael. "Whiteness and the Psychoanalytic Imagination." *Contemporary Psychoanalysis* 56, no. 4 (2020): 1–22.

Olsen, A. O. "Depression and Reparation as Themes in Melanie Klein's Analysis of the Painter Ruth Weber." *Scandinavian Psychoanalytic Review* 27, no. 1 (2004).

Orloff, Ann. "Gender in the Welfare State." *Annual Review in Sociology* 22 (1996): 51–78.

Owolade, Tomiwa. "The Narcissism of Anti-Racist Therapy." *New Statesman*, January 25, 2023. https://www.newstatesman.com/comment/2023/01/narcissism -anti-racist-therapy-helen-morgan-book.

Pandolfo, Stefania. *Knot of the Soul: Madness, Psychoanalysis, Islam*. Chicago: University of Chicago Press, 2018.

Pateman, Carole. *The Sexual Contract*. Stanford, CA: Stanford University Press, 1988.

Patterson, Orlando. *Slavery and Social Death: A Comparative Study*. Cambridge, MA: Harvard University Press, 1982.

Perry, Kennetta Hammond. "Black Britain and the Politics of Race in the 20th Century." *History Compass* 12, no. 8 (2014): 651–63.

——. "'U.S. Negroes, Your Fight Is Our Fight': Black Britons and the 1963 March on Washington." In *The Other Special Relationship: Race, Rights, and Riots in Britain and the United States*, ed. Robin D. G. Kelley and Stephen Tuck, 7–24. London: Palgrave Macmillan, 2015.

Phillips, Adam. "Keeping It Moving: Commentary on Judith Butler's 'Melancholy Gender/Refused Identification.'" In Judith Butler, *The Psychic Life of Power: Theories in Subjection*, 151–66. Stanford, CA: Stanford University Press, 1997.

——. *Promises, Promises: Essays on Psychoanalysis and Literature*. New York: Basic Books, 2001.

——. *Winnicott*. Cambridge, MA: Harvard University Press, 1988.

Phillips, Adam, and Devorah Baum. "Politics in the Consulting Room." *Granta*, February 14, 2019. https://granta.com/politics-in-the-consulting-room/.

Phillips, John, and Lyndsey Stonebridge, eds. *Reading Melanie Klein*. London: Routledge, 1998.

Pick, Daniel. *Brainwashed: A New History of Thought Control*. London: Wellcome Collection, 2022.

——. *The Pursuit of the Nazi Mind: Hitler, Hess, and the Analysts*. Oxford: Oxford University Press, 2014.

Pines, Malcolm. "Main, Thomas Forrest (1911–1990)." *Oxford Dictionary of National Biography*. Oxford: Oxford University Press, 2004.

Plotkin, Mariano Ben. *Freud in the Pampas: The Formation of a Psychoanalytic Culture in Argentina, 1910–1983*. Stanford, CA: Stanford University Press, 2001.

——. "Psychoanalysis, Race, and National Identity: The Reception of Psychoanalysis in Brazil, 1910–1940." In *Unconscious Dominions: Psychoanalysis, Colonial Trauma, and Global Sovereignties*, ed. Warwick Anderson, Deborah Jenson, and Richard C. Keller, 113–40. Durham, NC: Duke University Press, 2011.

Pontalis, J. B. "The Question Child." In *Reading Melanie Klein*, ed. John Phillips and Lyndsey Stonebridge, 79–89. London: Routledge, 1998.

Portuges, Stephen H. "The Politics of Psychoanalytic Neutrality." *International Journal of Applied Psychoanalytic Studies* 6 (2009): 61–73.

——. "Psychoanalytic Neutrality, Race, and Racism." *Journal of the American Psychoanalytic Association* 70, no. 2 (2022): 323–34.

Prince, Raymond, Sunny T. C. Ilechukwu, and Jock McCulloch. "Responses to Raymond Prince's 'John Colin D. Carothers (1903–1989) and African Colonial Psychiatry' [TPRR, 33(2): 226–240]." *Transcultural Psychiatry* 34, no. 3 (1997): 407–15.

Rada, Michelle, ed. "Psychoanalysis and Solidarity." Special issue, *differences* 33, nos. 2–3 (2022).

Rapoport, David. *Community as Doctor: New Perspectives on a Therapeutic Community*. London: Tavistock, 1960.

Rawlinson, Kevin, Nadeem Badshaw, and Matthew Weaver. "Windrush Scandal: Timeline of Key Events." *The Guardian*, March 31, 2022. https://www.theguardian.com/uk-news/2018/apr/16/windrush-era-citizens-row-timeline-of-key-events.

Rayner, Eric. "Introduction." In *The Ailment and Other Psychoanalytic Essays*, ed. Jennifer Johns, xiii–xxix. London: Free Association, 1989.

Reeves, Christopher. "Reappraising Winnicott's *The Piggle*: A Critical Commentary, Part I." *British Journal of Psychotherapy* 31, no. 2 (2015): 156–90.

Reich, Wilhelm. *The Mass Psychology of Fascism*. New York: Noonday, [1933] 1970.

Renik, Owen. "The Ideal of the Anonymous Analyst and the Problem of Self-Disclosure." *Psychoanalytic Quarterly* 64 (1995): 466–95.

——. "The Perils of Neutrality." *Psychoanalytic Quarterly* 65 (1996): 495–517.

Repo, Jemima. *The Biopolitics of Gender*. Oxford: Oxford University Press, 2015.

Reynolds, Wayne M. "Whatever Happened to the Fourth British Empire? The Cold War, Empire Defence v. the USA, 1943–57." In *Cold War Britain, 1945–1964: New Perspectives*, ed. Michael Francis Hopkins, Michael Kandiah, and Gillian Staerck. New York: Palgrave Macmillan, 2003.

Rickman, J. "Wulf Sachs, 1893–1949." *International Journal of Psychoanalysis* 31 (1950): 288–89.

Riley, Denise. *The War in the Nursery: Theories of the Child and Mother*. London: Virago, 1983.

Ringold, Evelyn. "Bringing Up Baby in Britain." *New York Times*, June 13, 1965.

Robcis, Camille. *Disalienation: Politics, Philosophy, and Radical Psychiatry in Postwar France*. Chicago: Chicago University Press, 2021.

——. "Institutional Psychotherapy in France: An Interview with Camille Robcis." *Hidden Persuaders Blog*, September 28, 2017. http://www7.bbk.ac.uk/hidden persuaders/blog/robcis-interview/.

——. "Jean Oury and Clinique de La Borde: A Conversation with Camille Robcis." *Somatosphere*, June 3, 2014. http://somatosphere.net/2014/jean-oury-and-clinique -de-la-borde-a-conversation-with-camille-robcis.html/.

Rodman, Robert F. *Winnicott: His Life and Work*. Cambridge, MA: De Capo, 2003.

Roper, Michael. "From the Shell-Shocked Soldier to the Nervous Child: Psychoanalysis in the Aftermath of the First World War." *Psychoanalysis and History* 18, no. 1 (2016): 39–69.

Rose, Jacqueline. "Black Hamlet." In *States of Fantasy*, 38–55. Oxford: Oxford University Press, 1996.

——. *Why War? Psychoanalysis, Politics, and the Return to Melanie Klein*. Oxford: Blackwell University Press, 1993.

Rose, Nikolas. *Governing the Soul: The Shaping of the Private Self*. London: Free Association, 1989.

——. *Inventing Ourselves: Psychology, Power, and Personhood*. Cambridge: Cambridge University Press, 1998.

——. *The Psychological Complex: Psychology, Politics and Society in England, 1869–1939*. New York: Routledge, 1985.

Rubin, Aline, Belinda Mandelbaum, and Stephen Frosh. "No Memory, No Desire: Psychoanalysis in Brazil During Repressive Times." *Psychoanalysis and History* 18, no. 1 (2016): 93–118.

Rubio-Marìn, Ruth. *The Gender of Reparations: Unsettling Sexual Hierarchies While Redressing Human Rights Violations*. Cambridge: Cambridge University Press, 2009.

Sachs, Wulf. *Black Hamlet*. Boston: Little, Brown, 1947.

——. "The Insane Native: An Introduction to a Psychological Study." *South African Journal of Science* 30 (1933): 706–13.

Sachs, Wulf, with a new introduction by Saul Dubow and Jacqueline Rose. *Black Hamlet*. Baltimore, MD: John Hopkins University Press, 1996.

Sadowsky, Jonathan. *Imperial Bedlam: Institutions of Madness in Colonial Southwest Nigeria*. Los Angeles: University of California Press, 1999.

Salter, Sir Arthur. "The Dead Hand: Reparation and War Debt." In *Recovery: The Second Effort*, 141–95. New York: Century, 1932.

Sánchez-Pardo, Esther. *Cultures of the Death Drive: Melanie Klein and Modernist Melancholia*. Durham, NC: Duke University Press, 2003.

Sandler, Joseph, Hansi Kennedy, and Robert L. Tyson. *Techniques of Child Analysis: Discussions with Anna Freud*. Cambridge, MA: Harvard University Press, 1986.

Sayers, Janet. *Mothering Psychoanalysis: Helene Deutsch, Karen Horney, Anna Freud, and Melanie Klein*. New York: Norton, 1991.

Scherlis, Lily. "Boundary Issues: How Boundaries Became the Rules for Mental Health—and Explain Everything." *Parapraxis Magazine*. https://www.parapraxis magazine.com/articles/boundary-issues.

Sears, William, and Martha Sears. *The Baby Book: Everything You Need to Know About Your Baby from Birth to Age Two*. New York: Little, Brown, 1993.

Sedgwick, Eve Kosofsky. "Paranoid Reading and Reparative Reading, or, You're So Paranoid, You Probably Think This Essay Is About You." In *Touching Feeling: Affect, Pedagogy, Performativity*, 123–53. Durham, NC: Duke University Press, 2003.

Segal, Hanna. *Introduction to the Work of Melanie Klein*. London: Karnac, 1988.

Segal, Hanna, and Donald Meltzer. "Narrative of a Child Analysis." *International Journal of Psychoanalysis* 44 (1963): 507–13.

Segal, Julia. *Melanie Klein*. London: SAGE, 1992.

Seshadri-Crooks, Kalpana. *Desiring Whiteness: A Lacanian Analysis of Race*. New York: Routledge, 2000.

Shapira, Michal. *The War Inside: Psychoanalysis, Total War, and the Making of the Democratic Self in Postwar Britain*. Cambridge: Cambridge University Press, 2013.

Sheehi, Lara, and Stephen Sheehi. *Psychoanalysis Under Occupation: Practicing Resistance in Palestine*. London: Routledge, 2022.

Shephard, Ben. "A Tale of Two Hospitals." In *A War of Nerves: Soldiers and Psychiatrists in the Twentieth Century*, 257–78. Cambridge, MA: Harvard University Press, 2003.

Shuttleworth, Sally. *The Mind of the Child: Child Development in Literature, Science, and Medicine, 1840–1900*. Oxford: Oxford University Press, 2010.

Sitze, Adam. "Treating Life Literally." *Law Critique* 18 (2007): 55–89.

Smyth, Jim. *Cold War Culture: Intellectuals, the Media, and the Practice of History*. London: I. B. Tauris, 2016.

Snediker, Michael. *Queer Optimism: Lyric Personhood and Other Felicitous Persuasions*. Minneapolis: University of Minnesota Press, 2008.

Solms, Mark. "The Establishment of an Accredited Training Institute in South Africa." *Psycho-Analytic Psychotherapy in South Africa* 18, no. 1 (2010).

Sommerville, C. John. *The Rise and Fall of Childhood*. New York: Vintage, 1990.

Soto-Crespo, Ramón. "Heterosexuality Terminable or Interminable? Kleinian Fantasies of Reparation and Mourning." In *Homosexuality and Psychoanalysis*, ed. Tim Dean and Christopher Lane, 190–209. Chicago: University of Chicago Press, 2001.

Spillers, Hortense. "'All the Things You Could Be by Now If Sigmund Freud's Wife Was Your Mother': Psychoanalysis and Race." *Critical Inquiry* 22 (1996): 710–34.

——. "Mama's Baby, Papa's Maybe: An American Grammar Book." *Diacritics* 17, no. 2 (1987): 65–81.

Spillius, Elizabeth Bott, ed. *Melanie Klein Today: Developments in Theory and Practice*, vols. 1 and 2. London: Routledge, 1988.

Spock, Benjamin. *The Common Sense Book of Baby and Childcare*. New York: Duell, Sloan and Pearce, 1946.

Stacey, Jackie. "Wishing Away Ambivalence." *Feminist Theory* 15, no. 1 (2014): 39–49.

Steedman, Carolyn. *Strange Dislocations: Childhood and the Idea of Human Interiority, 1780–1930*. London: Virago, 1995.

Sterns, Peter. *Childhood in World History*. New York: Routledge, 2006.

Stewart-Steinberg, Suzanne. *Impious Fidelity: Anna Freud, Psychoanalysis, and Politics*. Ithaca, NY: Cornell University Press, 2011.

Stoler, Ann Laura. *Carnal Knowledge and Imperial Power: Race and the Intimate in Colonial Rule*. Los Angeles: University of California Press, 2002.

Stonebridge, Lyndsey. *The Destructive Element: British Psychoanalysis and Modernism*. New York: Routledge, 1998.

——. "'Inner Emigration': On the Run with Hannah Arendt and Anna Freud." In *Psychoanalysis in the Age of Totalitarianism*, ed. Matt ffytche and Daniel Pick. London: Routledge, 2016.

Stovall, Natasha. "Whiteness on the Couch." *Longreads*, August 12, 2019. https://longreads.com/2019/08/12/whiteness-on-the-couch/.

Stuart, Douglas T. *Creating the National Security State: A History of the Law that Transformed America*. Princeton, NJ: Princeton University Press, 2008.

Sue, D. W., and D. Sue. "Barriers to Effective Cross-Cultural Counselling." *Journal of Counselling Psychology* 24, no. 5 (1977): 420–29.

Swanson, Maynard W. "The Sanitation Syndrome: Bubonic Plague and Urban Native Policy in the Cape Colony, 1900–1909." *Journal of African History* 18, no. 3 (1977): 387–410.

Tate, Claudia. *Psychoanalysis and Black Novels: Desire and the Protocols of Race*. Oxford: Oxford University Press, 1998.

Taylor, Frederick Kräupl. "A History of Group and Administrative Therapy in Great Britain." *British Journal of Medical Psychology* 31, nos. 3–4 (1958): 153–73.

Teurnell, Lena. "An Alternative Reading in Winnicott: The Piggle—A Sexually Abused Girl?" *International Forum of Psychoanalysis* 2, no. 3 (1993): 139–44.

Thalassis, Nafsika. "Soldiers in Psychiatric Therapy: The Case of Northfield Military Hospital 1942–1946." *Social History of Medicine* 20, no. 2 (2007): 351–68.

Trusscott, Ross, and Derek Hook. "The Vicissitudes of Anger: Psychoanalysis in the Time of Apartheid." In *Psychoanalysis and the Age of Totalitarianism*, ed. Matt ffytche and Daniel Pick, 193–204. London: Routledge, 2016.

Tubert-Oklander, Juan. *The One and the Many: Relational Psychoanalysis and Group Analysis*. Abingdon: Routledge, 2014.

Tubert-Oklander, Juan, and Reyna Hernández-Tubert. *Operative Groups: The Latin-American Approach to Group Analysis*. London: Jessica Kingsley, 2003.

Turkle, Sherry. *Psychoanalytic Politics: Freud's French Revolution*. New York: Basic Books, 1978.

Turner, Lou, and Hannah Neville. *Frantz Fanon's Psychotherapeutic Approaches to Clinical Work: Practicing Internationally with Marginalized Communities*. London: Routledge, 2020.

Twemlow, Stuart. "The Broadening Vision: A Case for Community-Based Psychoanalysis in the Context of Usual Practice." *Journal of the American Psychoanalytic Association* 61, no. 4 (2013): 663–90.

van der Horst, Frank C. P. *John Bowlby—From Psychoanalysis to Ethology: Unraveling the Roots of Attachment Theory*. Sussex: Wiley-Blackwell, 2011.

Van Dijken, Suzan. *John Bowlby: His Early Life: A Biographical Journey into the Roots of Attachment Theory*. London: Free Association, 1998.

Vaughan, Megan. "The Madman and the Medicine Man: Colonial Psychiatry and the Theory of Deculturation." In *Curing Their Ills: Colonial Power and African Illness*, 100–128. Cambridge: Cambridge University Press, 1991.

Vergès, Françoise. "To Cure and to Free: The Fanonian Project of 'Decolonized Psychiatry.'" In *Fanon: A Critical Reader*, ed. Lewis R. Gordon, T. Denean Sharpley-Whiting, and Renée T. White, 85–99. Oxford: Blackwell, 1996.

Viçedo, Marga. *The Nature and Nurture of Love: From Imprinting to Attachment in Cold War America*. Chicago: University of Chicago Press, 2013.

Viego, Antonio. "The Clinical, the Speculative, and What Must be Made Up in the Space Between Them." In *Dead Subjects: Toward a Politics of Loss in Latino Studies*. Durham, NC: Duke University Press, 2007.

Wall, Oisín. "Anti-Psychiatry: David Cooper and the Villa 21 Experiment." *Contemporary Psychotherapy* 7, no. 1 (2015).

——. "The Birth and Death of Villa 21." *History of Psychiatry* 24, no. 3 (2013): 326–40.

——. *The British Anti-Psychiatrists: From Institutional Psychiatry to the Counter-Culture, 1960–1971*. London: Routledge, 2017.

Walton, Jean. *Fair Sex, Savage Dreams: Race, Psychoanalysis, Sexual Difference*. Durham, NC: Duke University Press, 2001.

——. "Re-Placing Race in (White) Psychoanalytic Discourse: Founding Narratives of Feminism." *Critical Inquiry* 21, no. 4 (1995): 775–804.

Ward, Ivan. "Social Clinics and Analytic Boundaries," *Psychoanalysis and History* 24, no. 3 (2022): 369–73.

Webb, Alban. *London Calling: Britain, the BBC World Service, and the Cold War*. London: Bloomsbury, 2014.

Weber, Max. "Politics as a Vocation." In *Max Weber: Essays in Sociology*, ed. and trans. H. H. Gerth and C. Wright Mills, 77–128. New York: Oxford University Press, [1919] 1946.

Webster, Wendy. *Englishness and Empire, 1939–1965*. Oxford: Oxford University Press, 2005.

——. *Imagining Home: Gender, "Race," and National Identity, 1945–64*. New York: Routledge, 1998.

West, Elliot. *Growing Up in Twentieth-Century America: A History and Reference Guide*. Westport, CT: Greenwood, 1996.

Wiegman, Robyn. "The Times We're In." *Feminist Theory* 15, no. 1 (2014): 4–25.

Wild, Rosie. "'Black Was the Colour of Our Fight': The Transnational Roots of British Black Power." In *The Other Special Relationship: Race, Rights, and Riots in Britain and the United States*, ed. Robin C. G. Kelley and Stephen Tuck, 25–46. London: Palgrave Macmillan, 2015.

Williams, Charlie. "Public Psychology and the Cold War Brainwashing Scare." *History and Philosophy of Psychology* 21, no. 1 (2020): 21–30.

Wilson, Elizabeth. *Only Halfway to Paradise: Women in Postwar Britain, 1945–1968*. New York: Routledge, 1990.

Wilson, Elizabeth A. *Gut Feminism*. Durham, NC: Duke University Press, 2015.

Winnicott, D. W. *Babies and Their Mothers*, ed. Clare Winnicott, Ray Shepherd, and Madeleine Davis. Reading, MA: Addison-Wesley, 1987.

——. *The Child, the Family, and the Outside World*. London: Penguin, 2021.

——. *The Collected Works of D. W. Winnicott: Volume 5, 1955–1959*, ed. Lesley Caldwell and Helen Taylor Robinson. New York: Oxford, 2016.

——. "The Discussion of War Aims." In *Home Is Where We Start From: Essays by a Psychoanalyst*. London: Norton, [1986] 1990.

——. *The Family and Individual Development*. London: Routledge, [1965] 2006.

——. "Hallucination and Dehallucination." In *The Collected Works of D. W. Winnicott: Volume 5, 1955–1959*, ed. Lesley Caldwell and Helen Taylor Robinson. New York: Oxford, [1957] 2016.

——. *Home Is Where We Start From: Essays by a Psychoanalyst*. London: Norton, [1986] 1990.

——. "Morals and Education." In *The Maturational Processes and the Facilitating Environment*. London: Karnac, [1962] 1990.

——. "The Mother-Infant Experience of Mutuality." In *The Collected Works of D. W. Winnicott: Volume 9, 1969–1971*, ed. Lesley Caldwell and Helen Taylor Robinson. New York: Oxford, [1969] 2016.

——. *The Piggle: An Account of the Psychoanalytic Treatment of a Little Girl*, ed. Ishak Ramzy. London: Penguin, [1971] 1977.

——. "The Pill and the Moon." In *The Collected Works of D. W. Winnicott: Volume 9, 1969–1971*, ed. Lesley Caldwell and Helen Taylor Robinson. New York: Oxford, [1969] 2016.

——. *Playing and Reality*. London: Routledge, [1971] 1991.

——. "The Price of Disregarding Psychoanalytic Research." In *The Collected Works of D. W. Winnicott: Volume 5, 1955–1959*, ed. Lesley Caldwell and Helen Taylor Robinson. New York: Oxford, [1965] 2016.

——. *The Spontaneous Gesture: Selected Letters of D. W. Winnicott*, ed. F. Robert Rodman. Cambridge, MA: Harvard University Press, 1987.

——. *Through Pediatrics to Psychoanalysis: Collected Papers*. New York: Brunner/Mazel, [1958] 1992.

——. "The Use of an Object." In *Playing and Reality*. London: Routledge, [1971] 1991.

——. "Use of Two, Use of Black." In *The Collected Works of D. W. Winnicott: Volume 5, 1955–1959*, ed. Lesley Caldwell and Helen Taylor Robinson. New York: Oxford, [1965] 2016.

Winograd, Basia, dir. *Black Psychoanalysts Speak*, 2014.

Winter, Sarah. *Freud and the Institution of Psychoanalytic Knowledge*. Stanford, CA: Stanford University Press, 1999.

Wolpe, Harold. "Capitalism and Cheap Labor-Power in South Africa: From Segregation to Apartheid." *Economy and Society* 1, no. 4 (1972): 425–56.

Woods, Alexandra. "The Work Before Us: Whiteness and the Psychoanalytic Institute." *Psychoanalysis, Culture & Society* 25, no. 1 (2020): 230–49.

Yates, Sybille. "Review: Black Hamlet." *International Journal of Psychoanalysis* 19, no. 2 (1938): 251–52.

Young-Bruehl, Elisabeth. *Anna Freud: A Biography*. New Haven, CT: Yale University Press, 2008.

Zaretsky, Eli. "Melanie Klein and the Emergence of Modern Personal Life." In *Reading Melanie Klein*, ed. John Phillips and Lyndsey Stonebridge, 32–50. London: Routledge, 1998.

——. *Political Freud: A History*. New York: Columbia University Press, 2015.

——. *Secrets of the Soul: A Social and Cultural History of Psychoanalysis*. New York: Knopf, 2004.

Zeavin, Hannah. "Unfree Associations: Parasitic Whiteness On and Off the Couch." *n+1 Magazine* 42 (2022). https://www.nplusonemag.com/issue-42/essays/unfree -associations/.

Zelizer, Viviana. *Pricing the Priceless Child: The Changing Social Value of Children*. Princeton, NJ: Princeton University Press, 1985.

Index

antisemitism, 8, 53, 122; toward S. Freud, 153; genocide as result of, 82, 84–85; global fascism and, 109; in Great Britain, 153–54
anxious-avoidant attachment, 220
anxious-resistant attachment, 220
APA. *See* American Psychological Association
Appignanesi, Lisa, 11
Arendt, Hannah, 207
Argentina: clinical practices in, 9–10; Dirty War in, 9, 81, 121; Langer in, 5, 9; opposition to dictatorship in, 5; reparations in, 81
Argentinian Psychoanalytic Association, 9–10, 121
Ariès, Philippe, 257n52
Aron, Lewis, 18–19
art therapy, in Richard case study, 73, 73–74
Attachment (Bowlby), 210, 220
attachment theory, 17, 201–31; anxious-avoidant attachment, 220; anxious-resistant attachment, 220; in child psychoanalysis, 42; infantile attachment, 212; insecure attachments, 204–5, 208; natural, 220–21; parenting and, 205; secure attachments, 213–14; security feminism and, 27; Viçedo on, 210
Attlee, Clement, 280n35
Australia, clinical practices in, 9–10
Austria: clinical practices in, 9–10; Constitution of, 259n60; political transitions within, 53; transition to democratic systems in, 53–54. *See also* Red Vienna; Vienna, Austria
Austro-Hungarian Empire, 32, 53; industrialization in, 50
authenticity, 77, 84, 133, 137, 197
authentic sympathy, 83

authoritarianism, 18, 21, 38, 168, 178, 180, 259n58, 259n63; anti-Oedipal, 187; authority compared to, 52; global expansion of, 229; National Socialism, 54; Stalinism, 54
authority: authoritarianism compared to, 52; in child psychoanalysis, 38–56; in child psychoanalytic clinics, 38–48, 52–53; psychosocial function of, 47
autotheories, 134

"bad Hitler-penis," 68, 72–82
Badinter, Élisabeth, 210
Bailkin, Jordanna, 141–42
Balint, Michael, 172, 206
Bar-Haim, Shaul, 208
Barnes, Mary, 289n37
"Beating Fantasies and Daydreams" (A. Freud), 33
Bechdel, Alison, 134
Bell, David, 1, 170
Benjamin, Jessica, 14, 134
Bergmann, Thesi, 189
Berlant, Lauren, 14, 198
Bernfeld, Siegfried, 4, 32, 35–36
Bersani, Leo, 14, 79, 196, 244
Bertoldi, Andreas, 97, 112
Beshara, Robert K., 16
Bettelheim, Bruno, 36
Beveridge, William, 138
Bhabha, Homi, 16, 88
Bion, Wilfred, 168, 174, 182–84, 206, 208, 290n49, 290n51, 291n53
bisexuality. *See* unconscious bisexuality
Black Africans: double life of, 107–8; madness among, 6, 106, 246n6. *See also* African psychology
Black Afro-Caribbeans: fear of Black men, 152; integration failures in, 143–45; Moyne Report, 144–45; *My Mother Who Fathered Me* study,

144–45; Windrush generation, 141, 143, 149, 218

Black Anger (Sachs), 96–97, 109–10

Black Hamlet (Sachs), 96–97, 100–101, 103, 107–12, 118

"Black Mummy," in "Piggle" case study, 26, 128–29, 145–64

Blackness, 284n62; as corrupting presence, 151; Irishness and, 153; in "Piggle" case study, 128, 146–48; political activity connected to, 221; in UK, 146–48

Black Psychoanalysts Speak (Winograd), 21–22, 154

Black Skin, White Masks (Fanon), 127, 245n5

Black women: appropriation of body by white women, 88; maternal care by, 157–58; pathologization of Black immigrant motherhood, 218; symbolic murder of, 125–26

Blida-Joinville Psychiatric Hospital, Algeria, 6, 113, 178

Bloomsbury Group, 80

Bolsonaro, Jair, 21

Bose, Girindrasekhar, 113

boundaries: for S. Freud, 238–39; for Lacan, 238–39; in therapy speak, 237–38; weaponization of, 238

boundary-crossing, 17–18

Bowker, Matthew, 250n26

Bowlby, John, 3, 135, 189, 200, 294n8; *Attachment*, 210, 220; attachment theory, 17, 27, 203–13, 220–21; on domestic security, 213–28; early clinical career, 205; ethology and, 204–13, 295n15; feminist censure of, 209–11; instinct theories, 295n15; *Loss*, 210, 220; *Maternal Care and Mental Health*, 201–2, 204, 222; *Personal Aggressiveness and War*, 215; on psychological normality,

226–27; redefinition of women for, 208–9; *A Secure Base*, 205; *Separation*, 210, 220; Winnicott and, 201; World Health Organization and, 70

BPS. *See* British Psychoanalytical Society

Brazil, clinical practices in, 9–10; psychoanalysis in, 113, 234

Brennan, Teresa, 14, 173

Breuer, Joseph, 254n4

Brickman, Celia, 16, 122

Bridger, Harold, 183–84

British Anti-Psychiatrists, The (Wall), 180

British Nationality Act of 1848, 280n35

British Psychoanalytic Council, 232

British Psychoanalytical Society (BPS), 1, 2, 12, 21, 24, 35, 59, 60, 70, 99, 130, 172, 232. *See also* Main, Thomas

Bronfenbrenner, Urie, 206

Brook, Andrew, 301n15

Brown v. Board of Education, 5

Buhle, Mari Jo, 14

Bulldogs Bank Home, 4, 48, 56, 202

Bunselmeyer, Robert E., 267n71

Burlingham, Dorothy, 36, 189

Burnham, John C., 11

Butler, Judith, 14–16, 196–97

Buzby, Amy, 250n26

Cabernite, Leo, 10

Caldwell, Peter C., 259n60

capitalism, 5, 55; late-stage, 21, 205; Sachs on, 109; state-sponsored repression under, 38

Carothers, J. C., 105–6, 271n28, 272n29, 273n31

Case Studies in Hysteria (J. Breuer and S. Freud), 254n4

Cassel Hospital, in Great Britain, 26–27, 164; clinical work at, 167–77;

Cassel Hospital (*continued*)
  endowment of, 169–70; Freudian
  practices in, 172–73; methodological
  approach to, 168–69; organizational
  structure of, 170–72; psychoanalytic/
  therapeutic community at, 169–77;
  women at, 186–87
Cassel, Edmund, 169–70
Century of the Child, The (Key), 258n56
Chadwick, Edwin, 222–23
Chakrabarty, Dipesh, 16
Chavafambira, John: in *Black Hamlet*,
  96–97, 100–101, 107–12; as case
  study, 25, 91, 95–127, *102*, *115*,
  268n1; clinical case, 114–26;
  dehumanization of, 123–24; early life
  for, 100–101; early work for, 101–2;
  experiences of racism, 116–17,
  122–23; false accusations against,
  102–3; Freudian analysis and, 117;
  Hamletism and, 107–8, 110–11,
  117, 126; interracial relationships
  for, 103; Kleinian analysis and, 117;
  misogyny as element of, 125–26; as
  nganga, 95, 103, 117; nonracialism
  and, 118; Oedipal elements of,
  126; origins of difficulties, 108–9;
  in Rooiyard, South Africa, 95,
  104; self-determination and, 119;
  sociopolitical context, 114–15;
  transference in, 124; "traveling
  analysis" of, 96
Cheng, Anne Anlin, 16
Chettiar, Teri, 190
child psychoanalysis: attachment in,
  42; authority and, 38–56; conceptual
  approach to, 31–33; daydreams
  in, 42; developmental rubrics in,
  39; education and, 46; ego and,
  39–41; as future of psychoanalysis,
  31; id and, 49; instinctual life
  in, 45; Klein's wartime clinical

work, 57–91; mirroring in, 43;
  Object Relations field and, 59–60;
  obsessional neurosis in, 43–44; as
  political project, 38; popularity of,
  35; positive transference in, 40–43;
  reform movement in, 35; social
  authority in, 38–48; social contract
  theory and, 66; as social work, 4;
  superego and, 39–41, 44–46, 256n23
child psychoanalysis, during World
  War II: child's play, 59–69; Klein role
  in, 57–91; Object Relations theory
  and, 66; war games, 59–69
child psychoanalytic clinics, authority
  structures in, 38–48. *See also specific
  clinics*
children: adoption by LGBTQ persons,
  51; in British workforce, 49–50; ego
  for, 39–41, 49; liberation of, 52–53;
  reproductive futurity and, 50–51;
  superego for, 39–41, 44–46, 256n23.
  See also child psychoanalysis; child
  psychoanalysis, during World War
  II; mother-child relationship
child welfare, throughout Europe, 50
Chitty, Christopher, 195–96
Chodorow, Nancy, 14, 64–65, 134, 210
Civilization and Its Discontents (S.
  Freud), 46
civil rights movement, 149–50, 177
Cixous, Hélène, 14
Clarke, Edith, 144–45, 282n47
clinical psychoanalysis. *See*
  psychoanalysis
clinic as holding environment, 130, 159
clinics. *See* child psychoanalytic clinics;
  psychoanalytic clinics
Coates, Ta-Nehisi, 81
Cold War era: clinical psychoanalysis
  during, 177–85; communalism,
  198–200; counterculturalism and,
  179; Global South communism

during, 214; homosexuality and, 195; motherhood during, 213–28; psychoanalysis during, 27–28
collective psychopathology, 114
collectivity, 26, 71, 78, 169, 198–99, 272n29
colonialism: anti-Blackness and, 122; as civilizing mission, 106; "good enough mother" theory and, 129; madness as result of, 6, 106, 246n6; native populations and, 86–87; racialized nature of, 105; Sachs on, 109; in South Africa, 98. *See also* settler-colonialism
colonial psychoanalysis: Black madness, 6, 106, 246n6; British, 25, 91, 95–127; "good enough mother" theory, 129
Commonwealth Immigrants Act, UK (1962), 280n35
communalism, 198–200
complementarity, 133, 192–95
conscious individualism, 51
Cooper, David, 5, 168, 178; Villa 21, 179, 186
Copjec, Joan, 14
counterculturalism, 177, 179
Crake, Paul, 301n15
creativity, 72, 77–79, 87–88, 133
Crewe, Jonathan, 111
critical race theory, 13, 16
cross-racial clinical trials, 123

Dann, Sophia, 56
Danto, Elizabeth, 5, 36–37, 39, 48, 235
Dark Continents (Khanna), 15–16
Davis, Angela, 221
daydreams, in child psychoanalysis, 42. *See also* fantasy
Dean, Tim, 2, 14–15, 196
death drive, 14, 64
death instinct, 63, 65, 72–73, 79, 264n32

Death of the Family, The (Cooper), 178–79
decolonial: activism, 9; clinicians, 235; politics, 7, 114, 126–27; protest, 111, 126; psychoanalysis, 16, 18, 97
decolonization, 177; race and, 143–45; Winnicott on, 145–64. *See also* Chavafambira, John
deculturation thesis, 273n30
defamilialization, 71
dehumanization, of Chavafambira, 123–24
Deleuze, Gilles, 99
democracy, 31–56, 53–54, 134–40; social, 4, 27, 35, 53, 55, 70–71, 136–37, 169, 174, 182, 185–200; liberal, 18, 21, 24, 39, 48, 56, 177, 195, 203, 224
dependence, 39–42, 102, 130–31, 134, 137, 160, 171, 182
depression, 67, 78, 95, 235
depressive position, 58, 72–78, 80, 83–84, 86, 89
Der Derian, James, 215
Derrida, Jacques, 2, 119, 121
Desiring Whiteness (Seshadri-Crooks), 16–17
desubjectivity, 50–51, 88
Deutsch, Helene, 38
developmentalism, 8, 15
developmental models of mind, 63
Damousi, Joy, 11
DiAngelo, Robin, 299n4
Dictionary of Kleinian Thought (Hinshelwood), 84
Dijken, Suzan van, 217
Dimen, Muriel, 18–19
Dirty War, in Argentina, 9, 81, 121
discrimination, racial: in Great Britain, 149; in South Africa, 109; in UK, 283n58. *See also* antisemitism; race; racism

Gallop, Jane, 14, 250n26
Gay, Peter, 11
Gaztambide, Daniel, 16
Geissmann, Claudine, 264n32
Geissmann, Pierre, 264n32
gender melancholia, 16
gender psychology, gender roles and: dependence and, 130; gender-transitive mothering theory, 135; Main on, 185–99; maternal care, 130, 133–35, 138–40; mutuality and, 130, 133; postwar context, 131–45; recognition and, 130, 133; Winnicott on, 130–45. *See also* women
gender-transitive mothering theory, 135
gender tropes, 112
genuine sympathy, 83
"Geopsychoanalysis: . . . and the Rest of the World" (Derrida), 121
George, Sheldon, 17
Germany: clinical practices in, 9; monetary reparations by, 80–81; National Socialism in, 54, 225; transition to democratic systems in, 53; Weimar-era, 5. *See also* Nazi Germany; West Germany
Gerson, Gal, 58, 136–40, 250n26
Gherovici, Patricia, 16, 198
Gillespie, Sadie, 112
Gilligan, Carol, 14
Gilman, Sander, 10–11, 122, 126
Global North, 12, 235; psychoanalytic clinic practitioners in, 2
Global South, 16, 226, 235; clinical practices in, 9; communism in, 214
Golcman, Aída Alejandra, 113
González, Francisco, 198
"good enough mother" theory, 163–64; colonialization of, 129; methodological approach to, 128–30; racialization of, 129
Gordon, H. L., 106, 273n31

Great Britain: anti-psychiatry movement in, 180–81; antisemitism in, 153–54; Black Afro-Caribbean migration to, 141–45, 149, 218; boundary management in, 151; British Nationality Act of 1948, 280n35; British Psychoanalytical Society, 1; Cassel Hospital in, 26–27, 164, 167–77, 186–87; children in workforce in, 49–50; colonial psychoanalysis in South Africa, 25, 91, 95–127; Irishness compared to Blackness in, 153; multiculturalism in, 149; Northfield Military Hospital in, 168; postwar welfare state in, 70, 129, 136; psychoanalytic community in, 1; public clinics in, 5; Race Relations Acts, 149; racial discrimination in, 149; racist discourse in, 150–51; social democracy in, 185–99; welfare state in, 18, 27, 70–71, 128–29, 135–36, 138, 140–42, 169, 180–81, 189, 214; white supremacy movement in, 149; Windrush generation in, 141. *See also* Cold War era
Green, Emily, 162–64
Greenspan, Rachel, 119
Grewal, Inderpal, 17, 204, 212, 228–30
Grosz, Elizabeth, 14
Group Psychology and the Analysis of the Ego (S. Freud), 46–47
Guattari, Félix, 5–6, 26, 99, 164, 168, 178
Gubar, Susan, 250n26

Hale, Nathan, 8
Hamilton, James, 284n62
Hamletism, 107–8, 110–11, 117, 126
Hampstead War Nurseries, 4, 48, 202
Hampton, Fred, 221
Haraway, Donna, 210

Harlow, Harry, 205, 207, 219
Harrison, Tom, 183, 287n4
Hayes, Grahame, 122–23
Hayward, Rhodri, 191
Heimann, Paula, 172
Hietzing School, 36, 48
Hellmann, Ellen, 96, 98, 104, 116–17
hermeneutics of suspicion, 11
Herzog, Dagmar, 12, 194–95, 203
heteronormativity, 185–99; domestic
    containment and, 191; encoding of,
    194–95
hetero-sociality, 196–97
Hill, Jonah, 237–38
Hinshelwood, Robert, 76, 84, 170
historical trauma, 90
Hitler, Adolf, 57–58, 67–69, 73, 75
Hobbes, Thomas, 215
Hodges, Devon, 14
Hoffer, Willi, 35–36; as psychoanalytic
    reformer, 32
Homayounpour, Gohar, 16
homophobia: in British
    Psychoanalytical Society, 1, 21;
    clinical, 14; in psychoanalysis, 2
homosexuality: during Cold War era,
    194–95; Klein on, 265n37; S. Freud
    on, 15; typology of, 15
Homosexuality and Psychoanalysis
    (Dean and Lane), 2
Honneth, Axel, 250n26
Hook, Derek, 17
Hoover, J. Edgar, 221
Horney, Karen, 38, 206
"Hospital as a Therapeutic Institution,
    The" (Main), 170–71
Hug-Hellmuth, Hermine, 254n7; as
    psychoanalytic reformer, 32, 35. See
    also child psychoanalysis
Hungary: clinical practices in, 9–10;
    free public clinics in, 5
hypnosis, 113

id: for A. Freud, 49; war and, 49
identification, 14, 79; ethical pitfalls
    of, 85; paternal, 75; in Richard case
    study, 84
identity politics, 19
illusion and disillusionment, 130
India, clinical practices in, 9
Indigenous peoples: Aboriginal people,
    155; madness among, 6, 106, 246n6.
    See also Black Africans
Infancy in Uganda (Ainsworth), 219–20
infant development, 131–33
infantile attachment, 203, 212, 220
insecure attachments, 204–5, 208
instinct: instinctual aggression, 133;
    attachment instinct, 207–8; death
    instinct, 63, 65, 72–73, 79, 264n32;
    life instinct, 78–79 maternal
    instinct, 208, 210; instinctual need,
    47–48, 207–8, in Object Relations,
    63–64; sexual instinct, 39, 194
interbellum psychoanalysis, 37
internal representations, 64
International Journal of Psychoanalysis,
    112
International Psychoanalytic
    Association (IPA), 2, 9, 121, 232
interracial relationships, 103
Introduction to Psycho-Analysis for
    Teachers (A. Freud), 34
Introduction to the Technique of Child
    Analysis (A. Freud), 34
introjection, as psychological process, 79
IPA. See International Psychoanalytic
    Association
Irigaray, Luce, 14
Irishness, Blackness and, in Great
    Britain, 153
Isaacs, Susan, 70, 208

Jacoby, Russell, 11
Jenson, Deborah, 12

Johnson, Barbara, 250n26
Johnson, Boris, 21
Jones, Ernest, 5, 59–60, 255n12
Jones, Maxwell, 168, 172, 186
jouissance, 14
justice: global, 59, 82; political, 80,
    82, 85, 90; protopolitical theory
    of, 71; psychoanalysis and, 91;
    racial, 110, 123, 168; reparations as,
    81–91; reproductive, 233; social, 5,
    27, 37, 123, 127, 234, 240–41, 243;
    sociopolitical, 25, 59

Kandiah, Michael, 214
Keller, Richard C., 12
Kemper, Werner, 10
Key, Ellen, 51, 258n56
Keynes, John Maynard, 80
Khalfa, Jean, 245n5
Khan, Masud, 239, 286n96, 301n15
Khanna, Ranjana, 15–17, 97, 108
Kingsley Hall, 5, 178–79
Klein, Melanie, 3, 172; academic
    legacy of, 33; as apolitical, 70; in
    British Psychoanalytical Society,
    59, 70; clinical influences on, 58;
    Controversial Discussions and,
    72; on developmental models of
    mind, 63; deviation from classical
    psychoanalysis, 61; embrace of
    death drive theory, 65; A. Freud and,
    60, 63, 255n12; Hinshelwood and,
    76, 84; on homosexuality, 265n37;
    institutional legitimacy of, 60;
    interpretation of S. Freud's work,
    60; interpretive skills of, 68; John
    Chavafambira case study and, 117;
    Lacan and, 65; on mental health,
    265n37; metapsychology and, 65;
    methodological approach to, 24–25;
    on origins of superego, 65; Peter
    case, 62–63; *The Psycho-Analysis*

of Children, 62; psychoanalytic
    reform and, 35; relationality for, 64;
    reparations theory, 76–91; Richard
    case study, 57–59, 67–69, 71–82; on
    substitution of objects for words,
    61–62; on superego, 65, 67; two-
    body approach, 14; unconscious
    phantasy theory, 63–64, 260n5,
    262n17, 263n24; wartime clinical
    work of, 57–91; Winnicott
    influenced by, 130–31. *See also* child
    psychoanalysis; Object Relations
    theory
Kovel, Joel, 284n62
Kristeva, Julia, 14, 65
Kubie, Lawrence, 284n62

La Borde Clinic, 5, 168, 178, 180
Lacan, Jacques: academic legacy of,
    33; boundary-setting for, 238–39;
    egoistic self for, 133; on fantasy,
    194; Klein and, 65; psychoanalytic
    techniques for, 61
Laclau, Ernesto, 250n26
Lafargue Clinic, 4–5, 113, 168, 198
Laing, R. D., 5, 178–79, 289n39
Land Act, South Africa (1913), 103, 105
Lane, Christopher, 2, 15, 154
Langer, Marie "Mimi," 5, 8–10, 13, 121
Language of Winnicott, The
    (Abram), 159
late-stage capitalism, 21, 205
Lauretis, Teresa de, 14
Layton, Lynne, 19–21
Lazali, Karima, 16
Lebovici, Serge, 10
LGBTQ persons: adoption rights for, 51;
    Homosexuality and Psychoanalysis,
    2; trans rights, 51. *See also*
    homophobia
libidinal gratification, 79, 133
Linstrum, Erik, 12, 220

settler-colonialism, child-mother relationship to, 86

"Sex-Pol" clinics, in Vienna, 5

sexual abuse, S. Freud and, 10

sexual identity, 195–96. *See also* homosexuality; LGBTQ persons

sexuality: sexual normativity, 15, 169, 194; unconscious bisexuality, 14. *See also* heteronormativity

Shakur, Assata, 221

shame, 14

Shapira, Michal, 39, 48, 58, 69–70, 140, 191, 203

Sheehi, Lara, 16

silence, as white complicity, 120

Silverman, Kaja, 250n26

Simmel, Ernst, 5

slavery, in U.S., reparations for slavery debate in, 81

Snediker, Michael, 134

social contract theory, 66, 136, 215, 228

social death, 17

social democracy, in Great Britain, 185–99

Social Democratic Party, 4

Socialist Patients' Collective, 5

sociality theory, 198–200; collaboration in, 79; Frankfurt School and, 78; hetero-sociality, 196–97

social organization, S. Freud on, 47

social work, child psychoanalysis as, 4

sociotherapy, in Algeria, 168

Solms, Mark, 99

Soreanu, Raluca, 235

Soto-Crespo, Ramón, 65

South Africa: Black labor power in, 103; British colonial psychoanalysis in, 25, 91, 95–127; clinical practices in, 9–10; colonial governance in, 98; John Chavafambira case study, 25, 91, 95–127; map of, *101*; mass migration in, 97–98; Natives Land Act of 1913, 103, 105; Native Laws Amendment Act of 1937, 103; Pretoria Mental Hospital, 99; racial discrimination in, 109; racial justice struggle in, 110; racial segregation in, 97–98, 103–4, 270n18; scientific racism in, 107; Urban Area Act, 105; urbanization in, 97–99

South African Association for the Advancement of Science (SAAAS), 106–7

South African Psychoanalytical Association, 99

Spiller, Hortense, 14

Spitz, René, 189

Spivak, Gayatri, 16, 88

splitting, as psychological process, 23, 65, 85

squiggle game, 130

Stalinism, 54

state-sponsored repression. *See* repression

Stavrakakis, Yannis, 250n26

Staying Power (Fryer), 149

Stewart-Steinberg, Suzanne, 39, 48

Stoler, Ann Laura, 142

Stoller, Robert, 209

Stonebridge, Lyndsey, 65, 79

Stovall, Natasha, 120, 233

subjectivity, theory of, 39, 66

Sullivan, Harry Sack, 287n4

superego: in child psychoanalysis, 39–41, 44–46, 256n23; for A. Freud, 39–41, 44–46, 256n23; Klein on, 65, 67; origins of, 65; paternal, 52; tyranny of, 67

sympathy, 83

talk therapy, 107

Tavistock Institute of Human Relations, 173–74, 202

Taylor, Frederick Kräupl, 176

Thatcher, Margaret, 229
"Theory of Child Analysis, The" (A. Freud), 34
therapy speak, 237–38, 299n4
Three Essays on the Theory of Sexuality (A. Freud), 34
Tischler, Lydia, 188
Tosquelles, François, 6, 168, 178
Totem and Taboo (S. Freud), 54
touch therapy, 38
transference: African psychology and, 119; in child psychoanalysis, 40–43; in John Chavafambira case study, 124; positive, 40–43
transitional object theory, 130, 137–38
trans rights, 51
"traveling analysis," 25, 91, 96
Treaty of Versailles, 80
true reparations, 83, 85–86, 88
Trump, Donald, 21, 85, 216, 230
Two-Year Old Goes to Hospital, A, 189

Uganda, 219–20
UK. *See* United Kingdom
unconscious bisexuality, 14
unconscious conflict, 26, 129, 133
unconscious phantasy, 63–64, 206, 260n5, 262n17, 263n24
Ungar, Virginia, 301n15
United Kingdom (UK): Blackness in, 146–48; Commonwealth Immigrants Act, 280n35; A. Freud in exile in, 33–34; psychosocial approach to youth treatment in, 4; Race Relations Acts, 149; racial discrimination in, 283n58; Windrush generation in, 141. *See also* Black Afro-Caribbeans; Great Britain
United States (U.S.): civil rights movement in, 149–50, 177; clinical practices in, 9–10; critique of Freudian psychoanalysis in,

11–12; Moynihan Report, 145, 219; National Security Act, 297n45; racial segregation in, 5; reparations debate in, 81; September 11 terrorist attacks in, 20–21. *See also* African Americans
Urban Area Act, South Africa, 105
urbanization, in South Africa, 97–99
U.S. *See* United States

Vaughan, Megan, 106, 121, 271n28, 273n30
Vaughans, Kirkland C., 22
Vianna, Helena Besserman, 10
Viçedo, Marga, 210, 295n15
Vienna, Austria, 36–37. *See also* Red Vienna
Vienna Ambulatorium, 37
Vienna Psychoanalytic Society, 8, 33
Villa 21, 168, 178–79, 186
Vint, F. W., 106, 273n31

Wages for Housework Campaign, 187, 210
Wall, Oisín, 179–80
Walpole, Horace, 169
Walton, Jean, 14, 88, 154
war: ego defenses during, 49; id and, 49. *See also* Cold War era; World War II
War Inside, The (Shapira), 69–70
War in the Nursery, The (Riley), 135
Wayward Youth (Aichhorn), 31
Weber, Max, 54–55
Webster, Wendy, 151–52, 163, 221
welfare consensus, 177, 192
welfare state: children in, 50; in Great Britain, 18, 27, 70–71, 128–29, 135–36, 138, 140–42, 169, 180–81, 189, 214
Wertham, Fredric, 168
West Germany, Socialist Patients' Collective in, 5

white complicity, 120

White Fragility (DiAngelo), 299n4

whiteness: in clinical settings, 120; complicity and, 120; as culture-bound syndrome, 233–34; definition of, 233–34; postwar ideological construction of, 145; Winnicott on, 157–58

"white peril" trope, 155–56

White Racism (Kovel), 284n62

white supremacy movement, in Great Britain, 149

white women, appropriation of Black women's bodies and, 88

WHO. *See* World Health Organization

Wilderson, Frank B., III, 17

Wilson, Elizabeth, 139

Wilson, Harold, 280n35

Windrush generation, 141, 143, 149, 218

Winnicott, D. W., 3, 127, 179; archival drawings, *144*; BBC lectures, 4; Bowlby and, 201; Chodorow and, 64–65; clinical holding environment and, 130, 159; clinical legacy of, 133; on decolonization, 145–64; false/true self and, 130; feminist critique of, 140–41; A. Freud as influence on, 130; on gender psychology, 130–45; "good enough mother" theory, 128–30, 163–64; historical liberalism and, 135–36; illusion and disillusionment and, 130; on infant development, 131–33; Klein as influence on, 130–31; maternal holding, 132; methodological approach to, 25–26; on mother-child relationship, 129–33; mothering theories, 64,

135; "Piggle" case study, 128–30, 145–64; *Playing and Reality*, 157; political engagement for, 70; on race in psychoanalytic clinic, 145–64; on reproductive labor of women, 133–35, 151, 216, 223; squiggle game and, 130; transitional object theory and, 130, 137–38; universalization of psychology, 155; vocabulary for, 277n6; on whiteness, 157–58

Winograd, Basia, 21–22

Winter, Sarah, 11

Wittig, Monique, 13

women: application of psychoanalysis to, 38; Bowlby's redefinition of, 208–9; at Cassel Hospital, 186–87; reproductive futurity and, 50, 196, 217; reproductive labor of, 133–35, 151, 216, 223. *See also* Black women; femininity; feminist theory; gender psychology; white women

Work of Whiteness, The (H. Morgan), 242

World Health Organization (WHO), 70, 106, 201, 208

World War II: A. Freud after, 48; Klein during, 57; monetary reparations after, 80–81; Richard case study and, 67–70

Wright, Richard, 113, 168

X, Malcolm, 221

Yates, Sybille, 112

Young, Robert, 205–6, 209–11

Zaretsky, Eli, 18, 38, 58, 71, 203

Žižek, Slavoj, 250n26

GPSR Authorized Representative: Easy Access System Europe, Mustamäe tee
50, 10621 Tallinn, Estonia, gpsr.requests@easproject.com

www.ingramcontent.com/pod-product-compliance
Lightning Source LLC
Chambersburg PA
CBHW021847020426
42334CB00013B/227

9 780231 214957